THE ENGLISH DANE

Sarah Bakewell was born in southern England and grew up in Sydney, Australia. She now lives in London, where she spent several years as curator of early printed books at the Wellcome Library. Her first book, *The Smart*, about an amazing eighteenth-century con-trick, won wide critical acclaim.

ALSO BY SARAH BAKEWELL

*The Smart: The Story of Margaret Caroline Rudd
and the Unfortunate Perreau Brothers*

SARAH BAKEWELL

The English Dane

A Life of Jorgen Jorgenson

VINTAGE BOOKS

London

Published by Vintage 2006

4 6 8 10 9 7 5

Copyright © Sarah Bakewell 2005

First published in Great Britain in 2005 by
Chatto & Windus

Vintage
Random House, 20 Vauxhall Bridge Road,
London SW1V 2SA

www.randomhouse.co.uk

Addresses for companies within
The Random House Group Limited can be found at:
www.randomhouse.co.uk/offices.htm

The Random House Group Limited Reg. No. 954009
www.randomhouse.co.uk/vintage

A CIP catalogue record for this book
is available from the British Library

ISBN 9780099438069

MIX
Paper from
responsible sources
FSC® C018179

Printed and bound in Great Britain by Clays Ltd, St Ives plc

Contents

List of illustrations

7. John Sell Cotman, *Willliam Jackson Hooker* (1811). Victoria and Albert Museum, London.

8. G. S. Mackenzie, View of Reykjavík in 1810, from his *Travels in the island of Iceland (1811)*.

9. Jorgenson's *Placat*, 11 Juli 1809. Printed sheet.

10. Count Frederik Trampe. Miniature portrait reproduced in Jón Thorkelsson, *Saga Jörundar Hundadagakóngs* (1892).

11. Magnús Stephensen. Miniature portrait reproduced in Jón Thorkelsson, *Saga Jörundar Hundadagakóngs* (1892).

12. Jorgen Jorgenson: 'Oh! my wig!'. Watercolour with pen and ink, bound in his *Adventures of Thomas Walter* manuscript, British Library, London.

13. Jorgen Jorgenson: 'A prisonship in Capricornia' (i.e. the *Bahama*). Watercolour with pen and ink, bound in his *Adventures of Thomas Walter* manuscript, British Library, London.

14. Jorgen Jorgenson: 'Liberty triumphant'. Watercolour with pen and ink, bound in his *Adventures of Thomas Walter* manuscript, British Library, London.

15. Jorgen Jorgenson: *Travels in France and Germany*, presentation copy to W. J. Hooker. National Library of Australia, Canberra.

16. *Hobart Town 1840*. Lithograph from drawing by L. Le Breton, Allport Library, State Library of Tasmania, Hobart.

17. Jorgen Jorgenson and Norah on Ross Bridge, photograph by Jane Bakewell.

18. Memorial plaque to Jorgenson, outside police station in Oatlands, Tasmania, photograph by Jane Bakewell.

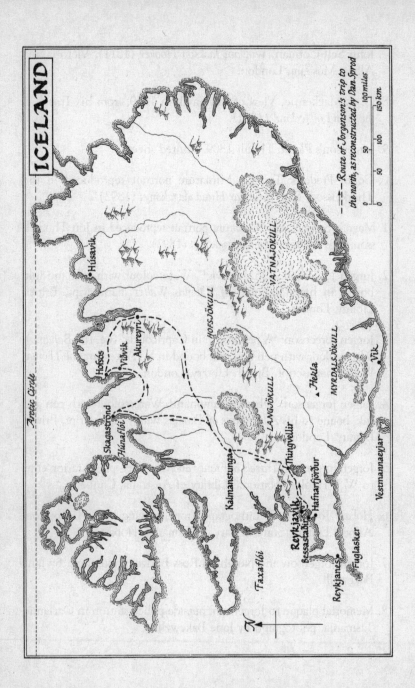

ICELAND

Húsavík

VATNAJÖKULL

HOFSJÖKULL

Hofsós
Viðvik
Akureyri

MYRDALSJÖKULL

Vik

Hekla

LANGJÖKULL

Skagaströnd
Húnaflói

Kalmanstunga

Þingvellir

Reykjavík
Bessastaðir
Hafnarfjörður

Vestmannaeyjar

Faxaflói

Reykjanes

Fuglasker

Arctic Circle

N

- - - ➤ Route of Jorgenson's trip to
the north, as reconstructed by Dan Sprod

0   50   100   150 km.
0   50   100 miles

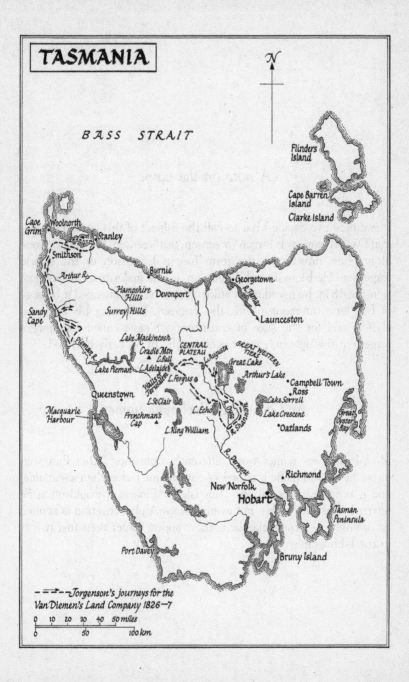

TASMANIA

N

BASS STRAIT

Flinders Island

Cape Barren Island

Clarke Island

Cape Grim • Woolnorth
Stanley
Smithson
Arthur R.
Burnie
• Georgetown
R. Tamar
Hampshire Hills
Devonport
Surrey Hills
Launceston
Sandy Cape
Lake Mackintosh
CENTRAL PLATEAU
GREAT WESTERN TIERS
Cradle Mtn. ▲ L. Ball
L. Augusta
Pieman R.
L. Adelaide
Great Lake
Lake Pieman
Walls of Jerusalem
L. Fergus ⊙
Arthur's Lake
Campbell Town
Ross
Queenstown
L. St. Clair
R. Ouse
Lake Sorrell
Frenchman's Cap ▲
C. Echo
Lake Crescent
Macquarie Harbour
L. King William
R. Shannon
Oatlands
Great Oyster Bay

R. Derwent
Richmond
New Norfolk
Hobart
Tasman Peninsula

Port Davey
Bruny Island

– – ⇄ – Jorgenson's journeys for the
Van Diemen's Land Company 1826–7

0 10 20 30 40 50 miles
0   50   100 km

A note on the name

It is difficult to decide what to call the subject of this book. His original Danish name was Jørgen Jørgensen, or Jürgensen, but Anglophone biographers mostly use the form Jorgen Jorgenson or the hybrid Jorgensen. He himself used 'Jorgenson' in the majority of his publications; in 1834, he noted in an affidavit that he had changed it because of his 'long intercourse with the English'. Following his authorial choice, and for the sake of consistency, I have called him Jorgen Jorgenson throughout, except occasionally in his early boyhood.

And a note on Icelandic names

Most Icelanders' names work differently from most other European ones: the second name is a form of patronymic rather than a surname, and is not used in isolation. Thus Ísleifur Einarsson would often be referred to as Ísleifur, but not as Einarsson. Alphabetization is applied accordingly, so most Icelandic authors appear under their first names in the bibliography.

Jorgen Jorgenson, aged around 28

Jorgen Jorgenson on a bridge

In Tasmania there grows a plant known as 'Horizontal'. It begins confidently, throwing up its first thin shoots. These shoots turn into branches, which become heavy and fall over to create new trunks, growing sideways. From them, more shoots appear, heading upwards and then toppling; these in turn sprout more and more entanglements, horizontal, vertical, diagonal. Eventually they create a maze of high trunks and branches heading simultaneously in all directions, perforated by moss-covered gaps dropping through to the ground below.

Horizontal is not the only botanical nightmare in the Tasmanian bush. There is *Bauera*, a shrub that laces into surrounding trees to form a knot of stalks that cannot be pushed or cut through even with a machete. 'Cutting-grass' drapes itself over the path like long, flexible razor blades. Ordinary shrubs and saplings crowd together so densely that, to a bushwalker following a track, they seem to form a wall on each side. Above the whole mess rise tall trees; when they fall they provide scaffolding for the vegetation to climb higher. Much of the land is mountainous, and between each ridge lurks a deep scrub-filled gully. The many rivers are fast and debris-laden, often full of leeches. The idea of leaving the path seems an absurdity. So does the notion that anyone succeeded in cutting the trail in the first place, and yet there it is.

This is one of the world's last great forest wildernesses, formidable even now. Hikers, loggers and dam-builders have made incursions, but for the most part it remains the same impossible tangle that enticed and defied colonists two hundred years ago.

Through the middle of this forest, however, unfurling over the eastern half of the island like an airstrip, there runs one stretch of easy pastoral land. Low hills display fields of honey-coloured grass, stroked smooth by the breeze. Sheep mow about; there are a few pylons and the odd farmstead. The road from Hobart to the north passes this way. It traces a line of towns, small and clean and conscious of their local history, with bungalow-sized museums and tourist information centres. This is the Midlands: the first area of Tasmania to be settled after Hobart and Launceston. Early maps show it as a streak of rural energy, busy with the names of farms and settlers' homes, while its clogged surroundings form blank zones marked only with the wide-spaced lettering, 'unexplored country'. On most islands, maps of later eras would show the named areas spreading and the unnamed ones retreating, but modern Tasmanian maps don't look that different from the early ones.

One of the oldest of these towns, Ross, sits near the main road about halfway along the Midlands strip. As you turn off to approach it, you pass over a low stone bridge that might seem more in place in Wales or a French provincial town. It looks too firmly planted for this landscape, too much at home. Yet there is a certain sternness about it, marking its true nature as an object of penitence and redemption. It was built by a convict gang in the 1830s, and two of the workers exceeded their orders by turning a plain bridge into an extraordinary piece of outsider art. Barely visible from the road, the bridge's sides sport an almost hallucinatory composition of Celtic carved motifs and gargoyle-like human faces, many of them portraits of famous local characters. The bridge's principal creator, Daniel Herbert, is here with his wife. So are the island's governor Colonel George Arthur, an Aboriginal Tasmanian, and a fearsome innkeeper named Headlam, known for his criminal propensities and dangerous dogs.

There are also two faces resembling figures on playing cards: a crowned King and his female companion. The woman has a long nose and a thin downturned mouth, and wears a puffy bonnet. Below her face is a composition which one expert on the bridge's symbolism has identified as a stew of androgyny motifs, all rampagingly sexual: a large cross, shapes resembling kidneys, a keyhole, a possible phallus, and something which, the expert writes, 'is presumed to be an anal symbol but may not be'.

Her companion, the King, is less weighed down with suggestive symbols. His face is pleasant: he has high cheekbones and a neat curly beard with a jaunty moustache. His nose appears snub only because it is chipped off; it lost its end in 1969. Under him are a donkey's head and some patterns representing primitive faces, together with a mass of melted, interwoven lines, rather like a nest of snakes or a growth of Horizontal. Mockery and absurdity are clearly the themes here, but the chaotic waves and lines also constitute a fair representation of the King's life and its tangled fortunes.

This is no allegorical or masonic figure, but another well-known Ross resident: a man often teasingly called 'His Icelandic Majesty' by those who knew him, and later dubbed the 'Convict King', the 'Little Napoleon', and the 'Dog-Day King', the last because his reign lasted only through the dog-days of a single summer. He is Jorgen Jorgenson, and the woman beside him is his wife Norah. The bridge commemorates him not only as a King, but as a celebrated local eccentric and a pioneer of Tasmanian exploration: he was one of the first men to cut a path through the great western wilderness, once nearly starving and several times nearly drowning in the process.

Had one stood in the midst of the north-western forests during the last few months of 1826, one might have glimpsed him hacking through the scrub, cutting his way not with an ordinary machete but with a long, lustrous sword, a beloved gift which would have looked more in place on a Napoleonic battlefield than here in the bush. When not wielding it, he liked to wear it slung over his shoulders in piratical style, even if it caught on branches and interfered with the fit of his knapsack.

In the evenings, one might have seen him lit by the setting sun on a mountainside, sitting apart from his companions to record the day's observations in his journal, before putting it aside to reflect on the sublimity of the view and on his lack of a true friend with whom to share his thoughts. The exhausted men with him were more interested in the meal roasting on their camp-fire, and even Jorgenson had to admit that, at the end of a twenty-mile struggle through scrub-bound gullies and freezing rivers, a feast of damper and pork was an excellent thing.

Two decades earlier, in 1803, Jorgenson could have been seen just a few hundred kilometres from this spot: a young man of twenty-three, fresh from helping to install Tasmania's first European settlement, striding through the southern hills on his own personal explorations. He was then a bright youth with an open, very Scandinavian face, full of high spirits and already powerfully built in a compact way. He was tireless, unable ever to tolerate physical or mental constraints without struggling to escape into action.

A much more dignified Jorgenson, though still a young one, had appeared in 1809 on an even more remote island, almost the exact geographical antipode of Tasmania: Iceland. There, His Excellency Jørgen Jørgensen sat in Reykjavík's Government House and frowned magisterially over a desk covered with draft proclamations and citizens' petitions; he decided each one's fate and stamped his papers with a Protector's seal of his own design, impressing the initials 'J. J.' on each red pillow of wax.

Yet it is in Tasmania, not in Iceland, that Jorgen Jorgenson's memory lives on with the most substance. He is petrified on Ross Bridge, but he is also remembered on a memorial plaque on a cairn outside the police office in Oatlands, where he once lived and worked:

> To commemorate
> Jorgen Jorgenson
> Once Lord Protector of Iceland
> Participated in founding of Risdon,
> Hobart and Port Dalrymple, 1803–1804
> Field policeman and constable,
> Oatlands under Thomas Anstey
> Police Magistrate 1827.

Another plaque in Campbell Town marks an inn where he was installed as a police spy, working in cahoots with his future wife. In the north-western town of Burnie, a street has been named after him, and in May 2001 the local library gave a free ice cream to every resident to celebrate his fame. A tree was planted in his name on a private estate, in an avenue commemorating pioneers. And, marking his presence at its foundation, he was once featured in the tourist centre at Risdon, though this has now become Aboriginal land and no longer serves up any form of invasion history. It was also once suggested that a 'Lake Jorgenson' be named after him in one of the areas he explored, but this was never taken up.

In fact, something less tranquil than a lake would seem more appropriate: a volcano or a bubbling hot spring. But Iceland, which has plenty of these, has never been inclined to memorialize Jorgenson. He is thought of with affection there, but not with pride, for he was an outsider and brought with him an air of quaintness and quirkiness: characteristics with which Icelanders dislike being associated. His own country, Denmark, also found him something of an embarrassment, though this may be changing. When the Danish Crown Prince, Frédérik, recently married the Tasmanian Mary Donaldson, he spoke warmly in his wedding speech of Jorgenson as another Dane who had once visited Australia 'with just as high hopes and just as much confidence'.

Jorgenson did not particularly like being considered an eccentric, but his own alternative vision of himself as heroic idealist and liberator rarely caught on. Instead, the emotion he usually evoked in others was fondness, mixed with exasperation. He inspired a range of literary comparisons, none of which he would have approved of. A man who knew him well in his finest hour, his employer Samuel Phelps, watched him blunder into one pratfall after another while lost in day-dreams of glory, and was the first to call him a Don Quixote. Phelps also described him as a miniature Napoleon; others have compared him to the fantasist Baron Münchhausen, to Benvenuto Cellini ('in his mingling of genius, high spirits, and madly irresponsible audacity'), and to the mythical jester Till Eulenspiegel. Constantly turning up in different guises and settings, he brings to mind Woody Allen's more recent creation, Zelig; one enthusiast's modern website calls him the Forrest Gump of the 1800s for the same reason. He has even been called a 'Tassie James Bond' because of his spying adventures.

In many ways he is like Ibsen's Peer Gynt, whose youth is spent in a mist of dreams: 'I'll be a King – an Emperor!' – to which his mother murmurs, 'I'd be satisfied if you could manage to mend the skag in your own breeches.' Or perhaps he is a Toad of Toad Hall, rushing pell-mell from one ill-fated enthusiasm to the next, popping up in paradoxical triumph at the end of each adventure. Appropriately for a seafarer, he has been described in terms of maritime rather than motoring mishaps, as 'a rudderless barque' who shipwrecked himself because of 'a lamentable lack of ballast, aggravated by culpably erratic steering', even when he had 'full sail and sun-lit seas'.

Some biographers simply whirl through his multiple selves: 'Sailor, whaler, explorer, privateer, naval officer, spy, author, dramatist, preacher, revolutionist, gambler, prisoner, convict doctor, police-constable, editor, exile, prospector, vagabond and King of Iceland – what a list!' There is something about Jorgen Jorgenson that drives people to enumerate, multiply, accumulate and replicate: to project endless versions of him, as if in an array of fairground mirrors. He even did it himself. In his own writings, Jorgenson adopted endless doubles and disguises, like a sprig of Horizontal throwing out shoots in all directions and always returning to somewhere near where it started.

1

A Danish boy

Jorgen Jorgenson leaped into the world in 1780, probably on 29 March, though the church registers give his birthdate as 7 April. Vigorous from the beginning, he muscled his way out of his mother's womb with such an appetite for life that the birth nearly killed her; she never recovered her health. In subsequent days, he proved a noisy, bellicose, turbulent baby, one who could never be swaddled prettily in fine linen and laid down in a cradle to sleep and be forgotten. He refused to be ignored. 'It was remarked, immediately after my birth,' he wrote, 'I made such an incessant noise that no one could rest near me, and for many days was I never done roaring.'

Jørgen was not the firstborn, but it was his arrival that really transformed the lives of his parents, Anna Lethe Brüün and her husband Jørgen Jørgensen. The paternal Jørgen was Royal Clockmaker to the Danish King, an appointment in which pride could be taken, and the family lived in a tall house at no. 77 Østergade – a respectable street in central Copenhagen, off the imposing Kongens Nytorv and close both to the harbour and to the palace. A dynasty of clockmakers was founded here, the business being carried on by sons and grandsons for generations. The Jørgensen name grew ever more eminent. But Jørgen the younger never made a clock. He was not born for minute, precise work, or for the fine-tuned manners of court life; his talents bore little relation to his father's.

Yet there were similarities. Adopting a fictional *alter ego* in his quasi-autobiography *The Adventures of Thomas Walter* in 1810, Jorgenson described his father as honest and good-hearted, with 'a warm temper', very much like himself. He could also be mean, however, and his wayward son considered him too judgemental – whereas Jorgenson himself had an almost unmanageable generosity of spirit, which often got him into trouble. His mother, meanwhile, had a 'virtuous disposition and sweet temper', but her poor health meant she was unable to attend much to her new baby. 'It would be injustice to my mother,' he wrote, 'to say she evinced more love for my Brothers and sister, than for me; but it was entirely owing to existing circumstances.' There is a gloomy undercurrent running here. Jorgenson, by nature a difficult baby, was pushed aside by both fragile mother and glowering father in his early years.

His mother could not nurse him, so a wet-nurse was provided. The strong peasant woman chosen for the job became as attached to him as any mother, and happened to be of a similarly obstreperous character to her charge. The infant Jorgenson often assumed that she *was* his real mother. He later wrote, significantly, 'I really think our temper and our constitutions on the whole are greatly influenced by what manner we are taken care of in our first infancy, and that it is far from indifferent, who is our nurse, and who is not; for otherwise I can not account for several oddities in my own temper, who is in many instances widely different from those of my parents and Brothers.' He thought of himself almost as a changeling. Claiming his nurse as a second mother in place of the real one amounted to a rebuke to his family, as well as an explanation for his 'oddities'.

There were to be five children altogether, all but one boys.* Jorgenson's older brother Urban, four years his senior, was everything he was not: delicate in health, painstaking, and obedient. Urban studied hard, and followed his father into clock-making; when he grew

---

* A daughter followed Jørgen in April 1781, and two more sons came a few years later. Jorgenson was fond of them all, though he never really knew the youngest, Marcus, except as a feisty toddler who used to kick his shins when playing. His one sister, Anna Catharine Frederica (known as Trine) had a weak constitution and needed a lot of care; the other middle brother Frédérik (known as Fritz) became a clockmaker too. So did Fritz's son Georg Urban Frédérik, also called Fritz, but this young man's heart wasn't in it: he seems to have had a streak of his uncle Jørgen in him. He abandoned the trade to become a comic artist

up he guided his own son into the same career. Jorgenson admired his calm good sense, though he could not resist laughing at a memory of how, when they were children, Urban was frightened by a bull and ran away so fast he became 'almost brokenwinded'. Jorgenson, by contrast, seemed hardly to feel fear at all.

It helped that he was naturally strong. 'At the age of four, I was able to beat any boy of six,' he wrote, 'and I was of such a fierce and violent disposition, that I attacked any one, who offended me.' His loyal nurse would often join in too, rising like an Amazon to his defence. But he was no thug. Along with his powerful physical presence, he had a warm, mischievous charisma which made adults and children alike smile. His younger brother Fritz later remembered him as 'the delight of his family and his friends, having always his head a little too much elated; he joined to that a heart so excellent, a courage so marked, a sense (ésprit) so lively, and a generosity so extraordinary, that at no time there was any question about himself, but totally and ever forgot himself when it concerned his friends'. Jørgen seemed more alive than the others in the family. As a creature of impulse, however, his path through childhood would not be easy.

The trouble started when he was sent to school at the age of four, his beloved nurse being dismissed at the same time. Suddenly he was expected to sit in his chair like the other children, and to keep quiet. This proved impossible, and he was constantly punished for cheekiness, for not knowing his lessons, and for fighting. He learned a lot about pugilism, as he said later, but nothing about how to read or write, though that deficiency would be amply made up for in due course.

During the next few years, his main form of rebellion was truancy. Each morning he set off as if going to school but instead explored the city, especially the harbour area near his house, where he would stand – a stout little dreamer – gazing for hours at Copenhagen's tall-masted

and make his living from cartoons gently mocking bourgeois Copenhagen life, before succumbing to alcoholism. He is evidently the true painter of a miniature, now held by the National Museum in Iceland, which has often been taken for a Jorgen Jorgenson self-portrait. Depicting a weird, angelic, golden-haired figure dressed in white and holding a palm leaf, it is an extraordinary image, and one rather regrets that it is not by Jorgenson. The sitter appears to have been Peder Otto Testman. I am indebted for this information to Lesley Albertson, and indirectly to Claus Bjerring.

ships, fitted out for journeys to the Baltic with coal and timber, to the West Indies for sugar and tobacco, to Africa for slaves. Copenhagen was a glorious maritime city. By land it could feel claustrophobic, being hemmed in with gated walls which were still locked every night after the mediaeval fashion, but to the sea it opened outward with generous abandon. It was (and still is) pervaded by veins of cool clean water, along which the goods of the world flowed in and out, enticing Jorgenson abroad like so many beckoning fingers. He began to dream of going to sea almost before he was tall enough to step in and out of a bathtub.

The school reported the absences to Jorgenson's father, who raged at the boy, comparing him as always to his impeccable elder brother. While the culprit was confined to his room in disgrace, a friend of the family – the director of Urban's more select and senior Efterslægtens school – happened to call, and suggested that Jørgen as well as Urban might benefit from the school's enlightened approach to education: it relied on appraisals and rewards rather than floggings. His father agreed, so in July 1787, at the age of seven, Jorgenson was enrolled there. He shared his class with a boy who became extremely famous in Danish literature, the poet and dramatist Adam Oehlenschlæger. Jorgenson evidently proved a memorable schoolmate, for Oehlenschlæger's memoirs relate several anecdotes of his mischief-making.

The director had been right: despite his initial backwardness, Jorgenson shone in the school. He caught up rapidly, learned to read and write, and raced ahead in all his classes, his intelligence and phenomenal memory making the work easy. All his life he had a talent for absorbing, remembering and reworking hoards of information; he mastered several languages and could always descant with only slightly dented erudition on classical and historical themes. Few would have guessed that his education only continued into his early teens.

But even as he excelled in study, he also continued to misbehave, and soon became the class clown. Adam Oehlenschlæger described him as a wit who played madman – an anarchical jester. He was particularly fond of baiting the teachers: in one of Oehlenschlæger's stories, Jorgenson challenged a boorish master who had been boasting of his global travels to say exactly where he had been. 'Bring me a map, and I'll show you,' said the teacher. Jorgenson went off, and with an air of straight-faced impertinence returned carrying a map not of the world but of Zealand, the local area around Copenhagen. On another occasion, he answered the question 'Where does saliva originate?' with the random reply: 'In the kidneys', and had to slide under the table to escape the torrent of slaps. He remained there, to considerable comic effect, while the rest of the class's examination continued. 'This Eulenspiegel has gone on in the same way ever since in his life,' remarked Oehlenschlæger, 'and it is very clear that the Icelandic revolution was a continuation of his fun and games.'

Out of school, too, he got into scrapes. Once, a classmate accidentally tripped over an old woman's market stall nearby and spilled her baskets of fruit. The woman complained to the school, and the boy was punished. A few days later Jorgenson took revenge. Seeing a coach pull up near her, he crept up and tied a piece of string from the coach's wheel to one leg of the stall. When the horses started off, the table flew out and fruit rolled everywhere, to the fright of the old woman, 'who thought the devil had hold of it'. The driver stopped and the string was discovered, but Jorgenson was long gone. He was eventually caught only because his guilty conscience led him to organize a collection among his fellows to compensate his victim.* Many of the pranks Jorgenson remembered committing had a similar quality: they combined a spirit of mayhem with a folk hero's drive to reverse wrongs and avenge the oppressed.

Jorgenson's fantasies took a flamboyant, romantic turn early on. In a later letter to his brother Fritz, he alluded to a secret moment from his childhood. 'My passions were all of stormy character,' he remembered, 'and when you least suspected or perceived it, my breast was agitated with a variety of deep thoughts all leading to raise myself to notice.' This arc towards glory had first been inspired when he saw a famous singer performing at the Royal Palace. 'All at once this songstress

* Perhaps stories about this incident helped to inspire Jorgenson's nephew Fritz Jürgensen, for one of his cartoons showed a mother saying to her little boy as they pass an orange-seller on the street: 'No, my boy, you keep your eight skillings and let the woman keep her oranges' – not noticing that her own cloak has caught on the basket and is spilling them all over the ground. The ghost of Jorgenson's schooldays also seems to haunt another Fritz Jürgensen cartoon, in which two boys are explaining to an adult how they came to be fighting: 'First I hit him first – and then he hit me first.'

occupied my whole mind.' He immediately wondered what he could do to elevate himself into a more glamorous realm, worthy of such a being. At first, he imagined himself becoming a German Count, the grandest figure he could picture. The reverie later flowed in a different direction, but the urge to do great things remained constant. 'I think you will smile at what I have above told you,' he wrote to Fritz.

At thirteen, Jorgenson was at the top of the highest class, studying with boys older than himself, some as old as twenty. He passed his final examinations with distinction, and this marked the end of the line. But his father was not sure what to do with a thirteen-year-old school-leaver, so he asked the director to keep him for an extra year: a mistake. Bored, Jorgenson directed his energies into making more trouble, until at last the school asked his father to remove him. Thus his scholastic career ended, not in precocious glory, but in ignominious expulsion.

For a while he lurked around the family house, perpetrating prac-tical jokes on neighbours and sliding into teenage depression. 'I became melancholy. I entirely changed, and shunned society, I loved to walk by myself, and if anyone asked me a question I seemed troubled.' The only event that cheered him up was a spectacular fire at the nearby Royal Palace later that year. He watched the drama from across the water in a Romantic ecstasy, abandoning himself to his era's distinc-tive lust for the 'sublime' – that exquisite mixture of terror and bliss that comes from witnessing destruction at a safe distance. The roaring flames were 'awful beyond conception', he wrote; they filled his mind with 'emotions of delight'. 'At night it was truly grand, and I stood looking on with unwearied pleasure as the devouring element continued its ravages. One after another the roofs of the beautiful halls fell in.' In his imagination, he saw the fire catching the portraits of dead Danish heroes in the Great Hall, so that they seemed to come to life and escape momentarily from their imprisonment on the walls, before blackening and withering to nothing. Meanwhile, the living king – the half-insane Christian VII – had been rescued from the palace only with difficulty. He thought the fire was one of his hallucinations, and would not believe that the building was really burning.

Jorgenson's father now decided to send him to a friend in the coun-tryside near Copenhagen, to calm down and reflect soberly on his future. Jørgen did come to his senses in his rustic retreat, but not in the way his father had intended.

Until now, he had been something of a junior revolutionist, like many of his generation: aged nine when the French Revolution broke out, he had grown up intoxicated with its ideals. 'I thought I saw the time of Greece and Rome renewed,' he wrote later. He had longed to be part of this rebirth, and to sign up for the Republican cause – which had erupted with force even in Denmark, although in reality the country had been inoculated against radical upheaval by a period of enlightened reform some decades earlier. Jorgenson's passion for revolution had provided an outlet for his mental ardour, but now, in Zealand, his enthusiasm began to dissipate. He had time to think; he would also have heard news of the mounting Terror in France, where the revolutionaries' dreams were becoming the people's nightmare. Local relatives may also have persuaded him to think differently: in his fictionalized *Thomas Walter* account, Jorgenson cast one influential adviser in the role of a venerable hermit, who became his mentor and also revealed himself to be a long-lost uncle. But the uncle's words were merely dramatizations of Jorgenson's own thoughts, which were moving in an unexpected direction. Instead of becoming a Jacobin, Jorgenson became an Anglophile.

While revolutionists often regarded Britain as irredeemably conservative, many on the Continent had come to see it as a haven of mercantile common sense, a place offering little ideological excitement but a striking degree of personal freedom together with great funds of economic and technological energy. As Jorgenson now came to believe, oppression was constitutionally impossible in Britain, for every man was his own king; the monarch merely ruled over a nation of private kings. The country was so strong that it need not fear invasion, and the robust character of the people and their sense of fair play seemed to Jorgenson to make internal turmoil equally unlikely. He was impressed when he heard that, on an English street, a crowd would stop a fight if a larger boy attacked a smaller one, while if the two were evenly matched they would watch without interfering except to enforce the rules of honourable combat. How could tyranny arise among such a people?

It was not the thrills of a stable political system that most attracted

Jorgenson, however. There was something else, which spoke to his childhood fantasies on the Copenhagen harbourside. Instead of the heat of revolution, Britain displayed a fervour for exploration, discovery and adventure. It offered access to the world's oceans, over which it had more control than any other country, and which it had filled with fast, beautiful ships. In place of revolutionary banners it offered billowing, wind-filled sails, which sped the dreaming mind of an adolescent as far away from the clockwork world of Østergade as one could get without flying to the moon. It offered heroes like Captain Cook, the published account of whose South Sea voyages Jorgenson had devoured and who now replaced the German count as a role model, together with Cook's scientific companion, the botanist Joseph Banks, 'a young gentleman of indefatigable curiosity and independent fortune' who had 'left all the pleasures his riches and rank entitled him to in his own country' to embark on his tremendous journey. Unlike military men, these seafarers 'had not the glory attached to the butchering of millions of our fellow creatures', but instead possessed 'the satisfaction of being useful to mankind, promoting trade and commerce, giving employment to the learned, and discovery of new knowledge'. Jorgenson's mind was now filled with exotic people, tropical scenes, and the imagined sensation of movement. In his dreams, he felt himself gliding 'in an immense ship along the smooth waters'.

England and the sea were then almost one concept. The same remained true for a century or more, and they still made a powerful combination when, almost a hundred years later, the young Pole Józef Korzeniowski happened to glance up while telling his tutor of his desire to travel, and saw his first Englishman, a vision of pink-faced, white-whiskered confidence wearing a silly suit and too-short socks. It was an epiphany: Korzeniowski was simultaneously seized by a determination to go to sea and by a passion for England. Like Jorgenson, he adopted the language as his own and took an Anglicized name, Joseph Conrad. He felt that the English language had claimed him rather than the reverse; there was an 'emotional surrender' in the discovery; an 'exulting, almost physical recognition'. What happened to Jorgenson was similarly visceral. Years later (when the image had lost some of its lustre) he wrote:

14

A Danish boy

From my earliest youth have I with inexpressible fondness doated on an imaginary vision, the creature of my own brain. Young as I was, I could not help contemplating with peculiar delight, the generosity, the desperate valour, and glorious love for liberty, which appeared to animate the breasts of Britons . . . I read every thing that could tend to nourish the growing principles in me, and at last became enamoured in the picture before me, that a flame was kindled within, which tho' now extinguished, has left such marks of violence, and has given such a turn to my mind, that I scarcely know myself again.

Having decided what he wanted to do – run away to Britain, and to sea – Jorgenson had one difficult task to perform: he had to return to Copenhagen and convince his parents to let him go. This was not easy. A life at sea was not a gentleman's life, and his father, an Anglophobe (unusually for a Dane at that time), demanded to know how the boy had got 'such romantic Ideas' in his head as to want to leave his own country and serve under strangers, 'especially such as were the most haughty and proud people in the world'. Jorgenson shrewdly worked on his mother instead, and won her support; thus, eventually, he brought both parents around. His father even helped to choose him a ship, seeking a recommendation from a friend.

So the fourteen-year-old Jorgenson signed up as an apprentice on the *Jane*, an English coal ship passing through Copenhagen on one of its regular journeys between Newcastle and the Baltic ports. It was a good way to learn the basic skills and acquire experience before venturing further; Cook himself had started out as a teenaged apprentice on a collier.

There was an emotional farewell with his parents and siblings – 'Oh! God! I shall never forget the scene' – but as soon as he was out to sea, Jorgenson apparently dismissed all thoughts of family and country, and showed no sign of regrets.

Jorgenson may have imagined smooth waters, but conditions in the Baltic and the North Sea were rarely like that, especially on the crossing to England, which he repeated many times. Travellers' tales describe the journey as tumultuous, with 'the fleeting clouds in the heavens: the screaming gulls wheeling above our heads, the flapping of the canvass, the rattling of the rigging about the mast', and the continual crash of waves against the ship's sides. The endless rocking made a landlubber's stomach 'move up and down, and glut like new butter in a bottle'. One Scandinavian traveller described how passengers would struggle to eat their meals:

> [I]t is droll to see all these spoons and knives and forks cruising in the air, steered by Fate and not by the hand which holds them, to see how an open mouth and a pair of hungry eyes follow all their movements and seem to pray devoutly for a fortunate voyage for them and their cargo to the desired haven.

For tourists it was entertaining if sickening, an induction into 'the sublime stir of nature'. For Jorgenson, it was a thrill that gradually became just a job, albeit one he never ceased to love.

He had much to learn: how to act quickly and obey orders, how to resist nausea, how to read the moods of the sea, and how to understand English. Every part of the ship had to be named and memorized; every eventuality must be perfectly understood so it could be prepared for. A large proportion of his next thirty years was to be lived on the sea: it became his profession and his element. The sea would flavour his character. All through life, he filled his talk with sailing metaphors, and a coarse streak of sailors' humour sometimes crept into his writings. Salt water flowed in his veins.

Life on the *Jane* took up the next four years – important years, from fourteen to eighteen, during which Jorgenson was transformed from a gauche and inconvenient son into a real sailor. One can picture him, a scruffy-headed, likeable boy, dressed in the wide-bottomed sailors' trousers of the day, rapidly picking up fluent (if heavily accented) English, and invariably full of energy. But he wrote little about this period, saying only 'I served my time out, and at the end of it had gained the reputation of a most perfect seaman', and 'I perfected myself in the knowledge of sea affairs and navigation.'

He did describe his first glimpse of the almost mythical country from which he was expecting so much. On seeing its coast from aloft on a mast, he felt flooded with 'a glorious joy'. At first it fulfilled his hopes in abundance: he made it a 'second home', one he considered a 'thousand times more dear to me than my native country'.

Between voyages he spent the winters in London, improving his command of the language and reading 'a great many books'. The famous city was everything he had imagined it to be: a dizzying wheel of commerce and activity. The London of the 1790s was just about to move from eighteenth-century elegance to nineteenth-century efficiency: it was hardly an aesthetically pleasing city, yet there was a kind of beauty in the sheer vigour of the machine's motion. It sucked people and goods in from all over the world, whirled them around and shot them out again: bought, sold, exploited, augmented. It was bigger than any single individual could take in. 'London is a giant,' wrote one visitor: 'strangers can only reach his feet.' There was an almost science-fiction quality to the sheer abundance and fatness of everything in its environs: another traveller observed cattle so fat as to be without wrinkles, pigs blown up like balloons, and human beings with 'hands swollen into round lumps of flesh' and 'calves as bulbous as a pumpkin'. Everything was oversized. 'Immense is St Paul's, immense Greenwich Hospital, immense the metropolis, immense are their parks, immense their possessions, immense their shipping, immense their wealth, and immense their debts.'

But amid this bloated plenitude there was also the clear air of freedom. Unlike in walled and gated Copenhagen, or almost anywhere else on the Continent, where one usually had to pass inquisitive guards to enter or leave a city, London was always open by land as well as sea. No one poked his nose into anyone else's business, and – as the caricatures in print-shop windows showed – no one was afraid to mock any public institution they wished: the government, the military, the Church, the royal family.

But there was also the English character to get used to, for in London there lived a people sometimes aloof, sometimes violently raucous. Jorgenson was to half-love, half-resent the English for the rest of his life, and to get to know them very well. He liked their strange combination of decency and misanthropy: for, as the wit Sydney Smith observed, Englishmen generally preferred not to engage with people at all unless their trading obligations required them to, or unless someone was in distress – in which case their generosity could be relied upon. Otherwise they preferred to be left alone by their hearth, to stare into the fire. 'They are content with Magna Charta and Trial by Jury; and think they are not bound to excel the rest of the world in small behaviour, if they are superior to them in great institutions.' Yet, for some reason, the ebullient Jorgenson came to feel at home among the English, while he never warmed to the more vivacious southern Europeans at all.

Perhaps this was partly because, like Conrad, he was so impressed by his first Englishman. The *Jane*'s captain, Henry Marwood, took him under his wing and more or less adopted him. Jorgenson lodged in Marwood's house when they were in Britain: he wrote later, 'I had often in his own house eaten his bread and drank his milk.' He became fond of his protective captain, and described him as 'a second father'.

Jorgenson was a young man of seconds: seconds which tended to supplant his firsts. English was to be his second language, and Britain his second country, the most important in his life. The departure on the collier marked a desertion more radical than his family could have foreseen: he would return to Denmark just once, briefly, but he was never wholeheartedly a Dane again. Nor did he entirely become an Englishman. He entered that twilight zone risked by all who leave the country of their birth, losing the ability to feel at home there but being only incompletely absorbed into their new homeland. For Jorgenson, the move tore up roots and destroyed whatever prospects he might have had for a simple life in the family clock-making trade. But it also opened up the world to him – a world towards which he was now borne, just as in his dream, on a ship sliding through deep waters.

2

Dreams fulfilled

The world had long been a constellation of travel and trading contacts, but by the eighteenth century a few particularly dense stars had developed a stronger gravitational pull, bending the lines of trade toward themselves. None was more powerful than Britain; as the nineteenth century went on, the experience of much of the world was to be conditioned by the ideals and interests of this small offshore island.

During Jorgenson's lifetime, Britain's confidence in its right and ability to play this role would just keep growing. By 1848, its Foreign Secretary Lord Palmerston would declare that, as Britain had been placed by God 'at the head of moral, social and political civilization', it was its inescapable task 'to lead the way and direct the march of other nations' towards the same exalted state. A government report on indigenous peoples came to the same conclusion: the Empire's highest purpose was to offer the world 'the opportunity of becoming partakers of that civilization, that innocent commerce, that knowledge and that faith with which it has pleased a gracious Providence to bless our own country'. There seemed nothing arrogant about this thought: it was the recognition of a duty, and the acceptance of a burden.

In the 1790s and early 1800s, however, when Jorgenson was first at sea, the main emphasis was not on moral improvement but on the promotion of trade. As Sir Walter Ralegh had once said, whoever commanded the sea also commanded the movement of goods – 'and hee that is Lord of the trade of the world is Lord of the wealth of the worlde'. It was Britain's aim to string this chain of maritime prosperity and influence across the globe, and nowhere was this more evident than in the barely charted waters of the Pacific, opened up by Cook in the 1770s and 1780s. This most beguiling of destinations was also one of the most commercially exciting, linking the Indian and Far Eastern colonies with South America and with Britain's new settlement in Australia, as well as offering up its own whale- and seal-rich waters. As a boy Jorgenson had been fascinated by the Pacific for its promise of adventure; now, like others, he was also to become fascinated by its promise of wealth and glory.

In 1798, finishing his apprenticeship on the collier, Jorgenson set himself to fulfil his original ambition and follow in the wake of Cook and Banks. He left the *Jane* and did his best to sign on to a South Sea voyage from Southampton. There were a few false starts – possibly including the alarming experience of being press-ganged into a navy ship and engaging in a sea battle or two before talking his way to safety again – but he did eventually find a place on the *Fanny*, a whaler and cargo vessel bound for the Cape of Good Hope, halfway to his destination and a good place to pick up a second ship for the rest of the journey.

Sailing on an intercontinental voyage was very different from nipping in and out of the Baltic. The trip to the Cape took several months; it could be longer if the winds were bad. A ship had to become a floating microcosm, able to support all on board for as long as necessary. Live pigs and poultry would often be taken on, as well as grain for planting, vast quantities of fresh water, preserved meat, ship's biscuit, potatoes and a daily allowance of rum for each sailor. The constant activity on board made it seem like a busy town on market day, albeit one populated exclusively by men and accompanied by the constant whump of flapping sails. The crew was kept busy scrubbing decks, washing clothes, performing drills and checking equipment – tasks imposed as much as anything else to preserve sanity.* They

---

* It did not always work: sailors sometimes succumbed to mental illnesses, including the calenture – a delusion that the ocean was a grassy field – or scorbutic nostalgia, in which intense vague longings alternated with a sense of physical disgust at the sight of the sea.

became extremely well-rounded in their skills: besides handling the ship, sailors could sew, cook, hunt, survey land, and entertain themselves. The only useful accomplishment often missing was the ability to swim, and Jorgenson was no exception. Years later, trying to ford rivers in Tasmania, he had to cross as best he could by stepping on rocks and wading.

Reaching southern Africa in April or May 1799, Jorgenson deserted the *Fanny* and looked for another ship; but here he seems to have been led astray. There follow eighteen or nineteen mysterious months during which (as he wrote) he 'engaged in different sea services, sometimes in private ships, and other times in regular men of war'. He hinted at dangerous and terrifying naval battles, but did not describe them in detail, and his miscellaneous 'sea services' apparently also included at least one spell as a hired seaman in a pirate ship, raiding vessels and ports far away on the west coast of South America.

Piracy was widespread in this period: certain forms of it were virtually regarded as a patriotic duty, for in war 'privateers' were licensed to capture ships and property belonging to the enemy, keeping the proceeds for personal profit. But the South American 'forced trade', as Jorgenson euphemistically called it, was rather different. Under the guise of trading with the local inhabitants, outlaw sailors would simply plunder coastal towns at will. It was armed robbery: a complete inversion of the liberating maritime commerce which Jorgenson was one day to bring with idealistic fanfare to Iceland.

In his published works he was circumspect, alluding only to a '*kind of trade* in the South Seas which could be of greatest use, but as it cannot be conducted openly, I would not dream of issuing anything public thereof, nor would it in my opinion be proper to do so'. He added: 'Because of the enormous profits which flow from it, no-one will write anything public about it, and everyone would like to keep to themselves what they know.' But in his more incautious private account he admitted to having sailed in a pirate ship which used to anchor off gold-rich towns in Mexico and Peru and threaten 'to blow down all the houses, if not permitted to trade uninterrupted with the inhabitants'.

This would have had a certain appeal to a bold young man with a few years' experience at sea, but it was foolhardy. South American piracy could be as dangerous for its practitioners as for its victims. Pirate crews faced summary execution, or, even worse, hard labour in the local quicksilver mines. There, one suffered slow mercury poisoning, the symptoms of which began with disturbing mental effects (memory loss, anxiety and a strange introverted shyness – the complete opposite of Jorgenson's qualities) and then progressed through various physical discomforts towards death. In his autobiography, Jorgenson described this gruesome punishment but said nothing of having risked it himself.*

By October or November 1800, Jorgenson was safely back at the Cape, and now he made it at last on to a more respectable ship bound for the new Australian colony in New South Wales. He must have sailed in one of two vessels which left within a month of each other: the *Lady Nelson* or the *Harbinger*. The evidence for each possibility is complex,† and would not be very interesting but for one point. If he sailed on the *Lady Nelson*, it was apparently as a convict, following arrest for mutiny on another ship – though he was liberated immediately on arrival, having impressed the captain by his seamanship. Whichever ship he was in, and whatever his status, he arrived in Sydney around the turn of 1801, and there did join the *Lady Nelson*

---

* In *Thomas Walter* he went to the other extreme, telling a bawdy, preposterous story of how he narrowly escaped capture, sought shelter with a melancholy eccentric in the jungle, and then saved himself by posing as a doctor and curing the local governor's wife of diarrhoea by applying scalding water to her buttocks – after which he was acclaimed as the greatest physician in Peru.

† The basic paradox is simple. Jorgenson himself asserted that he sailed in the *Lady Nelson*, but his description of the voyage does not match the *Lady Nelson* route; it matches that taken by the *Harbinger* a month later. (Both ships took a new short cut between Tasmania and the Australian mainland, but the *Lady Nelson* kept closer to the north side of Bass Strait, the *Harbinger* to the south.) Because of this key fact, it has generally been assumed that Jorgenson's memory was at fault, and that he was on the *Harbinger*. But the crew pay lists for the *Lady Nelson* do suggest (though not conclusively) that he was on board from the Cape. The *Lady Nelson's* captain also described taking on a convict there – 'a Dane, gigantic in his appearance'. The man proved to be 'an excellent seaman, active, willing, and occasioning no trouble', so the captain recommended his emancipation after they reached Sydney. This sounds very much like Jorgenson until one remembers that he was far from gigantic: convict registers give his build as medium and his height as either 5 feet 5½ inches (1.63 metres), or just over 5 feet 7 inches (1.67 metres). Nor does it solve the puzzle of the variant route description.

as a free, ordinary crew member, signing himself with the name he always adopted on British ships: John Johnson.

He stayed with this important surveying and exploration ship for several years, and in its service his boyhood dreams of adventure and discovery at last became a reality. As the *Lady Nelson* made its way from one unexplored harbour to another, charting coasts, laying down colonies and delivering stores, it also steadily bore Jorgenson himself upwards through the ranks, from common seaman to first mate. After his year or two of war, desertion, piracy and mutiny (or whatever subset of these approximated to the truth), this was just what Jorgenson needed: a chance at a nobler endeavour, in the spirit of his heroes Banks and Cook.

During 1801 and 1802, Jorgenson's new ship mostly conducted brief supply and exploration trips up and down the New South Wales coast on government orders, returning each time to Sydney to pick up further instructions and restock its stores, partly from its own vegetable patch on a little island in Sydney Harbour. Several of its journeys took it back the way it had come, into Bass Strait. The New South Wales government was interested in these southern parts because they were rich in treasure – a bounty of flesh rather than gold and silver. The south-eastern shores and islands supported a vast population of seals, whose fur and oil sold for good prices in markets all over the world.

In his writings on the South Pacific trades, Jorgenson enthused about these animals. There were two species: the fur seals, with their silky pelts, and the larger 'sea-elephants' or elephant seals, colossal creatures with fleshy probosces. These were valued for both fur and blubber, the latter being rendered down like that of whales to make oil. The *Lady Nelson* crew found thousands of them all over Bass Strait, particularly on King Island, where so many lay around on the beaches that they looked like giant, soft cobbles. The sailors collected oil and skins as samples, and also made cosy fur-seal hats and slippers for themselves. Both species were easy to kill, as they had no fear of humans. Jorgenson described the technique:

> The way to catch sea-elephants is very simple, one walks straight
> to where one sees them on the island and runs a harpoon in

under their heart, and thereafter a lance, of which thrust they usually die immediately. There is not the least danger walking close to them, one can even stand on their backs. They are so heavy that they cannot move quickly, and it can take them some hours to walk 100 paces.

The smaller seals were easy too: one needed only 'a knife, a steel or file and a large bludgeon' – the latter for killing them, the former for removing the skin, which was then preserved in salt. Jorgenson showed no sentimentality about this loveless trade, but no one would at the turn of the nineteenth century, least of all a sailor, whose first thought was likely to be for his own chances in the market. The *Lady Nelson* was not a commercial ship, but it did help to open the way for a seal rush. Companies such as Kable & Underwood of Sydney soon began to drop off teams of sealers all over the islands, leaving them for months before sailing back to collect them with their cargo.

It was these tough, isolated sealers who pioneered relations with the indigenous people of the area: they would take Aboriginal women as companions, often by arrangement with the men, and sometimes (not always) with the cheerful consent of the women. Meetings between Aboriginal Australians and more itinerant seaborne Europeans, such as Jorgenson and the other *Lady Nelson* sailors, were generally cautious affairs, driven by a mixture of curiosity and anxiety on both sides. In an all-too-typical encounter on the southern mainland coast in February 1802, a landing party, of whom Jorgenson was very likely a member, met a gathering of around eighteen people. The two groups amicably sat down to eat together, and exchanged gifts. The sailors swapped clothes for spears and a basket. Afterwards, however, their Aboriginal hosts indicated that they expected their spears back, though they did not return the clothes. They now seemed to want everything the sailors had, 'even to the last shirt'. The situation became tenser. The sailors asked by signs where good water could be found; there was no response. They got up and headed for their boat, but the ship's boy turned around just in time to see a man hurling a spear at their backs. It whizzed by, narrowly missing one of them. A larger group now came out from behind a fallen tree and spears clattered down on the boat. The sailors fired over the attackers' heads; it had little effect, so they fired directly at them and hit at least three before making a hurried getaway. It was a common pattern: the two sides would start on friendly terms, but some misunderstanding by one or the other would trigger violence, and all would end badly.*

In July 1802, after the *Lady Nelson*'s several voyages around the south-eastern coast, Jorgenson learned that they were to take part in an exciting assignment: they would accompany the explorer Matthew Flinders and his ship the *Investigator* on the next leg of his circumnavigation of the Australian continent, up the coast of northern New South Wales into what is now Queensland. This was a dangerous stretch, for it followed the Great Barrier Reef: Cook himself had nearly been wrecked there, and others had avoided it ever since. Flinders wanted to survey the coast from close to shore, but could not do so in his own standard ship. The *Lady Nelson*, however, had a revolutionary design. Instead of one fixed keel, it was fitted with three mobile ones which could be pulled up like skirts out of harm's way whenever the ship needed to pass over shallow sandbanks or coral outcrops. The design had not often been put to the test in the deeper southern waters, but it was just what was needed on the reef. Jorgenson was delighted: he would always take pride in having once sailed with the famous Flinders, and having shared in the glory of this great voyage.

The two vessels sailed together from Sydney on 22 July 1802 and raced northward, though in open sea the *Lady Nelson* tended to fall behind. Flinders had to keep pausing for it to catch up. He found this frustrating, but before long the *Lady Nelson* had its first chance to prove itself. To Flinders's satisfaction, it sailed several times into shallows the *Investigator* could not have reached, and surveyed hitherto unknown shores.

It did, however, suffer a few scrapes on sandbars in the process. Although it successfully freed itself each time by raising its keels as planned, it sustained some damage. More mishaps followed over the

---

* Differing notions of property were often the source of misunderstandings. Aboriginal communities operated a complex system of exchange, balancing gifts on one side with social obligations on the other: this included arrangements made over women, something few sealers realized. Meanwhile, the Australians tended to accept gifts and then help themselves to anything else they liked among their visitors' possessions – a practice invariably seen by the Europeans as theft.

coming weeks. The grinding shock of 'taking the ground' became horribly familiar to the crew – a sensation later described by Conrad as the feeling that 'your feet had been caught in an imponderable snare; you feel the balance of your body threatened, and the steady poise of your mind is destroyed'. The ground seemed to reach up through the sea and grab you by the ankles: it went against every sailor's deepest instinct, which was to keep ship and ground separate at all costs. But Jorgenson and all others on board had to put up with it for the moment, and to hope that any injury would stop short of complete shipwreck.

On one occasion, the main keel became so deeply lodged in the sand that it could not be lifted at all. When the crew dropped anchor, that stuck fast as well. The *Lady Nelson* strained and 'turned about violently', as if in agony, until at last the keel snapped off completely and floated up alongside them. The anchor remained stuck until the tide came in at nightfall; when the men eventually succeeded in raising it, they saw that it too was in bad shape. More delays followed while repairs were attempted, though little could be done. Yet somehow the ship managed to keep going.

As they continued sailing north, the land changed. First the smooth beaches of New South Wales gave way to entanglements of mangroves, gnarly treelets whose overground roots clawed into the mud along their entire length and made landing difficult. Fishlike mudskippers ran everywhere among the roots, as did small red crabs, each wielding one angry fighting claw. Later the ships reached the reef, and the coast changed even more dramatically: bright coralscapes became visible under the surface. Flinders thought these resembled a second Creation, in which things familiar from the ordinary world were reflected in fairy-tale form: 'wheat sheaves, mushrooms, stag's horns, cabbage leaves'. The outer edges of the reef were even richer, rising closer to the surface and revealing niches full of corals, sponges and sea cucumbers, laid out like cabinets of curiosities. Clams yawned open: when they shut they made a loud clack and sent a fountain of seawater erupting above the surface. It was a magical world – but one that threatened catastrophe to the ships above.

Sure enough, the *Lady Nelson* had another bad accident shortly afterwards, snagging its anchor on coral at the Cumberland Islands.

With help from the *Investigator*'s crew the men managed to pull it up by brute force, but one of its arms broke off in the process. This decided matters. The *Lady Nelson* had been useful along the reef, but Flinders now wished to hasten on northwards in open sea so that he could get past the tropics before monsoon season: the beleaguered ship would slow him down and jeopardize the whole project. He decided, with some regret, to send his brave 'little consort' back to Sydney.

This parting provided a good opportunity for Jorgenson. Before they separated, the *Lady Nelson* returned a first mate borrowed from the *Investigator*; its own temporarily demoted first officer resumed his usual job. This left the second officer's post free, and it was almost certainly now that Jorgenson made his leap into the officer's class. By the time they returned to Sydney he was second mate, and was then immediately promoted to first. Thus, at twenty-two, he found himself within a single step of making captain. As first officer, he also had to get used to exerting authority, and giving orders to men of all temperaments and ages. This he did, apparently with aplomb: leadership came naturally to him. He developed an air of confident command that was to remain with him throughout life.

While the *Investigator* sailed northwards alone (and successfully completed its circumnavigation, sailing back into Sydney Harbour the following June), the *Lady Nelson* began its slow limp home. It had no proper anchors left: the crew had to improvise a replacement from a hunk of iron-bark wood, weighted with two heavy guns. Jorgenson remembered this monster of an anchor as being 'one-third of the whole length of the vessel'. It was massively unwieldy, and tended to dry out when exposed to the air, so that each time they stopped they had to leave it floating in the water for a while before it would sink. Once soaked, it was difficult to lift aboard again. But the ship made it safely home, reaching Sydney on 23 November 1802.*

The *Lady Nelson*, with Jorgenson taking up his post as first mate, was now offered a second taste of glory and another chance to make its mark on Australian history. Again it was to go to Bass Strait, this time not to survey sealing territory but to help install the first permanent colonial settlement on the island of Tasmania. It took on board

* The triple sliding keel design was never used on ships again – it was insufficiently robust, as the *Lady Nelson*'s experience proved.

a small pod of free settlers, convicts and soldiers, together with their appointed Lieutenant-Governor John Bowen and all their stores and equipment, and delivered them in September 1803 to the chosen site at Risdon Cove, just inside the mouth of the Derwent River on the island's south-eastern corner.*

Like caterpillars placed in a cabbage patch, the new colonists immediately began chopping up vegetation, and they soon opened out a clear patch of ground. There was no sign of the Tasmanians, who normally entered this area only during kangaroo-hunting season. Nothing interrupted the work of transforming the land. Jorgenson and the rest of the crew helped the convicts and soldiers, but they were also granted time to trek around the surrounding hills and to hunt, adding fresh meat to the ship's supplies. For the first time Jorgenson was able to indulge his longing for exploration by land as well as by sea. He hiked through the formidable bush for miles, alone or with other crew members. According to a local legend (alas, probably untrue) he carried a Bible stuffed in one pocket and Johnson's *Rasselas* in the other, and from these he and a companion named many local landmarks: Bagdad, Jericho, Jerusalem, Lake Tiberias, and the River Jordan. He would certainly have enjoyed hacking through this difficult territory and working off his overflowing energies; idleness often troubled his mind, and a challenge like this was welcome.

Jorgenson and the *Lady Nelson* left the colony briefly in October 1803, but returned in early 1804 bearing a second group of settlers.† This time it transferred another brand-new colony *en masse* from Port Phillip on the mainland, where the appointed Governor David Collins had become dissatisfied with the land. (He may have given up too

* The government knew that the French were interested in Australia: a rival French expedition was going round the continent at the same time as Flinders, and it was obvious that France was considering staking an Australian claim. One major purpose of launching a new southern British colony was therefore to forestall any such attempt in the Bass Strait area. But Sydney also needed to branch out, so as to divide and reduce its own rapidly growing convict population.

† On the way, the ship sought shelter from stormy weather inside northern Tasmania's Tamar River, and there spent several weeks exploring. Jorgenson again hiked regularly into the bush, sometimes with Robert Brown, a botanist who had sailed with Flinders, or with the mineralogist Adolarius Humphrey, who once stopped to carve his initials on a rock near the river: 'A.H. 1804'. The writing is still visible today.

soon – this would later be the site of Melbourne.) He opted instead to move to the Derwent and join Bowen's settlement. In fact, it proved more of a takeover than a merger. Collins took one look at Bowen's windswept Risdon camp – Bowen was unable to argue its virtues, being absent at the time – and decided to shift the main colony a few kilometres upriver, to a place he named Sullivan's Cove. He was right: although Risdon had an attractive location, Sullivan's Cove was on the more sheltered side of the river, and had better water and soil. It also had a convenient little island, linked to the shore by a sandspit at low tide: perfect for landing stores. By the time Bowen returned to his colony, he found it had been drained of life by Collins's more successful version.

Sullivan's Cove did have its difficulties. A tall, humourless mountain (Mount Wellington) loomed into the mist above it, and the area was overgrown with scrub and fallen trees, concealing a mushy wet earth. The labour ahead was formidable. Collins's convicts were put to work immediately: 'spades, hoes, saws and axes were put into the hands of prisoners', wrote Jorgenson. The crew helped too: 'we commenced clearing away as fast as we could'. But again there was time for exploration. Energetic as ever, Jorgenson's instinctive response on seeing the nearby mountain was to climb it. He and Adolarius Humphrey struggled to the top, admired the spectacular view along the Derwent, and inched down again. It was an arduous excursion. The mountain's slopes were covered with the challenging Tasmanian flora: logs, strands of cutting-grass as long as shipboard ropes, and clumps of springy 'button-grass' into which the walker's foot sank deeply. A traveller who tried it thirty years later remarked that going up was not so bad, but descending again was 'one of the most difficult and exhausting things on earth'.

The following Sunday the settlement's new clergyman, Robert Knopwood, delivered an inaugural sermon on the prosperity to be hoped for in Sullivan's Cove. It worked: Sullivan's Cove did thrive, and became the permanent site of Tasmania's capital Hobart. The remains of Risdon were gradually abandoned, though it became the scene of one last infamous event towards the end of that year, 1804, when a group of Tasmanians passed by on their annual kangaroo hunt. They were shocked to see a scattering of unlikely-looking creatures pottering about their hunting grounds; the newcomers were equally amazed to see the huge Aboriginal party armed with hunting spears, and they panicked. An officer began shooting and a number of the hunters were killed – anywhere between three and fifty, according to different estimates. It was a grim incident, never to be forgotten, and it proved a portent of doom for the island's Aboriginal population, as Jorgenson himself was to agree when he eventually returned to the island twenty-two years later and learned of all that had happened in the interim.

Jorgenson and the *Lady Nelson* left the Derwent on 10 March 1804, ending a second stay of just under a month, and missing Bowen's return by four days and the Aboriginal encounter by some eight weeks. This also brought to an end Jorgenson's role in the founding of colonial Tasmania – a place he could never have dreamed he would one day return to in radically different circumstances.

Back in Sydney, he did one more short supply trip on the *Lady Nelson* before taking his leave of it in April 1804. He had been on board for just over three years, sharing its moments of fame and gaining in experience and rank. He was very likely the *Lady Nelson*'s longest serving crew member: he certainly outlasted all the captains. And now he became a captain himself.*

Jorgenson apparently left the *Lady Nelson* because he was headhunted: enticed away, with his knowledge of Bass Strait and its sealing opportunities, to a more lucrative job on a private vessel.

Whales and seals had come to dominate the Australian economy during the few years Jorgenson had been on the *Lady Nelson*: he later described the infant Hobart as 'enriching itself on their oleaginous remains', and indeed all of southern Australia now seemed to be floating on a sea of mammalian oil, and of money. The capture of whales off Tasmania was almost as easy as clobbering seals: the captain of a ship accompanying the *Lady Nelson* southward in 1803 had remarked that he took three sperm whales there 'without looking', so

---

* The *Lady Nelson* had one more notable moment after this, returning to the Tamar later that year to help found the first northern Tasmanian settlement at Port Dalrymple. In 1825 it was attacked by Malays near Timor: the ship was burned and sunk, and the crew were killed.

easy was the work. In calving season, southern or right whales even swam far up the Derwent River, to Sullivan's Cove and beyond. The noise of their blowing sometimes kept the settlers awake at night and, after whaling in the river began, farm animals would be fed on blubber when other food was scarce. By 1805, Collins was complaining that their pigs ate enough whale to make their pork taste like lamp oil.

The seal trade had flourished too, but in Bass Strait it was now slipping past its peak. By the 1810s it would be in total decline, for the simple reason that the sealers had killed all their product: the Strait elephant seal became completely extinct, and the fur seal population fell to almost nothing before recovering. Even by 1804, the focus of the trade was already moving back to where it had started, the bays of New Zealand, where seal numbers were still healthy. It was thus to New Zealand that Jorgenson now sailed, as captain of a new Kable & Underwood vessel, the *Contest*. He set out across the Tasman Sea in August 1804.

The untried ship developed a few technical problems, but on the whole it was a successful journey. Jorgenson's crew caught plenty of seals and returned to Sydney the following February with some five to seven thousand skins. 'We killed several thousands of these harmless creatures,' he reminisced later. 'It is indeed astonishing with what eagerness the sailors enter into this pursuit, knocking down the animals with their clubs, stripping them of their skins, and pegging them out to dry, or salting them down in casks, with the greatest zeal and perseverence.' It all meant money for Jorgenson: as captain he would have had the largest share of the profits.

He did not stay with the *Contest* for long. Having returned to Sydney, he signed up as first mate on a much larger ship, the *Alexander*. This was a typical South Sea whaler, and its commander, Robert Rhodes, was a typical whaling captain – rough, unprofessional, versatile, and extremely eager for profit. He and the *Alexander* had been at sea for years already, cruising around southern waters and loading up with oil and skins. It was time now to head for London and turn the loot to cash. This appointment would therefore spell the end of Jorgenson's first round of Pacific adventures, but there were still months of travel ahead. Rhodes seemed to be in no hurry to start his journey. The first of many delays took the form of a long detour from Sydney back to Tasmania, to take on even more whales at the height of the hunting season.

It is unclear whether Jorgenson was on board for this Tasmanian jaunt or not; if he was, there is a good chance that (as he proudly claimed) he was the first person ever to harpoon a whale inside the Derwent.* With or without him, the *Alexander* did well there: in three months Rhodes doubled his existing haul of oil to some two hundred tonnes, and took on a fresh shipment of whalebone. He also bought a few barrels of illegal rum to be smuggled to Sydney for a quick profit, for, as Jorgenson noted, there were frequent shortages in the colony and 'it was no uncommon thing to give ten guineas for a gallon of rum, tolerably diluted'. In Sydney, Rhodes also added even more to the groaning weight of cargo, taking on around fourteen thousand extra sealskins and over twenty-six tonnes of elephant seal oil, some probably acquired from Jorgenson's *Contest*.

The *Alexander* was as richly loaded as it could be, and looked set to make a fortune. But Rhodes proceeded to let it all leak away – literally. All the way home, he dallied in one port after another, often in pursuit of further elusive hunting or trading opportunities.† Every day cost money both in sailors' pay and in the physical degradation of the cargo. By the end, many skins had rotted so badly that they had to be thrown overboard, and much of the valuable oil was lost or ruined. As Jorgenson later wrote, good storage was one of the most important

* The *Contest* / *Alexander* enigma is almost as intriguing as the *Lady Nelson* / *Harbinger* one. The *Alexander*'s Tasmanian jaunt took place while Jorgenson was supposedly in New Zealand, but Rhodes's account books list him as being present on his ship. It *is* just about possible that he travelled on the *Alexander* briefly while delegating command of the *Contest* to someone else, later catching a lift in another vessel to be reunited with it before its return from New Zealand. The *Alexander* was indeed in the Derwent when the first whale was harpooned there – and if Jorgenson was on board he would have been the harpoonist, as this was the traditional job of the first mate.

† Whaling captains seemed particularly prone to being lured off their route by extra money-making schemes. In *Typee*, Herman Melville jestingly describes one ghostly whaler that never returned home at all, and was rumoured to have sailed for years from port to port, being last seen 'in the vicinity of the ends of the earth, cruizing along as leisurely as ever, her sails all bepatched and bequilted with rope-yarns, her spars fished with old pipestaves, and her rigging knotted and spliced in every possible direction', and presumed still to be drifting around 'somewhere off Buggerry Island, or the Devil's-Tail Peak'.

aspects of any whaling or sealing voyage: oil had to be run into barrels of the best quality, and properly cooled on the way in special tanks and lines. Otherwise, being warm and fluid, it would leak. Naturally any problem of this kind would become worse the longer it took to get home.

The delays began in Sydney itself, where Rhodes waited for ten weeks after his return from the Derwent. When he did set off it was only to detour to Norfolk Island for supplies: there he was caught trying to smuggle runaway convicts into the ship and was fined, losing another bite out of his profits. He then sailed to New Zealand again, apparently to pick up yet more sealskins. He also took on a couple of Maori passengers: two boys named Te Ina and Maaki, who joined the ship out of wanderlust and against the wishes of their parents, who feared they were being lured away for an English cannibal feast. Rhodes promised that both would return safely within eighteen months, but in fact one chose to leave the ship before reaching Europe and the other died in England. Neither ever made it back to New Zealand.

The ship now struck out into the real emptiness of the Pacific. There followed a long period of uneventful, open horizons, until they made their next landfall in June, at Tahiti. This does not seem to have been a scheduled stop: Jorgenson claimed that they were blown off-course by a gale while attempting to round Cape Horn. Some gale – but there may be a vestige of truth in this story, for if they were held back by bad weather they would have run short of provisions, and Rhodes did tell the missionaries on the island that he had come 'for refreshment'. If so, he had chosen the wrong place. The missionaries were in dire need themselves: shipping had been disrupted by the Napoleonic wars, and they had received almost nothing from home for a long time. In the end it was the *Alexander* that supplied them rather than the other way round, notably with two bottles of wine from Rhodes's small stock, for sacramental use.

There followed another ill-advised delay. The *Alexander* stayed in Tahiti for over seven weeks, restocking its supplies as best it could by curing local meat with sea salt, and squeezing sugar from canes using a gun carriage as a press. Jorgenson was fascinated but disillusioned by his Tahiti experience. Sailors calling there had traditionally regarded it as an opportunity for a few weeks of sex and relaxation, but the presence of the missionaries was changing all that. According to Jorgenson's description, they were as weird and withered a bunch of sour evangelical grapes as one could ever expect to find, and incompetent to boot. Most knew no Tahitian and could barely communicate with their flock; they did not understand Polynesian culture and had made very few converts. The futility of their attempt, combined with the difficulty many had in resisting Tahitian temptations themselves, seemed to be slowly but surely driving them out of their wits. At least two had become maniacal in different ways during the year or so before Jorgenson's arrival: one had been recently removed from the island in a state of collapse after giving away all his possessions and rambling from place to place loudly airing 'the most strange, and unaccountable notions and prejudices'.

Jorgenson considered the missionaries rude, crude and cowardly; they had no dignity of their own, yet showed little respect for others. 'They look somewhat like humble petitioners at a gentleman's door, and it is easy to observe, that they are men of no education, nor have ever conversed with any but the lowest classes of society. They seem to neither believe nor understand the doctrine they are trying to convey.' The majority were simply hypocritical: while preaching against extramarital sex and intoxication, they drank heavily and outfornicated the Tahitians. In their cups, they would contradict everything they said when sober. One openly cursed the miseries of a missionary's life, and another was heard shouting oaths against God because the chief's wife had rejected him. (Contrary to what most European visitors believed, sexual activity was subject to rigorous limitations and rules in Tahitian society.) The missionaries' records confirm that some of their number did have difficulty keeping to the right path: at least two gave up the fight, and set up house with Tahitian women. As one remarked, most of them had learned by experience how hard it was for young unmarried men to remain chaste in such a place.

But they were not all hypocrites; some were fanatical zealots instead. One, John Jefferson, seemed truly to believe the message he was preaching, and to struggle mightily against the temptations of the island. Unfortunately, the effort of resistance had turned him into a ghoul who spent most of his time shut up alone in his hut, mortifying his already gaunt flesh and uttering 'the most dismal and hollow groans'. Jorgenson thought he resembled a ghost, or the 'melancholy mad' lunatic illustrated in one of the two well-known figures at the entrance to Bethlem mental hospital – by contrast with the other 'raving mad' type, who resembled the missionary driven insane by lust. In fact, Jorgenson may have leaped to the wrong assumptions from Jefferson's cadaverousness: he had simply been in poor physical health for the last two years, after catching a cold-like infection from which he never recovered. He was desperate to leave the island because of this, and his superiors gave him permission to sail with the *Alexander*. But he and Rhodes fell out before departure, possibly disagreeing over which cabin he would occupy and how much he should pay. He decided not to go after all. A couple of years later he died on the island: several Tahitians attended the funeral, and the presiding missionary used the opportunity to address them 'on the subjects of Death, the resurrection and Judgement to come'.

Not surprisingly, the Tahitians were unimpressed by this glum theology, though they treated their guests tolerantly. They contented themselves with mild mockery, sometimes assembling near the church and pretending to sing along to the hymns 'with serious and long faces' before falling about laughing. It was an encounter between an exceptionally inept group of missionaries and a people as temperamentally and culturally unsuited to their message as could be imagined. The Tahitians' own traditions were far from Arcadian, including as they did brutal warfare, strict class divisions, human sacrifice, and infanticide. But they had no concept of either hypocrisy or evangelism. They could not understand why people would want to make a long dangerous journey just to torment themselves trying to propagate a religion.*

Besides the missionaries, the island also supported a raggle-taggle crowd of runaway convicts, deserting sailors, beachcombers and drifters who lived by working as mercenaries for rival Tahitian tribes. Forever at war, the Tahitians had a great appetite for European muskets and gunpowder, together with a firm grasp of the principles of commerce. To establish status they often stockpiled far more firearms than they

* This particular group of missionaries eventually abandoned the island, driven out by tribal warfare, though others returned later and had more success.

could ever use, so there was no limit to the number they would buy. The wars on the island were almost as interminable as the one still raging in Europe, although – just as in Europe – they were punctuated by truces, one of which was in force when Jorgenson was there.

The biggest pile of weapons belonged to the war-hungry King Pomare II, whose father Pomare I had started the trend. Pomare II was particularly shrewd at exploiting the European presence, missionary and otherwise, to consolidate his own power. Tall, massive and insatiable, he was a memorable character. Jorgenson described how he would demand brandy from the *Alexander* crew and swig it till he passed out – a habit that eventually killed him. On one occasion he boarded the ship and said: 'Master Christ, very good, very fine fellow; me love Christ like my own brother. Give me one glass of brandy.' He repeated this until he had drunk nearly a pint, whereupon he seized a leg of mutton from the table and began 'to gnaw it with his great and ugly teeth'. When they tried to remove him he demanded one more glassful, threatening to take back everything he had said about Christ if they did not comply. They still refused, so he carried out his threat: 'Damn Christ! Christ very bad; Otaheite God fine fellow.' He then jumped overboard and swam to shore. Jorgenson also noted that Pomare used to write threatening letters to the Mission headquarters in London demanding more and more muskets and ammunition: 'Should I be killed, you will have nothing in Tahiti. Do not come here when I am dead.'

In short, Tahiti was a depressing place: the encounter between Europeans and Polynesians seemed to bring out the worst in both sides. Sir Joseph Banks, who had visited Tahiti with Cook on the *Endeavour* almost forty years earlier, heard all about it from Jorgenson himself after the *Alexander*'s return, and wrote sadly:

Otaheite is said to be at present in the hands of about one hundred white men, chiefly English convicts, who lend their assistance as warriors to the chief, whosoever he may be, who offers them the most acceptable wages, payable in women, hogs &c.; and we are told that these banditti have by the introduction of diseases, by devastation, murther, and all kinds of European barbarism, reduced the population of that once interesting island to less than one-tenth of what it was when the Endeavour visited it in 1768. Surely these people will, if not otherwise provided for, soon become buccaneers and pirates.

Jorgenson's visit to the island was to trigger something of a personal crisis. It did not seriously damage his faith in God – that came later – but it did make him doubt the wisdom of the Church. He had grown up with a half-hearted Protestantism; until now his faith had been merely conventional, like many people's. But the scepticism which grew in him after Tahiti was to eat at his soul for years, and one way or another religion was a central problem for him from then on. A few years later, he published an intemperate book attacking 'the *ignorance*, *bigotry*, *violence*, and *indecent* behavior of these men, called missionaries'. He later disowned this work, but it was a passionate indictment and cast doubt over a much wider field than the folly of one group of ill-trained evangelists in Tahiti.

He believed that the Tahitians would respond if the Christian message were communicated straightforwardly in their own language. But the missionaries could not do this, and they alienated their listeners by constantly insisting on the superiority of their religion over others. Jorgenson felt that they should understand, instead, that 'the naked savage in the woods of New Holland is equally dear and equally as much under the protection of his gracious master as the most refined European. His soul is composed of the same precious materials as our's are, and perhaps in the eye of his maker he appears to be the more perfect being.'

Here Jorgenson was reviving the eighteenth-century notion of the 'noble savage', which proposed that people living in a state of nature were blessed because they were uncorrupted – a view adhered to by Banks himself as a young man in Tahiti, when he compared its people to denizens of Eden. But other remarks by Jorgenson also look forward to the very different philosophy of the Evangelical Christian movement, which was to become dominant among the administrators of the British Empire. According to this, all human beings were created equal and all were equally susceptible to the teachings of Christianity, but they stood, in effect, on different rungs of a ladder, climbing towards perfection. On the top were the British, though they did admit that they had not started there.* Everyone else was still on their way up, but there was hope for all: they would all reach the goal in the end.

It was an optimistic theory, especially if one was an Englishman or a would-be Englishman like Jorgenson. But, like many simple, exuberant theories, it foundered on the difficulty of applying it to the real world. The people clustered around the lower rungs also seemed strangely reluctant to climb on. Sometimes, like the Aboriginal Australians, they hardly seemed to notice that the ladder was there: the most profound rejection of all.

Whatever their reservations, the Tahitians were certainly curious about their visitors and their technology and habits. Like the Maori, they were keen to travel: when the *Alexander* finally left at the beginning of August 1805 several Tahitians sailed with them (though one of the Maori stayed behind). Two were specifically assigned to Jorgenson's care for the journey; he undertook responsibility for setting them up in Britain as well.†

The *Alexander* also delivered despatches from the missionaries to their head office at home, including a letter apologizing for their continuing failure in the objects of their mission. They had perhaps achieved some success with one minor goal, though: discouraging Tahitians from bestowing tattoos on their visitors. Unlike many South Sea sailors (including Banks) Jorgenson did not leave the island with one of those beautiful designs that a later visitor, Charles Darwin, thought ornamented their wearers 'like the trunk of a noble tree by a delicate creeper'.

The *Alexander* now successfully rounded Cape Horn, and brought to an end Jorgenson's long Pacific sojourn. More delays had to be endured before they reached home: three months were wasted in a port off Brazil, probably engaging in further trade. Another whale-ship's log-book

* The New South Wales missionary Lancelot Threlkeld noted that Rome had once been able to look down on 'the poor disarmed, dispirited, miserable Brutes, the White Aborigines of Albion's shore'.
† Jorgenson wrote that they eventually died in Britain and never returned to Tahiti, but the Mission's chronicles record at least three Tahitians who did return safely after sailing away on the *Alexander*. Thus, unless Jorgenson's charges were among the three after all, there must have been at least five altogether.

confirms their presence there, and even describes how, on Christmas Day, the festive season got the better of Jorgenson's dignity as first officer. The whole *Alexander* crew being swept away by a riotous mood, Jorgenson ran to the master's cabin of the other ship and hurled a bowl of beef stew through the door, thus proving that he still had something in him of the madcap schoolboy of half a lifetime ago, despite all his newfound responsibility and authority.

There was one final pause in St Helena while a convoy was assembled, in accordance with wartime travelling rules. They left at last with five other whalers for company on 19 April 1806, and arrived at Gravesend on 26 June, sailing into the commercial hurly-burly of the British dockyards with (though they did not yet realize it) a rotting, dribbling, dwindling cargo of oil.

Jorgenson was twenty-six: he had been seven years away from Europe and had over ten years of maritime experience. He had been promoted to first officer, and had even had his first command; he knew the whaling and sealing business, and was familiar with the southern colonies and their trade. He could call himself an experienced Australian bushman, and was a walking encyclopaedia of prices and markets all round the Pacific – from coconut oil to elephant oil, from guns in Tahiti to smuggled rum and convicts in Sydney.

He also had a treasure he had hoarded all through his Pacific travels, though regrettably it does not survive today: a journal of his experiences, full of notes on trading opportunities together with almost two hundred little drawings sketched to pass the time. He was sure he would be able to use this journal in Europe, perhaps to write a book, or to win some advantage from either the British government or the Danish one. Among all the ships in the South Pacific, he had never seen a Danish whaler, nor a Danish sealing squad. Yet the Danes had a noble fleet: they had staked colonial claims in Africa and the Caribbean. There was no reason why they should not join the money-making party in the Pacific. All they needed was encouragement from someone who knew how it was done. Thus, for the first time in years, Jorgenson's thoughts turned to his home country again.

3

English Jorgenson

They were safely back in Britain, but Captain Rhodes was in trouble. Most of his cargo was spoiled and, to make matters worse, the price of right-whale oil had fallen while they were travelling. He cleared no profit at all, and could not pay his initial investors what he owed them. At the insurance hearing, it was ruled that the disaster was caused by his own incompetence. He was held liable for the whole debt: around £5,000. As he could not pay, he was thrown in debtors' gaol, where he festered for years. The voyage that should have made Rhodes rich had ruined him entirely.

Fortunately Jorgenson had no share in this misfortune, and he probably still had some money from the *Contest* cargo – enough to support himself for a while as well as the two travelling Tahitians for whom he was responsible. The three briefly shared lodgings in Gravesend before moving on to London. It was not an easy cohabitation. Whenever Jorgenson wasn't looking, the Tahitians would sneak next door to the pub, where they were given what they assumed was free beer: 'Yes! Yes! Give us beer – very good, very good.' It was only when the final bill was presented that Jorgenson realized what they had been doing. Another problem was sex. They were used to making love whenever they felt like it, or so Jorgenson believed. One of the two, named 'Jack' in Jorgenson's account, was particularly fond of visiting Gravesend's numerous prostitutes whenever he had a shilling to pay them: in this case, it seems he did understand the finances of the transaction. Later, after they had moved to London, Jack made the mistake of offering two shillings to a fine lady who had stepped out of her carriage outside the zoo, and was nearly lynched by the surrounding mob. 'Look, look, two shillings,' he cried, and pointed to another woman passing by: 'I would only give her one.' Luckily the mob saw the funny side, but Jack was now annoyed, and harangued them: 'When you come to my country, don't I give you my mother, my wife, or my sister, and here you will not let me have a stranger.' It was a 'very bad country', he muttered.

London was overwhelming to Tahitian eyes, especially approaching it through the docklands from Gravesend. The Thames formed a highway of ships and docks all the way to the city, its banks clogged with shipyards and warehouses all staking their individual claims down to the water; there were no riverside footpaths for Sunday strollers. The river itself was almost as densely crowded, giving it a very different appearance from today. Visitors compared it to a forest rather than a waterway, so full was it of ships – all with their sails neatly furled and their masts sticking up like trees, only slightly swaying in the current.

Just as, along the fringes of the Thames, all was mud where there should be water, in the city all was smog instead of air. As one approached the centre, one penetrated ever more deeply into it: on a bad day, other pedestrians seemed to loom out of the murk ahead like dugongs in dark water. Sometimes you could not see the horses' ears at the front of your carriage, nor the edges of the road beside you. The houses were besmirched, and flakes of soot would settle on your clothes and skin like black snow. If one fell on your face and you thoughtlessly brushed it away, it would leave a greasy smear. Nothing more different from Tahiti could be imagined.

But on a good day, the city was more splendid than ever. It had grown even larger during Jorgenson's absence, and wealthier too, despite the hardships of war. No one would imagine that this was a country living under Napoleonic blockade. Along the West End pavements, shop windows were full of marvels: jewels, silks, books, maps, scientific instruments, meats, pastries. 'Here the costly shawls from the East Indies,' wrote an observer; 'there brocades and silk-tissues from China, now a world of gold and silver plate, then pearls and gems shedding their dazzling lustre . . . an ocean of rings, watches, chains, bracelets, and aigrettes, ready-dresses, ribbons, lace, bonnets, and fruit from all the zones of the habitable world.' But there was no time to stop and admire anything: the crowd swept on, hurrying along the right-hand side of each pavement while a stream of coach traffic ran down the middle of the street on the left. The busiest streets sported a complicated six-lane system of wheeled and pedestrian traffic, each lane obeying the unwritten laws of movement – and God help a stranger fresh from the Pacific who tried to walk on the wrong side, or who stood awkwardly staring into a jeweller's window. Not only was there nothing like this in Tahiti: there was nothing like it anywhere.

Jorgenson enjoyed the Tahitians' company, but he knew that he could not house or support them properly for long. He therefore turned to a grand personage he was sure would help: his old hero Sir Joseph Banks.

In the years since his voyage with Cook, Banks had become a one-man scientific institution, influential in politics as well as science, and a powerful supporter of all forms of discovery and research. President of the Royal Society and honorary director of the botanical gardens at Kew, he was still both vigorous and visionary, although his health was declining: by 1806 he was disabled by gout, which caused him agony and often confined him to a wheeled chair, though this did not slow him down much. In particular, he devoted great energy to promoting the interests of countries and people who had gained his sympathy during his travels, among them the two very different islands of Iceland and Tahiti.

His Tahitian friends formed a useful pretext for Jorgenson. He longed to meet Banks anyway, because he admired him and also because he was full of ideas about the Pacific trade, which he wanted to try out on Banks as well as taking them to Denmark. For the moment he spared Banks an airing of these ideas, and confined himself to describing the miserable conditions in Tahiti and soliciting his help with the two visitors. Banks willingly took them off Jorgenson's hands and later found a home for them, though, like many Polynesian travellers in Britain, they did not flourish in the unfamiliar climate and culture. According to Jorgenson, they both died within a few years.

Jorgenson stayed in London only for a couple of months, until late August 1806. Then, freed of his British responsibilities, he crossed to

Copenhagen and was reunited with his family for the first time in many years. He took with him his valuable journal, hoping to interest Danish investors in his South Sea expertise, which was rarer there than in London. Denmark had its own lively long-distance trading routes, shuttling between the Baltic, the Caribbean and Africa, although the most profitable part of this route, picking up slaves from the African coast, had recently been banned. It also had two small possessions in India, and seemed well prepared to plunge into the nineteenth-century colonial bonanza. But access to the Pacific was strictly controlled by the British, who discouraged incursions by other nations. Jorgenson knew ways round this, and he felt sure that Denmark could prosper in this new economic arena. Sometimes he despaired, once writing: 'I observe with regret that Denmark every way well situated for commerce lacks in that Spirit of commercial enterprize which alone can raise a nation to some degree of prosperity.' Decades later, he remained exasperated because the Danish flag was never seen in the Pacific and southern oceans. In 1806, however, he was confident that this could be changed.

Above all, he believed his country should imitate its fellow maritime adventurers across the North Sea by looking to a far-flung mercantile empire as befitted a seafaring nation, rather than getting embroiled in the quarrels of the Napoleonic mainland. Yet for the moment Denmark was doing well out of its situation in Europe. It was a neutral power, one of the four founding members in 1800 of the restored League of Armed Neutrality – a group of Baltic nations which used armed escorts to defend their right to trade freely around their ports, at a time when the two main belligerents were desperately trying to blockade each other. Of these nations, Denmark had the luckiest physical position, near the bottleneck through which all ships entering or leaving the Baltic had to sail. Everything passed by Copenhagen, and everything was taxed. But this good fortune was about to be crushed in a dramatic way neither Jorgenson nor anyone else could have foreseen, and from an unexpected quarter.

Jorgenson's family and friends greeted him with joy, as did many others. He was lionized as a patriotic hero: the first Danish explorer to have circumnavigated the globe.* No doubt many of his exploits improved in the telling, and his business ideas attracted as much attention as his

* If the South American piracy stories are true, he had actually been round twice.

adventure yarns. The young Antipodean sea-dog was 'much courted by all ranks', as he proudly wrote, and promised generous rewards in return for his advice. Even the Danish prime minister was interested, Jorgenson claimed, and wanted him to negotiate South Sea trading licences with the British, though this was never pursued. It was his finest hour in Denmark: his quick-witted brilliance in both writing and conversation paid off. Despite his rough edges, he was well informed, well travelled and confident: altogether an impressive young figure.

He enjoyed being flattered by the government, but he did not want to work for them: he had something more commercial in mind. Even less did he want to work for the French, which may have been proposed to him as well: he claimed they offered him control of the whole Danish fleet should the country come under French influence, as some expected it would. But Jorgenson was determined not to be co-opted against the British, from whom he had learned everything he knew: 'I could never be persuaded into the service of an usurper, who had no other view than to enslave the whole world, and especially to engage against a people, whom I loved and respected so much, and had been accustomed to look on as brothers.'

He did hope to put his knowledge to use, however. After showing his Pacific journal to friends for their opinion, he extracted from it the sections most interesting to a Danish audience and published them as a book. This was his literary debut. Working with speed and apparent ease, he filled the pages with advice for Danish traders: how to equip a whaling voyage, how much to pay the crew, what equipment to take for sealing, how not to lose one's entire cargo through slow leakage on the way home – and a few suggestive hints on how to get rich in South America. The result was published in Copenhagen in 1807, as *Efterretning om Engelændernes og Nordamerikanernes fart og handel paa Sydhavet* ('Observations on English and North American voyages and trade in the South Seas'), his only work in his own language. In the introduction, he pointed out proudly that if any foreigner came along after this claiming to have new information about profitable routes, they could say that one of their own countrymen had already told them all they needed to know. Jorgenson was discovering, for the first time, how to combine his flair for literature with his talent for absorbing practical information, to productive effect.

Having taken from the journal everything he thought of interest to Denmark, he wondered again whether portions of it might also do well on the British market. He wrote to Banks asking if he could send it to him for his professional opinion. Banks was always interested in writings on the Pacific, and agreed to look it over. Unfortunately, Jorgenson made a poor choice of postal methods. He gave the wrapped manuscript to a young Englishman sailing home on a ship that had called at Copenhagen for repairs – but this man turned out to be a criminal fugitive, who abandoned the package at the next stop in Göteborg while evading capture for a forgery. The journal disappeared, and Jorgenson never did publish anything in English on the Pacific trade.*

Meanwhile, with the first wave of fame subsiding, Jorgenson felt himself adrift in Denmark and somewhat confused. 'I had during my servitudes in British ships, fully imbibed the maxims, principles, and perhaps prejudices of Englishmen', he wrote. He did not attempt to conceal these new opinions from his old friends, but such candour did him little good even among his own family. His unorthodox opinions eventually transformed him, in many people's eyes, from minor national hero to something at the opposite end of the spectrum: a suspected traitor.

Denmark was a country with a strong Anglophile tradition, but this feeling was at its nadir in 1806 and 1807. Danes resented Britain's interference with their trade, and its constant stopping and searching of Danish ships in the Baltic and the North Sea. These insults had intensified since Britain and France had started trying to block the movement of goods around European shores – an attempt that had little success, for there were plenty of loopholes wide enough for whole fleets to sail through. The countries that suffered most from this tactic were not the two belligerents but the neutrals, whose profits were disrupted by the restrictions Britain and France each imposed on trade with the other.

* In fact, he may have retrieved the package successfully through contacts in Göteborg, but by that time war had broken out in Denmark and he could no longer post the contents to Banks so easily. Seventeen years later, a letter from Jorgenson to his mother mentions a journal recently mailed to him by the family. If this was the same, it probably ended up back in his hands, and was lost to history, like most papers in Jorgenson's possession.

At the same time, Danish admiration for Napoleon had been steadily increasing. Although he had done poorly at sea since losing much of his fleet at the battle of Trafalgar in 1805, Napoleon had rolled inexorably across the mainland, enjoying one victory after another against Austria, Russia and even the supposedly unbeatable Prussians. There weren't many dominos left to fall. No one in Denmark wanted to upset Britain, which was still so powerful at sea: the prosperity of any sea-trading nation depended on its benevolence, or at least its benevolent neglect. On the other hand, the future in Europe looked distinctly Napoleonic.

The recent runaway success only added to the glamour already radiated by Napoleon as a living emblem of self-creation and national revival. He had demonstrated how one decisive man could transform the scenery of a whole continent. His personality fascinated the government élite and ordinary people alike, in a way that went beyond normal politics, and his personal cult also inherited extra force from the French revolutionary cult that had inspired Jorgenson's own enthusiasm back in the 1790s. The philosopher Søren Kierkegaard described this period in a Denmark besotted by French ideals as one of vigour and energy, as opposed to the later onset of indolence and passive reflection. The latter was like the dull, incessant, undifferentiated striking of an out-of-order clock he had once heard at a friend's house (not a Jørgensen clock, one hopes) – but now the hours were marked with precise, firm strokes, like a drum beating out a march to war. It was a rhythm few could resist, though observers disagreed about how deeply this infatuation with all things French actually went. When one British visitor published his impressions that 'Danes of all conditions incline to French principles', another similar witness wrote 'nonsense', heavily underlined, in the margin of his copy.

For Jorgenson, this near-deification of a man he considered a vulgar usurper was a form of blasphemy. He derided a series of meetings and lectures held in Copenhagen while he was there at which Napoleon was spoken of as 'godlike' and as 'more than man'. Speakers were spontaneously 'moved by the spirit' and took turns to praise him like Nonconformists at a religious meeting: one said he was a finer general than Hannibal, another that he was a more virtuous statesman than Cato, a third that he was wiser than Socrates. Jorgenson thought it all absurd, and dangerous.

In his own way, however, he too was under Napoleon's spell. He was obsessed with the Emperor's aura of brute power, and would free-associate imaginatively about how Napoleon taunted those he conquered, or how after a battle he would allow his army's horses to trample over wounded men rather than take a slight detour to avoid them. Jorgenson analysed Napoleon's psyche: his flaw 'is not ambition, but vanity and silly pride; it is a certain intoxication, proceeding from the great power he has acquired, and which he himself has sufficient sense to perceive is not the effects of his own great genius nor abilities, but takes its source from the amazing stupidity of the human race, that suffers itself to be led by the nose by a single man.' He pictured the Emperor, after a day receiving humbled kings and ambassadors, returning to his room, locking the door, and turning on his heel 'laughing to himself at such a set of dull and stupid wretches'.

Fascinated though he was, Jorgenson vilified Napoleon in 1806 and 1807, and defended the protectionist domination of the British. He did so 'with some degree of heat,' as he wrote, 'which often involved me in discussions and disagreeable quarrels to no purpose'. So warmly did he speak that he became known as 'English Jørgensen'. No one was more displeased about this than his own father, a lifelong Anglophobe and now a supporter of France. But Jorgenson's rebellious attitude was increased rather than decreased by his father's disapproval: he argued constantly with him and with others at the family table.

His father said the British had no right to tax and impede neutral ships at sea; Jorgenson said they were entitled to defend their interests. His father called Albion perfidious: its political life was shallow, and its apparent generosity and offers of protection were just a hypocritical cover for self-interest in matters of trade. Jorgenson argued that its politics only appeared shallow in the light of European ideas to which the British themselves had never subscribed. Just as it was a mistake to confuse their reserve with haughtiness, he said, it was wrong to take devotion to moral and political principle for hypocrisy.

Above all, Jorgenson defended British rule over the seas, and praised the principle of mercantile self-assertion in general. The British were forced to control shipping around Europe, he said, because of the array of enemy nations trying to move material around the Continent to support themselves and to attack Britain, which had only itself to rely on. Ports likely to be used by such enemies must be blockaded if Britain were to survive, even if that meant interfering with neutral powers. As for the more general issue of British dominance, it was only natural: all through history one nation or another had controlled international trade, and such nations worked hard to keep that position. Britain had opened up the sciences of navigation and discovery, and created a network of global commerce: it should be entitled to enjoy the benefits. In any case, Denmark did the same, making all ships passing in and out of the Baltic pay a duty: it was in no position to criticize. If anything, Britain should be praised, for it enforced not a private monopoly but a general free trade around the seas, which it guarded for the benefit of all. The centre of a trading empire functioned like the heart in a human body: blood passed through it, receiving a boost: the energy of the centre promoted a vigorous circulation to all the extremities.

One evening over dinner, his father's friend the Danish Postmaster-General brandished (literally or metaphorically) a copy of the famous Dutch treatise on free trade, Hugo Grotius's *Mare Liberum* ('Freedom of the seas'). Jorgenson retaliated with the Englishman John Selden's *Mare Clausum* ('Enclosure of the seas'), which argued that nations had as much right to bring portions of the sea under private dominion as portions of the land. Jorgenson compared the Grotius treatise with 'that foolish work, which made such a noise some years ago', Tom Paine's revolutionary tract *The Rights of Man*. 'The principles in both are the same,' said Jorgenson, 'and perfectly consistent with reason, provided human beings could be divested of passion, but as long as this can not be done such maxims are impracticable.' In other words, the abolition of property rights both at sea and on land was simply incompatible with human nature.

Jorgenson's views were typical of the European Anglophile of the time: a type traceable to Voltaire and already encountered by Jorgenson in 1794. The battle-lines had been drawn on the subject well before Napoleon took power: a minority had become fascinated by the country's resolutely unimaginative but highly successful devotion to individual liberties, private property, and mercantile common sense. But now, as more and more countries tumbled into the Emperor's collecting bag, increasing numbers of dissenters – some of them French

– clung to resistant Britain as a symbol of hope. The exiled French writer Benjamin Constant even considered the Continent 'merely a vast prison, cut off from all communication with that noble country, England, generous asylum of free thought' – a case of a Napoleonic fog isolating the rest of Europe from its offshore island.

Constant was sure that the world would soon leave the era of war, which was 'all savage impulse', and enter a new era of commerce, ruled by 'civilized calculation' – a kind of global coming-of-age, which he passionately welcomed. Jorgenson welcomed it too. He was never an enthusiast for war, despite his hot-headed tendencies; what excited him was the steady, shining light of prosperity and freedom, not the flash of swords and roar of cannon on the battlefield. Even when people were denouncing him as a dangerous revolutionary, he would remain conservative and almost bourgeois in his convictions. He was a particular admirer of the anti-revolutionist Edmund Burke, a 'great genius', though he believed Burke's attack on the French Revolution was based on the 'wrong principles'. His final position as stated in the dinner party argument with the Postmaster was profoundly Burkean – and Hobbesian. 'I conclude', he said, 'the best form of Government is that, which is most able to prevent the vices and wicked inclinations of men to oppress and impose on their fellow creatures.'

As with the cult of Napoleon, continental Anglophilia tended to go beyond purely political matters, drawing its sustenance from personal temperament. You had to have a certain offbeat tendency to warm to the English character – which Jorgenson still did, even though he himself was everything the English traditionally were not: impulsive, warm-hearted, immodest and forthright. But Jorgenson's Anglophilia was about to be tested to its limits.

After losing at Trafalgar, France was desperately short of a navy, and Britain knew that it would do its best to replenish it. Neutral Denmark, meanwhile, was in possession of a fine fleet of naval and mercantile vessels, many of them unused at the moment and sitting in Copenhagen harbour. It was not hard to guess what France might do next, and Britain did guess it.

The British were not sure which was more likely: that Denmark would voluntarily throw in its lot with Napoleon, or that the French would seize its fleet without waiting to be invited. Denmark no longer had support from its defeated former Armed Neutrality allies Prussia and Russia, and it certainly was not strong enough to defend its fleet alone, so, in practical terms, it came to the same thing from Britain's point of view. Either way the result would be a re-fleeted Napoleon, something to be prevented at all costs. With a new fleet, he might succeed in his attempts to block Britain's flow of supplies, especially of timber from the Baltic – essential for shipbuilding. Access to colonies might also be affected. And now that things were already as bad as they could be on land, no threat to Britain's hard-won superiority at sea could be tolerated. As Jorgenson had argued, this was a simple necessity: if that advantage were lost, the war could end for Britain very quickly.

Strategy demanded that Britain pre-empt any seizure of Denmark's fleet by Napoleon. But there were problems. There was no way Denmark would agree voluntarily to join the war on Britain's side: it was still hoping to preserve its neutrality, and did not wish to attract immediate invasion from France. It certainly would not hand over ultimate control of its navy to the British, as would be required. Britain did ask, several times, but the proposal was rejected with outrage. That left just one other option, which was to do exactly what Britain feared France would do: invade Denmark and take its fleet away.

There were clear moral difficulties with launching an unprovoked attack and stealing a country's means of defence, especially when it showed no real sign of joining the enemy. Britain had already attacked neutral Denmark once during the war, in response to an argument over the Armed Neutrality arrangement in 1801. Under Nelson, its navy had pounded Copenhagen harbour without any formal declaration of hostilities. But in that case, at least in Britain's eyes, there had been some provocation: the Armed Neutrality was thought to be acquiring something of the belligerence of another enemy. Nothing of the sort applied here. Very few neutral countries were left now, and those few had little power and only one modest ambition: to survive.

The immediate pretext for British action was the reputed existence of a secret agreement buried in the first Treaty of Tilsit, signed that summer between France and the defeated Tsar Alexander I of Russia.

Besides the overt terms, there were a number of secret ones, not all of which have ever been identified; one of these was allegedly a promise from Russia not to intervene if Napoleon invaded Denmark. Britain would never reveal exactly why it thought this clause existed, but in any case it was clear that Russia could no longer defy the will of France, and that Denmark was unprotected by allies. In fact, Britain had already launched its fleet towards Denmark before any news from Tilsit could have reached London. Information from a Tilsit spy might just have clinched the details of what that fleet would do, but it is more likely that the rumoured clause was simply adopted to justify a decision that had already been taken.

While these anxieties were building, only half-understood by ordinary people in Denmark, Jorgenson was temporarily away from Copenhagen – he was staying with his sister in the nearby Zealand countryside, not far from the northern tip of the island. One day, early in August 1807, he looked up to see the familiar stretch of water in the Sound off Helsingør replaced with a dense brush of masts creeping towards Copenhagen. It was an eerie and unexpected sight: 'so formidable a fleet, was never before seen in these quarters,' he wrote later, 'for the whole of Sealand was surrounded with ships, which at a distance looked like impenetrable forests.' The arborescent Thames seemed to have come to the Sound, like Birnam Wood removing to Dunsinane.

The men on the ships were themselves unnerved by what they were doing, especially when a violent nocturnal thunderstorm broke out and they feared that God intended to strike them dead in the water or hurl their ships on the rocks. But they survived, and the next morning the whole fleet was at anchor in the narrow stretch of water, presenting a majestic but terrible scene to those on shore as well as to the naval men, one of whom later described it as a sight to inspire 'a sensation truly sublime'.

Expeditionary forces were landed, and headed for Copenhagen. They met only little resistance, though not for want of Danish bravery. At Køge, near the city, a hastily assembled army incorporating some seven thousand peasant volunteers tried to hold them back. These men were untrained and ill-equipped, wearing their own clothes and worst of all their own traditional wooden clogs, which made marching and running extremely difficult.* As Jorgenson later wrote, they were armed only 'with rusty old cutlasses, others with muskets without locks, but by far the greater number with instruments of agriculture'. They were up against one of the world's most sophisticated military machines; the battle was soon over.

By the end of August resistance was defeated, Copenhagen was surrounded and British forces had consolidated their positions on the land around the city and afloat in the Sound. Last-minute negotiations continued; more impossible demands were presented, ordering Denmark to hand over its fleet. All were refused.

The British soldiers waited, many of them billeted in accommodation in surrounding villages. One day in early September, a fire broke out in one of the buildings they were occupying, not far from Copenhagen. The British struggled to put it out, but were overwhelmed: the flames rose so high they could be seen from the city. Just as they were giving up, the soldiers were amazed to see rolling up to the base a corps of firemen in six specially adapted mobile firefighting vehicles. The firemen leaped out, and the British watched in further astonishment as they donned brass helmets with added flaps of leather covering their shoulders, and reeled out long leather hoses from their carriages. With well-drilled efficiency, they cleared the surrounding houses, pumped water through the hoses from a nearby inlet, and had the blaze extinguished in no time. They then rolled up their hoses and left again. The British had never seen anything like this: London had no professional fire service at all. Copenhagen, by contrast, had around five thousand highly trained firemen, whose skills and technical equipment had been perfected after the several conflagrations suffered by the city in the 1790s. It seemed as if they could deal with anything.

The British officers and men in the village were grateful, as well as impressed. But when they thanked the firemen, they did not – *could* not, without authorization from further up the chain of command – warn them of what was about to happen.

For, on the evening of that same day, 2 September, at about half

* A British traveller who was shipwrecked and captured in Denmark in 1809 once tried on a pair, having been told that they were warm. He found it was true: the exertion required to hobble along at even an ordinary walking pace warmed him up nicely.

past seven in the evening – just as the people of Copenhagen were strolling home or setting out to dine and visit friends – a fountain of stars rose from the British camps in the outskirts, and curved towards the city. The stars grew larger as they approached; some people noticed and stopped to watch the extraordinary sight. Others did not realize anything was happening until a rain of heavy, blazing missiles began falling around their heads.

These were rocket-propelled incendiary devices, each one a pointed metal cylinder a metre long, strapped to a stabilizing rod and tipped with burning fuel. When they landed, they stuck like fat arrows. They penetrated the roofs of houses and drilled straight through the floors, sometimes all the way to the cellar, and everything they touched on the way was ignited. Many people were caught in the open, and hit directly before they could find shelter. Some failed to see how dangerous the rockets were, and stood to watch instead of running, so there were far more injuries than there need have been. Even indoors, no one was safe. And the rockets kept coming, in volley after volley: thousands of them fell on the city that night.

This was a new and terrifying weapon. The British had learned rocketry from India, where it had been used against them in the late eighteenth century. Nothing inspires research more than being on the receiving end of a superior military technology: the Englishman Sir William Congreve started work in 1804 to improve the Indian design, and soon developed his new 'Congreve rocket', with enhanced range and accuracy, and able to carry either explosive or incendiary warheads – the former being better for battlefields, the latter for attacking ships, or domestic rooftops as in Copenhagen. They were not widely used in the Napoleonic wars, but Britain had used them before, on Boulogne in 1806. They later deployed them against the Americans in 1812, as immortalized in the 'Star Spangled Banner' lines, 'And the rocket's red glare gave proof through the night that our flag was still there'. In Copenhagen, they used them to force a quick surrender from a weakened city without engaging in any fighting through the streets, and without damaging the ships, which they wanted to keep in good shape for themselves. It was a devastating act, inflicting injury on civilians in an attack that was already morally suspect.

Copenhagen's fire service was quickly mobilized and struggled heroically, though it seemed that for every fire they put out another dozen would appear. The attack lasted all night, ending only at eight o'clock the following morning, over twelve hours after it had begun. Somehow the firemen managed to control and eventually extinguish the fires. During the following day, all was quiet. But there were injured and dead everywhere, and extensive damage to buildings. The government made no move to surrender, and no one doubted that the bombardment was likely to resume at nightfall. Many inhabitants collected their valuables and fled the city. All day the roads out of town were jammed with wagons and heavily laden pedestrians; by early evening they formed 'a train without end'.

As expected, at six o'clock that evening the attack began again. It lasted through the night, but seemed a little less severe than the first. This time people knew what was coming, so those who were still in town at all stayed out of the open. There were fewer casualties. In fact, the next day many thought the worst was over and even that the British might be running out of rockets: so many had fallen, it would not be surprising if stocks were low. How many rockets of this size could the British have? Encouraged, some of those who had left town headed home during the following day. And, as before, the daylight hours were peaceful.

But the British had not run out of rockets. That night, they launched the worst bombardment of all, a veritable Blitz, more intense than anything seen even on the first night. This time, the fires escaped the fire-fighters' control, and the individual blazes merged into a city-wide fire-storm. Many more lives were lost in this final attack; buildings were smashed and burned to ruins. The whole city seemed to explode. A British soldier in a nearby camp saw 'a complete volume of fire' on the horizon over central Copenhagen, illuminating the sky as bright as day: 'the glare reflected from the shells and rockets, shed a lustre on every object around.' One direct hit set fire to the steeple of the large Vor Frue church. It fell to the ground, killing several people at a blow and spreading the conflagration further. As a British poet later imagined it, the leaden sheets from the roof flowed down as molten metal, and the bells fell 'in showers upon the hallowed ground'. Each missile was a 'heaved volcano'; the narrow streets of the old city became 'double walls of fire'. It was a terrible foretaste of a much later European nightmare.

By the end of that night, many of the city's firemen were dead or wounded, including several of those who had gone to help the British troops a few days earlier. Many of the fire-carriages themselves had been destroyed. Others had simply broken down through over-use. And those firemen who were still unharmed were so exhausted that they could do nothing more to save their city. The fire burned on; the scene everywhere was one of chaos, pain and destruction. The injured were driven or carried to hospitals; some were struck again by more rockets on the way. 'The streets were filled with dead or lacerated horses', wrote one witness, before drawing a veil over the rest of the scene with a shudder: 'here I must conclude.'

Another night of this would have meant the complete destruction of the city, but when the sun rose on 5 September, the Danish government accepted the inevitable and sent an envoy to seek a truce. The bombardment was halted while they negotiated conditions: the Danes still hoped to avoid complete humiliation, but the British would accept nothing less than the unconditional gift of the entire fleet, together with naval stores and equipment. Denmark could not refuse. The agreement was signed two days later, on 7 September.

An estimated twenty-five thousand rockets had fallen on Copenhagen over the three nights. Almost two thousand Danes had been killed, out of a population of around a hundred thousand. Over three hundred houses were burned to the ground; another 1,500 or so were damaged. Jorgenson also noted that many of the dead were women and children, since they were more likely to be in the houses in the centre of the city, whereas after the first night many men had been stationed on the ramparts in an attempt at defence – where, ironically, they were safer.

It certainly destroyed whatever remained of Anglophilia in Denmark. 'A more distressing period Copenhagen never witnessed,' Jorgenson wrote. 'The fleet, her pride, carried off without a battle; the finest buildings razed to the ground.' The Copenhagen population proved indomitable, however, carrying on ordinary life as best they could and even strolling out to an outlying park to look at the British soldiers in the camp. The shops were replenished and the markets came alive with peasants bringing wares from outside the city; it soon looked almost normal despite the damage. But there was a muted air:

'the dejected countenance, and the mournful silence' prevailed, as a British soldier observed.

The British remained for a while, packing up Denmark's fleet. They took anything that floated – anything that looked as if it could ever be used against them in war: dozens of gunboats, frigates, brigs, all kinds of mercantile vessels. Only a few small craft, and a ship or two that happened to be out of the harbour at the time, were left untouched. They also raided the docks and naval storehouses, and seized everything they could use: sails, ropes, ammunition, provisions, charts and telescopes. It took six weeks to pack everything up. Secretly, however, the Danes were hiding a lot of their navy's possessions – including a thousand or so guns, and twenty-six thousand cannon-balls.

The action was regarded as an outrageous robbery and condemned in Denmark and across Napoleonic Europe – and in Britain itself. The House of Commons rocked with dispute and accusation; the MP Samuel Whitbread said bluntly, 'The English have behaved like shabby thieves.' There were calls for the man behind the attack, Foreign Secretary George Canning, to explain himself. Above all, there was a demand for evidence that any secret clause in the Tilsit treaty actually existed. Canning refused to give in, saying only that he knew for sure that the clause was there. He would not be drawn into revealing his sources, and indeed no proof has ever emerged. The truth seemed to be that Britain had no doubt that expediency necessitated a morally indefensible attack, but did not like to say so outright, and thus invented – or at least exaggerated – intelligence reports.

One anonymous critic, in a pamphlet of the following year called *The Real State of the Case respecting the Late Expedition*, roundly dismissed all the government's arguments about the necessity for the intervention and suggested that the real reason was simply because Denmark was weak: it was a risk-free way of showing off British power. He mocked Britain's sudden fear of the Danish fleet, which seemed to be inspired by its own victory at Trafalgar. The French fleet was destroyed, so 'we are all of a sudden to tremble because there are a few old ships in Copenhagen, and the Danes, our friends and allies, may peradventure be forced to repair and man them, and they may be put to sea, and may beat our veteran commanders, and our invincible seamen!' In return for a clapped-out navy, Britain had given France things of real value: the moral high ground, and the willing support of 'the whole Danish people, from the Prince to the peasant, exasperated against us, eager to join in any projects for our annoyance'. Worst of all was the blot on Britain's honour. How could it ever again stand as the world's beacon of freedom, justice and the rule of law?

Jorgenson, too, was shocked. He watched the events from his sister's farm, worrying about the safety of his parents and brothers, whose homes were in Copenhagen's worst-hit area near the harbour.* 'It is scarcely possible to conceive our feelings, that were in the country,' he wrote, 'on seeing night after night the place assaulted, which contained our father and brothers . . . For many miles could be seen the awful spectacle.' After Copenhagen surrendered, he went in to see the scene and to find his family – who were all safe. '[W]hat a horrible sight!' he wrote. 'Women, children, aged and young all were killed without distinction.'

It took a while for 'English Jørgensen' to absorb the horror and injustice, after spending months trying to convince people that the British were neither treacherous nor motivated by self-interest. He later said he understood the British strategy, but, he wrote, 'at this moment I forgot their just reasons for acting as they had done, and only contemplated the misery before me'. However good the reasons, he felt, it was surely 'extremely unjust, and against the laws of nations' to attack in this way, without a declaration of war and without provocation. He was later to speak of Denmark as a peaceful and inoffensive nation which was 'suddenly assailed by a formidable foe', and almost thirty years later he reminded his brother of how their country had 'proceeded onwards innocently and happily till that fatal hour when the war-hawks from the Westward crossed the Northern ocean, and in foul malignity, and under false pretences, perched upon our steeples, destroyed our honestly acquired property, carried off our best means of defence'. It removed the first brick in the edifice of his Anglophilia, an edifice that was eventually to crumble almost entirely.

On the other hand, Jorgenson also held the Danish royal and military administration to blame for making the disaster worse than it

* Paintings and engravings of the attack show the Jørgensen house surrounded by burning buildings, though not itself on fire.

need have been. They had concentrated too much on defending the south of the country (against the French) rather than the capital. They failed to act decisively when the British fleet first appeared but, conversely, they also waited too long to surrender once defeat appeared inevitable, causing unnecessary loss of life. Crown Prince Frédérik had actually issued the flamboyant, even murderous, order that the city should be defended at all costs, before himself fleeing to the safety of the country. Jorgenson was also critical of the decision to assemble the 'wooden clog' army at Køge to fight a battle they could not win. Abstract national pride could not be a justification for sending people to futile deaths.

Jorgenson's accusations formed part of his larger argument in a pamphlet published in 1811, *The Copenhagen Expedition Traced to other Causes than the Treaty of Tilsit*. Here he maintained that Denmark's flawless image was deceptive, and that the Danish government was itself unreliable: he was a firm opponent of the current regime, and suspected it of flirting with the French. Despite his initial revulsion, he also attempted to understand Britain's motivation. He concluded his meditation on the incident with a telling phrase: taking a neutral country's fleet may not be morally correct or even lawful, he said, but it could be considered '*politically just*', because it was essential for British security. He even considered it 'one of the greatest masterstrokes of policy that was ever planned or executed'.

Jorgenson's 'political justice' idea was slippery but astute. The British knew their action would drive Denmark into the French camp, but they regarded Danish enmity as of less importance than the dangers of a Napoleon strengthened at sea, at a time when Britain was already almost completely alone and defended only by its own navy. Coldly considered, it was a victory of British strategy, though it was a failure of diplomacy and of honour. It was one of those cursed pockets of history where there was no good choice available, only two bad ones. Denmark's extreme misfortune was that it had a weapon which it did not wish to use, and did not even regard as a weapon, but which might hold the key to the outcome of the sea war – and which each of the two great powers knew it was too weak to defend against the other. A good solution to this dilemma would be hard to imagine.

In one of his more illuminating judgements, Jorgenson went so far as to argue that it was Canning's duty to his country to do what he did, having seen the danger threatening Britain on the horizon. 'It is but a poor excuse for a Minister,' he wrote, 'when a great evil befalls a country, to say that he had foreseen it, but from motives of justice and honour did not prevent it.' There is a lot in this. Yet it remains far from certain that Britain was really obliged to use incendiary rockets against a civilian population as its means of assault. And however compelling the reasons, posterity will never look kindly on decisions taken in defiance of 'justice and honour'. It is surely better that it doesn't, lest such decisions be taken too easily.

Having checked on his parents and brothers, Jorgenson returned to his sister's farm. Reading between the lines, it looks rather as if he had fallen out with his father over the Napoleonic issue that summer, and had sought refuge with a more easygoing part of the family. The attack had changed Jorgenson's own feelings, but Trine was still better company than the elder Jørgen, who probably now had an intolerable fit of the *I-told-you-sos*. Trine's farm was quiet and consoling; Jorgenson seems to have been in a delicate frame of mind, and needed comfort.

The farm was near to where the British were camped while they worked on packing up the Danish fleet. For Jorgenson, with his fluent English and his general empathy with English ways, this meant a chance to get to know some of them and even to work as an occasional translator. In particular, he met Arthur Wellesley, the future duke of Wellington: 'I often conversed with him,' he wrote proudly later.

He always denied any suggestion that he turned traitor during this autumn, but his neighbours in Zealand automatically assumed the worst. The most virulent gossip was spread by the wife of the *Mare liberum*-wielding Postmaster, who was once present at a dinner party at which Wellesley arrived accompanied by Jorgenson: she had her husband spread rumours around court that Jorgenson was passing information to the British – something he denied. This was Jorgenson's first glimpse of life as a suspected traitor and spy. In fact, confusion seems to have affected his conduct during this time. Despite his aversion to their recent actions, he still felt at home with the British, perhaps more so than with Danes. He was not sure what to believe or which way his sympathies should lie. His adopted country had attacked his native one: it was not surprising that Jorgenson acted like a man divided.

In any case, British relations with the locals were mostly amicable, despite the underlying resentment at their presence. Many British soldiers felt sorry for their opponents and did their best to mitigate the insult by behaving decently. One wrote of his fellows, 'now every one says – *Poor Danes!*' Jorgenson also observed that the British troops clearly regretted the 'distresses inflicted on a people, who bore so great a resemblance to themselves'. There was a natural rapport between ordinary Danes and Englishmen, which Jorgenson once described by way of contrast with the mutual incomprehension that reigned during the later British occupation of the Spanish Peninsula. 'The similarity of Manners and Appearance of the lower Classes of Danes and English is remarkably striking', he wrote: their religion was similar, and unlike temperate southerners they both enjoyed a drunken spree from time to time. It was strange that the British should end up committing such an injustice against a people they found so congenial. It had been the same during the earlier attack in 1801, when Nelson had warmly addressed his call for surrender 'To the Brothers of Englishmen, the Danes'.

Wellesley in particular did everything possible to minimize suffering and to make sure that everything commandeered for the troops was properly paid for; in return, he was generally accepted with good grace. But Sir Home Popham, who took charge of the actual packing-up of the fleet, was hated. According to Jorgenson, Danes showed their dislike by giving his name to their dogs; but when one man came home to find his family had changed the dog's name from Sultan to Sir Home Popham while he was out, he brought his pistol and, with tears in his eyes, informed the dog: 'Sultan! for twelve years hast thou faithfully guarded round my dwelling, kept thieves from my door, and announced the approach of strangers . . . But now, hapless creature, thou hast been disgraced by the infamous name of an infamous man, and thou shalt no longer exist: if thou wert my firstborn, thou shouldst share the same fate.' Bang!

The British promised that they would leave as soon as they had what they wanted, and they did. On 20 October 1807, equipped, overhauled and packed with loot, the Danish fleet sailed out of Copenhagen in British hands, watched by many of the city's residents as it left the harbour.

As soon as they had gone, the Danish government threw in its lot with France, and declared war on the new enemy.

> Denmark does not deceive herself as to the danger or losses with which this war threatens her. Attacked in the most unexpected and dishonourable manner, exposed in an isolated province nearly cut off from all means of defence, and forced into an unequal contest, she cannot flatter herself with escaping a very material injury. Unblemished honour still remains for her to defend . . . Firm in an upright conscience, confiding in God, and the love and devotion of brave and loyal nations united under a mild sceptre, the Danish government trusts, that it will be able to acquit itself, without weakness, of the hard and painful task that honour and necessity have imposed on it.

The anti-Napoleonic Jorgenson did not approve of this new alliance with France, nor with the decision – however noble – to declare war on Britain simply as a response to wounded honour, when the result was so damaging to Denmark. It exposed Danish property in Britain to confiscation and its remaining merchant ships to capture at sea: the country's maritime interests were (literally in some cases) blown out of the water. As Jorgenson and others realized straight away, this was likely to prove the economic ruin of the country. And all to satisfy national pride, he believed – though it is hardly imaginable that Denmark could have responded otherwise. It was another impossible dilemma.

Unfortunately he was right, and the result was as many foresaw. Denmark fell into an economic collapse, and thus never became a major player in the global Monopoly game that was the nineteenth century. Its trade fell to near-zero, its currency was devalued almost out of existence, imports became prohibitively expensive, and inflation ran out of control, with all the attendant consequences in human suffering. By 1813, the state was declared bankrupt, having gone from prosperity to disaster in six years. 'Perhaps there never was a country which has, in so short a time, and to so great a degree, felt the effects of a change in affairs, as Denmark', wrote Jorgenson.

The country had its pride, however, and it also had anger. The British traveller James Macdonald found the Danes in 1809 violently patriotic, and convinced that their country was powerful enough to inflict real damage on Britain. When he remarked jestingly to a defiant Dane that the two nations were 'as wide of one another in political existence, as the fly is from the elephant or the whale', the man responded with fury, which taught Macdonald to be more cautious with his jokes. The British were regarded as robbers one and all, though many Danes came to dislike the French even more, especially once they started being billeted around the country. One landlord who had eighty-three French soldiers living in his house said that, rather than repeat that experience, he would sell everything he owned for half its value and move to another part of the world. They constantly demanded more luxurious food and wine than he was able to provide, and insulted his wife and daughter with 'gross and indecent language'.

But the Danes were not wrong in believing that they could hurt Britain. The country threw its considerable enterprise into rebuilding a new fleet from the hidden and salvaged scraps of the old one. A lot of timber had been secreted away, as well as guns and ammunition, and by supplementing these with plentiful donations from private citizens, they built up a fleet again with amazing rapidity. The few small vessels the British had not bothered to take were converted to armed gunships, and new ones were built from scratch. By the end of the following year Denmark had armed nearly 150 vessels, and these acted as a considerable annoyance to the British. Most were licensed as privateers: they seized British ships as lawful prize whenever they got the chance, thus providing a useful income as well as taking national revenge. Denmark continued fighting determinedly until 1814, when defeat by Sweden finally forced it to sign the Treaty of Kiel and end its involvement in the war.

Among the ships donated by private citizens was a merchant brig called the *Christine Henriette*: it was converted to a warship, renamed the *Admiral Juul* after the hero of a Danish victory over Sweden in 1677, and given a dual set of papers to help outwit the enemy – one in its old name as a mercantile vessel and one in the new as a patriotic privateer.

Suspicions against Jorgenson cannot have been too serious, for in December 1807 he was given command of the *Admiral Juul*, his expertise and his knowledge of British waters apparently outweighing any doubts. He had no choice but to accept and, despite his confused loyalties, he was unlikely to have been too sorry: it meant the chance to command a ship again, an escape from his judgemental father, and a smart new naval captain's uniform. He apparently had his portrait painted in this outfit, with its fine red and gold waistcoat, just before departure.*

It turned out to be a farewell portrait. When it was done, Jorgenson boarded the *Admiral Juul* for the second and last captaincy in his career. He never set foot in Denmark again.

Jorgenson's task was to attack British supply routes in the North Sea and the Baltic, which he did with considerable success during the first month or two of 1808, taking several ships. Then, in late February, perhaps inspired to over-confidence by his early victories, he sailed straight for the coast of Britain, evidently looking for unprotected merchant vessels to attack. Instead, he almost immediately met a thoroughly well-protected British warship, HMS *Sappho*, off Flamborough Head on the Yorkshire coast on 2 March 1808.

What was he doing? Some in Denmark later suspected that he was deliberately giving himself up to the British, which would have confirmed those rumours about his wavering sympathies. But this does not fit with the fact that, for half an hour, Jorgenson fought the British ship almost insanely, like David against Goliath, with all the firepower at his disposal – a life-threatening battle for himself and all on board, and considered so notable that it was reported in detail in the British newspapers.

The encounter began with the *Sappho* signalling to the unidentified vessel; when it received no reassuring response, it fired a shot across the *Admiral Juul*'s bows. In response, Jorgenson boldly ran up

---

* This portrait has been attributed to the school of the romantic artist C. W. Eckersberg, later a very famous Danish painter – one of his best-known works was a panorama of Copenhagen under the British bombardment. The picture was once thought to be of Jorgenson's father, but the uniform and age indicate that it must be someone of the next generation.

his Danish colours and fired back. The two ships approached each other to engage, sailing so close that, according to Jorgenson, his crew could plainly hear what was being said on the other deck.

Each ship's guns pounded the other's masts and decks from these terrifyingly close quarters, inflicting shattering damage. The *Admiral Juul* tore the *Sappho*'s mast and main shroud, and injured two of its crew. Jorgenson claimed that at one point the battle seemed to be going his way, and that he even tried to board the other ship: 'had we done so, no doubt our stout strong Norwegians and Danes would have been more than a match for the weather beaten men' on the *Sappho*. But the attempt failed, and now the *Sappho* steadily beat the *Admiral Juul* into submission. Two of the Danish crew were killed; the ship's masts and sails were so splintered and torn that it could no longer manoeuvre properly. It was completely outgunned, and eventually it struck its colours and surrendered. Jorgenson and his crew were taken prisoner; the ship was retained as British prize.

Despite the Danish fears, it is hard to read this battle as the act of a man who was deliberately handing himself over to the enemy.* There was no sign of timidity in his attack: his courage, as always, was complete and unthinking. In emergencies, Jorgenson was invariably fearless, and there is no reason to suspect idle posturing when he later wrote of the *Sappho* battle: 'it is very fortunate for man that the greatest and most trying moments of his life are generally of short duration, and often the work of a few moments. As Dr Johnson said, when his master could not get him to learn his lesson, he was flogged, and there was "an end on't;" and in the same way when a cannon-ball takes a man's head off, which he does not expect, there is an end of him.'

What does seem likely is that, as was equally habitual, Jorgenson

---

* Jorgenson did later make intriguing remarks suggesting that he had surrendered himself deliberately: he claimed that he had been given secret orders to sail troops from France to Denmark, so that they could launch an invasion of northern Britain from there. Unable to refuse these orders, but determined not to assist in a French invasion plan, he solved the problem by giving himself up. But this seems too colourful to be true, and Denmark is hardly likely to have entrusted such a mission to a man suspected of British sympathies. It is more likely that he made this up in order to impress British readers with his loyalty – for by this time he was very keen to explain the fact that he had once served against the country which he claimed was his preferred one.

plunged into action with very little calculation of any sort. One might conjecture that he had a subconscious desire to be captured. Perhaps the Danes were right, and it was an overt and conscious wish; but if so, the heat of battle seems to have taken over his mind as soon as the first shots were fired.

He was angered by the Danish interpretation. True, he did not admire his country's current regime, he wrote later, 'but fighting is one thing, and politics another'. He had engaged bravely with a stronger ship and defended his vessel to the utmost of his power. 'What then could Denmark desire more?'

When every other naval engagement has been blazed out in all Danish newspapers, mine is not mentioned, only in a manner to inflict infamy and disgrace. Whenever I think on such baseness, my blood rushes to my face, and I almost become intoxicated with madness! After having been twelve years in the British service; and never receiving a favor from Denmark in my life; after having reluctantly entered into a service I hated from principle, and still doing as much as the best man could, then to be accused of cowardice and treachery, is infamous in the villains that make the charge.

On his capture, Jorgenson was briefly detained as a prisoner of war in Yarmouth, but was then transferred to London and interviewed by Alexander Macleay, secretary of the Transport Board. After this formality, he was freed on parole, as was common for prisoners of war from the upper ranks. It meant that he could move around London as he pleased, on one key condition: he must not leave the country.

Apparently living on loans, he found lodgings at the Spread Eagle Inn, in Gracechurch Street near Leadenhall Market, a well-known coaching-inn which was to become his regular haunt while staying in London. It was an odd choice as a long-term home, since it was meant for casual travellers and was often crowded and uncomfortable, but Jorgenson seemed to be attached to it, and lodged there almost every time he passed through London.

One reason he liked it was because it was a good place to meet people – and now he pursued all sorts of chance social and commercial contacts. Some of these new friends prompted unwise investments: after winning a windfall on a lottery ticket, he borrowed another £1,000 to supplement it, and invested the whole lot in a cargo being smuggled into the Continent. It was a bad idea: the cargo disappeared, or was seized by the French, and Jorgenson lost both his winnings and the £1,000. 'Although I have wrote a treatise on the subject of trade and commerce,' he admitted plaintively, 'I am so little of a merchant, either by temper or inclination, that I am totally unfit for such speculations.'

He also met some more promising acquaintances, including two merchants from Iceland, Bjarni Sívertsen and Weste Petræus. They were in London not by choice, but because their ships had been seized in mid-ocean by the British in response to Denmark's entry into the war. Iceland being Danish territory, their ships were now considered fair prize. The two traders were being assisted by no less a figure than Sir Joseph Banks, who had visited Iceland as a young man and was still passionate about its welfare. Awaiting the results of this aid, the men had nothing to do but pass the time. They got into conversation with Jorgenson and told him about the predicament of Icelanders, isolated in their remote location and suddenly deprived of imports. Jorgenson was eager to find ways of recovering the £1,000 he now owed, and as always was interested in money-making ideas, especially those that sounded outlandish and risky. His ears therefore pricked up when Bjarni Sívertsen mentioned that he had a cargo of tallow in Iceland waiting for removal and that, as Icelandic shipping was still disrupted, a British trader might go and pick it up for a good profit, while also making money delivering much-needed imported goods.

There were a few obstacles: the British prohibited trading to enemy ports, while the Danish had a long-standing ban on foreigners trading with Iceland at all. Both nations would be likely to do everything they could to prevent such activity. Moreover, it was now heading into winter, a time when no sailor in his right mind would embark on a journey so far north. It was a crazy plan. Jorgenson loved it.

A while later, he made another chance acquaintance over dinner: a Huguenot-descended Englishman named James Savignac. Jorgenson talked about Iceland, and Savignac became very interested. He mentioned his acquaintance Samuel Phelps, who, as a soap manufacturer and all-round entrepreneur, could use the tallow for his soap and might also invest in a more general supply operation. The connections were made: the two men went to meet Phelps, an intelligent man with a steady gleam of money in his eye and an open business mind. Jorgenson liked him: he respected imaginative men of trade, whose willingness to take such risks kept the world turning. He presented his idea to Phelps persuasively: if Phelps provided a ship and the necessary Board of Trade licences, he said, he could offer a return cargo of over 150 tonnes of tallow as well as the sale of whatever goods Phelps sent on the outward journey. The enterprise could not fail. Phelps had no need to go himself: Jorgenson would undertake the voyage and act as translator, Danish being the language of official affairs on the island. He would also use his own connection with Banks to smooth the way to getting the necessary permits. Savignac would travel as Phelps's supercargo, taking charge of trade once they were on land.

Phelps was convinced; they agreed the deal. If successful, Jorgenson would get a third of the profits. If not, he would be liable for a third of the losses. Phelps did something else for him, too. Creditors were pursuing Jorgenson for his £1,000 debt; Phelps paid it off as an advance on profits, so Jorgenson was free to leave without people suspecting that he was trying to run away. Apparently Jorgenson did not tell Phelps that he was supposed not to leave the country anyway, because of the parole agreement.

Jorgenson next wrote to Banks seeking his support, repeating the arguments Banks himself had been urging on deaf governmental ears for some time. It was Britain's humanitarian duty, he said, to rescue Iceland and the other northern islands from their current predicament, for the British blockade of the North Sea was the cause of the problem. The best solution for the islanders would be if Britain took them over completely, but failing that, the government ought at least to issue licences and provide ships, so the disrupted supply routes could continue safely under British supervision. Jorgenson must already have known that his correspondent would agree with him: Banks had wanted Iceland brought under Britain's wing for years, and was particularly concerned about the present threat of famine. The British government did not respond to his arguments, so Banks threw his weight behind Phelps's application for the trading licence, while continuing to work towards freeing the other merchants. His support made a difference: Phelps was granted permission without difficulty.

And so, licensed and approved, Jorgenson and Savignac sailed from Liverpool on 29 December 1808, on a ship called the *Clarence*, captained by George Jackson. In the hold was a cargo of useful foodstuffs: biscuit, barley, rye, potatoes and meat, as well as a few inessential but saleable goods – coffee, sugar, tobacco, rum. There were also hats, and indigo, and one of the few substances Iceland did not need at all: salt. The crew were heading for a very cold island in the midst of war, at the beginning of a dark northern winter. And Jorgenson, a British prisoner forbidden to leave the country, was re-entering Danish territory, though with no intention of returning to Denmark's service.

He felt inspired by his new mission. Later he grandly wrote: 'By the advice and knowledge of Sir Joseph Banks, I planned an expedition to proceed to Iceland, to relieve the half-famished people of that Island from starvation.' The simple business opportunity had reinvented itself as a heroic rescue plan: Jorgenson's boyhood fantasy of himself as liberator and protector was about to emerge into glorious light.

4

Uprising in Reykjavík

Iceland is very alone. It lies 960 kilometres away from the nearest part of the mainland, and some 1,200 kilometres from Denmark, the country which governed it for centuries. It is beautiful and terrifying, a playground for devotees of the Romantic sublime. The island spits with volcanos, seethes with boiling water, and breathes sulphurous steam from hidden clefts. It also lashes with wind and snow, freezes with ice, and drenches with prodigious amount of rain, which often seems to fall from all directions at once, vertical, diagonal and horizontal. When the sun shines, the air is crystalline, but a more common type of day is better described by the phrases recurring throughout the travel journals of the Icelandophilic English designer William Morris: dark grey, dreadful grey, lightish grey, dark ashen grey, greyer than grey, light grey-blue, ragged grey, inky grey and woeful grey. The coasts are dangerous, and the water deadly. In the midwinter, the sun barely rises into the sky, and for most of the day the sea is as black and cold as outer space. An early visitor, the fourth-century BC traveller Pytheas the Greek, reported the eerie phenomenon of an ocean which seemed to have congealed into jelly, so close was it to freezing.

Yet, astonishingly, a sophisticated political and literary culture had already thrived on this island for almost a millennium when Jorgenson arrived on the *Clarence* in January 1809. Iceland had been an independent democracy for the first four hundred years of its existence, with its own parliament and legal system, but since the Norwegian King seized control in the thirteenth century it had been dominated by mainland masters: first Norway and then Denmark, which took over Norway and its territories in 1380. A commercial monopoly was imposed in 1602, limiting trading rights to Danish citizens. Icelanders were forbidden to buy goods from foreigners or even other districts without approval. This was painfully constricting, for they relied on all sorts of minor but essential imports, not least fishhooks. Many Danish merchants abused the system, fixing high prices and keeping their customers indebted to them permanently. But the Icelanders put up with it, knowing no other life. Most people barely used money at all, living by barter, though this did not save them from getting into debt. Jorgenson met a man who, to clear a small amount owed for a bottle of corn brandy, had allowed the local Danish trader to earmark the fattest sheep in his flock for himself, an animal worth far more than the brandy, and one the farmer could never afford to replace.

Sir Joseph Banks considered the Icelanders 'the poorest people in the European world'. They depended on fish and on small flocks of sheep, whose health and survival, often against the odds, were the main focus of farmers' energy. From sheep they took meat, wool for clothing, milk for butter, and fat for candle tallow – which would sometimes be eaten when times were really hard. The traveller Henry Holland saw children munching lumps of tallow on the street in 1810, and a sixteenth-century account told the possibly apocryphal story of an Icelandic woman boarding a trading vessel and devouring the ship's candles as if they were a wonderful banquet. Many years later, W.H. Auden made affectionate sport of Icelandic food in his and Louis MacNeice's *Letters from Iceland*. Of the two most popular kinds of dried fish, which were shredded and eaten with butter, he noted: 'The tougher kind tastes like toe-nails, and the softer kind like the skin off the soles of one's feet.' The soups were 'sweet and very unfortunate', and the smoked mutton was 'comparatively harmless when cold as it only tastes like soot, but it would take a very hungry man indeed to eat it hot'. Yet when he tried the sheep's udders pickled in sour milk he found them 'surprisingly very nice'.

Living conditions were austere. Almost no wood was available for building, and only the well-off could afford to import it (the richest imported entire houses as prefabs from Norway). Rural Icelanders lived in houses of stone or lava, buried in the earth nearly to the roof and insulated with moss and turf. Beds were filled with seaweed or, more comfortably, duck feathers; the whole family would sleep in intimate proximity. No fresh air was admitted in winter, and the frigid climate dissuaded people from washing either themselves or their clothes except on special occasions.

The weather, the remoteness and the constant hardship were bound to have an effect on the national character, which was of a substance even more indomitable than the dried cod. Some visitors found Icelanders 'serious' or 'morose'; the botanist William Jackson Hooker (who arrived with Jorgenson a few months after this first trip) observed a 'gloomy habit' hanging continually around them, not dispelled by their favourite entertainment of reading and reciting ancient sagas. The traveller Arthur Dillon's impression of an Icelandic musical evening in the 1830s was of 'mournful ditties' sung to the accompaniment of the longspiel, a zither-like instrument whose sound seemed 'by no means calculated to enliven their spirits; indeed, if its gloomy tones are capable of producing any effect, I should say that it is that of instilling a black melancholy into the mind'.

Others, however, thought them extraordinarily cheerful considering the rigour of their lives: they had an earthy sense of humour and, then as now, scenes of drunken merriment were common on Reykjavík streets. Many visitors also noted Icelanders' passion for their literature and country. Hooker found it strange that a land so stark and difficult could inspire such devotion, but that, surely, is exactly the reason for it.

In the early 1800s, no nationalist feeling had yet developed, in the proper sense of the term. But Icelanders' feeling for their island went beyond politics. Iceland was their world: its history and geography were the foundation of their being. Their language had hardly changed over nine centuries, so the sagas were as immediate to them as the day's gossip. Time crept glacially, or revolved endlessly in the slow circles of seasons and generations; the world beyond Iceland was merely a vague and not very interesting rumour. By the time it reached Icelandic shores, the surge created by far-off upheavals in Europe – the Revolution, the war, the treaties, the bombardments – had subsided to lapping wavelets. Yet the effects of these waves of history were real, and where life was so precarious it took only a minor disturbance in trade or transport to produce catastrophe.

The Napoleonic wars were especially damaging for Iceland.* They arrived on top of another disaster from which the island had not yet fully recovered: the Skaftá volcanic eruption of 1783, which poisoned a large area. Birds fell dead out of the sky, fumes rose from the ground, and the grass withered. Animals expired of strange diseases, their feet turning yellow. A fifth of the entire human population also died, from the resulting famine: around ten thousand people.† Denmark sent aid, but it was slow in arriving and rather ineffectual.

And now, in 1808, famine loomed again. Even before the official British and French blockades began, the North Atlantic had been dangerous for shipping. Now almost nothing was getting through. For about a year Iceland had received no imports at all, though one Danish ship called the *Justitia* had at last arrived from Norway and was still in port when the *Clarence* docked. Taking advantage of shortages, many traders had sold what remained of their stock in shrimp-sized quantities at whale-sized prices, but even these supplies were now running low. They were heading into deep winter, and there seemed no hope of more ships arriving until the spring.

The residents of Hafnarfjörður, the main port near the city of Reykjavík, must therefore have been astonished to make out a strange ship sailing out of the freezing darkness of 12 January 1809 – ostensibly an American vessel, for it was flying the flag of that country. (As was common in wartime, the *Clarence* had been given letters of marque, allowing it to operate as a privateer. This arrangement usually came with a set of false papers and colours, so the ship could disguise itself if necessary.) Those on board hoped the American flag would stop the

---

* In the wars of the following century, Iceland benefited from increased demand for its own exports; but in Napoleonic times, its export trade was insufficiently developed to take advantage of shortages elsewhere, and there was also a greater emphasis on blockading in the North Sea – which, typically, hurt the Icelanders much more than either the British or the French.

† The population declined from nearly fifty thousand to under forty thousand over the next three years; amazingly, by the time Jorgenson arrived it had recovered to nearer fifty thousand again despite the continuing hardships.

Danes on shore driving them away as an enemy before they could explain why they were there, but it was a misguided hope. When James Savignac disembarked, the island's acting Governor waved the American papers aside as irrelevant: the law forbade *all* trade with foreigners, whatever their nationality, and that was that. This particular official, the Supreme Court Assessor Ísleifur Einarsson, was a stickler for rules: although himself an Icelander, he was answerable for his decisions to the absent Danish Governor Count Frédérik Trampe, and he was as keen as any Danish official to demonstrate his dedication to duty.

The next day Savignac tried again, this time producing the genuine British papers. Unsurprisingly, this failed to improve the situation. He sent Ísleifur a letter full of vague threats; Jorgenson followed this with a gentler letter, in which he warned that certain preparations underway on the *Clarence* might prove harmful to the local inhabitants: as a Dane he felt it his duty to advise Ísleifur of the danger. It was an alarming suggestion, seeming to imply that the *Clarence* was about to open fire on the town – which, like the whole of Iceland, was completely undefended. But Ísleifur was not intimidated, and continued to refuse permission to trade.

Savignac did carry out his threats, but not by bombarding the town – something the *Clarence* lacked the weaponry to do even had those on board wished it. Instead, the crew boarded and seized the other ship in harbour, the *Justitia*, and held it to ransom. If the administration allowed them to trade, he told Ísleifur, they would release it unharmed; otherwise they would sail it away as lawful enemy prize. Ísleifur now had to ask himself which would anger his boss more: letting a valuable Danish ship go, or allowing foreigners to sell useful goods on the island. He opted to safeguard the ship. So, on 19 January, he signed a formal agreement lifting the Danish trading monopoly: the *Clarence* was permitted to sail on to Reykjavík, and trade its cargo at will.

The methods were aggressive, but the Icelanders stood to benefit from Phelps's goods. According to Jorgenson, they were overjoyed at the result, 'for not one of the articles on board the Clarence was to be had on the island for money, except salt and grain; the latter entirely in the possession of government, nothing to be had under twenty two dollars a barrel, so it might as well not be there at all . . . The natives themselves, with crying tears, begged Mr Savignac to remain and dispose of his cargo.' But when the *Clarence* arrived in Reykjavík, they found a different situation. Unloading their goods in a warehouse near the harbour, they waited complacently for their hungry customers to arrive. None did.

There were several reasons for this. Reykjavík was a town of only around three hundred permanent residents, most of them Danish traders or officials, or Icelanders connected with them in some way. Ordinary, rural Icelanders – the ones currently facing starvation – came into Reykjavík only in the summer, if at all. The town was therefore deserted of all except those who had no interest in dealing with the *Clarence*. Moreover, any Icelanders who might have been tempted did not dare to approach them, for they were 'terrified by the threats of government', as Jorgenson wrote. He was certain the Danes in town were conspiring against them. 'Government and the factors cared not in the least for the true welfare of the Icelanders, whom they had for many years imposed on', he complained: 'it was laughable enough to see a dozen of the greatest cowards, ever God created, keeping fifty thousand inhabitants in fear and dread, merely by threats'. But fear and dread were only an embellishment. The main problem was that most potential customers had no idea the *Clarence* was there.*

So they sold nothing, and, to make matters worse, none of the tallow they were expecting to take back materialized either. When Jorgenson asked the merchant's representative about it, the man 'only laughed'. Either the original information had been wrong, or the other Danish traders had sabotaged the deal. The *Clarence* remained through

* Count Trampe also claimed later that Phelps's cargo contained the wrong goods, being full of useless luxuries. That might be true, rejoined Phelps, if one considered such things as meat, grain and potatoes to be luxuries, as Icelanders might, having been deprived of them for so long. Nervousness of the Danish authorities probably did play a part: Jorgenson later quoted a letter he received from a local Icelandic priest, declining an invitation to dine on the *Clarence* because he was afraid to defy the government, who were 'over cautious' and gave 'wrong explanations of the law'. There was also a simpler aversion to strangers in general, and a tendency to take them for pirates – with good reason. Six months earlier, the island had been raided by a maverick British-licensed ship called the *Salamine*. Its captain, Thomas Gilpin, had stripped merchants as well as government offices of much of their property before sailing off in August, leaving both the traders and the ordinary people in shock.

February and much of March, but in the end accepted temporary defeat and sailed home. Savignac remained in the rented warehouse with the cargo, hoping to sell it once the spring came in. Jorgenson went home with the crew on the near-empty ship. Having no cargo in the hold, they had to take on stones for ballast, and this caused further expense. For, wrote Jorgenson: 'altho' Iceland abounds in nothing so much as stones, when the ship should take in her ballast, every stone taken for that purpose, was claimed by some factor or other, and the ridiculous sum of two hundred and thirty five dollars paid for them.'

Thus, the *Clarence's* total achievement had been to unload its cargo without selling it, to alienate the Danish administration, and to transport a load of useless and expensive rocks from Iceland to England. Leaving Savignac behind did Phelps's business little good either, because his character was so belligerent that he infuriated everyone he met. One of his first acts was to demand the use of an absent government official's house. If the keys were not handed over voluntarily, he said, he would simply break in and take it over by force. The house was given to him, but he made few friends on the island.

The considerably more charming Jorgenson meanwhile arrived in London and gave Phelps and his partners the bad news. Surprisingly, they 'appeared not much displeased, and put up with their loss patiently', and Phelps immediately began preparing a second expedition, better planned than the first, to try to recover his investment.

Jorgenson also wrote to Banks, sending him samples of tallow, down and wool, with a relation of the whole affair. He wrote eagerly: 'if I thought it could interest you I would in the course of a fortnight give you an account of the Iceland commerce from the year 1764 to 1784 with all imports and exports annually' – a typical Jorgenson project, and probably one he could have performed from memory. He called on Banks in person the following day to tell him more.

Banks took an interest in what Jorgenson had to say, and made notes of the conversation, later passing them to the Board of Trade. He particularly noted such matters as which articles were available in Iceland and which not, which Danes were present and in which offices, and how much money was available and where it was kept. He was interested in news of recent piratical activity, too, for this showed how poorly defended

Reykjavík was; and Banks had long been in favour of seizing Iceland and annexing it to Britain. He even added one astonishing extra suggestion: 'The owner of the *Clarence* offers to make the conquest.' Phelps's account confirms that he and Banks did indeed discuss this proposal.

The idea of annexation had been going around for some years, having first been proposed by John Cochrane in 1785: he suggested using Iceland as a convict colony and putting the prisoners to work as fishermen. Many similar schemes were to follow, some (though not Banks's) motivated by their authors' own commercial interests. What they all had in common was that they were ignored by the British government. Only once, in November 1807, did the Home Secretary show a spark of interest by asking Banks for a full feasibility study. When Banks supplied it, however, the government filed it away and paid it no further attention.

This indifference was not surprising, for even Banks was aware that there were few advantages to Britain in seizing an island which would provide little income and cost a lot to maintain, especially during wartime: as British territory it would have to be defended. It would benefit Britain only as an assertion of general dominance and as a psychological blow against Denmark, for, as Banks observed, Danes would feel the loss of an 'ancient Hereditary Dominion' more than that of their recent little colonies in India and the Caribbean. It was the jewel in their crown, especially now that a new Romantic nostalgia was stirring for Nordic history and sagas. The archaic Icelandic language was a sort of grandmother tongue to Danes, as to all Scandinavians and indeed to the English. Iceland was like a beloved but vulnerable aged relative, often neglected in practice but inspiring great sentimental devotion.

Banks pressed the annexation plan on the British government primarily as a moral duty, however, rather than as a move of real advantage to themselves. He had got the impression, when visiting Iceland in 1772, that the Icelanders were 'much inclined to become dependent on the Government of England', because Britain could find better markets for Icelandic produce than Denmark could.* Most Icelanders

---

* Banks lacked personal enthusiasm for their main potential export, dried and salted cod, but he showed himself a true imperial thinker when he suggested that it might do as 'some part of the subsistence of the negros in our Colonies'.

would have been surprised to hear Banks's theory: much as they suffered at the hands of Danes, they showed no signs of craving liberation through absorption into Britain's teeming empire. British writers were fond of quoting a supposed Icelandic proverb: 'When the Danes shall have stripped us of our shirts, the English will clothe us anew.' But the Icelanders knew that they were simply at the mercy of whichever clothier happened to be in town.

Banks was so optimistic about his plan that he drafted a letter to be sent to notable Icelanders with an invading ship, offering an even tougher choice than that which had faced Copenhagen.

> When I was in your country, the wish, I may say, of every man with whom I conversed, was to be placed under the government of England. This must now happen, either by conquest or by revolution; it is therefore sincerely to be hoped that the same disposition may continue to prevail; an instant acknowledgment of homage and fealty to the Crown of the United Kingdom . . . will do away with the necessity of conquest, preserve you from the excesses of an invading army, which no degree of discipline can wholly prevent; your women will remain inviolate, your children in security, your lives in safety, your property unaltered, and your laws unchanged, and your religion untouched.

He was keen to show that the takeover could be done very easily, even without local co-operation: '500 men with a very few Guns . . . would subdue the Island without striking a blow'. There was no army there, very few firearms, and only four officials of any standing, two of them bishops. Three of the four also lived very close to each other, so they could be captured together within moments.

Phelps and Jorgenson both supported Banks's idea: Phelps later wrote that it was 'much to be lamented' that Britain had never seized the island. Jorgenson too believed that annexation would be good for Icelanders, though they might need a couple of British frigates showing themselves along Icelandic coasts 'to enforce the inhabitants to do a thing beneficial to themselves, without exposing themselves to the displeasure of their own government'. But he was more aware than Phelps of the disadvantages to Britain itself. It was wiser, he believed, to impose a more subtle form of British control while treating Iceland as neutral: 'it is by neutrals England gains, not by taking possession.' Jorgenson may have been an unwise analyst of his own business interests, but he often showed an excellent grasp of politics and economics, and of the subtleties of colonial influence.

From Banks's enthusiasm for benevolent conquest, some have concluded that the ensuing events constituted a grand plot involving all the active participants together with Banks and dark powers in the British government. Yet the evidence points to governmental indifference to any such plans, despite the efforts even of a campaigner as influential as Banks. And as things turned out, Banks himself did not approve of what happened in Iceland that summer. He deplored it – rather to its perpetrators' surprise.

Visions of an Atlantic empire aside, there is no doubt that Banks cared about Icelanders' welfare, and so, when Phelps sought his help in obtaining a Board of Trade licence for a second supply trip, he was happy to assist. He also endorsed an added request that a government warship should sail to Iceland first, to liaise with the administration there and ensure that there would be no obstructions to trade: an exercise in firmness, possibly force, but stopping short of full invasion. The Admiralty granted this request, and on 1 May 1809 the sloop *Rover*, captained by John Francis Nott, was duly sent to Iceland, there to spend the summer cruising its waters protecting supply ships. Phelps liked this idea, and described the *Rover* in John-the-Baptist terms as being sent 'to prepare the way for us'. This was an exaggeration: it was meant as a general military escort for what was now becoming a regular British-licensed trading route.

By the time the *Rover* called at Reykjavík on 11 June 1809, the situation had changed greatly from that of the winter. The first of the Icelandic ships seized in Britain the previous year had been released, and was sitting in the harbour having unloaded a useful cargo of over four hundred tonnes of rye. More such ships were known to be on their way. And the Governor, Count Trampe, had returned from his long absence on the mainland, in another trading ship named the *Orion*. Trampe was horrified by what he found: Jorgenson's and Savignac's letters, a copy of the trading agreement signed with the

Clarence, and Ísleifur's hurried explanations of how he had been pressurized into signing it. 'I felt mortified', Trampe told the British government later. He immediately deemed the agreement invalid because it had been signed under duress: a fair point. It was further undermined, in Trampe's view, by the bullying behaviour displayed by Savignac ever since the *Clarence*'s departure. In any case, Trampe had arrived with new Danish government orders following the declaration of war, to which he added a fresh proclamation of his own, outlawing any agreement or trade with Britain on penalty of death. These orders were promptly displayed all over town.

Trampe's determination to enforce the ban was probably motivated by more than patriotism. He had his own mercantile interests on the island, and had arrived with his own cargo to sell. Trampe's goods were allegedly on the market for four times the price the *Clarence* had been asking: he was bound to resent competition from cheaper suppliers. As for the famine still raging among those too poor to pay, that did not seem to concern him much. Phelps rather melodramatically claimed that, on Trampe's return, Icelanders had come to him pleading for help and saying that they were trying to live on moss scraped from mountain rocks. Trampe supposedly replied, in effect, 'Let them eat seaweed.' There was still plenty of that on the shore, and Norwegians had once lived on it for nine months without complaining.*

The *Rover* arrived just a few days after Trampe. Captain Nott told the Hafnarfjörður officials that he came in peace, but Trampe sent a message forbidding him to step ashore, and protesting about Savignac's recent behaviour. At the same time, Savignac himself wrote to Nott complaining of ill-treatment and describing how the trading agreement with the *Clarence* had been overridden. Nott's orders were to provide protection for British trade: he had no doubt as to which side he should listen to. He therefore commanded Trampe to revoke his proclamation and restore the former trading agreement, else he would be obliged to impose it by bringing the full force of his well-armed sloop-of-war to bear on the port.

Iceland was still defenceless, so, like Ísleifur Einarsson before him,

* This story may have been based on a proposal made by the Chief Judge Magnús Stephensen, who had suggested in May 1808 that the Icelanders eat moss, lichen, seaweed, birds and even horsemeat (which was normally avoided) to avert famine.

Trampe had no choice. He gave in. A second trading agreement, informally known as the Nott Convention, was signed on 16 June, allowing
British-licensed traders to operate freely on the island so long as they
obeyed Icelandic laws. Trampe agreed to have it printed and displayed
in place of his own proclamation, and to send orders to officials around
the country informing them of the change. The next day, Nott sailed
away thinking everything was resolved. He remained in Icelandic
waters, but moved up towards the north-west, where he was incom-
municado and therefore knew nothing about the events in Reykjavík
a few days later.

The first thing he did not hear about was Trampe's alleged order to
officials, as soon as the British sails had disappeared over the horizon,
to ignore his last message and to reinstate his original trading ban. Nor
did he hear about the fact that, over a week after the agreement had
been signed, there was still no sign of the printed Nott Convention
appearing on Reykjavík's streets in place of the old death-threatening
ones. Trampe seemed to have agreed terms so quickly only because he
had no intention of abiding by them. He later denied this, and argued
that the printing took a long time because the island's only press was
far from town (it was a day or two's journey from the city). But other
documents rarely took so long, and Trampe undermined his own excuse
by noting that he had privately considered the Nott Convention invalid
anyway, since, like the earlier agreement, it had been signed under duress.

This, then, was the situation meeting Phelps's new ship the *Margaret*
& Anne, which sailed into Hafnarfjörður just four days after Nott had
left. (There is something of the bedrooms-and-hallways farce about the
comings and goings of ships in this port during June 1809.) Again the
ship had letters of marque, and again it carried a carefully chosen cargo,
this time assembled in the light of earlier experience, using a list sent
back with the *Clarence*. The result of this extra thoughtfulness is interesting, for the cargo it generated was less rather than more dominated
by necessary foodstuffs. It is unlikely that the people who were eating
moss off the mountainsides would be serving it from fine porcelain tureens,
or that they would drink moss-juice from any of the 14 dozen neat plain
wineglasses, 16 dozen stout ones, 6 dozen globed goblets, 5 dozen tumblers,
1 dozen large globed glasses, 15 dozen large best assorted wineglasses, 15
dozen assorted liquor glasses, 2 dozen common wineglasses, 8 dozen stout

ones, 5 pairs stout quart decanters, 6 oval ribbed liquor bottles, or 6 blue liquor decanters delivered by the *Margaret & Anne*. But, to be fair, the cargo also included potatoes, cheese, hams, cloth, fishing-lines, a salmon net, spades, nails and other practical goods. The inventory can be, and has been, used to support either side of the argument as to whether they were fulfilling their humanitarian mission. Besides, it was not unreasonable for Phelps to try to recoup his earlier losses by adding wineglasses for the rich as well as tools and foodstuffs for the poor.

For Jorgenson it made no financial difference this time: he was not sailing as an investor but merely as a hired translator to assist Phelps himself, who made the journey in person. Other passengers were on board too: the American Charles Vancouver and his wife,* and a young man who was to become a great friend to Jorgenson, the botanist William Jackson Hooker. His trip to Iceland was part of his apprenticeship, a journey to some region of scientific interest being an indispensable stage in any naturalist's training. He had been urged to try Iceland by Banks himself, who had paid his passage and given him plenty of advice and a letter of introduction to his oldest friend on the island, the former Governor Olafur Stephensen.[†]

Jorgenson and Hooker warmed to each other straight away. Hooker was an easy man to like. He was good-looking and intelligent, with a warm personality and an urbane, confident manner, although he was only twenty-four, compared with Jorgenson's relatively mature and much more well-travelled twenty-nine. He had a glorious career ahead of him: he was later to become Professor of Botany in Glasgow and eventually the first official Director of Kew Gardens. But for now he was just starting out; everything was new to him, and he brought a refreshing curiosity and enthusiasm to everything he encountered.

This journey should have been easier than that of the *Clarence*, but the *Margaret & Anne*'s trip was sickeningly rough: they were battered by winds and storms all the way. Off southern Iceland, they were nearly

---

* Agriculturalist and brother of the famous explorer George Vancouver, Charles was apparently working for Phelps as clerk or supercargo; his wife travelled along for the ride. Jorgenson came to detest the couple, for they turned against him during the events of the summer.

[†] Banks recommended Phelps too, describing him as 'a scientific as well as a commercial man'.

wrecked on a submerged rock: the ship was saved by Jorgenson, who was the first to spot breaking waves ahead of them. He raised the alarm just in time, and then raced from one part of the deck to the other helping the sailors turn the ship about. Hooker was impressed, and praised Jorgenson's expertise in his diary.

At last they rounded the south-western peninsula and headed towards Hafnarfjörður and Reykjavík. It looked very different from the scene of their first visit. This time they sailed into port on the year's longest day, 21 June, so instead of near-permanent night there was near-permanent day. Icelanders – the first Hooker had ever seen – rowed out in a boat to greet them. They struck up an urgent conversation in Danish with Jorgenson, and eagerly ate food given to them by the crew, even the ship's biscuit: they must have been hungry indeed. In return they offered snuff from narrow-necked vessels. Hooker had no idea why they were so agitated, but Phelps's account makes it clear that they were telling Jorgenson all about Trampe and the Nott affair. According to Phelps, they said they had come to meet the *Margaret & Anne* only at the risk of their own lives, and that they hoped for protection.

The ship continued towards Reykjavík, unusually not stopping at Hafnarfjörður, and there dropped anchor beside the other ship in port, Trampe's *Orion*. Savignac rowed out to meet them. More heated conversations followed: he too told Phelps and Jorgenson about the defying of the Nott agreement and the ongoing obstructions to trade. Leaving them to their debate, Hooker looked out from the deck and took in his first view of Reykjavík; the wooden warehouses belonging to the Danish traders, the low Icelandic houses so comfortably packed in turf that they could hardly be distinguished from the ground they stood on, a stone church with a wooden bell tower, and a large white building which Hooker assumed was the Governor's residence. In fact it was the prison.*

---

* The prison is still there, and it did eventually become a governmental building after all: it now contains the offices of Iceland's President and Prime Minister. Descriptions of Reykjavík by visitors like Hooker often depended on whether they had been to other Icelandic regions first. When the naturalist Henry Holland arrived in 1810, he found it 'mean, miserable and desolate', but after his voyage around the rest of the island it miraculously took on 'a certain semblance of magnificence – something of life, population and activity'.

A movable jetty of fir planks was floated out to the ship to help them disembark, and by four o'clock in the afternoon they were ashore. A hundred Icelanders, mostly women, gathered to welcome them. They had been drying fish: the shore was covered with lines of cod laid out in the sun, with more cod piled up nearby under heavy stones to keep them flat. The ever-observant Hooker was struck by the beach's black sand, actually fine-ground lava, and also by the women, who seemed 'stout and lusty, but excessively filthy'. They, or perhaps the fish, produced a 'strong and very rancid smell'. With nothing else to do while Jorgenson, Phelps and Savignac huddled discussing their crisis, Hooker watched the work on the beach and took note of every detail, including the women's thick high-waisted dresses, bound tightly across the chest, and woollen caps from which dangled long, wire-bound, pointed tassels. He even strolled behind one woman and stooped unobtrusively while she was picking up fish, to try to count the number of petticoats under her dress.

He was surprised to find Reykjavík so lively, but this was the town's busiest time of year: in these long light hours, Icelanders slept little and worked hard. The summer fair was just about to begin, and people from all over the island were setting out for town with whatever scraps of produce they had to trade. Hooker strolled among them with the other passengers, admiring the warehouses on Hafnarstræti, and the smart buildings on the city's main thoroughfare, Aðalstræti: a fine, wide street, but so covered with lumps of rock and lava that, had there been any carts or carriages in Reykjavík, none could have been driven down it. Here there were more merchants' houses, a smart little Government House, the bishop's residence, and the building Savignac had so unceremoniously commandeered. Hooker found them all charming, with their neat gardens fenced in with turf walls and kept free of weeds – in fact, mostly free of plants, since little would grow in Reykjavík's climate.

This part of town, like the warehouse area, was almost entirely Danish. It was only at the far end of Aðalstræti that a more Icelandic feeling took over, with a few turf cottages following the last Danish building, a tavern where traders gathered to play cards. Hooker later rented one of these turf houses from the local midwife. From then on, installed in Reykjavík and pleasantly oblivious to the concerns of

Jorgenson and the others, he settled down to his main business of hiking, riding, studying springs and volcanoes, and collecting plants. During his Icelandic summer he spent most of his time outside Reykjavík, and so witnessed only a few episodes of the drama to come, though he heard all about it from his new friend Jorgenson. Hooker got on well with everyone and gave a sympathetic hearing to all involved, but he was happy to remain an outsider in this restless, interventionist group of mercantile men.

While Hooker peeked at petticoats, Phelps, Savignac and Jorgenson were trying to decide what to do. Phelps was eager to unload his new cargo, but it was obvious that this would not be officially approved. Yet he had to sell his goods: if this cargo went the way of the other one, he was afraid he might be ruined. Savignac was bluntly aggressive as always, disinclined to brook restraint: besides being Phelps's employee, he seems to have had some financial investment in the cargo as well. And Jorgenson felt obliged to support Phelps, to whom he still owed money for the first cargo. He was also angered by what he saw as perfidy and tyranny on the part of his fellow Danes, from whom he dissociated himself completely. The three men worked themselves into a lather, each boosting the others' confidence. At some point during the four days following their arrival on 21 June, they came to a daring decision. By 25 June they were ready to act.

That day was a Sunday, and most people had spent the morning in church. By midday, the townspeople were emerging in no great hurry from the service, and milling near the church doors catching up on gossip, as departing congregations do. They paid little attention to the harbour area, so they did not notice a lifeboat being rowed from the *Margaret & Anne* towards the shore, bearing the ship's captain John Liston and a dozen sailors armed with muskets and swords. Nor did the Reykjavík churchgoers notice, or if they did they thought nothing of it, when the small gang of men disembarked and walked up Aðalstræti in a determined manner, followed by Phelps and the other strangers – all heading for the Governor's house.

Count Trampe was not in church that morning. He was sitting at home with the district administrator Hans Wolner Koefoed, the man whose house Savignac was living in. They had been discussing practical affairs, or perhaps just chatting. Few other people were in the house, for most servants had attended the service. The front door was unlocked.

Some noise made Trampe look up: he glanced out of the window, and saw the house 'surrounded by 10 or 12 men armed with firelocks and swords'. Before he could react to what he was seeing, an armed man (Captain Liston, as he later realized) charged into his sitting-room. He stood before Trampe, and announced that he was seizing him as a prisoner of war. Other crewmen marched in behind him, together with Phelps, at whose instigation Liston was evidently acting. Bringing up the rear came Savignac, also armed. Jorgenson was not yet on the scene.

According to Trampe, Savignac seemed almost demented. He shouted about the violation of the Nott Convention and said something about having proof of this in his hands, presumably a copy of Trampe's proclamation. Trampe asked to see this proof, but Savignac abruptly ran out again; after a few moments he darted back in, this time berating Trampe as a man without honour or faith who had broken the terms of the agreement. Again he said that he had evidence, but still he produced nothing. Lost for words, he left again.

Trampe tried to defend himself verbally and perhaps physically. Phelps claimed that the Governor seized a sword and threatened to cut his attackers to pieces, upon which Phelps 'gave him to understand that it was not so easily done as talked of or threatened', and disarmed him. Trampe's account mentions nothing about the sword. According to him he calmly asked the intruders by what right they thought they were taking him prisoner, what they wanted from him, and why he should not be considered protected by the Nott Convention just as they expected to be – since the convention specified that British traders must obey Icelandic laws. But his questions were ignored. Phelps told him there was no time for idle discussion, and Liston threatened that, if Trampe did not go with them voluntarily, they would take him by force. The choice was his.

Before Trampe could respond, Jorgenson arrived, apparently in just as over-excited a state as Savignac, and almost immediately rushed out again. Trampe took umbrage at this intemperate behaviour, and directed

his irritation primarily at Liston and Phelps, whom he obviously considered the responsible adults in the room despite their threats. But there
was little he could do. 'I found myself, unarmed as I was, alone with Mr
Koefoed . . . surrounded by a band of armed men, and having no assistance to expect from the unarmed and defenceless inhabitants, I found
myself, I say, in the most mortifying – nay more than mortifying necessity of surrendering to the dishonorable perpetrators of this shameless
outrage.' Sputtering but helpless, he gave himself up.

He was marched out of the house and along Aðalstræti towards the
harbour, under armed escort all the way. Hooker strolled into town
from one of his excursions just in time to see Liston, holding a drawn
cutlass, leading Trampe down to the shore, followed by the rest of the
armed sailors. They rowed the deposed Governor out to the *Margaret
& Anne* and there bundled him into a small cabin, which was to be
his prison cell for the rest of the summer. He was not left in complete
solitude. Later that evening his loyal secretary, a seventeen-year-old
Norwegian lad, came to the ship in tears begging to be allowed to
remain with his employer; this was granted.

Naturally the body of men forcing the governor to the harbour at
the point of a cutlass did attract some attention this time: everyone
was now out of church and on their way home. But no one inter-
vened. Jorgenson took this as proof that the Icelanders were secretly
pleased to see Trampe removed, and had no desire to risk their lives
trying to save him. He remarked particularly on one nearby group
of men holding metal-tipped pikes, normally used for walking on the
ice in winter: potentially lethal weapons. They must have brought
these out deliberately, as they were not normally used in this season.
According to Phelps, the men had been alerted by the few servants
who had escaped from the back of Government House. Yet they
made no attempt to do anything; they just watched the Governor
go. Perhaps they had not been expecting to see so many guns. It
would take a lot of devotion to attack an armed guard with what
were, in effect, spears. Jorgenson was right: Trampe had not earned
that kind of loyalty.

Many people would have assumed, too, that this was an action sanctioned by the British government. It seemed to be something arranged
over Icelanders' heads by forces too powerful to contest, even had they

wanted to.* As for the Danes, those living near their warehouses on Hafnarstræti would not have realized what was happening at first, since it was in a different part of town; those who did probably assumed they were up against both the British *and* the Icelanders.

The revolution was thus launched and accomplished within an hour. Trampe was secured. The remaining Danish officials made no move to resist: Liston's men warned those nearby to stay in their homes, and apparently they did so. There was no objection from the Icelanders in town. It only remained to formalize the change of regime, occupy Government House, swap the proclamations and appoint a formal replacement, and the transformation would be complete. It was a bloodless revolution – and an extraordinarily quick and nimble one.

The matter of the replacement was not that simple, however. The revolutionaries seem not to have discussed this in advance: they gave it their attention only now. Who was to take charge of Iceland? In fact, what had just happened? It was not even clear which country Iceland was now supposed to belong to: Denmark, Britain, or possibly even itself. Phelps claimed that a deputation of Icelanders called to beg him to 'hoist the British flag' and take the island under official British protection, but he was not sure he could legally do this. He told them that he did not wish to interfere in Icelandic politics; all he intended to do was to enforce the Nott Convention. This was an evasion of the issue, as he realized, but he could not claim the island for Britain without his own government's sanction. Besides, although he could imagine an argument for deeming the whole of Iceland legitimate prize by the terms of his privateer's licence, he suspected it might not be a sound argument. Could Iceland be treated as a sort of ship? 'I could clearly understand, that we were to annoy the enemies of our country wherever we found them, but whether we were to hoist the British flag on that island, the same as after taking an enemy's vessel, was what I could not decide.'

---

* Jorgenson and Phelps did nothing to discourage this belief. Trampe and the Icelander Gísli Konráðsson both wrote that Jorgenson was heard boasting of having been sent on British government orders; the chronicler Jón Espólín heard that Phelps had claimed something similar. This might seem to support the idea that the British really were behind it – but it is more likely that Jorgenson and Phelps played shrewdly on a popular misconception to shore up their own position.

It was because of this perplexity over British involvement that Jorgenson, rather than Phelps, was installed as the island's interim Governor. As a non-Briton, Jorgenson was not under the same constraints. Britain could not hold him responsible for any breach of law or etiquette, for he was not Britain's representative. He claimed not to be Denmark's representative, either: he seemed quite willing to act as a free-wheeling maverick. It was a relief to Phelps, for it removed all 'embarrassment' from his own position.

Jorgenson found that he rather liked the thought of becoming the acting Governor. He disowned 'all attachment to the Danish Government and interest', and indeed regarded it as his political duty to correct the evils he saw around him. He knew he could not easily return to Denmark anyway, with everything that had been said about the *Admiral Juul*, so he had nothing to lose. Nor did he see anything genuinely treasonable about acting against Danish interests at a time when the Danish King had already handed the country over to French tyranny. He wanted to assist Phelps, for he felt partly responsible for the losses on the first expedition, and he wished to help Icelanders in any way he could, despite being a Dane – or perhaps *because* he was a Dane. And of course the thought of becoming the islanders' figure-head and official liberator was not at all an unpleasant one.

Phelps claimed to consider Jorgenson's approach emphatically a '*farce*'; he remarked that Jorgenson 'had imbibed all the quixotism of a petit Napoleon'. (The Vancouvers, too, compared him to a 'second Buonaparte'; notwithstanding his disapproval of the French 'usurper', Jorgenson was pleased enough with this comparison to repeat it twice in his writings.) But this solution could not have been more conven-ient for Phelps. He was free to retreat behind the scenes and get on with making a profit from his two cargoes. Jorgenson meanwhile settled himself into Government House, and started writing the first of several far-reaching, magnificent proclamations for his newly independent island nation.

5

Jorgenson the Protector

Phelps was delighted to see scenes of celebratory trading following the revolution. '[M]ultitudes of people came to the town from all quarters,' he wrote, 'and such a scene of festivity and joy I never beheld! – It was a perfect camp for miles round; every family bringing their tents, with innumerable horses, and products of the island, which they exchanged for our goods . . . Dances and pleasure parties kept up the festive scene: – the Danes grumbling and working revenge, and the natives rejoicing!' In fact, what he was seeing was just the usual summer trading fair; if anything it was less lively than most years, as the winter's famine had taken the edge off it. The fair had nothing to do with the revolution, but it was perfectly timed: it brought Phelps customers, and he was able to sell his goods without interference.

Jorgenson paid little attention to the commercial side, in which he had no major investment.* Instead, he got to work on his first public document, which appeared early on the morning of the next day, 26 June: its main purpose was simply to announce what had happened. It began with the statement: 'All Danish authority ceases in Iceland.' Ten subsequent clauses ordered residents to turn in all weapons, public funds, and keys to warehouses; Danish merchants and officials were told to remain in their homes awaiting further instructions. Icelanders

* Except in a proportion of the sale of the first cargo, which would have done little more than clear his debt to Phelps.

were assured that they had nothing to fear, so long as they obeyed the terms of the proclamation and did not attempt to help the oppressive Danes who were its real target.

The proclamation ended, 'Shall these orders be speedily executed, it will save a great deel of unnecessary trouble, and the effusion of blood. But on the contrary, should any person act in opposition to what here is directed, he shall immediately be arrested, brought before a military tribunal, and shot within two hours after the offence is committed.' This sounds terrifying, but Jorgenson later claimed that he included 'expressions of severity' only out of political expediency. He did not mean them, and if his bluff was called he would have been incapable of carrying them out. Murderous tyranny was not in him. But, as he wrote, 'by appearing what I really was not, I managed the whole island with ease'.

A second, more detailed proclamation appeared on the evening of the same day, dictated in Danish to a secretary, then translated into Icelandic and sent to be printed at the island's only press – the same that had been so slow with the Nott Convention. It began even more boldly than the first, with the radical assertion: 'Iceland is free, and independent of Denmark.' After this it went on to list the ancient rights that were to be returned to the Icelanders after centuries of oppression: the right to self-government through their traditional Parliament or *Althing*, the right to trial by a jury of peers, the right to move freely around the country without travel passes, and the right to an independent flag. With this proclamation, wrote Jorgenson later, he sought to restore Iceland to its golden age, an age when government was free and no one could be condemned unjustly, and when the Icelanders were rich as well as independent – for they only 'became poor and cowardly under Danish government'.

As a first step to reassembling the *Althing*, the proclamation called for each region to elect a parliamentary representative, who must be an Icelander. This would take time, so meanwhile every official who wished to keep his job was ordered to write to Jorgenson notifying him of this intention, thus implicitly recognizing his authority. Anyone who did not write within the time limit (two weeks for areas near Reykjavík, seven for those further away) would lose his position.

Other clauses addressed Iceland's international affairs, declaring rashly that 'Iceland shall be at peace with all nations, and peace established on a firm footing with Great Britain, which will protect it', and that 'Iceland shall be set in a state of defence'. Both were little more than expressions of wishful thinking, since Iceland had nothing with which to defend itself and Jorgenson had no basis for promising Britain's protection. But other clauses seemed more carefully thought out. Indeed, Jorgenson showed considerable political flair, blending radical appeals to national pride with plenty of conservative reassurance. The proclamation emphasized that ordinary Icelanders would be safe, and that most aspects of life would carry on as normal, except for improvements to schools and hospitals. More pleasingly still, it offered a bouquet of financial incentives. Icelanders would be respited from half their taxes during the coming year, and all debts to the Danish government and Danish trading companies would be negated at a blow.

While Reykjavík was absorbing the new state of affairs and studying the proclamations, and while the strange news was gradually saddled up on ponies and despatched on its journey into the outlying districts, Jorgenson and his colleagues spent the day passing from house to house, in torrential Icelandic rain, collecting residents' weapons. There was not much to collect. When they had finished their wet tour of Reykjavík, their haul totalled only a couple of dozen small fowling-pieces for shooting birds, and 'a few rusty cutlasses'. These paltry confiscations did not greatly help their own plans to arm a defensive force for the island, but at least they made any counter-revolutionary uprising in town less likely.

They cannot have been too worried about the possibility of a rebellion, because on 27 June, the second full day of the revolution, Jorgenson, Phelps and Hooker left Reykjavík for the day to fulfil a prior engagement, leaving only Liston and his crew to watch the town. The day passed as peacefully as any other, Danes biding their time and Icelanders shaking their heads in amusement at the goings-on in Government House, while also passing on the good, if barely believable, news about debts and taxes to their friends.

The social engagement was a visit to Olafur Stephensen, a former governor and Banks's great friend – they had met in 1772, when Banks visited Iceland, and had corresponded (in Latin) ever since. Now retired, Olafur lived on a private island called Viðey, a short boat ride from town. Hooker had been up half the night botanizing in full sunlight, making up for the rain of the day before, so he felt a little dazed as they were rowed out to the island in the morning and greeted by the seventy-eight-year-old former Governor, dressed for the occasion in full Danish officer's uniform: blue pantaloons with spurs, a scarlet coat ornamented with gold lace and tassels, and a tricorn hat with a long white feather. Olafur was overjoyed at meeting Banks's protégés, and the mention of his old friend's name brought tears to his eyes. Hooker presented him with gifts sent by Banks; Olafur talked animatedly about the past while Jorgenson translated for the others. Conversation was light: the revolution seems not to have been mentioned at all. In mid-morning, they walked around the island admiring Olafur's sheep and valuable eider ducks.

Then, rather early in the day for Hooker's appetite, they went in for dinner. The table was set plainly: in front of each place were a plate, a single knife and fork, and a plain glass tumbler with a bottle of claret for each guest. A small interruption was caused by 'the breaking down of the chair upon which his Excellency had seated himself', but it was soon replaced, and everyone settled down to eat. The first dish was brought in: a large tureen of soup made of 'sago, claret, and raisins, boiled so as to become almost a mucilage'. They ate two full bowls of this each, not knowing if anything would follow and thinking it a good idea to fill up. But when the tureen was removed, two whole sliced salmon were delivered in its place, with a sauce of melted butter, vinegar and pepper. This was very good: the guests cleared their plates 'with some difficulty' and sat back feeling well satisfied.

Then another huge tureen appeared, this time piled full of hard-boiled tern eggs. A dozen were put on each of their plates, and a thick cream sauce was poured on top. Hooker begged to be excused from eating all twelve of his eggs, but was urged to try, and somehow managed to get through the plateful. The guests laid down their forks with relief – only to see coming through the door 'half a sheep, well roasted'. Their host insisted that they fill their plates with slices of meat, as well as with heaps of the accompanying dish of mashed and sweetened sorrel. They ate bravely; next came a dish of toasted waffles, each one 'about the size of an octavo book'. Olafur said that he would be satisfied if the guests ate just two apiece. The meal was finally rounded off with many generous slices of bread: 'Norway biscuit and loaves made of rye'.

All this time they were encouraged to drink plentifully of the wine, and to empty each of their bottles. Afterwards good coffee was served, and they felt confident that this meant the end of the meal, but 'a huge bowl of rum-punch was brought in, and handed round in large glasses pretty freely, and to every glass, a toast was given'. Whenever they flagged a new toast to Banks was called, and their glasses had to be drained and refilled so they could drink to his health. A second punch bowl replaced the first, and it was only with difficulty that they could persuade Olafur not to make them empty this completely as well. The feast finally ended with three cups of tea each.

After they sailed back to Reykjavík in the evening, the boat somehow staying afloat, Jorgenson offered Hooker a bed in Government House to save him staggering the few extra steps to his house – 'which I gladly accepted', Hooker admitted.

Serious revolutionary matters now needed attending to. Jorgenson was told of rumours circulating in nearby districts that Reykjavík's streets were 'stained with the blood of Danes and Icelanders'. He suspected someone was spreading these stories maliciously; certainly there seems not to have been any truth in them. The sailors providing the muscle behind the revolution were undoubtedly uncouth and intimidating, and Jorgenson's actions were an affront to the town's traders. But the streets remained peaceful. When his opponents spoke of rivers of blood, they seem to have meant it rhetorically: even his worst enemies never accused him of killing anyone, nor of ordering or approving any deaths. Jorgenson himself took pride in having given Iceland its liberty 'without a single drop of blood spilt, without a single man committed or sent to prison', and without even damaging the financial affairs of anyone other than the Danish usurers. 'I should wish in all history to see an example similar to this; no never.'

Is there any innocent blood crying vengeance against me? – If I have shed that of a fellow creature, either in a just or unjust

93

manner; let my head pay for it! If I have gained only one shilling at the public expence; let my right hand suffer for it! If I have enriched myself to the detriment of any one individual; let my left hand be cut off! If I have caused any one single person, or more, to be confined, for being opposite in principles to me, let me feel the horrors of perpetual imprisonment myself! But, if I have done none of these, let me enjoy that liberty, which I look upon as the only true good on earth.

Jorgenson dealt with the rumours by issuing a third short proclamation:

We are informed that certain evil-minded people have propagated false reports in the country, and have represented to the inhabitants that it is dangerous to travel from place [to place], and that a deel of blood has been spilt in the streets of Reikavig by the English. The inhabitants need not be under any apprehensions, and may rest assured that no violence will be committed against them, and that they are at full liberty to follow their lawful occupations without molestation, and it is hereby declared that all such rumours are entirely without foundation. – All persons that do, or shall hereafter spread such false reports, shall be deemed enemies to the state, and it will be necessary to treat all such people, who do not demean themselves as peaceable citizens, with the utmost severity.

By 'utmost severity', he seems only to have meant binding them over in court to keep the peace, for this was how he dealt with the particular 'sneaking fellow' he suspected of having originated these stories.

Two days later, he had to issue another *ad hoc* proclamation, this time in response to news that many Icelanders were reading earlier edicts as a licence not to pay off any debts at all. He set the record straight: 'It is hereby declared, that only such debt is remitted, which is due to the King, or to such Danish mercantile houses, whose principals are not residents of Iceland.' Danish merchants who lived permanently in Iceland with their families were still entitled to payment, and were invited to complain to Jorgenson if they did not receive it.

It is no wonder that Icelanders seized so eagerly on this one clause over all the others: debt and poverty were uppermost in their minds, and news of the abolition would have spread as rapidly as anything could in Iceland. Even with the added restriction, this particular rule continued to enhance Jorgenson's image in the popular mind.

As news travelled, people often saw other benefits to themselves and used the change of government to advance their own private causes. Jorgenson received many petitions, most airing grudges or requesting personal favours. He was asked to intervene with the bishop to facilitate several divorces, including one for a man whose wife had been imprisoned for sheep-stealing, and who had taken in a young woman to act as housekeeper in her absence. 'Nature, and these circumstances provoked me to an action,' wrote the man, 'the consequences of which was this, that the girl produced two little girls, after each other, whose father I am.' He now wished to join the mother of his children. Jorgenson supported him, and the divorce was granted by the bishop that summer.

It was only natural that most people's response to Jorgenson's idealistic proclamations was to look for personal benefits. High-ranking officials were no exception; foremost among those who saw the revolution as a chance to advance themselves and take a little private revenge was the island's Chief Judge, Olafur's son Magnús Stephensen.

Both Olafur's sons held office; his other son Stefán was a District Governor, while Magnús presided over the High Court. The Stephensen family had achieved very high positions for Icelanders, rising all the way to Governor in Olafur's case. But they were no ordinary Icelanders, being cultivated and highly Danicized. Magnús in particular had spent much time in Copenhagen and had there absorbed cosmopolitan, Enlightenment-flavoured ideas still alien to Iceland. He had a passionate love for his country, but most Icelanders did not return the favour. Many in this firmly Lutheran society distrusted his religious open-mindedness, especially when he tried to amend the traditional hymn-book, and they found him pushy and untrustworthy. Admirable though Magnús's intellect and patriotism were, almost everyone who met him agreed that there was something slippery in his character. Even the generous-minded Hooker later wrote to Banks: 'A man of greater talents or a more artful politician I never met with; yet the advancement of his own family and the aggrandizing of riches are, I fear, his greatest objects.' Jorgenson himself was sure that Magnús played 'a double part' in the events of that summer, and summed him up as 'a character universally hated by all parties'.*

Magnús took a contemptuous view of Jorgenson's posturing and proclaiming; but he did not want to lose his job, so he offered no resistance and quietly did all that Jorgenson required of him, which included co-operation in the High Court as well as the all-important job of printing Jorgenson's edicts, for Magnús owned the island's only press. This he did without demur, though he took care to leave a paper trail implying that he had resisted every step of the way. He trod a fine line, refusing to defy Jorgenson openly but laying a good foundation of excuses for the future; he knew that Jorgenson's regime could not last for long.

In fact, though he would not later have admitted this, Jorgenson's arrival was by no means an unmitigated evil for Magnús. However much he disapproved of Jorgenson, he personally detested Trampe and was secretly delighted to see him removed from office and thrown into a cabin on the *Margaret & Anne*. Hooker noticed this, telling Banks that 'there was not a single man in the whole country who so truly rejoiced at the deposition of the lawful Governor' as Magnús did; the later visitor Henry Holland also observed that, when a toast was proposed to Trampe's health, Magnús seemed reluctant to raise his glass.

Though no proof ever emerged, Jorgenson suspected that Magnús used the opportunity to undermine another personal enemy too: Ísleifur Einarsson, the man who had acted as Governor during Trampe's absence. Ísleifur was a conservative, Magnús a reformer: they had always disliked each other, though they had been obliged to work together at the High Court. In early July, Jorgenson was passed an anonymous report accusing Ísleifur of masterminding a conspiracy to launch a counter-revolutionary coup to return Trampe to power. He was surprised, since Ísleifur seemed acquiescent enough, but he duly

* Magnús had earlier played a double part in Denmark too, albeit from humanitarian motives – he wrote secretly to Banks from Copenhagen in 1807, after the outbreak of hostilities between the two nations, seeking his help in restoring the Iceland trade under British protection.

had the Assessor arrested with several others. The suspects were confined in Government House for nine days while Jorgenson investigated the allegation; when no evidence emerged, he released them. He concluded that the report had been sent in out of 'malice'. Only later did he suspect Magnús. Meanwhile, Magnús himself lay low and did as he was told; Jorgenson left him alone, and everything went on peacefully.

There was no other sign of organized resistance. Most officials wrote pledging to continue in their posts, and activity on the island continued much as usual, except that the once-powerful Danish traders were stripped of their goods and money. The convocation of the *Althing* seemed a long way off, but this was not Jorgenson's fault. No one had initiated local elections for representatives yet. Indeed, many districts had not even received the proclamation: they knew nothing about Jorgenson's arrival.

The fact that officials complied does not mean they were happy about it. Danes were naturally reluctant, but many rural Icelandic administrators were displeased too, for they had long since come to a personal understanding with the regime. They could not afford to lose their jobs and therefore sent in their letters, but they often continued to complain in private. As Hooker noted, 'it seemed to them absurd that an island, to which nature had denied all internal resources, should be proclaimed in a state of independence'. There was a feeling that Jorgenson had no idea what he was talking about, and did not understand local conditions. Some expressed discontent by delaying their replies until the last minute. One disarmingly admitted in his letter that he had waited to see what other people would do first: 'I kept back my opinion, till I saw some of those much higher in office than myself, declare their sentiments on the subject.'

Magnús Stephensen tackled the problem in his own way by asking Jorgenson to *force* him to write his letter, another sign that he was thinking ahead. If anyone later asked why he had collaborated, he could point to evidence of duress. But Jorgenson refused to co-operate. He pointedly included a clause in his next proclamation stating 'that several officers, from fear of Danish government, wish to be forced to retain their offices, though they fully approve of our late proceedings', and decreeing 'that all such people, who are not animated by sufficient patriotism to serve their own country, are permitted to leave the island, and go to Copenhagen'. So Magnús wrote his letter in the normal way.

Only a few officials expressed outright opposition. An unusually forthright response came from Jón Guðmundsson, Regional Governor of one of the southern districts. 'Who are you?' he asked Jorgenson.

You are born a Danish subject . . . But what are you now? You have not become a British subject, yet you have ceased to be what you were and should be, and also ceased to be a human being. Whoever and whatever you are, you have insulted me by assuming me foolish enough to be seduced, cowardly enough to be fearful, and dishonest enough to ignore honour and duty.

If Jorgenson and his crew appeared in his territory, he warned, they would be treated as outlaws. 'Avoid Denmark, there you will find no grave. Everywhere you will be cast out, hated, banished, cursed. In the end you will drown in an ocean of hatred.'

The poet Finnur Magnússon, who worked as a clerk in the Treasury Office, wrote his letter to Jorgenson but then spent the summer working privately on an epic poem of derision. This enjoyed considerable success later, as a sort of poetic souvenir. When it was recited with musical accompaniment at a ball the following year, the whole party sang along. The following excerpt gives a flavour:

He pretended that he served the English King: that he depended on the protection of his armies.

He armed brothers against each other: terror seized the remainder of the people;

Who had never before beheld the sword or blood, and unwillingly submitted to the insolent yoke.

He more powerful raised fortifications; and erected his standard black as hell.

He took a lordly title; having dared to assume possession of the supreme power.

He pretended that our people wished for these things; and that they all demanded these tumults.

Again the blood and terror seemed to be figurative, and Jorgenson's revolutionary flag – which was unveiled shortly after this – was white and blue as a cod in water, rather than black as hell. His handling of the Ísleifur Einarsson affair hardly suggests a colossus wading thigh-deep in gore. He did bring a certain 'tumult' to the island, yet most people seem to have felt neither terror nor joy, but rather a sort of amused indifference.

Rural Icelanders had no political framework in which to make sense of Jorgenson's rhetoric. They were sceptical about what he claimed to offer them, not because they considered him a dangerous usurper but because nothing in their experience prepared them for such sudden political transformations. His proclamations did not stir their blood to a revolutionary fervour: for the most part they weren't sure what a revolution was, or what national independence or liberation were. They cared primarily about their sheep and their families, and their response to wider events was like that of the rural Norwegian described in *Peer Gynt*, whose extreme heroism in the face of natural disasters was matched by total indifference to abstract military and national glory.

> His horizon was narrow. Apart from the few
> Who were nearest to him, nothing else existed.
> The ringing words that rouse other men's hearts
> Meant nothing to him, more than a tinkle of bells.
> Mankind, fatherland, the highest ambitions
> Of men, were only misty figures to him.

There was to be a powerful Icelandic independence movement later on: its great hero, Jón Sigurðsson, was born two years after Jorgenson's revolution. But the time for organized rebellion had not yet arrived. Even on the Continent, the golden era of national liberation movements was yet to begin. Had Jorgenson launched his revolution a few decades later, the response among Icelanders might have been different indeed.

But it wasn't just that Icelanders could not make sense of Jorgenson. Jorgenson actually did not make much sense. He was a stranger, and the disgruntled officials were right in thinking that he understood nothing of their country. He did not speak the language; Icelanders did not know him, and he did not know the Icelanders. And, as Jón Guðmundsson had demanded to know, who was he? On the one hand he seemed to be working for the British, but on the other he was undeniably a Dane: why was he turning against his own people? He was an enigma to his newly acquired nation.

Jorgenson did not preside over a reign of terror, but he did support his regime with military force – first using the *Margaret & Anne*'s sailors, and then by creating a proper national army, composed entirely of Icelanders except for its supreme commander: himself. It was, admittedly, a very small army. At first it consisted of just six men; two more joined later and brought the total to eight. All were volunteers, but several were recruited from the handful of inmates in Reykjavík's prison, the doors of which Jorgenson had dramatically thrown open. He reallocated the same building for use as a barracks, so some of his soldiers simply stayed where they were.

Jorgenson claimed that 150 Icelanders had offered their military services, but that he had to confine himself to eight because he did not have enough weapons to arm more. He did manage to give them green uniforms, according to Hooker, though it is a puzzle where these came from. They were supplied with horses, and the green mounted militia was sent out to roam the countryside, its main task at first being to gather more weapons from outlying villages.

It was at this point, if it had not already done so, that the revolution went to Jorgenson's head. Informants told Trampe, still in his shipboard prison, that Jorgenson had usurped the count's aristocratic manner as well as his position in Government House, and was – as Trampe later put it – 'spreading about him a magisterial dignity for which he did not appear at all to have been born'. Jorgenson was enjoying himself, dictating innumerable letters and orders from his gubernatorial desk, inspecting his troops, and laying on occasional entertainments to get to know the locals, with one of whom, the young woman Guðrún Einarsdóttir Johnsen, he evidently started a brief romance. This way of life gave him delusions of grandeur – delusions that soon tempted him into making the most infamous blunder of his brief career, the one that led to his being known later in life as 'His Icelandic Majesty'.

This came to light most obviously in Jorgenson's fifth and most radical proclamation, released on 11 July. It has been described as being 'in the French revolutionary spirit', and even as going beyond it: a strange twist of history for the Burkean Jorgenson. The most significant clause was in a spirit far from that of *égalité* and *fraternité*, however, for it read:

That we Jörgen Jörgensen have undertaken the management of public affairs, under the name of Protector, until a settled constitution can be fixed on: with full powers to make war or peace with foreign powers.

Jorgenson had already taken a few steps in the direction of the royal 'we'. His two recent brief proclamations had begun 'We are informed' or 'We have learned' – *Vi have erfaret* in the Danish originals. But it remained possible that he might have meant 'We, the administrative body at Government House'. There was no such ambiguity here. The proclamation may have declared him 'Protector', but he was pronominally announcing himself as King.

Later he denied such 'foolish ostentation', and tried to argue that the error had crept in only when the proclamation was translated into Icelandic: his secretary was used to translating royal orders from the Danish monarch, and had used 'we' by mistake. But this does not stand up to a moment's scrutiny. The words are too similar in both languages to have confused a linguist like Jorgenson,* and in any case the plural also appears in the Danish versions, presumably as dictated by himself. He used the form in several letters and other documents written around the same time. There is no denying it: Jorgenson was beginning to think of himself as a royal personage, though he never called himself King in so many words, contrary to later legend.

The preamble to the proclamation stated that he had been forced to take the step of declaring himself Protector because the parliamentary representatives for the *Althing* had not yet been nominated. It was only an interim measure: he promised that he would lay down

* Icelandic has *vér* for 'we', Danish *vi*; Icelandic for 'I' is *ég*, while Danish is *jeg*. Both languages also use a reflexive form for 'undertaken', so the words *os* and *oss* also appear, meaning 'us', rather than *mig*, or 'me'.

the office as soon as the representatives were assembled, an event scheduled for 1 July of the following year. A constitution would then be drawn up, Jorgenson would resign, and the 'poor and common people' would 'have an equal share in the government with the rich and powerful'.

This sounds admirable, but other clauses show tell-tale signs of dictatorial flamboyance:

2. That the military have nominated me their commander by land and sea; and to regulate the whole military department in the country . . .

4. That the great seal of the island shall no longer be respected, but all public documents of consequence shall be signed by my own hand, and my seal (:J:J:) fixed thereunto, until such time the representatives shall assemble, and provide a proper seal . . .

6. The situation we now are in, requires that we should not suffer the least disrespect to our person: neither that anyone transgress the least article of our proclamation, which has solely in view the welfare of the inhabitants of this island.

Other clauses repeated some of what had already been promised in the earlier proclamations. It was again stated that the country would be set in a state of defence, and that 'a person shall be invested with full power to conclude a peace with his Majesty the King of Great Britain'. All Danish property must be handed over for public use, and all Danish storehouses closed and sealed: district governors were instructed to take charge of this. Officials who 'from motives of patriotism' had sent in their letters of acquiescence would keep their jobs, but those who had not would be suspended; when the opportunity arose they would be sent to Copenhagen, and in the meantime must promise to keep the peace.

A new flag was decreed, to a design depicting three white cod against a blue background. Suiting actions to words, Jorgenson immediately had a flag sewn up displaying this motif, and it was raised over the town on top of Phelps's warehouse. Like Jorgenson's royal language, this rather attractive-sounding flag was to attract considerable mockery later, and it became a symbol of the absurd presumption of the whole enterprise – although it was actually based on a traditional Icelandic symbol. A similar split-cod motif was later used for Reykjavík's city emblem.

Again, this final proclamation showed the mind of a well-rounded politician at work, with well-calibrated doses of pomp and pragmatism. Jorgenson proved himself particularly shrewd by including a clause promising to raise the salaries of the clergy. ('Poor fellows!' he later remarked; 'Some of the pastors had not more than twelve pounds a year to live upon.') In the following Sunday's sermons, the pastors were suitably grateful and 'preached resignation and contentment under the present order of things'.

Despite his ignorance of Iceland, Jorgenson seemed to have an intuitive awareness of what people everywhere want in life: a decent income, freedom from debt, and a bit of showmanship to smile at. Bread and circuses, in short. It was very different from Trampe's style of government, which was blandly patrician. Jorgenson himself knew very well what he was doing. 'All the measures I adopted were of course of a popular description', he wrote. As one modern commentator has noted, Jorgenson 'had the natural instincts of a statesman as well as a strategist. He could, of course, bluff in the grand manner, and this was an infinitely valuable qualification for both callings.' Indeed, Jorgenson's claim that he finely calculated each of his moves smacks of later rationalization: it seems more likely that, with his flair and confidence in dealing with all kinds of people, he simply took to benevolent dictatorship as one to the manner born.

The last clause in the proclamation repeated something already decreed in one of the earlier documents: that Icelanders would be free to travel on the island as they pleased, without a pass. This, like the flag, was considered particularly outrageous by his enemies: the very soul of anarchy. Both Trampe and the Stephensen brothers later expressed shock at the idea of letting Icelanders wander around freely. No wonder, for it meant that they would no longer be obliged to buy all their goods from their local trading monopoly – though no one mentioned this. Instead, Trampe and the Stephensens concentrated on law and order. Without travel restrictions, 'robbers, murderers, troops of thieves, and criminals of all sorts' could commit their depredations and escape unpunished. The idea that people could 'ramble across and along this country, without passport, which certainly is unheard [of] in others', was both dangerous and preposterous, they said.

It was unheard of in Denmark, but not in Britain, which imposed no constraints on travel. In fact, on examination, quite a few of Jorgenson's supposedly revolutionary reforms turn out to reflect the principles, not only of Icelandic tradition, but also of modern British mercantile democracy, as adopted so passionately by Jorgenson in his teens. And, in spirit if not in words, Iceland had now been given something else considered essential to a British-style constitution, whether it wanted it or not: its own island King.

Having settled in, created the flag, set up new administrative systems and issued his orders – all within two and a half weeks – Jorgenson next set out on a grand tour, to meet rural Icelanders in the island's north and to check that his laws were being applied. He was away for about twelve days, in mid-July, and he covered a remarkable distance, mostly through pleasant hills covered in heather and bilberry and criss-crossed by cold, fast-moving streams. This was a picturesque side of Iceland, but not a terrifying one: there were no glaciers or lava flows, though Jorgenson was impressed by the outlines of snow-covered mountains in the distance. Black rocks lay scattered everywhere among the rusty yellows of the hills, and the scene was invariably capped by low clouds overhead. It was three weeks past the solstice: only a few hours of twilight and darkness broke up the long days of travel.

With Jorgenson went the majority of his army: five of them. There was also a guide, and a team of the stout, pony-like horses of the island, tough steeds with fringes falling over their eyes. The horses travelled in a convoy, each linked to the next by a plait of tail hairs: they resembled an Arabian camel caravan, except that they trudged through wet grass up to their thighs instead of over hot sand. The new Protector must have made a strange sight, mounted on his low horse, emerging from the mist with his five green-clad soldiers behind him. No one was expecting him, and few had any idea who he was. But there was natural hospitality in the countryside, so he met with a gracious welcome almost everywhere. Icelanders were glad that someone wanted to listen to their problems, and as news spread at each village, more and more people would gather to make 'bitter complaints against the Danish merchants'.

Danes and Icelandic officials were less pleased to see him, especially once they realized that he was there to separate them from their profits and positions. There were a few confrontations: at Thingeyrar on the northern coast, a quarrel with a Björn Olsen ended with Jorgenson aiming (though not firing) his pistol, and in Akureyri a Danish trader tried to drive him away by force; both disputes were resolved amicably. In Höfðakaupstaður, two Danish traders – both accused by locals of profiteering – objected to Jorgenson's interference and wrote letters of complaint to the governor of the northern district, Stefán Thórarinsson. When Jorgenson met Stefán in person later on the journey, a serious altercation took place. Stefán refused to hand over public funds; Jorgenson intimidated him by having his men pile brushwood around his house and threatening to set fire to it – with plenty of help from willing locals, as he took pains to point out later. The threat was not carried out, and again all ended peacefully.

When Jorgenson returned to Reykjavík, weary from his disputatious trip, he found that Phelps had been busy in his absence with projects of his own. He was building a fort on the shore, using six antiquated Danish cannons dug from the sand nearby. In this, he seems to have gone beyond what was intended by the order that the island should be defended, for Jorgenson expressed displeasure; but Phelps had his way, and the fort was completed and armed. Once, the Icelanders on watch there saw a ship out to sea, and rushed to man the rusty guns, but the vessel disappeared from view again.

The other activity occupying Phelps was the continuing confiscation of Danish property, and in this too he had become over-zealous. Trampe believed that Phelps took advantage of Jorgenson's trip away from town to 'plunder whatever could prove a profitable cargo', prioritizing his own business interests. There were also complaints that he forced merchants to engage in trade, selling them goods or swapping cargoes which they did not want. Jorgenson felt that Danes on the island were imposing on Trampe with such stories, probably because they hoped for compensation. But there do seem to have been differences between Phelps and Jorgenson on this point. Jorgenson himself was always offended by any suggestion that he was only in it for profit, and he went to great trouble to support his defence by including long tables of expenditure and receipts in his *Historical Account* – tables which do bear out his claims. His own motives were complex and personal; Phelps was a simpler soul.* His interest was undoubtedly in raking up profit: there would have been little other reason for him to be there.

What Jorgenson's tables seek to establish is that almost every *riksdaler* of the money collected from traders and officials was earmarked for legitimate government expenses: paying people's salaries (including those of the cheered-up clergy) and improving public services as promised in the proclamations. Such reforms seem to have been genuinely intended, though it is hard to judge the matter since he had no time to put them fully into effect. He did set at least one of them in motion, ordering improvements to the run-down Latin School at Bessastaðir near Reykjavík, academically the best in the country, but with physical conditions as dreadful as any London orphanage. Jorgenson and Hooker visited it together, and found the rooms filthy, the food unhealthy, and many of the boys ill, yet still sleeping in threes in box-like beds stuffed with seaweed (though this was not unusual in Iceland). The school's famous library was depleted and disorganized, and everything in it was covered in dust. Jorgenson immediately ordered the creation of a new governing committee, and allocated a thousand *riksdaler* for cleaning the building, buying better food and new bedding, and increasing the salaries of the teachers. The whole experiment came to an end before these orders could be carried out, however, and the school was just as bad in 1814, when the visitor Ebenezer Henderson found the same filth, the same seaweed beds, and the same dark and dusty library.

Real reform might have taken place here and elsewhere, vindicating Jorgenson's claims to philanthropy; but the island would never discover whether any good might come from Jorgenson's regime. Nor did it ever find out whether he would have fulfilled his promises to convene the *Althing* and retire gracefully from office the following year, thus

---

* Though not that simple: in 1818 he published two weighty volumes entitled *The analysis of human nature*, concerned mainly but not exclusively with social and economic issues.

proving that he was not merely playing King after all. His plans were about to be put to an abrupt end, by the North Atlantic's self-appointed watchdogs, the British.

The ship that had been seen far out to sea from Phelps's fort returned to Reykavík on 14 August, and now revealed itself to be the British sloop-of-war *Talbot* – a replacement for Nott's *Rover*, which had completed its Icelandic tour of duty. The captain, a cool-headed, aristocratic Anglo-Irishman named Alexander Jones, had not intended to stop here, which was why it had only been seen in the distance at first. But when he called at other ports he heard strange stories about what was going on in Reykjavík, and came back to investigate.

Sure enough, the first thing Jones saw as he approached was Jorgenson's fishy flag, a national symbol unrecognized by any other country, waving merrily over the town. A messenger then rowed out to him with a letter of complaint smuggled from Count Trampe (through the Vancouvers, the American couple who had taken to visiting him secretly). Trampe's letter recounted the story of the uprising and described his own sufferings. He was never allowed out for exercise, and from the porthole in his cabin he could see just one thing: Jorgenson's flag, a form of mental torture. He would rather see even the British flag than that, he said, and he begged for Jones's help in overthrowing the usurper and restoring the rightful state of affairs.*

Captain Jones responded cautiously at first, not wanting to release a Danish prisoner of war without good reason, but the injustice of the present situation seemed clear. He ordered Phelps and Liston to transfer Trampe to more comfortable accommodation on his own ship, though he technically remained Phelps's prisoner of war. Jones then investigated each of the principal actors in turn, summoning them on board the *Talbot* to explain themselves, and asking them for written reports describing all that had happened. Trampe voluntarily produced a long document putting his side of the story; Phelps was asked to do the same, though he failed to present much except a few informal notes.

* Jorgenson disclaimed responsibility for Trampe's inhumane imprisonment, blaming it on Phelps. He also alleged that Magnús Stephensen had privately urged Phelps to keep Trampe as strictly confined as possible. Hooker later remarked that he thought this the worst part of the whole revolution, though he was unsure who was responsible, Jorgenson or Phelps.

Jorgenson, seemingly the central figure in the whole scene, was left to one side, since he was not answerable to the British government. The full brunt of responsibility appeared to fall on Phelps after all, despite his precautions. When Jorgenson was eventually asked for a written account, he did not produce one: a rare instance of his *not* writing a voluminous manuscript when he had the opportunity to do so. 'During all those doings, I remained quite passive', he noted, explaining that he had not wished to come out openly against a representative of the British King, and thought it wiser to keep quiet. He was undoubtedly right.

Meanwhile, someone else on the island saw that this was the moment, not for keeping quiet, but for thrusting himself forward: Magnús Stephensen. He and his brother Stefán presented Jones with a highly coloured version of the summer's events, and set to work on a document called 'Being a Remonstrance against the conduct of Phelps and Jorgen Jorgensen'. This systematically repudiated each clause in Jorgenson's proclamations, saving a special tone of astonished fury for the most revolutionary ones. Independence, the creation of a republican government, and the peculiar flag all filled Icelanders with repugnance, they assured Jones. Evoking a familiar image from anti-revolutionary texts of all kinds, they portrayed Jorgenson's government as a world turned upside down, a topsy-turvy society in which 'drunkards and unlearned were invested to high posts' while worthier individuals were persecuted, and private property was stripped from its rightful owners. Republican government of this kind was 'a very chimera and quite inapplicable here', they concluded; 'only fools and turbulent heads' could wish for such a thing.

Jones accepted their evidence with interest, as he did everyone else's, although he privately saw through Magnús's motivation. A judicious man, he refused to be hurried until he had everything he needed to make a decision. Even so, it was clear to everyone from the start that his arrival must mean the end of the revolution, and that the whole mess would have to be referred to London. Hooker expected departure so imminently that he dared not venture far from Reykjavík in case he missed the boat, and so had to spend his time in relatively uninteresting hikes around Reykjavík and in tedious 'balls and festivities'. (At one of these balls, if Jorgenson is to be believed, Mrs

Vancouver lost her wig to a hook in a chandelier; but this story may have been his comic revenge on her and her husband for having collaborated with Trampe.)

Jones laid out his preliminary judgement in a letter to Phelps of 19 August, and followed it with a more formal ruling the next day. He stated that Phelps had far exceeded the limited authority conferred by his letter of marque, by taking over an island which did not have full enemy status and which could not be construed as lawful prize. Moreover, he (as well as Jorgenson) had transgressed international law 'by assuming an authority which no Subject of any Realm whatever can have a right to, namely that of declaring this Island free, neutral, independent, & at peace with all nations'. Phelps had also offended by appointing a Governor who was not merely a Dane, but who had recently fought against Britain – a Governor, moreover, who had gone on to issue proclamations 'signed in a Regal manner', and to display 'a flag as yet unknown' within sight of Jones's ship, which was disrespectful to Britain as well as to his own country.*

Jorgenson would therefore be removed from power until the King's pleasure was known; both he and Phelps must go to London and present themselves before the Admiralty. Trampe would also go to London, but as a prisoner of war. That left Iceland without a Governor, and Jones chose to hand temporary Governorship to the men who were still the obvious candidates despite their transparent ambition, and who also had the advantage of being Icelanders: the Stephensen brothers. The more modest Stefán would take charge of religious matters; Magnús would govern everything else.

This arrangement was formalized on 22 August 1809 with a written agreement which abolished all Jorgenson's proclamations, returned Danish property to its original owners, reinstated all sacked officials in their posts, and restored the Nott Convention. Free trade would continue

---

* Jorgenson claimed that, far from his flag insulting British honour, it was Jones who perpetrated this insult by allowing the Danish colours to be hoisted a few days later on 27 August, while the British colours were flying on board the *Talbot*. Moreover, while the colours were raised, Captain Jones received three cheers from the Danes in town. This struck Jorgenson as an extraordinary breach of etiquette, as indeed it was: 'I really believe, that he is the only British captain, who has ever been cheered by the ennemies of his country.' It is further testament to the sheer oddness of the entire affair.

under its terms, and British subjects would henceforth be entitled to live and do business on the island so long as they obeyed local laws.

Phelps and Jorgenson had no choice but to accept Jones's decision. If they did not, it was clear, they would find their independent nation independently at war with Great Britain – starting with Jones's heavily armed warship, much more powerful than the *Margaret & Anne*. Jorgenson felt deeply disappointed, and believed that his intentions had been misunderstood. He was sure the Icelanders would suffer more than anyone. Confiding in his new friend Hooker, he shed tears over what he called 'my poor unfortunate Icelanders': the first time he had wept since leaving home fifteen years earlier, he said. He also thought Jones had been influenced by Trampe's aristocratic manners, Trampe being 'more of a courtier' than he was.

In truth, Jones sympathized with Jorgenson. 'Poor Jorgensen was a good natured mad man,' he wrote in a less formal assessment of the situation later, 'nobody's enemy but his own, and in this business the greatest sufferer of all.' The person he considered most to blame for the whole affair was actually neither Phelps nor Jorgenson, but Savignac – who somehow remained even further out of the limelight than Jorgenson during the investigations, and was the only principal player not to be sent to London. (He remained in Iceland long after the events of that summer, continuing in his bullying ways and regularly violating hunting laws by shooting eider ducks without permission; Henry Holland was told the following year that everyone in Iceland feared him.) Jones thought that Savignac had whipped up the revolution to further his own business interests, and Trampe and Hooker both had similar suspicions.*

Once the agreement was signed, there was nothing further to be done except to assemble all those who were going to London and send them on their way, together with a mass of documents for the Admiralty

---

* Jones later even wondered if Magnús and Savignac had been in on the whole thing together: this is unlikely, but they did apparently engage in a crude conspiracy the following year. During another Phelps-run trading venture to Iceland, again captained by Liston, Phelps's agent Michael Fell heard that Savignac and Magnús were planning to ship Phelps's goods from his Reykjavík warehouse to America and there sell them for their own profit. He challenged them; they barricaded themselves inside the warehouse and threatened that anyone who broke in would be 'cut in pieces'. In a strange reprise of the *Margaret & Anne*

and the carefully folded flag. The preparations took just a couple of days, and the *Margaret & Anne* set sail on 25 August, exactly two months after the uprising. On board were Phelps, Hooker, Trampe, the Vancouvers, two Danish prisoners of war taken from Trampe's old ship the *Orion*, and an officer from the *Talbot* entrusted with delivering Jones's evidence. The hold contained Hooker's painstakingly assembled collection of botanical specimens and journals, plus two Icelandic dresses which he was taking home as gifts or souvenirs, and also Phelps's entire return cargo of tallow, oil and wool, worth between £35,000 and £40,000. Phelps had done well out of the revolution after all, and, as his cargo was considered the legitimate object of trade rather than plunder, he was allowed to keep it.

The only item missing from the heavily laden *Margaret & Anne* was Jorgenson, who sailed instead on the *Orion*. Trampe's ship was valid prize under the *Margaret & Anne*'s letters of marque and was now Phelps's property, but there was a shortage of available seamen to sail it home, so Jorgenson joined it as an unofficial crew member. The only Dane on the journey who was not a prisoner, he was being treated as an unusual, rather perplexing special case.

The first day was stormy, with a strong wind. As often happened at sea, the two ships became separated soon after sailing, and followed different routes around the dangerous rocks near the south-western coast. The *Orion* fell behind at first; it started catching up after taking a short cut between offshore islands, but was still out of view by nightfall.

Early on the second day, at about six or seven o'clock in the morning, the passengers on the *Margaret & Anne* woke to the smell of burning. They ran out on deck, and there saw a terrifying sight: thick smoke billowing out of the hatchways. Panic ensued. The ship was so overloaded that the boats would not take all the passengers, and in any

uprising, Liston for the second time had to storm ashore with a party of armed sailors. He marched to the warehouse, broke in, and disarmed the two men. The ship's cannon was fired, sailors with muskets and swords ran around the city's warehouses, and Reykavík fell briefly into total confusion. If recent French history had already repeated itself as farce in the Jorgenson revolution, this was a case of its repeating itself yet again – as pure sleaze. But Magnús and Savignac did not remain so cosy for long, for Magnús later joined his voice to those accusing Savignac of having engineered the 1809 revolution.

case the crew could not launch them properly in the rough seas, though they struggled to do so. Sheets and sails were wetted and thrown over the flames, but the fire devoured them. All on board faced a terrifying death – a choice between burning or drowning.

But then, just as the passengers were giving up hope, they saw a welcome sight: the sails of the *Orion*, rising over the horizon. While those on the *Margaret & Anne* continued fighting the flames and trying to launch its boats, the *Orion* made its way alongside, and Jorgenson himself leaped aboard the burning ship.

According to Jorgenson's own account, nothing had been done properly by those 'two boobies', the captain and first mate of the *Margaret & Anne*. They had not worked the pump or applied proper hoses to put out the flames, and they had made a mess of evacuating the ship. 'All was consternation and dismay. Nothing was attempted, and even the boats were not hoisted out. Twenty minutes more, and all would be too late.' It was already too late to extinguish the blaze, but Jorgenson immediately 'set the crew to work' launching the boats and rescuing the passengers and crew; he even managed to remove the various cats, dogs and sheep on board. 'When I saw all living creatures secure from harm I left the vessel, and took them on board the *Orion*.'

Jorgenson's account might seem self-serving, but Hooker – always willing to give credit to others – was in no doubt that he had saved their lives, and he praised Jorgenson as their single, fearless rescuer, a whir of activity who helped everyone across to the other ship in relays. Soon the *Margaret & Anne* was cleared of all but a few sailors, who remained to cut open the decks and make one last effort to extinguish the flames, before they abandoned ship themselves.

Most of the passengers' possessions were lost, except what they could carry. Hooker lost almost everything: his specimens, most of his journals, and one of the dresses, though somehow the other survived. The written despatches from Jones were rescued, but the flag burned. And Phelps lost all his cargo. Just as he had been congratulating himself on recovering from the *Clarence* episode and escaping prosperously from the whole débâcle, he found himself confronted with poetic justice after all.

But Hooker knew they were lucky to be alive. 'We were but too happy to escape with our lives and with the clothes upon our backs, and even for this we were . . . indebted to the extraordinary exertions of Mr Jorgenson at a time when nearly the whole of the ship's crew seemed paralysed with fear.' Jorgenson was the man of the hour: as always, in a crisis he revealed himself to be a cool thinker and a man of almost crazed courage. It was only in the ordinary business of life that he tended to make wrong choices and go to pieces; in emergencies he knew how to act.

Just as they had all reached safety, the wind fell, so the *Orion* was becalmed and had to stay watching the final slow destruction of the *Margaret & Anne* for the rest of the day. The flammable cargo of wool, tallow and oil kept the ship burning for many hours, the wool acting as wicks and the oil and tallow as fuel – the whole thing became one giant lamp. As it burned further, the ship's guns started going off, nearly shooting the *Orion*. As Jorgenson remembered: 'what with the crackling of the masts, the firing of the guns, the sails burning fiercely, the sight was truly sublime'. Hooker described how the burning tallow and oil boiled over and ran in cataracts of fire down the sides of the vessel; the clouds of smoke were greater than the steam from Iceland's Geyser. Even after the breeze got up and ushered the *Orion* away in the evening, they could still see the *Margaret & Anne* burning from miles away. Its copper bottom floated on the water 'like an immense burning cauldron, long after the shades of night had come on'.*

The passengers on the *Orion* were still in danger, for it was perilously overcrowded, and another storm might have sunk them. As it was they certainly could not make it to Britain. There was nothing for it but to return to Reykjavík, where Jones and everyone else in town were very surprised to see the *Orion* waddling back in with its extra passengers.

Several days were spent in Reykjavík preparing for a second attempt, and a few changes took place during this time. Phelps and Jones freed Trampe to go on shore and gather up the documents he wanted so he could press a case for compensation in Britain.† Magnús Stephensen

---

* The fire may have been started deliberately by the two Danish sailor prisoners, though that seems a risky form of sabotage: rumours soon started circulating to that effect, and during the following day Hooker noted that they confessed to it.
† Trampe was actually freed from his prisoner of war status at this point, and could have stayed in Iceland had he wished – but he chose to go to Britain in search of recompense for his sufferings.

meanwhile wrote urging Jones not to send Jorgenson with the others but to hand him over for trial on the island itself, according to Danish and Icelandic laws: a move that would probably have resulted in his being hanged as a traitor. Fortunately for Jorgenson, Jones declined.

When they departed again, Trampe and most of the passengers sailed with Jones himself on the *Talbot*. The *Orion* left shortly afterwards, with Jorgenson, Phelps and the officer bearing Jones's papers. All went smoothly, and the two ships arrived in Britain on 19 and 20 September respectively.

During their journey home, the first signs of tension between Phelps and Jorgenson appeared. 'I never told you,' wrote Jorgenson in a letter to Hooker later, by which time he and Phelps had fallen out completely: 'Phelps and I got a fighting, on our passage home.' The officer from the *Talbot* had to separate them, 'crying: Now! Now! What damn nonsense, what damn nonsense? come! come.' According to Jorgenson, Phelps was drunk and was making wild claims about his losses, saying they were worth not just thirty or forty thousand, but more like a hundred thousand pounds. 'I laughed, and could not help saying that his bragging under our present circumstances was ridiculous.' Phelps caught him by the neckcloth, twisting it and nearly choking him. Jorgenson claimed that he refused to be drawn into the fight – 'for you know, I might have put out my foot, and tript up his heels, and laid him on his fat arse, but I considered the cabin floor, and his own bulk. – I said not a word, I put up with all very quietly.' It was a sign of trouble ahead for Jorgenson: almost everyone except Hooker would turn against him.

In Britain, Jones sent his reports to his commanding officer. Trampe and Phelps each travelled to London to put their respective cases there: Phelps to his insurance company, Trampe to the Admiralty requesting financial compensation as well as personal revenge against the revolutionaries. (Neither got what he wanted.) Jorgenson meanwhile headed off to visit Banks. He was hoping for sympathy from that quarter, but he did not get it.

News of the affair now reached the world outside Iceland, but it created little stir even in Denmark, which had more pressing problems to worry about: the war and the looming recession. Britain's attention was also engaged elsewhere. In any case, Jorgenson was already deposed by the time news arrived: the drama was over. There were brief reports in the Danish press, and the government took the trouble officially to condemn Jorgenson as a traitor. If he attempted to return to his country now he would face immediate arrest, but he knew he could not go back, and had no intention of doing so.

The story survived, in several countries, but primarily as a form of comedy. By comparison with the epic turmoil in mainland Europe, this was a dolls'-house drama, conducted on a shoebox-lid stage by a tin-soldier Napoleon. An article in Charles Dickens's periodical *Household Words* in 1856 dubbed Jorgenson 'the very least of all the Cromwells' and added, 'Perhaps there never occurred a smaller revolution.' Visitors to Iceland in 1810 were told of the previous year's turmoil as something 'laughable' and 'ludicrous'.

Even now, Icelanders learn about Jorgenson mainly as comic relief in school history lessons, and his best-known incarnation there has been in a knockabout musical variety show called *Thið munið hann Jörund* or 'We remember Jorgenson', first performed in 1970 and broadcast on Icelandic television in 1994. A few take him more seriously; others feel considerable fondness for him. Two Icelandic visitors to Tasmania in 1987 were quoted in the local paper as saying they were there to research the man whom Icelanders had 'taken to their hearts', and who was still popular because he 'was kind to the Icelandic people'.

Almost the only person ever to see the revolution in a grander heroic light was Jorgenson himself.* Writing to his brother Fritz years later, he explicitly related it to his boyhood fantasy life, and to his early vision of glory while listening to the concert at the Royal Palace. For two short months, he had been transformed into something even finer than a German count, his first naive image of greatness. He had become a true Protector, a sort of angelic counterpart to the diabolical Napoleon. Like angels, many Jorgensons could have danced on the head of a single Napoleonic pin – but Jorgenson had no dreams of conquest on the stage of Europe. He dreamed of liberating the downtrodden, and of being admired for it.

Leaving aside the liberator fantasy, and also disregarding his sense

* He was not quite the only one: Inði Einarsson's 1936 play *Síðasti Víkingurinn* presented the story as one of freedom's noble struggle against tyranny, on the model of the Spanish Civil War – but this never had the popular appeal of *Thið munið hann Jörund*.

of obligation to Phelps, Jorgenson's true political motives are harder to fathom. He was a lifelong conservative, yet here he was, suddenly playing revolutionary. The precise cause of this shift is never spelled out in his writings. In his first account of the events, however, he did point out a telling paradox in the things people were saying about him:

> I am at one and the same time accused of having assumed Regal power, and of having established a Republican form of gover[n]ment in Iceland. Now, this is a direct contradiction, for if I have assumed Regal power, I can not have established a Republican form of gover[n]ment; and if I have done the latter, I can not have assumed Regal power.

Which was it, then? Jorgenson claimed, with good reason, that it was neither. What he actually conducted was not a revolution at all, but a restoration, returning Iceland to its rightful owners and bringing back its old rule of law. Even if the upheaval in Iceland was considered a true revolution, he was no revolutionary. In later life, he sometimes took pleasure in presenting himself as one: he once claimed to be proud to call himself a republican, a name the British considered synonymous with 'rebel, traitor, disturber of all legitimate government', and he congratulated himself on frightening the British into believing that he would 'render Iceland a nest and refuge for all discontented people in Europe'. But there was little sign of such thinking in 1809. He may have acted against political and economic tyranny, but he did so initially to defend the trading rights of bourgeois entrepreneurs like Phelps, and to advance his own belief that Iceland would be better off with Britain's protection than Denmark's. He had even previously maintained that Iceland would benefit from being woven entirely into the mercantile tangle of Britain's empire – hardly a revolutionist's ideal.

What he really desired, as he explained to Hooker the following year, was that both Denmark and Iceland should be liberated from pernicious alien powers and returned to their true selves, something that, strangely, could best be achieved in Iceland through transferring it to some sort of British influence. He wrote:

[Y]ou know, that no man can love your country more than I, yet did I not by any means wish to sell Iceland to England. No! No! I meant to make it independent, such as I would Denmark itself, and by making it friendly to Britain, promote its own welfare.

This was what he meant, too, by his constant denials that he was a traitor. 'To love the country in which I am born, and to be a patriot are two distinct things', he wrote. He never wavered in the former, although he loved Britain equally, but he rejected patriotism – defined as blind allegiance to his country's national interests even while it was under the control of an illegitimate government. And, although he told his family several times that he had 'no personal feeling' against the Danish King, he did doubt that the monarch (now Frédérik VI, who had succeeded his insane father in 1808) could really be considered King so long as he placed himself under the dominion of the French. 'I will maintain, that, I am not obliged, if I do not cho[o]se, to adhere to a person who makes me dependant on a foreign usurper.' In such a situation rebellion was not merely an option, but a duty.

His love for his country, though probably genuine, was certainly idiosyncratic. He later assured his mother that he had not acted vindictively against the Danes on the island: 'I treated my countrymen with the greatest humanity in the world.' But he did seem to take the Danish traders' abuses almost personally. Had they been of any other nationality, he might not have felt so incensed. One senses him deriving a kind of satisfaction in operating against Danes' interests: it was a way of proving that he was not one of them.

With all his peculiar obsessions, could Jorgenson ever have made a good ruler in Iceland? Would he have handed over power to the *Althing* the following year, as he promised? One can only speculate. The matter was given serious thought by just one contemporary writer, the anonymous author of a pamphlet called *Memoir on the Causes of the Present Distressed State of the Icelanders* in 1813. The writer's verdict was mixed, and his attitude to Jorgenson ambivalent: he called the regime both a 'free government' and a 'usurpation' within a single sentence.* His

---

* The indecision over Jorgenson is the least of the pamphlet's confusions: it first asserts that immediate British annexation is desirable and then reverses this conclusion in a hasty appendix. The author's identity remains a mystery.

conclusion was reasonable, however. Lasting improvement would have required, in addition to 'extraordinary talents' on Jorgenson's part, capital investment and support from abroad. Jorgenson would have been unlikely to succeed in raising the latter, no matter how well equipped he was with the former. In any case, 'the rank absurdity of declaring the independence of Iceland [from] all foreign government, was no favourable prognostic of that gentleman's sense'. It was probably good that the attempt was cut short, for there could be little hope from 'an authority, which promised every thing, and had obviously the ability to perform little'.

This seems a fair assessment. But others have suggested that, had Icelanders responded differently, the unexpected uprising could have provided the spark for a genuine independence movement. The Danish authorities were wrongfooted, the proclamations created a fresh legal foundation: it was the perfect opportunity. But it was too soon, and Jorgenson was just a little too eccentric. *Everyone* was wrongfooted, not just the Danes. And so, as one historian has put it, Jorgenson arrived, abolished Danish authority, proclaimed independence and announced the restoration of ancient freedoms: the Icelanders accepted it cheerfully. Two months later, he was arrested and deposed, the ancient freedoms were removed again, and the Icelanders accepted that cheerfully too. It could hardly be otherwise; successful revolutions are rarely untimely.

Yet it was not by any means futile, for it did open up a chink in Icelandic affairs. The island's trade became free again (though there continued to be terrible shortages), and the power of the traders' monopolies was significantly reduced. The British government's puzzle over how to handle Phelps and Jorgenson also produced useful results.* It brought Iceland's more generally perplexing situation to their attention, with help from Banks, who saw the affair as an opportunity to nudge Iceland's problems into full view. An Order in Council of

---

* Its solution to this particular problem was to declare the revolution an unedifying farce, but to deny that it could be considered a criminal matter in Great Britain. Trampe's appeal for financial compensation was rejected, as was his request that Jorgenson be sent to Denmark for trial as a traitor. Phelps also escaped punishment, and was allowed to continue trading to Iceland, which he did intermittently over the next few years – amazingly still being solvent after the first two disastrous expeditions.

7 February 1810 extended formal British protection to Iceland and the Faroes, and granted their citizens the special status of 'Stranger Friends' while in British territory. Icelandic ships could now resume trade under full British protection, and Icelanders could even travel to Britain without fear of personal capture or seizure of their goods.

Technically, Iceland was now governed by Icelanders, but it lacked administrative autonomy. In 1810 Trampe (who still considered himself the rightful Governor) sent orders from Denmark deposing the Stephensen brothers; perhaps surprisingly, they went without a struggle.* Their place was taken by three other prominent men, two of them Icelandic: Ísleifur Einarsson (who thus got the better of Magnús Stephensen in the end), and the District Governor Stefán Thórarinsson, the one Jorgenson had met on his northern tour. The third man was the island's Danish Treasurer, Rasmus Frydensberg. All three had been associated with Trampe, so this was no great advance on the pre-Jorgenson regime, and in 1813 they were retired and another Dane was appointed. In fact, throughout the Napoleonic era it was Britain who retained true control. As British officials privately agreed, Danish authority on the island was now 'exercised only by sufferance'; if they did not co-operate with British interests in the North Atlantic, it would be taken away from them.

Independence did eventually come to Iceland, in response to the liberation movement led by Jón Sigurðsson, but it came piecemeal. The *Althing* was partly reinstated in 1840: it remained answerable to Copenhagen and had little real power. In 1874, a constitution was drawn up and the *Althing* took control of domestic affairs. Iceland became a sovereign state in 1918 and acquired its own flag, but it kept the Danish King and foreign affairs were still managed by Denmark. This lasted until 1940, when Denmark fell under German occupation and lost control even over its own defence: the *Althing* assumed full responsibility for Icelandic politics to avoid sharing Denmark's subjugation.

---

* Magnús wrote to a British correspondent: 'I am very glad and happy, being relieved of the troublesome Government'; in the same letter, he also took much of the credit for overthrowing Jorgenson. Trampe never returned to Iceland. Over the next few years he became caught up in scandals of his own involving suspicious export deals in Norway, but held a post as District Governor in Trondheim until his death in 1832.

In the same year, Britain feared that Germany would seize the island and use it as a submarine refuelling base from which to launch attacks in the North Atlantic. Iceland could not have defended itself, and Britain's strategists realized – just as with Denmark in 1807 – that they must pre-empt this possibility. It was done with slightly more delicacy, though not much. A detachment of unflagged British battleships appeared off Reykjavík without warning, so that Icelanders were not even sure whether their invaders were British or German until the crew stepped ashore and posted a declaration on the walls in garbled Icelandic, explaining what they were doing. Iceland protested, but could do nothing to stop it. After a year the British moved out – only to be replaced by a similar force of Americans.

A few years later, still in the middle of the Second World War, Iceland finally achieved full independence. It became the Republic of Iceland on 17 June 1944. There was just one hitch: the Americans forgot to leave at the end of the war and maintained their base there through the Cold War years to the present, irritating many Icelanders, though others appreciated the boost to local employment.

The two twentieth-century wars affected Iceland very differently from the great nineteenth-century one. They created increased demand for Icelandic fishery exports, and made it astonishingly wealthy. From having been, as Banks reported, the poorest country in Europe, it transformed its economic fortunes as radically as any nation in modern history. At the time of writing it has the second highest standard of living on the planet, after Norway – being ranked well above Denmark, in eleventh place, and the United Kingdom, in thirteenth.

6

Prisoner

The Icelandic summer had laid the foundations of a warm friendship between Jorgenson and Hooker, and in Britain they started writing regularly to each other. Hooker seemed to be Jorgenson's only remaining ally: his enemies all formed a united front against him, however much they disliked each other, for he made a perfect scapegoat. The only good news was that, once Jorgenson had made his initial report to the Admiralty, the British government seemed willing to leave him in peace. He moved into his usual haunt at the Spread Eagle Inn, and told Hooker complacently, 'they never trouble me about anything.' He did not know that this was Hooker's doing: he had written to the Secretary of the Transport Board asking that Jorgenson be treated with forbearance.

Jorgenson had hoped for equal support from his other powerful friend Sir Joseph Banks, and at first he seemed to have it. Banks asked him to dinner and listened to his account of the affair with interest, but it did not last. Trampe soon sought out Banks too, and from then on everything Banks wrote about the revolution showed the imprint of Trampe's opinions. Jorgenson suspected that the deposed Governor received a more favourable hearing because of his superior social class. The urbane, well-born Banks did like Trampe's 'fine manners', and found him 'a Man of quiet disposition well informed moderate & reasonable', implicitly the result of good breeding. Jorgenson himself

121

was no peasant, but he was not a count, and his years at sea had added a crusty layer to his demeanour and speech. In fact, Banks was making even finer distinctions between the protagonists: he wrote to Hooker, 'my mind is, that Jorgensen is a bad man, Phelps as bad, & that Count Trampe is a Good man, as good I mean as Danes are when they are good which is by no means so good as a good Englishman.'

Jorgenson was defiant: 'Thanks to God! my name is plain Jörgen Jorgensen.' The 'sen' at the end meant that he was a true Dane, not an imported German fake like Trampe: it showed that he was 'descended in a direct line from those great and glorious people, that once . . . conquered England.' He was hurt at Banks's abandonment of him, and thought it an injustice unworthy of such a man. Hooker did try to mediate: he was in an awkward position, feeling indebted to Banks for funding his trip but fond of Jorgenson, and thankful to him. As he wrote to Banks, 'I feel my situation with regard to Jorgensen a very peculiar one. His exertions on board the Orion most undoubtedly saved my life and those of the rest of the passengers of the Marg. & Anne.' Moreover: 'his pleasant manners and goodness of heart have excited in me a friendship for him which I should be glad to make use of in his behalf.'

Meanwhile, Jorgenson learned that he was not to be let off as easily as he had thought. Almost a month after arriving in London, he was arrested at his inn and brought before the Transport Board, apparently at the instigation of Trampe, who had just arrived in London and was petitioning the British government to punish the revolutionaries. Trampe did not get his wish, but he had the satisfaction of seeing Jorgenson deprived of freedom. The specific charge had nothing to do with Iceland, however. Jorgenson was arrested for having violated the parole he had given the previous year, which clearly stated that he must not leave the country. He always claimed that he had never agreed to this arrangement, mainly because the parole letter sent to him in 1808 had been addressed to the 'Captain of a French Privateer', which he was not. But the government saw things more straightforwardly.

He was taken at first to Tothill Fields Prison in London. 'I can not think I will be kept long here', he wrote brightly to Hooker. He was right. Soon he was transferred to somewhere far worse: the prison ship *Bahama*, reserved for housing prisoners of war. Hulks like this were notoriously unhealthy, overcrowded places, feared by all Britain's enemies. They were designed to operate in permeable levels, like Dante's Hell crossed with Snakes and Ladders: new arrivals would start in the lowest and worst deck, but good behaviour or powers of influence could move them upwards, while bad behaviour precipitated them downwards again. The reality was more corrupt and chaotic, and prisoners were largely left to manage themselves. Whatever hardships Trampe thought he had endured on board the *Margaret & Anne*, wrote Jorgenson to Hooker, it could have been nothing to this.

Life on the *Bahama* would be unpleasant for anyone, but for Jorgenson it held extra terrors. Many of the inmates were Danes, and they already knew all about him.* They had heard the rumours about the *Admiral Juul* battle, and they knew the stories about Iceland in their most exaggerated versions. So, as Jorgenson told Hooker: 'you may see my situation is extremely perilous and disagreeable.' He could not escape his fellow prisoners, and 'no marines or Englishmen dare to come down among them': there could be no protection by the authorities. According to Jorgenson, one British officer who had ventured below decks on a similar hulk had been released only after being held hostage for three days, and he emerged with the word 'Buonaparte' burned across his face with gunpowder.

Jorgenson was confined on the *Bahama* for ten months, in fear for his life at every moment, yet somehow – by some fortune or talent – he managed never to receive a stiletto between the shoulder blades. Moreover, living in such conditions and lacking either reference materials or an English dictionary, he used the time to produce drafts of a long *Historical Account of a Revolution on the Island of Iceland in the Year 1809* and the autobiographical *Adventures of Thomas Walter*, both of which were completed by May 1810. He seemed surprised himself, and pleased: he knew few people could have written anything in such a place. In the dedication to *Thomas Walter* he excused the grammatical errors that had crept in by explaining, 'every moment do I set in dread some one or other tumbling over me, and spoil all I have

---

* The captured *Orion* sailors may have circulated stories of his activities in Iceland, and Scandinavian newspapers smuggled on to the ship also contained reports of his being damned as a traitor by the Danish King.

wrote. It is impossible for me to collect myself . . . for the prisoners are generally always swearing, cursing or fiddling.'*

In fact, his 1810 works contain remarkably few errors: disregarding a few distinctive usages like 'also' for 'therefore', and the spelling of 'prisoner' with two 'n's, the English in both is admirable. Jorgenson had lived half his life in the company of Englishmen. He read widely in the language, and English eventually became more natural to him than Danish: years later, he even used English to write to his own family. Such mastery was a source of pride to him, and he once took offence on reading an uncommissioned editor's claim that his 'exotic style' had required amendment. Any exoticism was a matter of personal expression, he retorted, not of linguistic failure. What he did evidently still have, unlike many Scandinavian English-speakers, was a strong accent. It was imitated years later in a Tasmanian newspaper, again to his annoyance: 'I am not responsible because the English have taken it into their heads to pronounce some of the letters of the Alphabet in a manner different from all other European nations.'

The *Historical Account* was circulated to various readers, including Banks, who hated it. Hooker read it with interest, but feared that it might contain libels: there were several mischievous stories about the Vancouvers, for example. He was probably more entertained by *Thomas Walter*, which Jorgenson presented to him as a personal gift. It told much the same story as the *Historical Account*, but with extra memories of his earlier life and an elaborate framing fantasy in which a balloon flight goes wrong and transports the narrator to a parallel universe.

Two other works by Jorgenson were also doing the rounds at the time: manuscripts he had written earlier, possibly even in Iceland. They were both plays. One was a frothy comedy called *Robertus Montanus, or The Oxford Scholar*, about a country boy who returns from studies at Oxford and upsets everyone in his village by questioning their traditional beliefs, before being set straight by a spell in the army. The other play was a tragedy based on a scandalous event of 1804, when the exiled Bourbon duc d'Enghien was charged with conspiring

---

* He was not the only person to manage extraordinary feats of concentration in the hulks: a group of French prisoners spent their time building exquisitely detailed model ships out of animal bones saved from their meals.

to assassinate Napoleon, and executed – though almost everyone was sure he was innocent. Unusually, Jorgenson presented him as a genuine conspirator, the better to use him as a mouthpiece for his own anti-Napoleonic opinions. He also borrowed the Duke's predicament to explore the feelings of someone called by the voice of destiny to be his country's liberator, a theme to which he was naturally drawn. The play contains many other echoes of Jorgenson's own adventures, not least in the fact that one of d'Enghien's first actions is to sit down and draft the first three proclamations he plans to issue after overthrowing the tyrant. But there are times when it seems to be Napoleon, rather than the Duke, who really fascinates the author.

There is more to these plays than uncontrolled fantasy and wish-fulfilment. Jorgenson was clearly trying to build a career for himself as a writer, and to produce works that would entertain and edify the public and bring him commercial success. Alas, his plays did not take him far. But he had other projects in mind too: he wanted to produce an English version of his Danish work on the Pacific trade (though he never did), and he became interested in the ancient Scottish poetry of 'Ossian', which had inspired a cult all over Europe after its publication in 1760: Napoleon himself was said to carry a copy wherever he went. Most people now thought it a hoax, but Jorgenson proposed to prove it authentic in a book on Nordic mythology, which he was sure would sell well in Britain.

He was right about the market opportunity: a vogue for Scandinavian mythology was to sweep the country later in the century, and Jorgenson's book could have been a slow-burning bestseller. But he was wrong about Ossian, whose poems had been written by their 'discoverer' James Macpherson. Jorgenson was set straight on this subject (and thus put off the entire Nordic project) by a friend of Hooker's, Henry Jermyn – an eminent antiquarian to whom Hooker had mentioned the plan. Jermyn became a patient friend to Jorgenson; his advice to ditch Ossian was the first of several helpful interventions.

Despite his literary enthusiasm, or perhaps because of it, Jorgenson was suffering from the effects of his imprisonment. Friends noticed that he looked unwell. When he was brought to the Guildhall to give evidence at Phelps's insurance hearing, his appearance was shocking:

Captain Jones saw him there and told Hooker that Jorgenson looked 'so miserable and so altered' that he 'could not bear to go near, or meet him'. More seriously still, Jones heard a rumour that Jorgenson had recently poisoned himself. Jorgenson did mention having 'once been poisoned', and it is possible that he attempted suicide while on the *Bahama*: he was certainly unhappy enough. On the other hand, it would not be surprising if someone else on the *Bahama* poisoned his food.

His emotional state was unsteady, as his letters of this period show. He often sounds reckless, bitter or paranoid, though his persecution complex was partly justified: his enemies really were out to get him. (Phelps, for one, tried blaming Jorgensen to help with his own insurance claim, though the attempt failed and he lost his case.) As early as November 1809, Jorgenson had written to the Secretary of the Transport Board, Alexander Macleay, from whom he hoped for practical help: 'I am rather getting very ill . . . My mind is so agitated and my situation so distressed, that I have no rest neither night nor day.' When he saw the English shore he had once loved so much, he felt 'almost intoxicated with madness'.

> Comparing my former situation with my present, makes me almost senseless and stupid; I am sick and weary indeed; when the poignancy of my grief forces tears to my eyes, I am not in this place permitted to let them flow freely, for here I have not the melancholy pleasure to be by myself, and would not wish to be thought a milksop; tore away from ever[y] thing that's dear to me, the loss of my liberty and the uncertainty in which I am, make me entirely unhappy.

His head, 'once full of romantic notions', was now bent low. He longed for death, and if Napoleon himself stood over him with an axe he would feel no fear, so much did he crave oblivion. Things became worse: in December, he was 'quite senseless' for three days, and later he realized that his letters to Hooker during that time had contained things 'inconsistent with sound reason and good sense'.

The disturbance was to recur during the following decade: he had a severe relapse in 1815, and in 1820 he wrote to Lord Castlereagh –

himself prone to suicidal depression – 'I am weak in the head, sometimes subject to an afflicting malady and if I am treated harshly I must perish.' The illness affected both body and mind, causing severe stomach and bowel pain with a kind of mania. He remained convinced that the problem was physical, and that it dated back to the poisoning. Inadvisable though it generally is to guess at diagnoses of past ailments based on patchy personal descriptions, one cannot help wondering if Jorgenson suffered from acute intermittent porphyria, similar to the more severe version thought to have afflicted George III. The symptoms frequently include abdominal pain and mental agitation. It recurs periodically, and can even be triggered by poisoning, though the underlying cause is genetic. But porphyria is rare, and the case may have been simpler. Jorgenson's current problem, confined and in fear of his life, still trying to assimilate the exhilarating experience in Iceland, would be enough to disturb anyone's equilibrium.

In mid-September 1810, while Jorgenson was still in disarray, someone cruelly told him that the only way he would ever get away from the *Bahama* would be by dying or escaping. He sought Macleay's advice again. 'If you think there is foundation for what he said, let me know so, for it is better to know the worst than to live in suspense.' The letter went on to discuss other matters, but at the end he added miserably: 'Damn the fellow he has quite put my pipe out.'

In fact, within days, Jorgenson was freed after all – a release engineered by Macleay and Hooker with the tacit approval of Banks, for even he was feeling sorry for Jorgenson by this time. Jorgenson was so overjoyed that he borrowed fifty pounds from the prison's moneylender and, as he left, gave the money away as a parting gift to everyone he knew in the ship: a typical act of rash generosity. He was apparently expecting to collect an old debt in London, but this did not materialize, so he ended up indebted himself again. Still, he was free, and alive.

His release was not unconditional: he was again on parole, and was only supposed to stay in London for a few days before going on to Reading, a town set aside for the accommodation of paroled enemy officers. Had he found a job on a ship in the meantime, he would have been allowed to leave; there was no ban on his leaving the country this time. He tried, but failed, mainly because he seemed reluctant to consider any post below the rank of captain. Even first mate was not good enough. When Hooker advised him to settle for a mate's position if necessary, Jorgenson wrote back almost hysterically:

My dear friend need not be apprehensive . . . I am going to adhere closely to what you have mentioned in your letter, and look out for that situation you pointed out to me, which is perhaps the easiest obtained, and shall do all I can to obtain it: still my very goodnatured friend, altho' I am extremely happy to think myself almost released, still was it out of my power to prevent tears starting in my eyes on reading the word mate, but I do not think myself entitled to object to anything . . . I shall be careful how I act, and you shall not hear a word about the Iceland business nor any thing relating to it . . . no man shall ever hear my name more mentioned, for I shall then retire and go out of the way, many thousand of miles from hence, to bury my head from the sight of the world, for I do not see I have any more business in it. But let not those my expressions give you any concern, for I feel deeply all what I owe to my friends and my own character, and tho' being mate of a merchantship, will deeply wound me, still will I bear every thing with manly fortitude . . . so when I have done all required no one can blame me, if I have no more to do with a world in which I have met with such bitter disappointment, and by so many misrepresented.

Far from relieving his wild despair, the sudden freedom seems to have inflamed it. He finished: 'excuse me if this letter is incoherent in places, for I am not quite well.' Two days later he wrote again penitently, saying that he wished he could retrieve the first letter from the post. 'But when things come suddenly over one, the best man may be taken aback (a sailors phrase).' It was in his character to fly off the handle like that, he explained contritely, but it never lasted long. 'I may despond as much as anyone for twelve hours, but then when I rightly looked at things, I soon come round again.'

Not finding a job, he gave up and travelled to Reading, taking a carriage which whizzed along at an average of eight miles (12.8 kilometres) an hour: 'glorious fun for a sailor'. His next ten months or so

were spent in this staid provincial town. It did not suit his temperament, but was certainly an improvement on the *Bahama*. He lodged
at an inn with the suitably seafaring name of the Upper Ship, well
away from other Danish officers. There the scribbles on the inn's toilet
walls cheered him up. He transcribed the funniest into a notebook. 'I
laughed above an hour at them', he told Hooker: they were 'full of
solid wit and humour'. A few lines later he added: 'N.B. Is it a proper
expression, to apply: <u>solid wit and humour</u>?' He seemed suddenly
ebullient.

He was short of money, though: he had been living on loans from
Hooker for some time, and now he asked for more. It was an emergency. The lenders in the *Bahama* were agitating for repayment of his
parting loan, and they were men with a long reach. 'This presses me
very hard, and makes me very uneasy.' He asked Hooker for 'brotherly advice', and for £35. 'It is only the true friendship you have shewn
me, that emboldens me, to impose on you now.'

Hooker did help him, but his patience would not last for ever. He
urged Jorgenson to get work on a ship, as mate if necessary; Jorgenson
hedged. Hooker also advised him to give up all thought of publishing
his *Historical Account*, on which he was still working, for it could get
him into even more trouble. 'No! No! my dear and goodnatured fellow,'
Jorgenson replied. He had no intention of libelling anyone. It was
only that, on the *Bahama*, he had felt the need to swagger in his
writing, to keep his spirits up.

By now Hooker was at work on his own *Journal of a Tour in Iceland*,
and Jorgenson rather insincerely promised not to publish his account
if Hooker thought it would interfere with his own book's prospects.
A long epistolary debate ensued about this over the next few months.
It amounted, in effect, to the following conversation:

JORGENSON: Truly, I promise not to publish my book if you
    think it will damage yours.
HOOKER: Very well, thank you.
JORGENSON: No, I insist: I am serious. If you think it will be
    bad for your book, tell me and I will abandon the idea at once.
HOOKER: That is very good of you: I am grateful.
JORGENSON: No, I couldn't possibly bring myself to publish

this book if it would hurt you in the slightest way – even though its value and interest to the nation would be immeasurable, and even though I have worked on it so very hard for such a very long time with such very great hopes for its success, and the publishers in London are clamouring for it.

HOOKER: Good, that's agreed then.

In fact, Jorgenson's book was never published, though Hooker did nothing to suppress it. Had it come out, it might have affected Hooker slightly, as the *Tour*'s account of the revolution and of Iceland's history and politics leaned heavily on material borrowed from Jorgenson. But Hooker was not yet considering commercial publication anyway – this first edition was only for circulation among friends – and most of the book concerned quite other matters: botany, vulcanology, zoology, and travel anecdotes like the story of Olafur Stephensen's formidable lunch. His motives in dissuading Jorgenson from publication seemed to have been decent. Eventually Jorgenson did give up, and turned to other enthusiasms. He was enchanted with Hooker's book when it appeared, and in later years re-read it many times, possessing, borrowing, losing and reacquiring numerous copies.

Jorgenson continued to write prolifically on other matters in Reading. He told Hooker in October, 'I am writing as much here as on board the Bahama, for I cannot be idle, and though it may be nonsense, it keeps the devil out of mind.' His graphomania was a strange compulsion, halfway between therapy and addiction, and it remained so for the rest of his life. He compared it to the 'drinking and pleasures' to which other people resorted to escape their thoughts. In another letter a few weeks later he added, 'You laugh perhaps in your sleeve to think I should be writing on so fast, and so much, but I am of too busy a mind to remain inactive, I must either write, fight, go to sea, or do something, I do not care which, so I am interestedly employed.' Again in December he wrote: 'I am obliged in a manner to fly to books and by penning down my own thoughts, to divert the emptiness within.'

But his scribbling also had a more practical purpose. He was still working through his literary apprenticeship, trying one field after another: tragedy, comedy, fantasy, politics, history, autobiography. The only area he seems never to have dabbled in, perhaps surprisingly, is poetry. By the end of 1810 he had added to his works an Orientalist, Utopian fantasy on the model of Montesquieu's *Persian Letters*, called *Description of the Kingdom of Shandaria and Adventures of King Detrimedes*. Set mostly in an imaginary Central Asian kingdom, it also described the King's experiences as a traveller in Europe – a perfect vehicle for satire. Through Detrimedes's naive observations, Jorgenson mocked European national habits, the inconsistency of politicians, and the absurdities of war. He had Detrimedes reflect, for example, on how the Christians of the West were so cowardly that they threw 'iron balls filled with combustibles, called bombs' into towns full of civilians instead of fighting in the field. The King particularly remarks on the dullness of the English, and their habit of ridiculing foreigners who cannot speak the language well. But an English traveller in Shandaria later corrects him and explains that many foreigners grow to love the English as much as once they hated them. Detrimedes listens to this, smiles, and says:

> [L]et me make one remark to you. – Do you not think that when we consider the short time we have got to live, and then contemplate the immense space of time hereafter, it is scarcely worth the trouble man takes to support either this claim or that: and that it would be much better not to take such heed about the present, but look into futurity; and therefore like a good soldier, not quit our post without orders, but believe that alwise providence has placed us into such a certain situation for some wise purpose or other?

Jorgenson strikes a strangely incoherent yet touching note here, simultaneously dismissing futile cross-cultural argumentation and warning against suicide – an idea which may have been still playing on his mind. The whole conversation also reflects the unease he was beginning to feel about nationality. By 1810 and 1811, Jorgenson was losing his certainty about all things English. He still felt no sympathy for the current Danish government, and often waxed sycophantic towards British authorities in his writings, for his fate lay in their hands. But a different sentiment sometimes crept rebelliously into view from behind his attempts at flattery. He was becoming disillusioned with his second country: writing to Hooker in December 1810, he described the 'flame' of his early fondness for Britain as quite extinguished. This twist of an Anglophile's fate was partly the result of unfortunate timing. His years of service on British ships had come to nothing – 'and for what?' Merely for getting stuck in Denmark while on a visit to his family, and being caught up on the wrong side of a war he could not avoid: a chance circumstance that spoiled his relationship with both countries. Trying to do his duty by both, Jorgenson had satisfied neither. He became not a stateless man, but a man of two states, both of which regarded him as an enemy. No wonder he felt himself splintered by inner demons.

He thanked God, though, that he had found 'one friend, an Englishman, equal true, faithful, indefatigable . . . and that is you my dear Hooker'. This friendship sustained him; he poured out affection in his letters. In one of the earliest, he described the 'peculiar pleasure' he took in communicating his thoughts to Hooker: although they had not known each other long, he said, he felt a bond of friendship which depended not on time but on 'something else, something like what the french call – je ne sais quoi'. A year later, he was writing: 'I see good nature in every thing you say and do, and the longer I am acquainted with you, the more I love you. Pray, is that a proper expression to a man in this country?'

In one letter from Reading, Jorgenson said he missed Hooker so much he could not sleep. He kept getting up early and going to bed late: 'which proceeds from being such a short distance from you, and not confined, for I think it hard not to see you; Yes! I think it hard not to be able to embrace, to shake hands, with you my glorious friend: – I have loved, – I have loved deeply indeed, but never did I with such eagerness wish to see any person, as I do you now. God! how happy I shall be, when I see you the first time.' Later he spoke of 'a strong and lasting interest in my heart, much greater than perhaps you are aware of', sentiments 'of a very serious nature though not altogether unpleasant', and 'a number of friendly sensations in my breast towards you, not very easily described'. These passionate declarations are intriguing, though it would be a mistake to jump to over-hasty conclusions. They certainly give some idea of how unmanageably

Jorgenson's emotions flowed, and how in need of company and comfort he felt during these years.

As a friend, Jorgenson could be overwhelming, and he was exhausting financially as well: he continued to embarrass Hooker with frequent requests for money. But his expressions of adoration were in his nature, he said: he could do nothing by halves.

> And do not dear friend wonder that Jörgensen should thus at times break out in such extacies, for when the torrents are pouring down from the mountains, or the raging gale blows upon the shore, you cannot expect the ebb and flood to flow in regular succession, and the river will swell above its usual limits, and with impetuous force carry every thing away on the neighbouring banks.

Although Hooker felt both sympathy and gratitude, the friendship was less important to him than it was to Jorgenson. He was busy, and had much else to think about: working on his *Tour*, perfecting his studies, and planning a second botanical expedition. He hoped to go to Ceylon, though Jorgenson kept talking him out of this with ghastly descriptions of epidemic diseases and dangerous natives: 'is it worth your while to go all that way, for the sake of a few plants?'*

Jorgenson was allowed a trip to London in December 1810, and spent Christmas there with Hooker. He probably also visited a publisher, for he travelled with a pile of papers. Jorgenson's hopes for Shandaria and the other fictional works were dashed, but he did publish two more works during this time, both on a vanity basis, though he claimed to have plenty of subscribers to fund the investment. One was his controversial analysis of the British attack on his country, *The Copenhagen Expedition traced to other Causes than the Treaty of Tilsit*, a

---

* Hooker never did make it to Ceylon. Instead, he involved himself in business, buying a share in a brewery which proved a good investment. Jorgenson fretted that 'the eagerness of gain, the anxiety of losing, and many such like circumstances' might ruin his friend's character. 'I know but few merchants, who are not complete monsters.' This was a change of tune: Jorgenson had once thought highly of the mercantile class, who promoted understanding and courtesy between nations and brought people the necessaries of life in the cheapest manner. But since his falling-out with Phelps, he had come to hate merchants 'most heartily'. His picture of the moral excellence of British capitalism was curling around the edges.

work guaranteed to make his fellow Danes in Reading fume.* The
other was the Tahiti book, which was every bit as infuriating to most
of the English in town because of its attack on religion in general and
Methodism in particular. With two publications, he thus managed to
upset almost everyone. As so often happened when Jorgenson tried to
advance himself, his impulsive honesty took over and ruined everything.

He originally intended to call the Tahiti book *The State of the
Missionaries on the Island of Othaheite in the year 1806, and the reasons
why Christianity cannot be introduced in any part of the globe, unless
supported by fire and sword*. Even before he saw the book, Hooker was
alarmed by the title (which was later toned down), and thought
Jorgenson was wrong to suggest that Christianity could be imposed
only by force, or that it had no innate appeal for the majority of
humanity. Jorgenson replied that if Hooker did not like the title, he
had better brace himself before reading the whole thing. Through a
fictional 'enlightened pagan', things would be said that cast doubt even
on the most fundamental dogmas. Indeed they were, for among the
pagan's arguments in the book are assertions that the first five books
of the Bible are a forgery and that Christ was merely human.

It is not clear how far Jorgenson's theological doubts went. In a
later work he described a crisis of faith experienced by 'a friend' at
the age of thirty, just his age now. Hitherto he had thought little about
the subject, merely accepting the doctrines into which he had been
born. But as he approached the mid-point on life's path his beliefs
were overturned, not by what he had seen in Tahiti (though that may
have started it) but by picking up a volume of Gibbon's *Decline and
Fall of the Roman Empire*.

He was not alone in this experience: the book had unplugged and
drained many shallow pools of stagnant belief in the thirty-five years
since its first volume had appeared. Gibbon's main target was the
assumption that Christianity had triumphed because of its inarguable

---

* Only two copies of this pamphlet can be traced, one in the Cambridge University Library
and one (located by Jørn Dyrholm and Lesley Albertson) in the Danish State Library in
Århus; it was hitherto thought lost. This paucity suggests either a small print run or a
lot of readers tearing up their copies in disgust. It was anonymous, but the identity of its
author seemed to be well known.

and luminous truth, any encounter with which was expected automatically to produce conversion. Instead, he argued that early Christianity was successful because certain elements in its doctrine made it replicate effectively; in effect he compared it, *avant la lettre*, to a virus. These victorious elements were fanaticism, evangelism and intolerance of other religions: just as a cold makes its carrier cough and sneeze, Christianity made its adherents evangelize and crush competitors in a way other Classical religions did not. Luminous truth had nothing to do with it.

It was a powerful idea, and it turned Jorgenson's world upside down. His faith was 'staggered'; he became 'entangled in the mazes of a labyrinth'. He lost all sense of value, and began to act like someone who lived only for this world: being naturally 'of a warm imagination, and under the influence of strong passions', he fell into many errors. The crisis would prove the source of his salvation, for his meaningless childhood faith was eventually replaced by a profound sense of God and of the literal truth of Scripture, which liberated him from his mental torments. But that lay ahead. These early years of the 1810s were a period when all Jorgenson's old assumptions – about justice, about the British, and about religion – were crumbling at the same time.

Even by the time the *State of Christianity* was published, in March 1811, he was already thinking of it as a 'foolish work'. Having spoken his mind, he was now changing it. But he was delighted at the way it irritated the Reading bourgeoisie. He told Hooker in April that he was being denounced from the pulpits – a splendid result. 'The reason for my writing, was, to vex the hypocritical rascals in this town, who never leave a fellow-creature in peace. You cannot conceive how full Reading is of religious hypocrites, who are continually preaching against the wickedness of other nations.'

He enjoyed teasing the Reading burghers in other ways, too. They were 'rather thickheaded, though they are hospitable, civil, and in fact good fellows'. Most of the time they were 'immersed in Canal-bills, buying of wheat, barley, religion, pshalm [*sic*] singing, and methodism'. At least they provided him with a good social life, inviting him to dinners, breakfasts and soporific evenings at the Reading Institution with its excellent library. In many ways their solid good humour impressed as well as amused him. How 'ridiculous' it was, he wrote, for anyone to imagine that Napoleon could ever conquer such a bluff, prosperous people.

By the spring of 1811, Jorgenson had finished all his literary projects and was casting about hungrily for more: he considered writing a history of modern Denmark, or an account of the current state of Great Britain, or an expansion of the Iceland account into something three times longer and 'more <u>historical</u> and <u>philosophical</u>'. – 'Ha! Ha! Ha!' he wrote to Hooker: 'I am now laughing, and I know you do.' He went on: 'I am not going to confine myself this week to this single letter. No! No! – I have nothing to do this week, as my publication is finished.' Two days later: 'I am obliged to write and write, so I may forget my melancholy thoughts, and yet I am not clear but what I write may do me more harm than good, for when I do write, I write boldly, indeed I write as I think.'

But then, just as he was almost coming to enjoy Reading life, and to put it to good effect, he was released. By the summer of 1811, he was living as a free man in London and could do whatever he liked. It was the worst thing that could have happened to him.

7

Spy

At first Jorgenson moved into his usual lodgings in London, but by September he became entangled in debt, and was confined in a sponging-house, a sort of private semi-prison. He also started losing his hold on Hooker, who became exasperated by his constant pleas for money. Jorgenson complained that arrest and imprisonment were nothing compared to the misery of receiving Hooker's latest 'cold note' refusing a loan. Their relationship never really recovered, and much later he chided Hooker: 'you treated me severely . . . Indeed the unhappy sensations I felt in your cool behaviour completed my destruction, for I cared not what I did.' He paid off his debt instead by borrowing money from a former landlord, and thus freed himself from the sponging-house.

Deprived of Hooker's sympathetic attention, Jorgenson started writing to someone else: the Whig politician Samuel Whitbread, a well-known champion of underdogs and worthy causes. Jorgenson obviously hoped to become one of the latter. It did not quite come off, but Whitbread gave him a reasonable hearing and sent him money on at least one occasion.

Jorgenson's first approach was not well planned. He sent Whitbread copies of his two contentious pamphlets on Tahiti and Copenhagen. In reply, Whitbread advised him not to try this again when trying to attract sympathy from unknown correspondents. Jorgenson's covering letter was also confused and intemperate. Like other letters written to Hooker during this time, it shows the influence of alcohol. He later admitted: 'I do not think I was sober for three months on a stretch, and so violent was I that scarcely a day passed over my head, but I got into some scrape.' At the same time, he acquired an even more destructive addiction: compulsive gambling. This had taken control of him once before, when he was briefly imprisoned in Tothill Fields in 1809; he had since shaken it off, but now he met some old prison acquaintances who led him astray again. It was to ruin him almost completely over the next few years.

With his wild swings into brio and optimism, his unending faith that some great deed would save him from trouble, and his inability ever to take the long view, Jorgenson was a classic gambler. He knew he was not good at it, because he could not keep a cool head, and he once said that he had not won at the gaming tables more than seven times in his whole life. But that never stopped him trying. Looking back later and honestly assessing the ravages of his twin addictions, he decided that the gambling was the worse of the two. Drinking affected primarily the body, in his view, but gambling altered the victim's psyche in terrible ways. 'When once this horrid vice has obtained possession of the heart, it absorbs and surmounts every other passion.' Gamblers were 'careless of life' and could not be trusted, for 'their minds become repositories of the darkest thoughts, and the most dangerous designs: they are alike incapable of private friendship and of public virtue: dice and cards occupy their minds by day, and haunt them in their dreams by night'. The irony was that they did not start out as monsters, but the opposite: it was those with the warmest and most generous dispositions who were most susceptible. Misers were never seen at the table, unless they were there to lend money to addicts at high interest rates.

Jorgenson's debts piled up. He tried everything: hiding from public view, seeking help from Whitbread, borrowing and risking more and more in the hope of a big win. Eventually all evasive manoeuvres failed, and he was thrown into the King's Bench debtors' prison on 21 December 1811. He wrote to Whitbread from there, on the following day: 'You will perhaps be a little surprised at receiving a letter from me from this quarter.' He explained that he had been just about to leave for a seaport when he was told that his father had died. Wondering if he was due an inheritance, he delayed his departure to find out more, but while he was thus hesitating his creditors caught him.*

Jorgenson was deeply affected by his father's death, but in a strange way, reflecting the confusion in his filial feelings. An obsession was born: he came to believe that he himself was destined to die at the same age as his father, which so far as he knew was sixty-three. The thought tormented him, although he could not understand why it worried him so much: he knew most people at thirty-one would consider sixty-three a reasonable age, and too far off to worry about. But his 'fatal and fearful' *idée fixe* continued to haunt him, and even to threaten his sanity at times. He was only freed from it when, much later in life, he learned from his brother that his father had actually lived to sixty-five: this broke the spell. Jorgenson never mentioned it, but he may have known from his wide reading that he was not alone in dreading the age of sixty-three. Known as the Grand Climacteric, it was traditionally feared as a numerologically doom-laden point in life, being the product of the two equally fateful numbers seven and nine. Perhaps Jorgensen's real fear was that he, the rebellious son in exile, would somehow still be subject to his father's dominance.

On 1 January 1812 he was freed again, and he hid from his remaining creditors in the tranquil backwater of Bloomsbury for some time. He wrote to Hooker in April saying he was calm and sober. He had been taking a tonic medicine which had made him healthy and 'as happy as a King' – an odd simile, perhaps, from someone who had lived much of his life under two monarchs who were both dismal lunatics: Christian VII of Denmark and George III of Britain. 'The physic has driven all ill-humours out of my body, cooled my blood, and my frugal mode of living restored harmony and peace to my mind which had for a long time been in a tumultuous state. – All topsy-turvy. – You see, like the magnetic needle always pointing to the true North, so do I always return to my friend Hooker, when I have any thing to communicate.'

A creditor may have learned of his hiding-place, or Jorgenson may have thought travelling would help his writing career, for he next appears a few weeks later on the Iberian Peninsula. This was a key

* His father did leave him some money, but the war and Jorgenson's status as traitor meant he could not claim it yet; he received nothing until many years later.

battleground in the interminable Napoleonic wars: by the early summer of 1812 the French were being slowly beaten back by the British, Spanish and Portuguese armies, as well as by the world's original guerrilla forces. Jorgenson apparently hoped to work as a kind of war correspondent, reporting either for newspapers or for the Foreign Office – to whom he did send documents on his return, via Whitbread.

These ideas did not come off, but he whiled away several months travelling around Spain assessing morale and absorbing what information he could. His most interesting reflections concern the reasons why British troops failed to win the hearts and minds of locals, even those who were supposed to be allies. With his stereoscopic vision as quasi-naturalized Englishman and disillusioned foreigner, Jorgenson was well equipped to understand the problem, which he ascribed to religious disagreements and other forms of culture clash. Even where the French plundered and abused the Spaniards, he said, they did it with a certain 'adroitness, and good Discretion' that won them sneaking admiration from fellow Latins. Billeted with families, they would charm the inhabitants, especially the females, while the British stayed aloof and proper in their military encampments. British taciturnity made them 'bad companions to loquacious Beings':

The common English neither know nor care how to accommodate themselves to the customs and manners of Foreigners. Even in other Countries they expect the natives to submit to their humours. – As long as they are perfectly sober, their good-nature and generous Temper prevent them from giving Offence, but they are not social till they are well acquainted with People. When inflamed with Liquor, they become noisy, quarrelsome, and treat the Natives with infinite and mortifying Contempt . . . The Sobriety of the Spaniards and Portuguese is remarkable, Intoxication is a Vice held by them in perfect Abhorrence. The English take little pains to learn the language of the Country, but they generally obtain enough to bestow improper names on the Inhabitants. With much real good-nature and humanity (for they seldom or never commit murder or ill-use women) they are looked upon with horror, whilst their more cunning and insinuating Enemies, the French, are well received.

After a few months in Spain, Jorgenson found himself either hired or press-ganged into service on board a British navy ship, under his usual seafaring name of John Johnson. This ended with his being invalided out and transferred to a military hospital on Gibraltar. It is not clear what happened: he sometimes said that he had been injured in battle, receiving 'a severe wound in a dark and stormy night' off Cape St Vincent. But at other times he hinted at a different cause, perhaps a return of his former ailment.

Writing to Hooker from Gibraltar, he said: 'my principal illness proceeded from the gloom of my mind, which prevented me from getting better of my bodily distemper. – I could never get over the sad blow I received once' – a reference to Hooker's abandonment of their friendship. He seemed to be in despair: 'a deadly and slow poison consumes me gradually and runs through my veins. – Sickness preys upon my vitals.' He gave Hooker all his personal details, including the name under which he was sailing, and told him he had written his final instructions ready to be forwarded 'should I haul home my Topsail-Sheets and set sail for the next world'. It is not clear whether he was contemplating suicide, or merely fearing that his illness would carry him off. His letter ended: 'farewell my boy, and think sometimes on your old friend Jorgensen, who tho' guilty of imprudent actions at times, perhaps still is a good-natured fellow.'

But there are hints of something even stranger. Having met Hooker on his return to Britain and suffered pain after the long coach journey back to London, he alluded in a letter to a private conversation that had taken place between them: 'Perhaps you will see the Propriety of keeping the Nature of my Wound a Secret: Mr Jermyn partly guessed my Case, to you I tel it, as I hold no secrets from you, I should however be sorry to have it farther abroad.' One can only wonder what this might refer to. If a venereal disease is meant, the use of the word 'wound' seems odd. It is possible, instead, that the injury was caused by a suicide attempt.

Whatever the cause, he made it through his crisis and was transferred to a Portsmouth hospital ship, which was almost as hellish as a prison hulk. It was an incentive to rapid recovery. He had himself discharged as soon as possible, and set out to tour all his old friends in the countryside: Whitbread, Hooker, Jermyn, and Hooker's friend (and later father-in-law) Dawson Turner, who had occasionally written him letters. Hooker himself was away on holiday in Torquay when Jorgenson first called: he wrote from there, and this is the only example of his side of the correspondence that survives, as it somehow ended up in the Foreign Office's files rather than among Jorgenson's personal possessions. His tone was a little too blithe, considering the difficulties Jorgenson had been through. 'My dear Jorgensen, Your letter has afforded me and my friends much entertainment. We have been highly interested in your adventures and have feelingly participated in your misfortunes . . . The country here is uncommonly beautiful and we have all enjoyed ourselves extremely.'

They did meet sometime in the spring of 1813, and Jorgenson may have stayed with Hooker for a while. His autobiography describes an occasion when he was sitting writing at a table in his friend's house, wearing his sailor's clothes, presumably the short jacket, neckerchief and bell-bottom trousers usually worn in the navy. (He had no money to buy others.) A visitor asked Hooker who the 'strange-looking man' was. 'Oh! that is the King of Iceland,' he replied.

Back in London, Jorgenson sent his Spanish documents to Whitbread, and also hinted at something else the British government ought to know about: a story he had heard from an old prison acquaintance, who in turn had heard it from a French prisoner of war. When he revealed the full details in a report to the Colonial Secretary, the Earl of Bathurst, it turned out to be the very thing the British in Australia had been fearing for years: a threatened French invasion. Four heavily armed French frigates were apparently to be sent that November to the Falklands, there to meet an American ship – the United States now being also at war with Great Britain. All five would sail together to Sydney, sneak up the Hawkesbury river and attack the city from the rear, recruiting any convicts who would join them on the way. Once they had seized Sydney and all its subsidiary colonies, they would use New South Wales as a base for further attacks on the Pacific Islands and South America. It seems a wild plan, but it was far from implausible. The French had considered moving on Australia several times: similar plans were concocted in 1806 and 1807, and in 1810 Napoleon himself had told the French Governor of Mauritius to prepare for an attack on Sydney from his island. The schemes had been abandoned each time, because more urgent matters in Europe stole Napoleon's attention and resources.

Bathurst affected indifference, and forwarded Jorgenson's report to Governor Macquarie in Sydney with a dismissive covering letter. In fact, he took it more seriously than he let on. A paper was sent from the Colonial Office to the Admiralty shortly after this, headed 'Suggestions for defeating an attempt reported to be in preparation against New South Wales by a Squadron of four French and one American Frigate'. In Sydney, Macquarie also noted that French ambitions in Australia were well known, and that Jorgenson was knowledgeable about Australian ports and sea routes. 'Under this impression, I shall be as much prepared as circumstances well permit to resist any sudden excursion or descent of the Enemy on this country.' He asked for reinforcements, and reminded Bathurst that he had already asked for more military support anyway, but had yet to receive it.

If the Falklands plan did exist, it went the way of previous schemes. Napoleon was now on the defensive in Europe and could not afford to send frigates and men to the other side of the world on an expansionist mission. Jorgenson's predictions had been wrong, but his report did bring his name to the attention of 'friends of influence', as he put it, and this proved of use to him in the future.

For the moment, however, he was relatively friendless. Creditors caught him again: the summer of 1813 saw him imprisoned first in a sponging-house and then, from 18 August, in the Fleet Prison. There he met old acquaintances, including James Savignac, who had returned from Iceland and fallen into financial difficulties, and his own former Icelandic companion Guðrún Johnsen, who was now attached to Savignac. Jorgenson was not particularly pleased to see his former colleague, but they agreed to share a cell to save rent. On the first evening, they enjoyed an 'Icelandic' reunion dinner to rival that at Olafur Stephensen's house. 'I do assure you that we were not less supplied with victuals and drink than we were at the old Stiftamptman's table,' wrote Jorgenson to Hooker happily: '18 pots of porter and 2 bottles of gin were drank immediately after dinner and much more during the course of the Evening.' But Hooker had fallen silent, irritated by Jorgenson's innumerable recent requests for money, and did not respond.

His companions gave Jorgenson one interesting piece of news: they showed him a copy of the *Danske Statstidende*, the Danish government gazette, announcing that the King had granted him a pardon in response to a last request made by his father a few hours before he died – a sign that the elder Jørgensen might exert a benovolent posthumous influence after all. Jorgenson wondered whether this meant he could now return to Denmark, but it still seemed risky, and he was stuck in prison for the moment anyway. He never did go back; nor did he feel any less anxious about his father's death.

Savignac was a bad cell-mate. As Jorgenson grumbled, he never got up before two in the afternoon, and when he did he would heave his Icelandic feather bed into a high cupboard so that it scattered dust everywhere. His rowdy habits made it hard for Jorgenson to write – for, as always when imprisoned, he turned to literature for consolation. Just as on the *Bahama* he had worked on the *Historical Account* and *Thomas Walter*, and in Reading he had 'amused' himself with the *Copenhagen Expedition* and the *State of Christianity*, so now: 'To divert my unpleasant reflections on myself, and the more to reconcile me to my fate, I set myself down to write a history of the Afghan Revolution, with the particulars of which I had by accident become intimately acquainted.'* He also wrote a manuscript on Russia, considered trying a book about Icelandic birdlife, and resumed work on his *Historical Account*, sending Banks a revised version and trying again to get it published.

While in the Fleet, Jorgenson wrote his last letter to Whitbread. It began again with the surely erroneous supposition: 'You will perhaps be surprised at receiving a letter from me dated from this place.' Whitbread seems not to have written back, and Jorgenson finally gave up. Whitbread had his own insurmountable difficulties: less than two

---

* This work does not survive – nor does the Russia manuscript – but Jorgenson summarized the story in his autobiography. It concerned an uprising led by the Afghan prince Mir Mahmud in 1722 against the Persian Sultan, who had oppressed his people for years. Like Jorgenson, Mir Mahmud had left his own country as a young man: since then he had lived a semi-prisoner in Persia, as the Sultan's protégé. After some years, he asked permission to go home and persuade his own people to offer themselves willingly as subjects, rather than paying a forced annual tribute. The Sultan gladly agreed, but it was a trick: when Mir Mahmud returned it was at the head of a great Afghan army, which captured the regional capital Isfahan and took the Sultan prisoner. 'These facts were hardly known at the time I wrote my little history', wrote Jorgenson proudly. The story can be interpreted as another sign of his disillusionment with the British.

years later, he committed suicide while in the grip of depression and paranoid delusions.

Jorgenson eventually admitted defeat with Hooker too: there was a four-year gap before he wrote again. Thus, after the autumn of 1813, he was without his two most influential (if sceptical) correspondents. But he had other ideas in mind, and was building up contacts at the Foreign Office. He sent Under-Secretary William Hamilton several minor reports and suggestions in 1814; these were not taken up, but they did make an impression, for in May 1815 Hamilton apparently engineered Jorgenson's release from the Fleet and recruited him to the British intelligence service.*

At first he was simply employed to translate documents from Scandinavian languages into English. This could have kept him happily engaged for years, but was perhaps a bit too tranquil for his taste. Before long he was transferred to a very different kind of work. He was sent to rove the Continent, now assumed to be permanently at peace following Napoleon's abdication and exile to Elba (though war had broken out again before Jorgenson actually made it across the Channel). His task was to assess morale and detect new market opportunities for Britain, a classic post-war activity. As before, his espionage achievements actually amounted to little more than glorified tourism, yet the British government did consider it of sufficient value to pay him a modicum. Information about morale and business was far from worthless, especially to a country whose prosperity was based on trade, and whose strategy was currently to promote a balance of power between Continental nations while appearing to take no interest itself: a delicate policy requiring subtle and reliable information.

So Jorgenson's pockets were filled, and he was despatched across the Channel in June 1815 although – as he admitted in the auto-biography – he lost the first payment gambling in London and had to sail as a hired hand rather than as a passenger. He left his ship in

---

* That Hamilton did use Jorgenson is confirmed by an exchange of letters from 1820, when Jorgenson turned up at the Bow Street magistrates' court apparently seeking a loan and dropping a string of impressive Foreign Office names. The puzzled officials wrote to Hamilton, who confirmed that Jorgenson had once performed 'services' for which he had been paid. 'He has met with misfortunes in life, and I believe is sometimes induced to do acts of which he soon repents', he added. 'He is a man of Education and some ability.'

Ostend, collected more expenses, and set off immediately for his first destination: the field of Waterloo.

Jorgenson liked to claim that he witnessed the battle of 16–18 June itself, from a safe distance. This was probably untrue. More likely, he witnessed only the aftermath, which was terrible enough. Days after the fighting had ended, wounded men were still lying on the muddy field waiting for rescue among the dead horses, human corpses, trampled helmets and feathers, and lost weapons. Survivors and locals helped to clear the battle zone; carts piled with casualties streamed towards nearby towns. 'The cries and groans of the mutilated soldiers pierced the heart,' wrote Jorgenson, 'some imploring a drop of water to quench their thirst; while others begged to be put to death.' Civilians roamed the area, hoping to find missing husbands and sons; others gathered out of journalistic curiosity – including Jorgenson. The battlefield became a tourist destination, as well as a target for thieves and morbid souvenir collectors, almost before the fighting had stopped.

Nor was it only to Waterloo that tourists were flocking. The British wasted no time in arranging the Continental tours they had been unable to enjoy for most of the last two decades – Hooker and the Turners had been among the first, conducting a Grand Tour during the temporary peace in 1814. An *Edinburgh Review* piece on Jorgenson's published travelogue noted sarcastically that the Continent was now overrun with English sightseers just like him, 'full of romance' and eager to see things closed to them for a generation but now 'as invitingly open to the sober citizen and his worthy family, as Margate or Brighton'. But they did not all travel on government pay as spies, and they did not all travel on foot, as Jorgenson did most of the time.

Jorgenson remained in the Low Countries for six weeks and then, in late July or early August, made his way through the chaos of northern France towards Paris, a city to which he took an immediate dislike.* It was vivacious enough, but Jorgenson found that Parisians only bothered to turn on their famous gallantry for people they thought worth-

---

* He also learned that Parisians still nurtured a great love for Napoleon, a love he put to the scientific test by buying a snuffbox with a miniature of the ex-Emperor on its lid, and carrying it everywhere to observe reactions. People invariably said 'Ah!'; women would take it from him and kiss it.

while, or from whom they wanted something. To a poor stranger in unfashionable clothes, they were supercilious. Jorgenson's clothes were considered particularly risible: throughout his French travels he wore a 'short grey coat' resembling the outfit of a Quaker, a fact that later inspired a rumour that he had witnessed Waterloo in deliberate Quaker disguise.

He returned the favour by excoriating France in his travelogue, disparaging in particular those things the French took most pride in: fashion, women and food. As for their politics, he thought the people too frivolous to appreciate true liberty, despite their revolutionary veneer: they could only be ruled through force or appeals to their vanity. In general, he was not in sympathy with the Latin temperament, whose distance from the Anglo-Saxon one he had already analysed in Spain. He snorted at the whole notion of French style, which he compared with the weightier substance of the northern nations. In Paris, seeing a tragedy performed by a famous actor who flung himself about and contorted his body like a Harlequin, Jorgenson thought the play ridiculous – though an acquaintance pointed out that for the French it was merely lifelike. He was much more impressed later by a performance in Berlin, in which scenes were acted in 'the silent agony of despair', and feelings were communicated almost entirely through the eyes. Jorgenson would have agreed with Madame de Staël's remark, 'A Frenchman knows how to talk even if he has no ideas. A German always has more in his head than he knows how to express.' (He himself seemed to have plenty of both powerful emotion and verbal facility.)

Just one aspect of Paris impressed Jorgenson: the legalized gaming houses, which were grand and well regulated. They were a bad influence on him, however. He played 'desperately', and the experience unhinged him so that he had another of his alarming relapses. It hit him on his second visit to the city, as he returned into a hot Parisian September from an excursion to the south, and was again marked by the double symptoms of mental distress and abdominal pain. Thrown into 'an unaccountable frenzy', he went out into the nearby woods of Boulogne, and there:

> I built a little hut of branches of trees, I tore my clothes, and remained unseen for four days, when I was taken up naked, but

147

by order of the angelic and accomplished Dutchess of Angoulême I was placed in a <u>maison de santé</u> – I was convinced my illness proceeded not from the brains, for whenever I was taken ill, I was for some days previous plagued with a cholic, this was the case in London; and so it was at Paris. – I told my case to Mr Lafont the physician, and that I had once been poisoned, since which time I had experienced often excruciating pains in the bowels. – He comprehending my case, applied bleeding, purging, blistering, and hot baths with a most rigid diet. – I was cured and cooled in 6 weeks, but could not set out on my voyage before the 2nd of December.

Even at the time of writing this in a letter to Henry Jermyn, over a month later, he was not fully himself again: 'notwithstanding the favour I receive from the persons of the highest distinction in Europe, I am not quite easy in my mind. It was the same in London, whenever I began to get ill I played all manner of Pranks.' Still, somehow he managed to make sober contact with his British employers in Paris and to pick up funds and his next instructions – which were to proceed through Germany towards Poland and Russia.

Predictably, he lost much of the money in a Parisian casino, together with his shirt, so he had to leave the city on foot with his overcoat buttoned up to the neck to keep out the December cold. Walking gave him insight into local conditions and opinions, though perhaps chatting with other travellers in carriages would have done just as well. It was certainly an endurance test. Despite the discomforts, notably the slippery ice underfoot on the smooth new French highways, he often covered thirty kilometres a day, when he was in full stride. He also picked up a travelling companion, a dog named Cartouche. Jorgenson now looked like (indeed he was) a scruffy vagabond, complete with dog. He often had difficulty in finding lodgings for the night or being served at inns, but, resourceful as ever, he usually managed to bluff his way in eventually. 'I had lived long enough to learn not to starve in a Christian country', he wrote.

In one village, he presented himself as an Irish Catholic pilgrim on his way to Jerusalem. This worked well: the French liked the Irish because they perceived them as fellow Anglophobes – 'which is of

more service to a man in France than the best letter of recommendation'. For some reason, he never told anyone he was Danish, and
usually presented himself as an Englishman. No one seemed to notice
that his accent in French was different in flavour from the usual *rosbif*.

He regularly lodged in inns full of soldiers, and in one case of a
group of rowdy wagoners who sang republican songs and shouted '*Vive
l'Empereur!*' all night. Once he met a detachment of soldiers heading
for Châlons-sur-Marne to report for duty: 'men of a merry disposition,
singing the whole of the way, and wishing for a war again'. Many were
sure the story of Napoleon's St Helena exile was a lie, and that he
was at this moment marching on France at the head of an army of
Turks, or else leading an Irish rebellion against Britain. They teased
Jorgenson because of his coat, and called him 'Monsieur le Curé', but
he won them over by buying plenty of wine at the inn they shared
that evening. This helped to reconcile them to the English: cheered
by the wine, one soldier declared that their old enemies were 'brave
and generous fellows'. He would even like to take a trip to England,
he said – but preferably 'in company with 100,000 armed Frenchmen'.
The other soldiers roared at this.

As Jorgenson approached German territory, he noticed that the
countryside took on a more Nordic feel, and the people seemed heavier
but more good-natured. They were less inquisitive and did not ask
questions of strangers, possibly something to do with the amount of
smuggling going on in the area. He reached the border on New Year's
Eve, having covered some four hundred kilometres by road in under
a month, and crossed to Saarbrücken for the beginning of the new
year of 1816.

Jorgenson entered Germany with low expectations, mostly derived
from French travel books which portrayed Germans as dull and glut-
tonous, but he was soon to find his ideas transformed. At his first
major city, Frankfurt, it was raining heavily: he arrived 'miserably wet,
not knowing what to do', and penniless. With his usual bravado, he
talked his way into a fine-looking inn and ordered their best meal,
not yet knowing how he would pay for it. The next morning, strolling
around town, he happened to see one of his father's clocks in a shop
window, and introduced himself. The owner, a Scotsman named
Alexander Fraser, was delighted to meet him and turned out to be

extremely helpful, lending Jorgenson money to clear his bill, putting him up in his home, and introducing him both to his own patron the Grand Duke of Hesse and to the British representative in town, who topped up Jorgenson's funds.

Jorgenson stayed with Fraser for several weeks, and even engaged in a confused flirtation with his host's daughter Maria, who gave him a curl of her hair in a locket when he left. An offer of marriage seemed to be expected; he hesitated at first, but later wrote from Berlin proposing to her after all. This was foolish: as he admitted later, he had mistaken for love a feeling of sentimental fondness after seeing her 'just in a short apron attending upon her father with the utmost care and tenderness in the hour of sickness'. He had been flattered by her liking for him, too. 'I was dressed in a very old fashioned manner, was 16 years older than the girl, nor could I conceive what any woman could see in me.' She accepted his proposal, and was despatched to her aunt's house in Scotland to await his return after his travels. But it ended miserably: when Jorgenson did get back to Britain he fell into his gambling ways, and failed to contact her. Later, he felt extremely guilty about it, and asked Hooker to trace her, but with no success.

None of this is mentioned in his published *Travels*, where he instead told an amusing story about asking a young lady to dance at a Frankfurt ball – presumably a different young lady, for she rejected him most disrespectfully:

> To my utter confusion, shame, and vexation, the lovely creature answered me, with the utmost affability of manner and sweetness of voice, that she had once taken a solemn oath never to dance with a person who was in the least degree bow-legged. I had never, till then, thought that there was any defect in my legs, which had safely carried me over so many leagues; and I could not help thinking that the lady intended to divert herself at my expense.

He watched grimly as she spent the evening dancing with 'a tall thin person, at least six feet high, and monstrously knock-kneed'.

Jorgenson spent the rest of his Frankfurt time polishing up the first section of his journal to send to Jermyn for safekeeping; he also wrote Jermyn a long letter extolling the cultural riches of Germany, to which his eyes were now opened. He particularly admired the Grand Duke's splendid private museum in nearby Darmstadt, full of antiquities and curiosities, including a set of bizarre cork replicas of great buildings in Rome and Berlin. From then on, he was full of nothing but praise for Germans and their lands.

He travelled eastwards, meeting many impoverished journeymen on the road – tough itinerant craftsmen looking much like himself, dressed in rags and invariably accompanied by dogs. (One man gave Jorgenson a useful training tip: to win the devotion of a new dog, you should stride energetically for a few hours with a piece of bread under your armpit, then give the bread to the dog – it would never leave your side.) Reaching Weimar, he visited the library where the great Goethe worked, but probably did not meet the man himself, though he later claimed he had. Next came Leipzig; here his dog Cartouche had its leg broken by a cartwheel. Jorgenson tried to take the injured animal on to Berlin by carriage, but it died on the way. 'I was left solitary in the midst of Germany,' he wrote sadly, 'without either a friend or companion.' He felt bereaved, but was pleased with his first sight of Berlin. It was magnificent; the Prussians seemed reserved and proud at first, but this impression disappeared once one got to know them, just as with the English.

Berlin inspired him to a paroxysm of name-dropping. In the *Travels* and the autobiography alike, he claimed to have met all sorts of celebrities, though not the same ones. They included 'the old Marshal Blucher, who was passionately fond of his pipe and a game at whist', and the eccentric Anglomane Count Hermann von Pückler-Muskau, who had all his servants dress in English clothes, filled his gardens with grazing sheep, and kept a special carriage with oval wheels in which he would take unwanted guests for a fast ride around his property to put them off staying longer. While Jorgenson was there, Pückler-Muskau made a balloon ascent accompanied by a female 'aeronaut' to whom he presented five hundred crowns as a gift in mid-air.

Jorgenson was supposed to continue to Warsaw but did not make it; instead he compiled a fake report for his employers based on hearsay from Poles and stayed in Berlin for another seven or eight months, surrendering himself to gambling. It was another of his low points. Only the need to flee creditors set him moving again at last, and in

November 1816 he trekked back via Dresden to Hamburg, where he stopped for some time to prepare his travelogue for publication, looking back with pleasure on his wanderings through the German country-side but glossing over his months of mayhem in Berlin.

As the author of the *Edinburgh Review* piece commented of the *Travels*, there was a paradox in Jorgenson's responses. His journey through France seemed to go smoothly (Jorgenson said nothing about his breakdown in his book), yet he railed against the French all the way. In Germany, he encountered hardship and was often treated inhospitably, but he praised the country to the skies. Jorgenson's attraction to all things German seemed to be purely instinctive, and it shone forth despite earlier feelings of resentment over excessive German influence in Danish politics. He thought the people frank, good-willed, and as 'open and warm-hearted as the sun at noon-day' – rather like himself, in fact.

Sometime in the first half of 1817, he returned to London with his completed manuscript in hand: it was published very soon after his return, under the name 'J. Jorgenson', his first use of the Anglicized spelling. He wrote throughout as an Englishman, using 'we' and 'us' whenever he referred to the English, and adopting English prejudices with gusto. This near-stateless global wanderer chose to speak as one of the stout and insular John Bulls who had so amused him in Reading: it seemed almost a deliberate disguise, although he made no real secret of his identity.

The book attracted more mainstream attention than Jorgenson's previous publications, probably because there was so much British interest in the newly accessible Continent. But the *Edinburgh Review* writer sighed wearily over the number of 'What I did on my Grand Tour' accounts currently on the market, and noted that Jorgenson accomplished little out of the ordinary apart from all the walking. He also made fun of Jorgenson's fondness for digression. The description of Waterloo was singled out for particular criticism: 'he might just as well have arrived the year after; for not one fact does he conde-scend to impart, that may not be found in the Gazette, – unless indeed it be those matters which he takes from Rollin's Ancient History, and Plutarch's Lives, touching Scipio and Hannibal,

Leonidas and Caesar, with all of whom, as well as with Plato, he occasionally claims acquaintance.'

The reviewer did not realize how lucky he was: there would have been far more of that sort of thing had Jorgenson's publisher not brutally slashed it. Jorgenson sent some of the excised texts to Jermyn: 'the great Frederick's panegyric on Voltaire – the Speech of Gustavus Adolphus on his departure from Sweden for Germany – An account of the departure of the Princess Ulrica from Berlin . . . These pieces were expunged by the booksellers from my work, for what reason I know not.'

He also reported to his government sponsors, and sent them a paper entitled 'Observations on Smuggling', which was apparently 'much approved of' by the Chancellor of the Exchequer. A similar paper, sent to the Foreign Office, was also well received, and it seems he was generously paid for both. But he wasted the money, and fell into gambling again. The next three years, from 1817 to 1820, blurred into one 'continual whirl of misery and disappointment at the gambling table'. By 1820, it seems he was *persona* no longer *grata* at government offices: an attempt to warn of a supposed Cato Street-style conspiracy to assassinate leading politicians was simply ignored. Looking back years later, he wished the whole stretch of time could be blotted from the records of his existence – which it could easily have been, for the allusion in his own autobiography is the only trace it has left on the world.

Besides government payments, his only other earnings came from casual journalism: he wrote one piece about an infamous incident in which two Britons named Robert Ambrister and Alexander Arbuthnot were summarily shot in America on suspicion of having sided with the Seminole against the US colonists, an execution which caused outrage in Britain. Jorgenson was particularly proud of his article: it was the only achievement from this period he looked back on with any satisfaction. Like himself, the two men had been accused of taking sides against a people they were supposed to consider their own. No wonder their fate aroused his sympathy.

Through Jermyn, Jorgenson made contact with Hooker again, though Hooker's first letter was censorious. 'I am much obliged to you for the candour with which you express your sentiments with respect to me', replied Jorgenson stiffly. He only wished to correct a few misconceptions, the main one being that he could get a job at sea any time he wanted to. In fact, he was not free to sign up on a ship, for the government might send him to Russia or South America on hush-hush business at any moment. 'We only wait for some important information before it is decided whither I may go.' He scolded Hooker for inconstancy: 'if any difficulties I have been in have been the cause of forfeiting the good opinion of my friends, I will not take a single step to be reinstated in their good opinion, I wish for no such friends. – I stand on a rock: you are not to wonder how I have got into difficulties, but rather how I have got over all as I have.'

On calmer reflection, he went on, he still thought of Hooker as his dearest friend, despite their ups and downs. He had been re-reading Hooker's *Tour in Iceland*: it brought back memories with overwhelming force. He longed to share his latest adventures with his old friend: 'I have thousands of things to tell you – wonders indeed.' But, as he concluded in a rare moment of introspection:

> strange as it may appear, there are some curious peculiarities attached to my character which baffle the penetration and judgment of my best friends and welwishers, and which indeed puzzle my own mind to such a degree at times that even in my most solitary hours and in the midst of the deepest meditation I cannot understand myself. – These peculiarities have sometimes been considered in a strong light, and rendered my friends suspicious of my reason. – Yet after taking a careful and repeated survey of my own mind, I think Genius may often be mistaken for madness. (My good natured friend do not smile at my presumption, I talk to myself when I talk to you.) Genius frequently acts so entirely under the influence of imagination, as to do things so utterly irrational, that if it be not the effect of an absolute want of reason, it is certainly that of a deriliction from reason, and produces the consequences of madness. – If I am not right in my present manner of arguing, I am at a loss to judge of myself.

But he had learned (at least in theory – he had difficulty putting it into practice) that this state of mind was not the best route to happiness, and that extraordinary powers of mind were of no use if they were not well applied. He had 'foolishly rejected' his many opportunities to advance his fortune in the world; yet he still hoped to make up for lost time and was still convinced that he possessed 'a good and feeling heart'. Only one thing gave him real regret: the thought that he had lost Hooker's friendship.

And that is the last we see of Jorgenson for two and a half years. He whirled around in his uncontrolled 'misery and disappointment' until, on 25 May 1820, he found himself hauled up before the Old Bailey on charges of theft. They were not serious charges, but they were to have momentous consequences.

8

In a dreadful scrape

According to the evidence heard against Jorgenson at his Old Bailey trial, he had taken the bedding out of his rented room in Warren Street – a mattress, a bolster, some blankets and a quilt – and had pawned it for cash at a shop around the corner, as if it were his own property. He had thus robbed his landlady, Sarah Stourbridge. She testified in court that she had begun to worry about Jorgenson when he failed to pay rent for several weeks and refused her access to the room, even though he had moved in with aplomb as a prosperous gentleman with Foreign Office connections. She finally broke in with the help of a constable on the morning of 8 May 1820: they found Jorgenson at his desk, eating breakfast and writing. When they pulled back the cover of the bed, they saw that it was stripped and empty. The constable's testimony to the court confirmed the landlady's story; a trader who later bought the bedding from a local pawnshop agreed that it matched Mrs Stourbridge's description.

Jorgenson delivered his own 'exceeding long and unconnected defence', according to the *Old Bailey Sessions Papers*, and 'complained of improper administration of justice in this country'. But it was to no avail. The evidence against him was overwhelming, and he was found guilty. The sentence was the standard one for petty thievery: seven years' transportation.

He was not packed off to a convict ship straight away, but taken to wait in Newgate Prison, next door to the court. There he set about writing letters to anyone he thought could help him. To the Foreign Secretary, Lord Castlereagh, he explained that he did not want a pardon; he actually *wanted* to be transported. But he would rather transport himself, as he put it, to a destination of his choice, instead of being sent on a convict ship to a hot country, where his precarious mental balance might be destroyed. He even asked for the same amount in cash as it would cost the government to ship him to Australia, to help with his self-transportation expenses. With incredible chutzpah, he thus managed to spin a standard plea for clemency into one of his habitual requests for money. It did not work. Castlereagh, a cool man not easily won over by unorthodox appeals, annotated the letter 'No answer' and ignored it. (Secretly nursing a mental instability of his own, he later went the same way as Whitbread, falling into paranoia and depression and cutting his own throat with a penknife.)* Oddly enough, however, Jorgenson did eventually get at least part of what he wanted.

His desire for banishment seemed genuine. Bridging another long gap in their correspondence, he explained to Hooker that he had approached Castlereagh not to seek a pardon, but to avert one. 'This may appear strange, but it is absolutely necessary I should leave the Kingdom. I am always wise every where else, and mad in London.' In fact, whether it was good for him or not, he was left to wait in Britain for many months, a favour apparently arranged for him by friends. They also procured him a comfortable cell in Newgate and generally mild treatment. He was not sure who his well-wishers were, and the prison authorities would not tell him. Perhaps his former Foreign Office employers were still helping him after all.

He had plenty of time to think. 'I write this letter near the midnight hour,' he whispered in a letter to Hooker: 'all here is silent, and hush: as I have a room to myself I can enjoy candlelight all night.' The quiet surroundings put him into a reflective mood: he thought a lot about his lost friend. 'You say I have nothing to ask your forgiveness for,' he

---

* The English at this time were known for their gloominess and suicidal tendencies. Depressive disorders had long been known as 'the English malady'. This image, which seems to be associated with national prosperity, transferred itself to the Scandinavians only in the following century.

wrote; 'you think so, but I feel otherwise; and this feeling is a source of great grief to me . . . Why did I not follow a tranquil plain path?' Hooker was moved, and did write back, ending years of silence. Jorgenson also wrote to his family in Denmark, and received anxious letters from his mother and from his brother Fritz, who agreed to make a thermometer in a silver case as a present for Hooker.

During his reflections, Jorgenson's mind turned to religion. He came to the conclusion that his long period of misery had begun with his Gibbonian religious crisis in 1810. His loss of faith had made him too confident; he had assumed 'that reason was a match for impetuous passions and a warm temper'. This was a great error. He now began to see that only faith could hold back the 'torrent of overruling inclinations' in his character; without it, all was 'emptiness and confusion within'.

In September, Jorgenson got a good job as assistant in the prison hospital, helping the surgeon, Dr Box, and supervising the patients' basic physical welfare for a fee. Like everything in Newgate, this job was run as a business, and it required capital investment: he was expected to buy eating utensils and other equipment from the outgoing assistant, a man named Nathaniel Davis. Jorgenson begged Hooker for a loan of £25 to fund this, though he had promised to ask for no more. Hooker was so angry that he cut off the correspondence again. Jorgenson apparently never did raise the money: he took over the job, but made a bitter enemy by not paying Davis. At least he now had a chance to learn useful medical skills, both from Dr Box and from books. 'I have now studied with unceasing application, and I have got completely through Doctor Cullan's system,* as well as several authors of distinguished eminence. Such knowledge may perhaps be of service to me sometime or later.' (It was.) He also won the personal friendship of Dr Box, who warmed to Jorgenson and thought highly of his abilities. With his quick wits and good memory, Jorgenson must have made an excellent medical student.

Naturally, he reverted to his usual prison hobby: writing. During these first months of imprisonment he produced two versions of a report to the government on the South Seas, a pamphlet on criminal

---

* i.e. that of William Cullen (1710–90), whose *First Lines of the Practice of Physick* was a standard text.

law, and a revision of another prisoner's manuscript on Madagascar, though unfortunately these works are all lost. Madagascar particularly interested him, and it became the preferred destination in his self-transportation plan. In October 1821, a year and a half after his arrival in Newgate, he wrote to tell Hooker that he was shipping out at last. The Home Office had approved his release, on condition that he leave the country within one month and stay away at least until the period of his original sentence had expired: that he transport himself, in other words. In 1808, his parole had stated that he must not leave Britain. This time, it forbade him to remain there. What both sets of conditions had in common was that Jorgenson ignored them.

He did take the trouble to request a two-week extension on the grounds that he was awaiting a package from Copenhagen with papers relating to an inheritance. 'I lead a quiet and tranquil life,' he added. 'Of me there is no fear now.' The application was denied, but he stayed on anyway. According to his autobiography he became caught up in gambling again and forgot about the problem, being swept away in the usual hurricane and losing his newfound tranquillity and circumspection. When the authorities eventually caught up with him, almost a whole year after his release, it was because his new enemy Nathaniel Davis happened to see him (or perhaps tracked him down deliberately) and turned him in.* He was arrested on 28 September 1822, and faced a second Old Bailey trial on 4 December, on a charge of being feloniously at large before the expiry of his original sentence.

It was not a complicated trial. Jorgenson was all ready to defend himself: he claimed to have prepared a written defence a hundred pages long and assembled seventeen witnesses. But he was advised to change his plea to guilty, to improve his chances of receiving clemency on appeal. He did so, presenting no defence at all, and was sentenced to death: the inevitable judgement for someone who had absconded from transportation.

Awaiting execution, Jorgenson was sent back to Newgate again, and

---

* Davis really had it in for him: Fritz later said that Davis had got hold of the family's address in Copenhagen and tried to blackmail them, claiming that he had secret evidence against Jorgenson. He did not get what he wanted, so turned Jorgenson in. Afterwards, Davis continued to harass him by sending letters to the prison and generally doing everything he could to damage his position.

succumbed to a kind of furious despair. He wrote to his mother on Christmas Eve, having received another letter from her as well as one from his elder brother Urban. His letter is long and emotional, and written in crabbed handwriting to eke out the paper available. He was distressed to learn that the worry had made his mother ill: 'You should remember that you have many others to live for apart from just me', he wrote. He only hoped that his brothers and sister would make her happy enough to outweigh the misery he had caused. She had sent him £5, for which he thanked her, but he urged her not to send more: 'your Jørgen will never wish to rob his mother in her old age'. All he wanted were affectionate letters. 'I can take anything except the lack of tenderness and affection from those I love.'

She had apparently reprimanded him for his actions against Denmark, so he now defended himself, protesting his loyalty to King and country despite everything. 'It is a duty I owe to you, to justify myself in the best possible way, so that you may know that you are not the mother of a monster.' He wished she would not reproach him so much, and was bothered by a remark she had made about his having a guilty conscience. 'Now understand me rightly, again. I have the same feeling in me that is natural to every good man. That is, I know I am not as deserving of God's mercy as I, and all others, should be.' But that did not amount to a feeling of guilt, particularly for the offence he was now being punished for, which was an absurd one. Why should it be a crime to draw breath in London rather than in Paris, or any other place? And in any case, 'What have I to do with England's stupid laws?'

At times, he sounds angry even with her. 'How can you know what relation I have with my God?' he demanded. 'How dare you judge your own son . . . and have you no belief in the upbringing you have given me?' But he added that, whatever happened to him, and even with a hundred nooses around his neck, he still had a good heart, and had done many good things in his life. 'Love your son as he loves you and that is all I will ask here on earth.'

He wrote to Hooker as well, telling him of his sentence. 'Again in a dreadful scrape. I am cast for death.' Since his condemnation, he had felt so despondent that he had not even troubled to send in an appeal for mercy, although he knew he must do so. He could not stir himself. Nor could he afford it: there was the old money problem again, for one must pay to get a petition drafted and to collect signatures. 'I am isolated, and solitary, and range over in my mind this morning to whom I could apply to help me to procure the parchment, paying a man a triffle to write a petition . . . I could not figure to myself any one that would assist me in this matter but him who was once so friendly to me. – Yet I am now so accustomed to wretchedness that I even fear to be disappointed in this my last request to you.' If Hooker would not help him, he would do nothing more. To his mother, too, he wrote that it cost money to submit a petition for mercy. Everything in Britain, even life and death, was so entangled in expensive formalities and matters of etiquette: 'it almost drives me mad'.

Hooker could not ignore such a letter, and he did more for his old friend than merely lending him money for the petition. He submitted one himself, urging the authorities to commute the sentence, and he used his influential contacts to make sure it went through.

It worked: Jorgenson's life was saved. The sentence was again changed to transportation. This time it was for life, and he would not be allowed to undertake it himself: he would be sent to Australia on a convict ship like everyone else. Again, however, the journey was postponed for a long time. He ended up spending another three years in Newgate and did not leave British shores until the end of 1825, a delay again resulting from intervention by friends, including the Berkshire MP Charles Dundas (whom Jorgenson had met in Reading) and the Newgate surgeon Dr Box. His own family also did what they could to help. Fritz wrote to Box praising Jorgenson's good qualities, and the surgeon forwarded the message to the prison governor and to Robert Peel, the new Home Secretary. Peel seemed to be persuaded, especially as he was 'not unaware of the good name and esteeem' enjoyed by Jorgenson's family in Denmark. Jorgenson's respectable background may not have helped him much after Iceland, but it was apparently helping him now.

Jorgenson went back to his job as hospital assistant and continued studying medicine. By 1825 he was able to boast: 'I have had to administer nearly forty thousand doses of medicines to outpatients, attended upon upwards of nine hundred patients admitted, and watched over the sick more than 200 nights of that time.' He also volunteered as an amateur preacher, composing and delivering sermons to other prisoners. His income from all his activities was good: he had his own large room, with plenty of light for writing, and he assured his mother that he was well fed and clothed. Important Newgate visitors often spoke to him, including all kinds of do-gooders, for, as he told his mother, 'It is now fashionable in England to be, or at least to pretend to be, a philanthropist.' Most notable of these were the Quaker prison reformer Elizabeth Fry and her brother Joseph John Gurney, both of whom took a particular interest in his case.

He seemed glad to be back in touch with his family again. In June, he urged his mother to keep him informed about everything that happened to them: 'Everything is interesting to me.' He wondered whether his youngest brother Marcus would get married soon ('a long engagement is dangerous and not good'), and he showed avuncular concern at the news that his niece, Fritz's daughter, had been to the theatre – 'but do you think that she should go to the theatre? The theatre is a bad place for a young girl.'

Despite his requests that they not impoverish themselves, the family also sent him money, which he admitted was useful. It was advantageous to dress and live well, even in prison, and especially to make it obvious that he came from a well-off family. As he wrote to his mother, 'even though there are many generous-minded Englishmen, they are more likely to show friendship to those they think are fairly respectably situated in life. They believe our family is not merely respectable, but rich, and that is how I have received many services that I would not enjoy if they thought differently.'

The experience of being condemned to death, though it threw him into despair, also propelled him through the last stretch of his religious trajectory from shallow convention, through doubt, to profound belief. He prayed for enlightenment and received it. Afterwards, he found himself filled with a fresh zeal not only for prayer but for theological disputation. This new enthusiasm kept him sane in an unnerving situation, and even brought him long-term relief from his obsessions, his addictions, his 'unmanly fears', his psychosomatic illnesses, and his general feeling of being out of control.

Jorgenson's medical and religious activities impressed the authorities: his sermonizing was particularly welcomed, partly because the official chaplain of Newgate was lazy and did only the minimum necessary to keep his job. At the same time, the new convert developed his theological reflections by working on a book which was eventually published, after he left Newgate, as *The Religion of Christ is the Religion of Nature.**

The views expressed in the book were considered inflammatory by many in the prison and elsewhere. They were well known even before publication, for Jorgenson broadcast his thoughts fearlessly in his sermons and in a long pre-publication notice of 1825. He presented himself as a militant defender of revealed religion against all who tried to set up human reason as a substitute, the very error he now believed had wrecked his own life for so many years. This meant primarily Deists, a loose confederation united by the belief that God did not intervene in the everyday world, and that everything after Creation proceeded purely according to the laws of science. As there was no continuing divine involvement, there could be no miracles, and even Scripture was questionable since it could not have been inspired by direct revelation. For Jorgenson all this was heresy of the worst sort, and he attempted to prove it wrong using a range of historical, scientific, literary, archaeological and anthropological arguments.

The book was less formidable than many in Newgate had been led to expect, for it was severely affected by Jorgenson's usual weakness for digression. He meandered through all sorts of odd topics, arguing that rationalist thinking was in error in each case.† But there were also genuinely poignant passages where he touched on the subjects that troubled him most: death and the immortality of the soul.

---

* He left the manuscript with Elizabeth Fry: somehow it found its way from her to the publisher Joseph Capes, who added a biographical preface largely cribbed from Hooker and issued it without Jorgenson's knowledge.

† For example, he scoffed at the idea that meteorites were bodies floating in space which were occasionally pulled to Earth by gravity. He also devoted several pages to the fashionable science of phrenology, which claimed the ability to discern character through the study of cranial bumps. He had once been intrigued by this, he said, but had rejected it after reading of a pair of twin brothers who, though identically bumped, could not have diverged more in character and behaviour. One was a criminal who ended up on the gallows, the other an upstanding pillar of the community – rather like Jorgenson himself and his brother Urban.

Jorgenson could not contemplate without horror the materialist suggestion that human beings lived and died like animals, becoming
'confounded with the grossest matter' after being laid in the soil. That
would mean that 'generation after generation follow each other in
rapid succession . . . for no other visible purpose than to look about
them for a few moments, then drop into the grave'. He would have
been moved by Bede's comparison of a human life to a sparrow that
flies accidentally into a banqueting hall full of feasting guests and great
blazing fires, but a moment later flies out through another doorway
into the cold emptiness of winter again. If that is all there is to life,
wrote Jorgenson, he would rather be a block of stone or a creeping
reptile.

Instead, he described how he had found all the comfort he needed
from living by the simple moral instructions found in Scripture. Indeed,
it all came down to one command: to do as you would be done by.
The truth and beauty of this Golden Rule outweighed any number of
volumes of rational argumentation and could untie any mental knot,
however tortuous. He derived his sense of security from it, and also
his love of scriptural dogma, for: 'In my opinion, the moral truths
contained in the New Testament, firmly establish the truth of all the
other parts.' This may not have convinced his Deistical opponents,
but it seems deeply felt and has a touching simplicity – which then
gets rather lost in the book's subsequent arguments.

When the book eventually came out it received several reviews,
including one in the *Gentleman's Magazine* which snootily found it
of interest mainly for having been written by someone in a 'peculiar
situation'. A Deist writer in the *Sydney Gazette* was more irritated by
Jorgenson's wandering logic and self-righteousness: 'he does but too
often snatch a theological cudgel from the armoury of his spiritual
comforter, and lay about him stoutly, endeavouring to break the heads
of those who perhaps feel most for him.' Both reviews picked holes
in his evidence, and the *Sydney Gazette* wondered about his access
to scholarly sources. 'Is Newgate so well provided with books and
instruments?'

One thing Newgate was certainly well provided with was Deists,
and this created something of a problem for Jorgenson. Religion was
a delicate subject which he did not handle with delicacy. In his sermons

1. A contemporary view of Østergade, the Copenhagen street where Jorgenson was born. His house, no. 77, is the third on the right.

2. Sullivan's Cove, later the site of Hobart, in 1804. The ship in harbour is probably the *Ocean*, which assisted the *Lady Nelson* in transferring Lt.-Gov. Collins's colony there.

3. The *Lady Nelson*, in which Jorgenson sailed for three years, outlasting all other crew members and rising in rank from common seaman to first mate.

4. A watercolour by Jorgenson, depicting the double shipwreck of the *Porpoise* and *Cato* in 1803. He was a talented artist: his many early travel sketches do not survive, but in 1810 he presented his friend William Jackson Hooker with a series of striking watercolour drawings, including this one.

5. The British bombardment of Copenhagen with incendiary rockets in 1807. The Jørgensen house is visible on the right in Østergade, on the other side of the square.

6. The encounter in 1808 between Jorgenson's Danish privateer *Admiral Juul* (right) and Britain's HMS *Sappho*. Two Danes were killed and both ships were severely damaged before Jorgenson struck his colours and surrendered.

7. William Jackson Hooker,
Jorgenson's best-loved friend,
as a young man in 1811,
two years after Jorgenson
met him on the journey
to Iceland.

8. A view of Reykjavík in 1810, the year after Jorgenson's revolution.

9. The fifth and most radical of Jorgenson's revolutionary proclamations, opening with the royal phrase 'We, Jorgen Jorgenson', and marked with his Protector's seal ('J.J.').

10. Count Frédérik Trampe, Iceland's Danish governor: he was easily captured and deposed without bloodshed by the 1809 revolutionaries. 11. Magnús Stephensen, Iceland's Chief Judge and, after Jorgenson's removal, its temporary co-Governor with his brother Stefán.

12. 'Oh! my wig', a mischievous watercolour by Jorgenson depicting an alleged mishap at a Reykjavík ball. The lady is Mrs Vancouver: she and her husband had opposed the revolution and secretly assisted Count Trampe. This picture is Jorgenson's revenge.

13. Another Jorgenson watercolour showing the British hulk *Bahama*, in which he was imprisoned after the Icelandic adventure.

14. 'Liberty triumphant': the long-suffering hero receives his reward after tyranny and oppression have been overcome.

15. A copy of Jorgenson's *Travels through France and Germany*, inscribed to William Jackson Hooker. The title page carries a contemptuous extra note by Hooker's son Joseph: 'Died a ticket-of-leave man in Tasmania'.

TRAVELS

THROUGH

FRANCE AND GERMANY,

In the Years 1815, 1816, & 1817.

COMPRISING

A VIEW OF THE MORAL, POLITICAL,

AND

SOCIAL STATE OF THOSE COUNTRIES,

INTERSPERSED WITH

NUMEROUS HISTORICAL AND POLITICAL

Anecdotes,

DERIVED FROM AUTHENTIC SOURCES.

By J. JORGENSON, Esq.

Died a ticket of leave man in Tasmania in 1840. J. D. Hooker

LONDON:

PRINTED FOR

T. CADELL AND W. DAVIES, STRAND.

1817.

16. Hobart in 1840, much transformed from the 1804 camp shown in Plate 2.

17. The Ross Bridge in Tasmania, with decorations carved by creative convicts in the 1830s. Jorgenson appears here as the King, with his wife Norah as his companion, the Queen.

TO COMMEMORATE
JORGEN JORGENSON
ONCE LORD PROTECTOR OF ICELAND
PARTICIPATED IN FOUNDING OF RISDON,
HOBART AND PORT DALRYMPLE 1803-1804
FIELD POLICEMAN AND CONSTABLE
OATLANDS UNDER THOMAS ANSTEY
POLICE MAGISTRATE 1827

18. The memorial plaque to Jorgenson outside Oatlands police station, Tasmania.

and the printed prospectus he attacked Deism in the most undiplomatic way, direly warning that this 'dreadful mischief' was responsible for all the ills of society: the increase in crime, the loosening of moral principles, the destruction of bonds between people, the disappearance of charity, and the rising tide of insubordination. Many of his listeners took this personally.

There was another complication. Some Deists (not all) united their religious radicalism with a similar radicalism in politics, none more so than the followers of the freethinker Richard Carlile. Newgate had recently received an intake of his 'shopmen', rounded up on suspicion of subversive activity (Carlile himself had been sent to a different prison), and they formed a powerful clique. They continued to publish Carlilite journals and pamphlets using outside contacts, and wielded much influence among the general prison population, who were attracted to their anti-authoritarian politics. The Carlilites could hardly fail to be aware of Jorgenson's attacks on Deism, and they were not amused. His *laissez-faire* politics did not improve his position, especially as he was apparently given to proclaiming the fact that he came from a wealthy family in Denmark. Having once feared for his life as a traitorous revolutionary, he now feared for it as a bourgeois conservative.

Jorgenson suffered a pummelling in Carlilite publications. His enemies accused both him and Box of mismanaging the hospital, and Jorgenson was described as a drunkard and, even now, a persistent gambler. He was even accused of attempting to poison his enemies using hospital medicines. He angrily denied it: 'the Radical press of England, with all its base and ignoble concomitants, attacked me for several months, with all the virulence of malice and scurrility of language ever used by that press'. They 'never ceased their machinations', he claimed, until they had undone his comfortable position in Newgate and got him removed, first to a prison hulk and finally to Australia.

In reality, it was probably not the Carlilites but his friends who had him removed, for they were concerned about his physical safety. In October 1825, after Jorgensen had spent a total of four years and three months in Newgate (as well as the intervening ten months of illicit freedom), it was ordered that he be transferred at last to the prison hulk *Justitia* to await transportation. The change was something of a shock. The *Justitia* was much like the *Bahama* in which he had been so miserable sixteen years earlier, although at least it was not full of vengeful Danes. Nor were there any Carlilites, it seems. Jorgenson's life there was not dangerous. He was kept apart from the tougher types of prisoner and spared the usual daily labour in the dockyards: all he had to do was wait.* After a month or two, he was transferred to the *Woodman*, a convict transport going not to New South Wales, as most did, but to the very colony he had helped to found back in 1803 and 1804: Van Diemen's Land. It departed on 6 December 1825, carrying Jorgensen and 149 other prisoners.

Jorgenson's autobiography vividly described the scenes on departure, all bustle and lamentation. Families came to call out their final farewells; the convicts themselves were raucous and distressed: 'it appeared as if ten thousand demons had been let loose'. As they sailed out of port, Jorgenson watched his last view of the English shore recede over the horizon. 'I stood in silent agony, taking a last and lingering view of those shores, the sight of which had on so many former occasions afforded me delight.' It was his first time at sea as a passenger since his return from Germany in 1817; memories of life as a sailor were even more distant. 'I saw myself an exile and a captive on that element on which I had once been a commander.'

At forty-five, Jorgenson knew he was leaving Britain, and probably Europe, for ever. Despite his mixed feelings about his two homelands, this saddened him. He later took issue with those who pretended that transportation to sunny climes was so attractive that convicts would actually commit crimes to achieve it. 'Let every man examine the emotions of his own breast,' he wrote, 'and see whether in the abstract, and under any circumstances, he would wish to be torn away from the scenes of his youth . . . from all his old friends and . . . relations . . . and to be placed in a sunken and degraded class, among strangers in a distant land!' No, prisoners dreaded transportation as a kind of death,

---

* Again, this was the result of friends' kindness: the MP Charles Dundas was still helping him, and Hooker and Dr Box may have exerted their influence too. As for his being sent to Van Diemen's Land rather than Sydney, this may have been arranged in accordance with his earlier plea that he be allowed to live in a cooler climate – or it may have been just luck.

and would do anything to avoid it: the remoteness and uncertainty of the destination filled them with horror. For Jorgenson, the destination was familiar and remoteness was something he actually craved. Yet the prospect of life as an exile – in fact as a *double* exile – was hardly comforting.

The atmosphere of lawlessness continued throughout the journey. The convicts were confined below decks most of the time, and left to their own devices. The thieves among them (the vast majority) stole anything they could get their hands on: 'boxes, and parcels of tea and sugar, were torn from under those who possessed any'. When Jorgenson opened a trunk in his berth, a silk handkerchief was snatched from it and, while he looked around for the culprit, other light fingers removed almost everything in the box before he could slam it shut again. Those with greater bravado dominated those with less; a brutal pecking order soon emerged, as in any prison society.

But he only had to endure a day or two of this before being rescued. Dundas and a sympathetic Home Office official had written to the captain asking him to find useful work for Jorgenson on the journey, and to treat him with special consideration. He was therefore removed from convict quarters soon after departure and given a job as assistant in the ship's hospital, together with cabin accommodation and permission to stroll on deck whenever he wished during the daytime. Thus Jorgensen bobbed up high above the crowd as usual, a reward partly due to his diligence in Newgate, and partly to his ability to win the sympathy of friends. This was the pattern of his life. He was always being flung from one antipode of fortune to the other, first rising through his intelligence and warmth of character, then descending into misery after some self-induced mishap.

The *Woodman* journey proved to be one of his finest moments. Some weeks out of port, a contagious fever broke out on the ship. It killed four convicts, followed by the ship's surgeon himself, who heroically said nothing about his illness until he 'dropped down dead from his chair' one day. As second-in-charge in the hospital, and the only person with medical knowledge, Jorgenson was called on to cover all the surgeon's duties until they reached a port where a replacement could be recruited: the Cape, still five weeks' journey away. According to his own account, he wiped out the terrifying fever during those five weeks by applying treatments he had learned from Dr Box. One naturally suspects him of boasting, yet the records of the ship's eventual arrival in Hobart bear him out perfectly: 146 convicts arrived in good shape, and the only four not to survive the journey were the four who had died already.

9

A species of gloomy delight

After nearly five months at sea, the *Woodman* sailed into Tasmania's Derwent river on 29 April 1826, and returned Jorgenson to the town whose birth he had witnessed so long ago. The *Hobart Town Gazette* noted the arrival, adding that twenty-two of the convicts on board had been sentenced before, mostly to Australian transportation. It singled out for special mention 'a native of Denmark, named Jorgen Jorgenson, formerly a dispenser of medicine in Newgate, and well known to most of the prisoners in the colony. He is a very intelligent man, and speaks several languages. He was here at the first formation of the Colony.'*

The Derwent settlement was now twenty-three years old, half the age of Jorgenson, who had turned forty-six during the voyage. When he had seen it last, it had been little more than an assortment of tents stapled to the edge of a forest. Since then Hobart Town (or Hobarton) had not merely changed: it had come into existence out of nothing. Where once there had been scrub, fallen trees, mud and flood debris, now there were straight roads, theatres, banks, offices, a neat church, a neat prison, and a Government House considerably more imposing than Reykjavík's.

The settled zone had also spread up the valley into the country's

---

* This has been cited as evidence that Jorgenson had been transported as a convict on the *Lady Nelson*, but (assuming it means to include Jorgenson among the twenty-two at all) it is probably just a reference to his having absconded from 'self-transportation' – which was how his present offence was described in the convict register.

interior. Van Diemen's Land was still primarily an open-air prison, now containing almost seven thousand convicts, but free settlers had been moving in too, and they were gradually changing the country-side. Unlike convicts, they arrived with money and hope, as well as with wives and children, valuable sheep, and all kinds of home comforts. Many had become wealthy, for Antipodean wool fetched good prices in London. 'Vast tracts of land have been brought into cultivation,' wrote Jorgenson later, 'the surface covered with millions of sheep, stately mansions and public buildings gracing the towns and the estates of the settlers, stage-coaches running from one end of the island to the other.' He was impressed, and for a moment it made him proud of his adopted country again: 'Britain, and Britons alone, could bring about so wondrous an achievement, – such a monument of the stupendous energies of a mighty nation.'

In many ways the transplanted northerners felt at home. The climate was more familiar than that of hot, red mainland Australia: Tasmania was woody and wet, and its distances were on an English scale. But it suffered fierce winters, and the settlers were everywhere haunted by reminders of its remoteness: the strange animals, the impenetrable mountain forests, and the indigenous people, who by 1826 were changing their policy of cautious acceptance and becoming more belli-cose. Even Hobart was far from comfortable: there were unpredictable shortages of imported goods, and between the smart buildings the streets were still 'one continued succession of ponds and holes of water, into which a passenger goes "splash," enveloping his legs in mud and filth', according to complaints in the papers. The town felt cosmopol-itan – the port often contained a dozen ships from all over the world – but that also meant gangs of drunken sailors and whalers on sprees. The country outlaws known as bushrangers had terrorized rural settle-ments for years. Floggings and hangings were common: around a hundred executions took place in Hobart in the three years preceding Jorgenson's arrival. Indeed, five thieves and killers were hanged just after the *Woodman* docked, while its convicts were still waiting to disembark.

This unloading process began on 6 May, and took two days to complete. The routine was always the same: first a couple of officials would go aboard to take down each person's physical description, place of origin, occupation and sentence. Then they were brought ashore to the Prisoners' Barracks, and subjected to a bracing speech by the colony's Lieutenant-Governor, currently Sir George Arthur.* After this, a sort of job market took place. Private settlers and merchants had earlier submitted requests for workers of various types – farmhands, building labourers, clerks, maids – and the officials now went through the list of convicts matching each one to a suitable employer. The convict would work for this employer until no longer needed, or until issued with a 'ticket of leave', a preliminary semi-pardon which permitted the recipient to change employment at will.

In effect, this 'assignment system' was a form of centrally managed slavery. Yet it worked well and was popular with settlers and administrators alike. It could be popular with convicts too, as an alternative to working on a chain gang, but that depended on individual luck. Given a good employer, a convict could expect reasonable comfort, healthy food, generous reports and rapid progress towards a ticket of leave. With a bad employer, life could be made so miserable that the prisoner would seek oblivion in drunkenness or even try to escape, and liberation could become an ever-receding possibility.

Every convict in Van Diemen's Land was in perpetual motion, heading upwards to freedom or downwards to ever more unpleasant punishment. Co-operative deeds and useful public services were rewarded by tickets of leave, measured out with careful consistency. Incidents of intoxication or insubordination (such as 'neglect of duty and going to bed in the middle of the day', or 'refusing work and singing obscene songs', to sample a couple from the conduct records) resulted in fines or floggings. More serious offences could land the convict in one of the island's penitentiary camps, like that at Macquarie Harbour in the remote west, where conditions were so ghastly that inmates were said to murder each other just to be executed and find release in death. The horror of these places was always impressed on new convicts by Lieutenant-Governor Arthur, for he was a believer in the well-managed application of dread as a preventive against disorder and worse difficulties. Convicts should live in fear of Macquarie Harbour, he believed; the criminal classes back home should fear the thought of Van Diemen's Land in general. That way, on

* The title of Lieutenant-Governor reflected the subordination of the Van Diemen's Land colony to New South Wales, which had a full Governor.

average, good order would be maintained and everyone would be happier, both here and in Britain: the quality of life would be improved.

Arthur was not a cruel man. His main qualification for the job had been his campaign against slavery in his previous post in Honduras, and tough punitive policies actually formed part of his philanthropic ideal. But he was guided by reason rather than sentiment, and his frigid manner made it hard for many to see his good qualities. There were always chilly winds blowing in Government House during his administration: dinners and balls were noted for their parsimonious tedium, in contrast with those of the previous Lieutenant-Governor, William Sorell, whose party expenses had raised eyebrows. Arthur sought to turn Van Diemen's Land from a frontier outpost into something more serious, a kind of factory for the reform and improvement both of human nature and of the land.

One advantage of Arthur's reward-and-punishment machine was that it worked. Much of the amelioration in living conditions noted by Jorgenson on arrival was the result of the Lieutenant-Governor's rigorous crime policy. 'We can now walk the streets of an evening without fear of having our brains knocked out', wrote one newspaper editor: 'This is what we like.'

This success was due not only to motivational principles, but also to Arthur's efficient sytem of espionage and surveillance. He turned the whole island into a sort of 'panopticon' – the imaginary circular prison invented by Jeremy Bentham, where inmates were liable to constant observation from a central hub. They need not actually be watched all the time, for they knew that they always *could* be, and would therefore police themselves. The twist in Van Diemen's Land was that observers lurked on all sides as well as in the centre, for generous rewards ensured that convicts were often willing to spy on each other. An early settler panicked by the approach of an Aboriginal hunting party had once vividly described the sensation with the words, 'they looked at me with all their eyes'. By 1826, Van Diemen's Land had indeed become an island full of eyes. Rational and efficient as it was in principle, it had an air of the uncanny about it.

From his first hour in the Prisoners' Barracks, Jorgenson was a creature set apart. He had a sheaf of letters of recommendation from eminent friends, and he had his brilliant performance in the ship's hospital to top off his earlier achievements in Newgate. Even without these, it was obvious that he was a different sort of man from the other 145 on board. He was older than most, better educated, and more widely travelled; he even had two extraordinary claims to fame on the island. He had been present at the foundation of the colony – unlike almost all of the settlers and administrators, let alone the convicts – and he had his own (admittedly peculiar) experience of island governorship, not something many people could boast of. If he never saw himself as a convict among the horde, it is hardly surprising, for no one else saw him that way either.

With his legend surrounding him like an aura as he stood with the other prisoners awaiting assignment, Jorgenson's lottery throw in the employment market naturally turned out to be a winner. Instead of being assigned to a remote sheep farm upcountry, he was appointed to a comfortable job as clerk in the Customs House in Hobart.

In reality he had no talent for bookkeeping, as he admitted, and the job did not suit him well, but it stood him in good stead for a different reason. After a couple of months in the office, he noticed other employees behaving suspiciously, and worked out that a major banknote forgery operation was underway. Knowing the value of this information, he reported his observations to the Chief Police Magistrate, and the culprits were arrested and punished.* Jorgenson was declared a hero, and expected a good reward. A group of merchants in town offered him £50 by way of thanks, equivalent to five years of his convict clerk's salary, but he shrewdly turned this down. He hoped to receive something better: a ticket of leave, or even a full pardon. His new supporters duly organized a petition, urging that he be pardoned both for his action and for his ethical stance in refusing the £50.

But Jorgenson and his claque had forgotten one thing about Arthur's reward policy: it had to be administered with rigorous consistency, lest other informants develop unrealistic expectations. If everyone could

* Just one man was executed as a result, the twenty-six-year-old Thomas Childs. He was not among those actually reported by Jorgenson, but the four men initially arrested gave information against Childs to save their own lives. Childs was the only one left when there was no one else to turn in. He tried to face the gallows bravely and maintained a resolute silence until the end, but then, as the noose was being adjusted around his neck, he lost his composure and cried out, 'I am sure I shall go to heaven, I can see heaven.'

get a pardon within a few months of stepping off the boat, there would soon be no convicts left. Arthur therefore felt obliged to maintain a strict attitude, and Jorgenson's petition was ignored for the moment. He did eventually get a ticket of leave, but it took a while. For the moment he got a different reward: a new job.

This was partly for practical reasons. Having turned informer in a high-profile case, he needed protection, and the safest solution was to send him to a remote part of the country until the scandal blew over. He may also have requested a more challenging assignment himself, wanting to try some of his old skills. His name was therefore passed to Edward Curr, the Hobart agent of the Van Diemen's Land Company, a private organization devoted to exploring and developing the Tasmanian wilderness. Curr took Jorgenson on and gave him a most unusual job for a convict. He hired him not merely to join, but to lead, a party of explorers into the north-western forests in search of good land and a livestock route from the settled areas to new company-owned agricultural territory near the coast.

The Van Diemen's Land Company was a young, aggressive and thoroughly commercial concern. What they expected from their vast northern land grants was rich farming territory for sheep and cattle. What they actually got was inaccessible, wet, overgrown country tortured by harsh winters and cursed with poor soil, though no one realized this yet. The land *looked* lush enough, but this was deceptive. It fooled even the company's most experienced surveyor, Henry Hellyer, who named two areas the Surrey and Hampshire Hills in the hope that they would become copies of the English originals. A few years later almost all of the five thousand sheep installed there were dead, frozen by the cold and hunted by feral dogs and the island's 'tigers' or thylacines. And this was one of the more pleasant zones in the company's territory: worse areas still awaited exploration.

In mid-1826, Edward Curr and the company investors were still optimistic, and most of the surveyors were out exploring all corners of the new territory, expecting to find good land. There was thus a temporary shortage of personnel, which was what opened Curr's mind to considering Jorgenson. It was a risk: Jorgenson had no experience of land-surveying, though he knew how to navigate at sea, and he was a convict who did not even have his vital ticket of leave yet. But he had established his loyalty in Hobart, and he had letters of recommendation from company officials in London (one being a relative of his patron Charles Dundas). His courage was beyond question, and as a former sea captain he was a proven leader, as his natural air of command confirmed. There was also the fact that he had been in Tasmania before, and had explored informally on the Tamar and Derwent rivers, as well as travelling with Flinders. Moreover, it was clear from his list of publications that he was literate and would have no trouble producing the detailed reports Curr always demanded. (Indeed, in later years, less bureaucratic employers often had trouble getting him to *shorten* his despatches.)

So, on 25 August 1826, Curr wrote informing London of the new expedition: 'This party will be under the conduct of Mr Jorgen Jorgenson, who has been strongly recommended to me by Captain Dundas to whom I refer you, and upon whose ardour and perseverence I place much reliance.' He gave Jorgenson written instructions and a copy of the only map in existence, drawn up by the surveyor Thomas Scott two years previously – though this was almost completely devoid of information. It showed a scattering of landmarks tentatively identified from a distance, including the distinctive mountain now known as St Valentine's Peak, which Scott called 'Peak like a Volcano'. A few possible routes were marked out, but the rest consisted of a large space marked, 'This part of the country unknown'.

Jorgenson's task sounded more straightforward than it was. He was to start by going to a farm on the River Shannon run by the settler and newspaper proprietor James Ross, who would help him requisition supplies. Two companions would go with him, Andrew Colbert and Mark Logan, both also convicts.* Each man would be paid a good wage of half a crown a day, though they had to buy their own thick clothes and boots, which would be ruined on the journey.

* Colbert was often referred to by Jorgenson and others as 'Black George', but he was not Aboriginal: he was an African-American, identified in the convict registers as an American of black complexion and a former drummer by profession, probably in the British Army – which often recruited escaped or freed American slaves. Colbert was not the only convict of African origin in Tasmania. Indeed, the eminent settler and District Chief Constable Gilbert Robertson, a later colleague of Jorgenson's, was of mixed race: his mother was a West Indian slave.

When all was prepared, they were to cross the Shannon and set out over St Patrick's Plains towards the Great Lake, then head north-west into the unexplored wilderness area. Through this zone, they must pioneer a route to the coast, preferably one wide and clear enough for a stock route to follow one day.

The three men thus left Hobart at the beginning of September 1826, and made their way towards the outlying settlements near the Shannon. At every inn, they heard alarming stories about what they were heading into. The winter and spring of 1826 had seen the foulest weather in local memory: 'the oldest inhabitants of the Colony could not recollect such heavy floods as then inundated all parts', wrote Jorgenson later. There were bushrangers to beware of: one particularly desperate character called Dunne had been rampaging through the area in recent weeks. But, as Jorgenson wrote with his usual bravado, they were more afraid of 'the fleas in the Kangaroo rugs' than of any human attackers.

The flooding was a more serious problem, as they realized when they reached James Ross's farm and saw the Shannon in full torrent. The river had become a monster: it looked completely impassable. They assembled their supplies and waited for an opportunity to cross, but the water kept rising rather than falling. Jorgenson passed the time by browsing through Ross's books and transcribing quotations from Flavius Josephus, and by listing their equipment and provisions. They would carry about seventy pounds each (over thirty kilos), a substantial load, though it would lighten as they consumed the great hams and hunks of pork and mutton with which they started out. Jorgenson also carried something lighter but very important: his journal, which he wrote up every evening once they were underway.*

They took dogs to help them catch kangaroo, guns for hunting and for self-defence against any white or Aboriginal attackers, and machetes

---

* This journal went through some adventures of its own. It was later left at the home of George Scott, brother to the map-maker Thomas, and his servants apparently used some of its leaves to light pipes from the fire. The rest was retrieved by an unknown rescuer, who added a note explaining what had happened. In fact, some of the missing material may have fallen victim not to pipe-puffing servants, but to Jorgenson himself. On one of his trips, his party lit a fire on a mountainside which got out of control: part of the journal was lost in their hasty retreat. Much does survive, however, and his other compiled accounts fill the gaps.

for hacking through scrub. And it was now that Jorgenson acquired a new possession of which he was very proud: his heavy sword, presented to him as a gift by Ross, a man with whom he seemed to strike up another of his easy, warm friendships. He wore this colossal piece of metalwork slung across his back on all his bush journeys, and kept it close by him for the rest of his life: it often featured in later descriptions, and would add greatly to his legend. In everything Jorgenson does after this point, one must always think of him with his sword at his side, or hanging from his bedpost, or across his shoulders.

Although the water remained high, Jorgenson eventually decided to move on from Ross's farm anyway, and to start along the Shannon's banks in roughly the right direction. Two weeks were now lost in following the river up and down, searching for a place to cross. It looked like 'a complete sea', and the weather kept worsening: as they headed out into St Patrick's Plains (still on the wrong side of the river) it started snowing heavily. They often waded into the numbing water, trying to make it to the other side. Once Jorgenson was pulled off his feet by the weight of his pack (and sword presumably), combined with 'the wind blowing downwards exceedingly strong'. He could not swim and was in danger, but somehow scrambled back safely, though he shivered from the cold for hours afterwards. A few days later, he and Colbert tried to cross together, and were nearly carried off again. This time Jorgenson cut his hands and feet on the rocks. The wounds became infected, and caused him pain: 'My hand much inflamed, not being able to use my thumb and little finger.'

They kept trying, however, and every evening Jorgenson would set off on extra investigations by himself while his companions rested. One evening he went so far that he got lost: 'dark came on, the heavens were overclouded'. The others had to find him by scouring the bush shouting and whistling. It was worth the alarm, for he did find a crossing-point that night, and the next day they all forded the river successfully. But they were now much shorter of supplies than they should have been, and far out of position.

They strode across the plains and made it to the Great Lake by nightfall – one long day's journey. That evening they caught three kangaroo, and enjoyed the landscape, though it was still freezing. 'Delightful prospect. White gums mostly . . . Marshes not ankle deep.'

The country beyond the lake looked to Jorgenson like fine grazing land for sheep and cattle; the next day they struck out towards it, heading north-west across the marshes of the Central Plateau. The ground was both boggy and icy, and the wind was still strong. But what lay ahead of them was worse, for they would soon enter the area shown as a blank on Scott's map, aiming for his 'Peak like a Volcano' – actually just one peak in the long, impenetrable range called the Walls of Jerusalem.

Before they got that far, however, they had to pass another river, the Ouse, and it too turned out to be far more swollen than they expected. It blocked their route completely. Just as torrential as the Shannon, it also had steep cliff-like banks which made any approach impossible. Again, while the other men rested from the day's walk, Jorgenson took a solitary hike upriver. No crossing could be seen, but he came to the foot of a snow-covered mountain where the river bent sharply to the west, and wondered if it might lead them to the coast without their having to cross it at all. He climbed the nearest ridge, and from the top had an uninterrupted view beyond the mountains towards the north-west. Again he thought he saw good land there, of the kind Curr wanted.

The next day they followed the river, but it soon bent away from the west again and then entered a narrow gorge: 'two stupendous rocks, between which the water precipitated itself with amazing impetuosity and great roaring'. At sunset, from the top of the gorge, Jorgenson took his bearings. To the east were plains and the rest of the Great Lake, which they had skirted on the southern side. To the north were two high mountains. To the west, on the horizon, a series of ridges led to the 'Peak like a Volcano'. It was a magnificent, terrifying panorama, all wide plains and high jagged mountains in their torn cloaks of snow. The beauty of the landscape moved him, and he had a lonely consciousness that he was the only one of the three men who could really appreciate it. He missed having a kindred soul with whom to share his 'thoughts and contemplations'. Years later, he wrote to tell his lost friend Hooker that this wilderness reflected the cast of his own mind, and even reminded him of his years at sea:

Often, when ascending the loftiest summits far above the Clouds,
I beheld with a species of gloomy delight, the ranges and tiers

178

beneath my feet, appearing like the waves of the mighty ocean troubled and agitated when the gale sweeps furiously over its surface. The terrific desolation around me as far as the eye could reach in the Horizon struck the mind with inconceivable awe and astonishment, but alas! I had no one by me who could participate in my feelings.

Jorgenson still hoped to find a path through this unearthly scene, and he did not forget his pragmatic duties. None of his sublime personal reflections appeared in his journal, where he wrote instead, for Curr's benefit: 'Abundant feed for sheep and cattle and a considerable proportion adapted for cultivation. Even on the top of the heights good feed is found, and everywhere the kangaroos are swarming in flocks and are large and excellent eating.'

They spent such an uncomfortable night in the cold that it was actually a relief to get up in the morning. Over the following days, they continued battling the Ouse. They tried to cross at a set of falls, wading in tumultuous water up to their waists and fixing rope on poles across the torrent, but this failed. Logan heroically tried to swim across, but gave up; 'in all reasonableness the attempt ought not have been made.' Jorgenson himself had another accident: a rock gave way as he was climbing up the side of the chasm, and he fell 'several fathoms headlong down'. Fortunately he was caught in some bushes, perhaps snagged by his sword, and this saved him.

By 29 September, he concluded that they could not hope to get across the river before their provisions ran out, and that the expedition should be abandoned. It was the right decision: had they managed the crossing and made it as far as the Walls of Jerusalem in such weather, they would surely have died there. Instead, exhausted and unaware of how much worse things could have become, they set off back to civilization, pushing through deep snow and struggling each evening to light fires in the damp. Fortunately the return crossing of the Shannon was simpler than the first, for they found a tree newly down across the river and made it quite easily to Ross's farm. There, they found everyone in turmoil: the bushranger Dunne had just passed through, as had been feared, and had robbed every hut in the area, including Ross's. By this time Jorgenson and his two companions looked like bushrangers themselves, with their guns and tattered clothes, not to mention the blade on Jorgenson's back.

Jorgenson and Colbert stayed with Ross while Logan travelled to Hobart to deliver the report and present Curr with a list of supplies and equipment needed for a second attempt. Curr, always hard to satisfy, was unconvinced by Jorgenson's praise of the land glimpsed beyond the Ouse, and disappointed that the trip had failed. But he understood the reasons for giving up, and applauded Jorgenson's willingness to try again. He sent Logan back with revised instructions, a freshly annotated sketch map, and a stern reminder: 'I trust you will continue to push forward with alacrity.'

Jorgenson re-equipped his party; they picked up fresh dogs, and set off again on 11 October 1826, following the same route. The weather was still grim, but the floods had eased, and this time they made it across both the Shannon and the Ouse with just a few days' delay. On the other side of the Ouse, they camped, and the next morning climbed a rocky outcrop to assess the land ahead. The view was good, but when Jorgenson tried to take bearings he found his compass needle reeling crazily around the dial: the explorer A.L. Meston, retracing Jorgenson's journeys over a century later, had the same experience. The rock was powerfully magnetic, and threw the compass off.

The little team continued towards the looming Walls of Jerusalem, wading through many smaller streams. They were permanently drenched from river water and rain, and their wet clothes pulled against the windward side of their bodies as they walked. In one particularly violent river, two of the dogs were nearly swept away. But at last they left the plains. The land turned into a bumpy mess of hills and valleys, strewn with stones. There were no kangaroo to hunt, so they had to live off their rapidly declining provisions. No trees were found with branches big enough to build shelters: they camped as best they could among the rocks. Rain poured down, and the little firewood they could rustle up was too wet to burn properly.

The next day brought them to the foothills of the Walls of Jerusalem, and now 'difficulties of no ordinary description' crowded in upon them. They had to walk through snowdrifts a metre and a half deep in places, jumping from rock to rock to avoid sinking. More snow continued to fall, 'in masses'. Pausing to look ahead, they saw that their troubles were only beginning. Between them and the next mountain lurked 'a frightful chasm' – 'a bottomless gulph!' – thickly packed with snow-covered scrub and draped in a strange heavy fog. The whole landscape looked impassable, and appearances were not deceptive. Although they are not forbiddingly high, the Walls of Jerusalem are not called walls for nothing. Routes exist, but they are clogged and difficult to nego-tiate, and the rest of the range forms one huge system of glacial hollows and slabs of rock, many with intimidating 'organ-pipe' formations running up them. With the benefit of maps a modern climber knows that the landscape just keeps getting worse, but Jorgenson did not have this advantage, and tried to advance in different directions, turning and detouring, hoping at every step for an improvement that would never come.

Stuck in a gully full of scrub when darkness fell that night, the party had to camp there – three tiny figures buried in a crook of the land-scape. The weather the next day was worse than ever. They hacked onwards, heading for a river they had glimpsed through the vegeta-tion. After much 'painful walking', they at last came to its banks, and managed to cross using a fallen pine tree. Veering away from the range, they followed this river to its source, a large lake: things seemed to be looking up. But this clearer landscape produced a fresh hell of its own. Instead of tangled scrub, they now found themselves in a deso-late nothingness.

'The dreary and barren country around us supplies nothing for food', wrote Jorgenson gloomily: 'even the crows had deserted this inhos-pitable region: our dogs were in danger of starving.' They fed the dogs out of their own sparse provisions, and spent a terrible night in the cold without sufficient dry wood to keep the fire going. Jorgenson's horror comes through in his report, although his overt concerns remained practical. 'No carts can ever cross in this direction; neither can sheep, nor cattle, be driven across, even in the summer season.'

More snow fell the next day; their clothes had been so badly torn in the scrub that they provided little protection. That night a gale blew in from the west. It was so cold that 'the snow on the two ends of the log of wood, which was burning in the middle, would not melt'. Another heavy fall that night raised the snow level by over half a metre; dawn presented 'a scene of desolation and terror'. Fog descended, too, leaving the explorers disoriented, lost in their own fear.

Jorgenson felt that they needed to descend to lower country as a matter of survival: 'every moment would increase our danger'. He gave up all thought of pressing on. They must just get out of the high country and back to the familiar world before they all died. But, trying to rouse his companions for the journey, he found that Colbert had been 'seized with a species of lethargy' and at first could not be persuaded to get up at all, a dangerous sign. Somehow Jorgenson got him in motion, and they slowly set off. All three men's feet were too numb to walk. Jorgenson cut strips of cloth to wrap around their boots to help them keep trudging through the snow.

And so they retreated, and as they descended away from the high ground the country eased. Life was reborn. By the following day, they were relieved to see kangaroo: a welcome sign of normality, and a source of fresh meat at last. The next day brought even more 'swarms of *Brush* and *Forest Kangaroo*'. They managed a good day's journey before camping on the shores of Lake Echo – which Jorgenson believed was Lake Fergus, twenty kilometres away, though he added: 'I could scarcely flatter myself, that after having observed no marks to steer by for four days past, my reckoning should be so correct.' The next day they saw cattle tracks, and at last reached proper settled territory on the River Clyde.

It had been a failed expedition, but they had to congratulate themselves on simply being alive. They rested for a few days, then all returned to Hobart on 1 November to collect nine weeks' pay. Colbert and Logan were apparently discharged, for they did not accompany Jorgenson on his subsequent trip.

Curr could be contrary. Last time, Jorgenson had sent him a glowing report on land seen from a distance, and he had expressed reservations. This time Jorgenson sent him a damning assessment of this sodden, labyrinthine wilderness based on close observation; yet Curr again insisted on reserving judgement, writing in his despatches: 'I shall not indulge in any vain conjectures on this head.' He commended Jorgenson's willingness to try yet again, however, and hoped that the knowledge gained on the first two trips could still be put to good use.

By Curr's usual stern standards his assessment of Jorgenson's efforts was remarkably positive. He did not seem to feel that Jorgenson had exaggerated his sufferings, or that he should have carried on further. This judgement was right, for Jorgenson had done a commendable job, despite mistaking some of his bearings. When A.L. Meston retraced parts of his journeys between 1927 and 1948, most of the territory still being unknown, and pieced together a reconstruction of where Jorgenson had been, he concluded that it was a 'quite creditable piece of exploration'.* Having shown where Jorgenson went wrong, he also showed why. Jorgenson was working from an almost blank map in almost zero visibility; his attempts at interpreting the landmarks he thought he saw, and deducing his bearings from them, were entirely reasonable. On the other hand, he also became his own worst enemy, as usual. He was so keen to impress Curr that he obscured genuine, careful exploration work under a blanket of bombast.

In one sense, nothing positive came out of Jorgenson's journey across the plateau, but his work was not wasted. He helped to prove an important negative: that the land was of no practical agricultural use, and that it was not feasible to transport stock across it. As the later explorer C.J. Binks has remarked, land-surveying in the Tasmanian west was 'largely a matter of negatives, of battling the country and the elements only to demonstrate that rich lands and mineral bonanzas did not exist' – while adding, in the process, a few hard-won, uncertain details to the maps of the day.

Roads were eventually built through nearby areas, though at first only near the coast. Just one was laid through the wildest part of the north-western interior, but it ran south of the Walls of Jerusalem. There is still no road through the wilderness where Jorgenson's expedition nearly died of exhaustion and exposure, and it does not seem too rash to guess that there never will be.

---

* Meston's conclusions, in quick summary, were that Jorgenson made several errors of identification: he thought he had seen Frenchman's Cap and Lake St Clair, but was wrong in both cases – he was much further to the north-east, and had never actually left the Central Plateau. His 'Peak like a Volcano' was the Western Wall of Jerusalem; and his 'bottomless gulph' was the gorge of the River Mersey. The lake in the desolated area was either Lake Ball or Lake Adelaide.

10

A rogue in grain

Jorgenson spent a few months in Hobart and Launceston, writing up his journal and doing clerical work for the Van Diemen's Land Company. Then in February 1827 he sailed to the company's new headquarters at Circular Head in the island's north-west corner, where the town of Stanley now stands, to join a new party for a third trip into the wilderness. This time they would try the journey the other way, starting from the west coast and penetrating inland as far as the place where his earlier party had given up, completing the loop.

The operation was larger and more complex than the previous ones. Curr wanted the overland group to be accompanied on the coastal stage of its journey by a whaleboat, which would sail alongside and keep it supplied with provisions. Six men would travel in the boat, and four would walk: Jorgenson, two juniors named James Dunn and Thomas Jones, and a more experienced company surveyor named Clement Lorymer, who was nominated the party leader. Jorgenson did not seem too pleased about this: he found it hard to relinquish his habit of leadership. His own account often seeks to create the impression that he was still leader himself, though it is strange that he was so keen to claim responsibility, for the trip was a disaster.

Lorymer was one of Curr's key men, but he was young and impulsive, and more than a little unreliable. He had once gone missing for ten days just before an expedition was due to depart, and at best his execution of his duties stopped short of rabid enthusiasm. His surviving travel journals serve mainly to emphasize how diligent Jorgenson was by comparison, in physical endurance and energy as well as in journal-keeping. On survey trips, Lorymer frequently stayed in his hut because he felt ill, or because hostile Aboriginal groups were about, or because the weather was inclement – excuses many people might find reasonable enough. But Jorgenson would never have been deterred by such things.

On 1 March 1827 the four-man party set off. The boat detoured around Cape Grim and, after a day or two, caught up with them. The plan was then to walk southward along the beach until they spotted a good route or reached the mouth of the Pieman River, about 160 kilometres away. There the boat would leave them, and they would strike out inland. Lorymer and Jorgenson argued almost daily about how close they were getting to this point. Invariably Lorymer thought they had travelled at least twice the distance estimated by Jorgenson. The first quarrel occurred when they camped the first evening: Lorymer said they had walked over twenty miles (thirty-two kilometres), while Jorgenson thought it was more like eleven. Modern maps confirm that, in these arguments, Jorgenson's figures were usually closer to the truth. Jorgenson's account suggests a good reason for this. According to him, Lorymer paced out his distances by counting each step as a full yard – almost a metre – even when walking through thick undergrowth.

The next day it was again Jorgenson who showed himself the more skilful bushman. Spotting a tea tree bush, he advised his companions that fresh water must be nearby and, sure enough, they soon came to a lagoon full of wild duck. Refreshed from the water, they walked on towards the coast, and for the next few days followed a beach beaten by a 'prodigious surf', the whaleboat trailing them out to sea and landing wherever it could. The shore became increasingly rugged. No game was seen anywhere; they had dogs with them as always, but there was no successful hunting yet. At first no people appeared, either, though they saw traces of Aboriginal huts and fires.

Jorgenson then went off by himself for a couple of days to explore a mountain inland, and while he was away Lorymer and the others encountered an Aboriginal group of around twenty on the beach. Both sides were equally surprised to see each other, but the meeting was friendly: spears and guns alike were laid aside. Four or five young women in the tribe seemed particularly vivacious, full of jokes and laughter. Everyone parted 'on the best terms', Jorgenson was told.

But the next morning, a couple of the white men woke up with a burning desire to follow the group and abduct some of the lively young women for themselves – not an unusual practice among the whites in the north-west. They ran into the bush with guns at dawn; fortunately they found no trace of their quarry, and they 'returned in the evening, wet, cold, and hungry, cursing their ill luck, and regretted that they had gone on a fool's errand'. Jorgenson rejoined the others that evening as well, and heard the story. No more people were seen on the journey.

They walked on, fording the many rivers that poured down into the ocean from the ranges inland, and passing one stretch of spectacular sand dunes, as high as mountains. Lorymer was sure they would reach the broad Pieman River soon. Indeed, he thought they should be there already. But there was no sign of it, and Jorgenson again accused him of mistaking his distances. Lorymer believed they had travelled 125 miles (200 kilometres) around the coast; Jorgenson correctly maintained that they were far short of this.

The next time the whaleboat landed, they discussed what to do. They were behind schedule; the boat was now due elsewhere. Jorgenson also thought he had recognized a mountain inland from his earlier travels, and was confident that he could find a way through to the Central Plateau from here, without going as far as the Pieman at all. The four men therefore packed up all the supplies they could carry, buried more near the beach in case they needed them on the return journey, and struck out with their dogs into the mountains of the interior.

The first few days' hiking took them into the Norfolk Range, up and down one tough rise after another, and through fern-filled gullies between each spur. At night they could find no level land to camp on; it was very cold, and there was little dry wood for burning. They spent several nights huddled in blankets around paltry, smoky fires while Jorgenson and Lorymer continued arguing about the distance they had travelled, before settling down to try to sleep as best they could, bracing themselves against rolling downhill.

Continuing, they came to the bank of a river they all thought must be the Pieman at last; it was actually one of the Pieman's tributaries, the Donaldson. They crawled down its banks and crossed with difficulty over slippery rocks. Broken trees lay criss-crossed and tumbled everywhere, a sign of violent floods in the past. The climb up the other side was tougher than they expected: it was nearly dark when they reached the top, and then they found themselves stopped by a single, massive fallen tree, as high as their heads and extending far into the darkness on each side. They waited until the moon rose before attempting to continue. When it came, the milky light showed them a ruined, inhuman scene: fallen trees, rocks torn from the earth – 'a complete wreck of nature'. Everything pointed to some furious flood, even this far above the river. They feared that they were stuck behind the giant tree, but one of the men, Thomas Jones, managed to lift himself up. By clinging to branches on the other side and feeling the ground with his feet, he found a spot clear enough to jump into.

In his journal, written in the midst of this tangle by moonlight, Jorgenson wondered whether humans had passed through this country before. It seemed abandoned by animal life, and almost malevolently determined to repel intruders, every rock and tree being 'well calculated to arrest the progress of the traveller, sternly forbidding man to traverse those places which nature had selected for its own silent and awful repose'.

The next day, in rain and high wind, they made their way up another mountain, the Longback. From the top, they saw scrub and chasms below them. These did not look bad from a distance, but as they descended they found themselves sinking into an almost solid growth of brushwood. The ground was steeply tilted, and it was almost impossible to keep their footing as they slashed through with sword and machete. Somehow they kept going, but they only made two miles that day. Dunn injured himself, and could walk only slowly.

It became apparent that, even if the rest of them could struggle through gully after gully to the other side of the range, which still seemed to stretch endlessly in front of them, there was no way Dunn could make it. Between every mountain there would be a pit full of snares: the higher the mountain, the deeper the gullies. The dogs were starving. Soon the men would be too, and there was no game to be had in this thick scrub. In any case, such land could never be used for stock and carts, and it was certainly no good for pasture. Jorgenson now realized how lucky his earlier party had been to be twice blocked before they reached the heart of this wilderness.

And so, once again, the journey was abandoned. The men returned through the scrub and re-climbed the mountain they had just negotiated. The next evening Jones went hunting with the dogs and caught two wombats. This success cheered them up so much that they briefly wondered, while the wombats were roasting, if they should carry on a little longer. But the meat tasted foul: they decided to stick to the original decision. Jorgenson later advised his readers that only 'absolute necessity' could ever justify eating a wombat.

It took them a long time to get back to the coast, struggling through rain all the way. The dogs were weakening: even when game was seen, they had trouble catching it. The best hunter of the three, Fanny, was heavily pregnant. Hunger had driven the second-best, Spring, into the habit of eating anything he caught himself before the humans could take it. One day, hunting with Spring, Lorymer and Jones saw him gnawing at a kangaroo, and one of the two men stupidly fired his gun, perhaps only meaning to scare the dog off. Instead, he killed him. They had now lost their only remaining hunter. The third dog was useless, and had difficulty even in walking. Jorgenson later said that Lorymer was responsible; in fact, a report by Curr suggests that it was Jones who killed Spring, and that Lorymer rather nobly took the blame.

At last they made it back to the bay where they had buried their extra rations, and spent a cold night there, but at least now they had bread, and flour to make damper. They headed slowly back along the coast, enduring a fierce wind full of sand all the way. The weather was worse than on the journey down: most places where the boat had landed before were now unusable. They passed the sand dunes again and, incredibly, Jorgenson found the energy to climb them. At the top he discovered that the wind had hollowed them out inside, so that a man standing at their centre could see nothing but sky. The sand around him resembled 'an ocean agitated by a strong breeze'.

They passed a fine Aboriginal hut which they had not seen before, large enough to accommodate a dozen or more people. Jorgenson was impressed, and described it as 'a complete piece of Gothic architecture, the shape of a dome, and presenting all the first rudiments of that Science'. Its wooden struts had been carefully 'steamed and bent by fire'; the low entrance was perfectly designed to afford protection from the wind. He thought highly of the coastal tribes' craftsmanship. Indeed he thought well of them in general. 'The natives seem an inoffensive and friendly race,' he wrote. 'Frank and generous treatment may render them of some service to White men who should visit this quarter.' But honourable treatment was something they rarely received, as the exploits of Jorgenson's own companions testify, and explorers in the area never sought Aboriginal expertise.

Even the restocked supplies soon began to disappear, and the men had to ration their bread and flour. All the sugar had been used up some time ago; now they ran out of tea as well. They tried improvising with local herbs, but 'the miserable trash produced lassitude, weakness, and great looseness'. Fanny gave birth to her pups, which were either lost in the bush or quietly disposed of by the humans. And still it kept raining: 'The sea was in a violent agitation, and the rain pouring down.' After another day or two of this, Jorgenson's journal entries lost their vigour, degenerating for once into mere notes. 'We felt the cold keenly – frosty in the night.'

A few days later the weather improved a little and they revived, only to be halted almost immediately by a swollen river, which was now far wider than when they had passed it before. They crossed it by building a raft out of spars from a shipwreck, conveniently found strewn on the beach nearby. The raft was so heavy that only one person could cross at a time; they pulled it back across using a rope made of blankets, for they had no proper rope.

By 5 April, just over a week after returning to the coast, they had used up the flour and had only scraps of bread left. The two dogs, now looking skeletal, loped into the bush and reappeared with blood around their jaws. Jones was sent off with them to search for remains of their forbidden kill; he came back with skin and a piece of tail from a kangaroo, but with only one dog, Boxer: the one who could not hunt. Jones said that Fanny had run off (perhaps searching for her lost pups), but Jorgenson was sceptical. 'From the manner in which the fellow told his story, there could be little doubt of his having kicked the bitch in his savage disposition; for it was his practice when the dogs would

189

not show [i.e. give up the game], to beat them unmercifully with the butt end of a musket.' Even Boxer abandoned them a day or two later.

On 6 April, the men solemnly shared out the last bits of bread. Walking on, they caught a glimpse of Circular Head, but here they made a serious mistake, trying to head directly for it instead of following the coast around. They thus became embroiled in an expanse of scrubby mudflats, divided by endless rivers and channels. This route was far slower and more tiring than the longer one around the coast. The closer they came to Circular Head, the worse the difficulties became. 'On this and the following day, the party often stuck fast in the mud, and some of them, through weakness and exhaustion, seemed inclined to remain in that situation and let the tide flow over them', wrote Jorgenson. There was no fresh water either, as the flats were salty. Dunn, still suffering from his injuries, became so thirsty that he drank sea water, which sent him half mad.

On the 7th, they arrived at the Duck River, at a place now called Smithton. This was only twenty-four kilometres from Circular Head, but the river was deep and fast, and the men were halted in their muddy tracks. They gathered enough branches and river driftwood to build another raft, and tied a blanket-rope to it as before. But it was difficult even to launch it safely: they slid from the slippery banks into water up to their waists every time they tried. They cut more wood to construct a makeshift launch platform: the raft was placed on the platform and Jorgenson boarded it with a pole in his hands, to push himself off. But as soon as he slid the raft off the platform, it sank. Only the pole, which he was still holding and which stuck fast in the mud, saved him from drowning, and at last he managed to haul himself back on land. What struck him most about this drama was the inactivity of Thomas Jones, who had been making 'brags' throughout the journey that he was a strong swimmer who could cross deep rivers with a knapsack on his back, though they never saw him doing so. He made no attempt either to cross or to save Jorgenson when he was hanging on to the pole for dear life.

Lorymer now wanted to try swimming across himself, without the raft, but the others talked him out of trying it at such a broad point. They walked upstream a few kilometres but found no improvement; it was now late, so they camped for the night. Lorymer woke up the next morning full of renewed determination, and insisted on trying again at the original place downriver. It was worth the risk, he argued. If they did not try something soon, they would become too weak to do anything at all. It was now Sunday morning, and they had not eaten since Friday.

They returned to the previous day's spot and Lorymer 'asserted with much confidence that altho' he was not a good swimmer, yet he could strike out well, and swim several yards', which was all he needed: there seemed only to be one stretch in the middle that was really deep. He stripped, tied a length of blanket-rope around his waist, and waded through the mud into the torrent. At first he seemed to make good progress, but as soon as he reached the deep middle section he sank abruptly out of view. When his companions tried to pull him back the blanket tore, 'and after rising twice he sank', never to come up again. Jones was urged to plunge in and save him but, to no one's surprise, 'the wretched fellow stood aghast' and admitted at last that he could not swim.

They stood staring at the river for a long time, hoping that by some miracle Lorymer would emerge. He did not. They searched downstream for his body, but there was no sign that anything had happened at all. Either he had been swept further downriver, or his body had washed up out of view on the other side. There was nothing more to be done. The three men eventually abandoned the spot, and trekked back upstream towards the place where they had camped. They kept going, too weak from distress and hunger to ponder up further solutions, and a kilometre and a half beyond the camping spot they found a fallen tree across the river, on which they crossed easily.

On the other bank they returned to the scene of the drowning, but there was still no sign of Lorymer, so they headed onward again and reached the spit of land leading out to Circular Head. They were now just an hour or two away from the settlement, but after two and a half days without food they were so desperate that, when they saw gulls picking at a raggedy fish-tail on the beach, they fell on the tail eagerly, scorched it quickly over a fire, and devoured it. At about three o'clock that afternoon, they reached Circular Head and safety.

Curr passed on his own cool analysis of the disaster in his report to company officials a few days later. He accused the party of losing their nerve after Dunn's injury and of wasting time on the way back; the shooting of the dog had also been reprehensible. Nor could he understand how they had got into such trouble on the final stretch of their route, when they were only a short distance from home. Lorymer's death was entirely avoidable; 'The rest of the party crossed without difficulty on a tree about four miles higher up, and subsequent researches shew that they might have forded the River with ease in two other places very near the spot where Mr Lorymer was drowned.' He did add that the only person fully to blame for this was Lorymer himself, for he 'exposed himself to the danger without any occasion and in opposition to the advice of the people with him'.

Jorgenson criticized Lorymer too, but laid even more blame at the feet of the company and of Curr. No party should enter an unknown part of the bush without having proper rope with them, he wrote, reasonably enough: 'had we been provided with lines, Mr LORYMER would not have been drowned. We asked for them before leaving Circular Head, but they could not be obtained.' They should also have had better hunting dogs. There were several excellent dogs at Circular Head, but they had been told these were needed for another expedition: a trip to nearby Cape Grim, which Jorgenson would consider a mere 'party of pleasure'.

Jorgenson turned completely against Curr after this: he questioned his organizational expertise and accused him of overplaying the innate obstacles to Tasmanian travel. It was difficult all right, but this was no Siberia or Sahara: so long as expeditions were properly planned it should be possible to traverse any part of the island without danger to life.*

He had his reasons for sniping at Curr, for Curr had also turned on him. The official judgement that Lorymer was to blame for his own death might seem to imply that Jorgenson had acquitted himself adequately, but the failed expedition led Curr to look more sternly at

---

* Jorgenson also had fun with a book Curr had published about Tasmania several years earlier, apparently 'to beguile the tedious hours of a gloomy winter's passage round Cape Horn'. 'This is one of the most singular and extraordinary reasons we have ever seen given for writing a book,' he remarked. 'Because time hung heavy on his hands, the world must have the benefit of his gloomy cogitations' – as if he himself had never written a book for that reason.

Jorgenson's previous explorations. In a despatch to the London office he cast aspersions at Jorgenson's honesty, suggesting that his earlier report had been 'in part a fabrication' – surely an unfair suggestion, despite Jorgenson's errors of identification.

Jorgenson's career as explorer had been marked by misfortune: his three journeys had achieved only negative results, and Lorymer's death – the only one to take place among early Van Diemen's Land Company explorers, despite the dangers – should never have happened. It took the edge off his enthusiasm; much as Jorgenson enjoyed bush life, it may have been a relief not to be sent immediately on a fourth attempt. Besides, he had another idea in mind: his travels had given him a perfect subject for his first Tasmanian book.

Perhaps Curr would have entrusted Jorgenson with another expedition after all, but, typically, Jorgenson sabotaged his own chances before the question of his next trip arose. On 7 June 1827, in Circular Head, he learned that his partial pardon – the ticket of leave he had applied for the previous year – had been granted. So great was his jubilation that he ran out of the company office without a word of explanation, picked up a boat to Hobart, and proceeded to get drunk and disorderly, a misdemeanour for which he was fined five shillings. He was lucky: the punishment could have been the removal of his ticket of leave, just days after receiving it.

The company still expected him to report for duty at their Hobart office. Although Jorgenson was free to choose his own employer, he was obliged to work out a period of notice like any other departing employee. But he did not show up. Later, he struggled to explain his folly to himself:

> I can scarcely tell how it was that on my arrival in Hobart Town I did not attend at Mr Curr's office; I was sent for several times, but declined. The allowance made me was certainly very good, and I could have no reasonable grounds for quitting the service. It is true, that on two occasions Mr Curr, when in an ill-humour, had spoken harshly to me; yet after all my conduct was too hasty . . . I have since reflected that the Company's agent behaved himself towards me with great lenity.

Lacking a job, he lived on his back pay for a while and put his energies into his writing project: an idiosyncratic, book-length account of the Van Diemen's Land Company and his own explorations. This appeared in instalments in 1828 in the *Colonial Advocate*, a paper recently founded by the island's foremost publisher Andrew Bent. Jorgenson's account was widely read, for there was considerable interest in the company, and it later appeared in separate form with a London imprint. It gave him a chance to vent his feelings about Curr and to promote his own adventures, albeit anonymously, for all convict writers, even ticket-of-leave men, had to be discreet. Arthur forbade them from writing for the press.*

Jorgenson also wrote other pieces for Bent, including a disquisition on phrenology in which he mentioned that the Phrenological Society of Edinburgh had requested a cast 'of the skull of an individual in this Colony, who, although now almost forgotten among the wild woods of Tasmania in his very humble station of life, has figured in courtly scenes, and made much stir on the literary and political world of Europe'. Despite his dismissal of phrenology in the *Religion of Christ*, Jorgenson was sufficiently flattered to be intrigued, as anyone would be.† But he did not respond to Edinburgh straight away, or if he did nothing came of it: 'by some mismanagement and blunder the thing was not at that time effected'. Seven years later he asked Hooker to find out if the society still wanted his bumps, but whatever interest had existed in 1827 had evaporated by 1834: alas, no bust of Jorgenson was ever made.

Jorgenson was to work for Bent again in later years. Yet they never saw eye to eye on politics, for Jorgenson became a supporter of Arthur,

* This ban was ostensibly to prevent convicts undermining their employers through the public papers. In fact, it was part of Arthur's generally repressive approach to press freedom. He did all he could to destroy editors and publishers who disagreed with him, and none suffered more than Andrew Bent himself, who was imprisoned several times and had newspapers confiscated as fast as he could start new ones up. The *Colonial Advocate* lasted only a few months, closing in October 1828.

† Phrenologists were often interested in people they regarded as exceptional: George Combe had written about the famous murderers Burke and Hare, and about the killer and compulsive liar David Haggart, whom he examined both alive and after execution. Haggart's skull was more convenient for study than the living cranium of Jorgen Jorgenson on the other side of the world, but distance did not seem to deter the Phrenological Society's enthusiasts.

while Bent was one of the Lieutenant-Governor's most vocal opponents.* Jorgenson wrote in a job application that 'in the whole Colony
there exists not a person better affected towards the government than
myself', although of course he would say that in a letter seeking government work. But the praise continued in his other writings, even after
Arthur had left the island. He often said such things as 'Colonel Arthur
succeeded in making Van Diemen's Land an *honest* country', and he
observed that the Lieutenant-Governor only seemed strict and tough
because these were the qualities needed in a tough country. He was
amazed to see how a place could be transformed by one gifted individual – an almost Napoleonic phenomenon. Perhaps Arthur struck
him as the kind of leader he could have been himself in Iceland: a
wise despot, sometimes stern but never brutal, and always driven by
the highest philanthropy.

One of Arthur's radical tactics for maintaining order was his creation
of a new kind of Field Police, staffed by convicts as well as free
employees. This increased police numbers while also encouraging keen
convicts to work towards liberation. The job was difficult, dangerous,
physically exhausting and guaranteed to inspire resentment among
fellow convicts: it was perfect for Jorgenson. He realized this sometime in early 1828, and applied for a post as Convict Constable in
the Midlands town of Oatlands, working for the local Police Magistrate
Thomas Anstey. He got the job, and travelled to Oatlands to start
work in May.

Field Police work gratified Jorgenson's enthusiasm for Arthur's policies, and also used a wide range of his talents: for spying and detecting,
for bush-trekking, and even for report-writing. It kept him busy, which
was important. There was nothing he loved more than to be out
striding over the wildest countryside in pursuit of a hunch or a tip,
often getting up before dawn and leaving his fellow constables behind:
it was not unusual for him to start at two or three o'clock in the
morning. As he wrote once to Anstey, 'I could not remain inactive if
I would . . . I could wish my whole time to be filled up.'

---

* Jorgenson and Bent eventually fell out, and Jorgenson successfully sued for unpaid wages.
He later found a more congenial employer in the man who had given him his sword: the
pro-Arthur publisher James Ross. In the 1830s Ross hired Jorgenson for work on his own
Hobart Town Chronicle, and issued the *Shred of autobiography* in his *Almanack*.

Most people would have been nervous of hiking alone through thick bush, but the temperate Midlands held little to scare a man who had recently tried to slash his way with a sword over the Walls of Jerusalem. The hills around Oatlands were already well developed as pasture, supporting a growing population of sheep, which were mostly ear-tagged and left to wander freely as in Iceland, though some farmers put up fences. Between the open fields there were patches of forest, however, some of them on mountainous 'tiers', and these were the problem areas. They made convenient hideouts for the two main types of violent attacker: hostile Aboriginal tribes, now increasingly given to looting and raiding settlements, and gangs of white sheep-thieves and bushrangers, who could be ruthless if disturbed. Jorgenson describes how one man, unfortunate enough to have witnessed a cattle-thieving gang at work, was 'wrapped up in a green bullock hide, and roasted alive by a large fire'. Physically this was gentler territory than the west, but in human terms it was fiercer. A list of place names mentioned in Jorgenson's autobiography gives a flavour: 'Murderer's Plains, Murderer's Tier, Deadman's Point, Killman's Point, Hell's Corner, Four-square Gallows, Devil's Backbone'. Many landmarks were also named after individual bushrangers, like the several Brady's Lookouts, or Mike Howe's Marsh (later misheard as 'My Cow's Marsh', a version that stuck in some guidebooks). Yet farmers lived in these areas, often with wives and small children. The nearest neighbour could be miles away.

Life in the bush suited Jorgenson, and it did him good to feel a sense of mission. The combination of beauty and danger exhilarated him, and again he felt as if his own invigorated state of mind was reflected in the landscape around him. 'Although the service was some-times severe,' he wrote, 'travelling by myself, and enjoying those contemplations which the sublime and beautiful prospects of nature inspire, yet this mode of life was so suitable to my disposition, that I scarcely was ever more happy.'

It was not just in the bush that he faced danger. Another part of his job involved sitting in pubs listening for information, especially in 'sly grog-shops': unlicensed liquor retailers which invariably became hotbeds of criminal conspiracy. (Surprisingly, no one in the Midlands seemed to know at first who Jorgenson was, and he was able to work incognito for some time.) This was pleasant: Jorgenson was never averse to sitting in pubs. But as time went on and people began to guess his true role, the work became more risky. Convicts followed a reverse morality to that of ordinary folk: as Jorgenson explained in his autobiography, if one heard someone described as a 'fine man, he will do what is right', this meant a character who would join in any criminal scheme and would never help the authorities, even on pain of death. But if a man was said to be 'a rogue in grain, and would be glad of a chance to injure anyone', he was probably a law-abiding citizen. In this mirror world, Jorgenson was now unmistakably a rogue in grain, and he knew that anyone who sought revenge could easily follow him into the bush and knock him on the head or sink a musket ball in his brain, then dump him in a wooded gully.

On his first day, he almost lost the job because he could not find the country house of his new employer Thomas Anstey: when he finally arrived, a day late, a plain, stout man 'dressed somewhat like a farmer who looks after his own fields' stomped out of the back door and greeted him brusquely. Taken aback, Jorgenson realized that he looked just as bad, with his 'fustian jacket, and a pair of trowsers of the same stuff, nothing the better for long wear, a stock around the neck, with sundry holes in it, and a broad-brimmed straw hat on my head, which from long service, having been buffetted about in various ways, presented a most grotesque appearance.' There was also the sword slung across his back, as always. The two ungentlemanly figures eyed each other nervously.

Jorgenson's first impressions of Anstey turned out to be misleading: he was a fair employer and a kindly man, admired by all who knew him. Meeting him was another step forward in Jorgenson's Tasmanian career. Anstey once remarked that he had only contempt for ne'er-do-wells, but he clearly did not think of Jorgenson this way. Indeed, Jorgenson was not a ne'er-do-well so much as a do-well-at-first-but-then-mess-it-all-up, a fact that was to become fully evident only later in his Tasmanian life. Anstey soon discovered his employee's weaknesses, but he also liked him. He respected his energies and talents, and his relatively subtle understanding of the Aboriginal people, who were to become a central concern of Anstey's over the coming years.

Jorgenson proved him right, and got off to an excellent start. By May of the following year, he was able to announce to Arthur that, by exerting himself 'in a manner never before done by any prisoner of the Crown in this Island', he had helped to capture over fifty livestock thieves and outlaws in a few months. His greatest coup was the capture of several members of a large sheep-thieving gang led by one William Sheldon. Working with police at nearby Campbell Town, Jorgenson captured two of the gang on 1 December 1828: William Axford and his girlfriend, an Irish runaway convict named Norah Corbett or Cobbett – a woman who was to transform Jorgenson's life, not entirely for the better. Both prisoners were confined in Oatlands Gaol, and pressure was put on them to improve their own situation by giving information against their colleagues, who were still at large. Axford was not particularly co-operative, but after a day or two Norah Corbett caved in and agreed to 'split' – to give evidence as a Crown witness – and to collaborate with Jorgenson in laying traps for other gang members.

A twenty-three-year-old milkmaid from County Cork, Norah had been in the colony since the previous August, having been transported for life for theft. The registers describe her as five foot four inches (1.6 metres), with dark brown hair, brown eyes, and a scar on her right arm; she was illiterate, and always had to sign official documents with a simple cross. Her prison report described her bluntly as 'Bad', but the ship's surgeon, for whom she had worked as cook during the journey out, had considered her 'Good', likely to make a valuable servant 'to any farmer wanting a woman of her abilities'. The prison's damning assessment was more accurate. She turned out to be a persistent offender and an alcoholic, continually in trouble for drunkenness and unauthorized absences. When drunk, as she was whenever she had the opportunity, she also tended to become violent. In mid-1828, she absconded from her employer and vanished; her name appeared in newspaper lists of convict runaways for many months, sometimes with a note that she had 'escaped apprehension by being disguised in male attire'. In fact, she had taken up with Axford and joined Sheldon's gang in the eastern bushland near Oyster Bay, a place where it was easy to disappear, at least until Jorgenson got on the trail.

Now that she was a government witness, Norah was released from gaol and placed in Jorgenson's charge: it was his job to protect her from revenge, ensure that her evidence remained uncorrupted, and deliver her to court in good shape. Meanwhile she was also installed as a decoy at the nearby Campbell Town Inn, a haunt of outlaws, who did not realize that it was actually run by another police constable. Jorgenson, still being unknown in Campbell Town, moved in as well.

One by one, over the following weeks, most of the rest of the gang were rounded up. When not at the inn, Jorgenson continued combing the surrounding hills in search of Sheldon, who was eventually captured not by him but by Gilbert Robertson, Chief Constable of a different district. Meanwhile, the news gradually leaked out that Jorgenson and Norah were both police spies. Jorgenson himself was used to the dangers of this, but Norah was not; it was now her turn to experience the terrors of being a 'rogue in grain'. A report in the *Hobart Town Courier* in March 1829 noted: 'Serious fears have been entertained here during the last two days that Jorgan [*sic*] Jorgenson, and a most important witness, named Norah Corbett, under his charge, will be put to death by some of the murderous wretches denounced by this woman. Her important disclosures render her life of immense value to the community.'

The same issue of the *Courier* also passed on a rumour that Norah Corbett was 'lamenting deeply her breach of promise of marriage with Mr William Elliott': probably a mistake for William Axford. She was unlikely to be lamenting it that much, for, while she and Jorgenson were staying together at the Campbell Town Inn, a romance began. It quickly became serious, at least on his side, and she seemed to have no objection. She said once that he asked her to marry him as early as December 1828, just weeks after their first meeting. The marriage was actually delayed for two years,* but all evidence suggests that Jorgenson fell in love with Norah at first sight, with all the irrational passion of a man approaching fifty who (so far as we know) had never really been in love before.

Sheldon and his gang were tried at Hobart's Supreme Court over a series of days in May; Norah appeared as a witness at three of the trials. Both she and Jorgenson needed guarding. In a petition to Arthur later that month, Jorgenson described how his work had earned him such 'ill-will and hatred' from criminal networks on the island that

---

* There may have been a falling-out. Norah sought permission to marry someone else in the meantime, a John George Houskie, but the marriage never took place.

his life had almost become a burden, and he felt 'harrassed beyond conception'. Naturally he made particularly heavy weather of it to Arthur, as the purpose of the petition was to seek a conditional pardon, the next step in the ascent towards freedom. Thomas Anstey added his own note supporting Jorgenson, and remarking, 'In the many signal services rendered by Jorgen Jorgenson to the Community, I consider his to be one of those rare cases in which a Convict may, without presumption, ask the Government for his Emancipation.'

But before he had a chance to send it, Anstey was obliged to cross out his own note and scrawl the amendment, 'All rendered abortive by the sentence passed on Jorgenson in Hobarton on the same day!' Jorgenson had suffered another of his typical reversals, just when everyone was admiring him most.

What had happened was (Jorgenson said) no fault of his own. He and Norah had travelled to Hobart for the trials, and Norah was ordered to lodge in the Waterloo Tavern during their stay. Jorgenson did not think it was a good idea to put her in a pub. He feared that she would go off the rails and lose her ability to testify calmly, and even that her enemies would ply her with drink and talk her into changing her evidence. 'I do know, and I know it from long experience, that she will be tampered with,' he wrote; 'she will not take money, but her feelings and her fears will be called into action. I know it.'

But he could do nothing except watch her closely and beg the publican to prevent her drinking anything until the week's hearings were finished. For a while, all seemed to go well. The first morning session passed uneventfully, and she drank only porter at lunchtime: it was stronger spirits Jorgenson was worried about. She made it through the afternoon session as well, but then, as she left the courtroom, a man 'actually came out in the street with a full glass to her', and other suspicious types gathered round and hustled her off to the Waterloo Tavern. Jorgenson followed them and saw what he had dreaded: Norah sitting among nine or ten men with a glass of gin in front of her.

He had fretted about her losing her cool, but in fact he was the one to fly into a rage. He rushed in, pulled Norah from her chair, and swore and raved so violently that an officer was called. At the magistrates' office, he was charged with drunkenness, violence, the use of indecent language, and what Jorgenson himself described as 'certain very unmannerly actions'. He could not justify his behaviour or produce witnesses in his defence, so he was pronounced guilty. Later he claimed that he could have defended himself, but did not wish to damage Norah's character and credibility in the middle of the trials: he kept quiet in order to preserve his own 'handy-work'.

The magistrates recommended his suspension from the Field Police, but he later managed to avert this by writing to Arthur and other authorities pointing out that such public disgrace would both encourage criminals and deter the honest from joining the police. People would think, 'Here is this busy fellow been exerting himself for sixteen months in bring[ing] depredators to light, and now what has he gotten for his pains?' He also denied that he had been drunk: no one had ever seen him the worse for wear on duty, he pointed out.

> In the man who is giving himself up to the habits of intoxica-
> tion there is always some interruption of intellect and labour,
> some nervous affection about him . . . this is not the case with
> me. – I never in my life drank before dinner, and never after
> dinner till all my work was over, and if required I have gone on
> writing the whole night. And the same in my journeys through
> the Island.

His aggressive actions were merely the consequence of being placed in a difficult situation with 'a wild Irish girl'. The witnesses had mis-interpreted his demonstrative body language: 'by the manner of throwing out my arms, and by speaking with eagerness and vehemence on any subject which greatly interests me, people who do not know me think me excited by something else than the interest of the thing that I have at heart.' The only thing exciting him in this case was his highly developed sense of responsibility.

Jorgenson got his job back, though his application for pardon was delayed. The twelve sheep-thieving trials turned out well: Norah gave the rest of her evidence competently and the affair ended with several convictions – although there was obviously a lot of 'splitting', for sentences were light. Even Sheldon turned Crown witness, and was imprisoned for just a few months. William Axford pleaded guilty, and together with four other defendants was sentenced to seven years' imprisonment.

The case over, Norah was assigned to a series of households in remote country locations, to keep her out of further trouble and protect her from reprisals. In Jorgenson's later application for permission to marry her, he said that he could not help looking 'with infinite compassion on a human creature . . . who is continually harrassed, and exposed to the utmost danger . . . The unfortunate woman knows no safety from insult and ill-treatment except in the far recesses of the Bush.' She behaved well and was granted her ticket of leave at the end of that year, on 26 December 1829.

Meanwhile, Jorgenson went back to Oatlands and to police work, which from now on concentrated not on bushrangers and livestock thieves, but on a much more elusive and sophisticated type of opponent.

11

The unknown

The Aboriginal people of Tasmania had been cut off from those of the mainland for eight to ten thousand years, after the land bridge to southern Australia became submerged. Living on in isolation, they developed different physical characteristics – wool-like hair, reddish-brown skin, heavier facial features – and also a different culture. Their technology was perhaps the simplest in the world, though it was well adapted for life on the island. They lost some mainland techniques, ceasing to make bone tools or to fish with spears, though coastal shellfish formed part of their diet and they were skilled in diving to collect it. At some stage in their history they had produced rock art; they also continued to decorate their own bodies with incised lines and circles, just as mainlanders did. Otherwise little is now known of their sense of art, community or spirituality. The total population was small, but apparently stable: they probably numbered somewhere between two and seven thousand when the Europeans arrived in the late eighteenth century. A few decades later, under the invaders' influence, their numbers had fallen to just a couple of hundred. And by the end of the nineteenth century, they had ceased to exist as a full, independent race, surviving only through descendants of mixed blood.

To this day, no one is sure exactly what caused this catastrophe, since official records confirm only a few hundred Aboriginal deaths.

It is obvious that this is not the whole story. As Jorgenson himself wrote in his history of the subject, archives shed insufficient light on the truth of events and personal accounts by white colonists could not be relied upon: they were as likely to deny killings they did commit as to exaggerate those they did not, out of bravado. He could only conclude: 'I feel convinced that some very barbarous and wanton acts of cruelty have been by some of the brutal part of our population committed on the Blacks, but in the absence of positive proof I cannot as a faithful historian place on record as a fact that which I can only express as an opinion.' The same constraint applies today. The popular supposition that the decline was caused by whites engaging in large-scale massacres for sport is not generally accepted, though all writers agree that unprovoked shootings formed part of the story. Other factors probably included disease, debilitation, demoralization, failures of understanding, administrative incompetence, and some other terrible Factor X. As the historian James Boyce has argued, there remains a 'deep mystery' in Tasmania which cannot be adequately tackled by explanations pretending to certainty; any attempt to do so without recognizing the mystery 'dismisses the unknown, treating with contempt the empty tomb that confronts every history rooted in Van Diemen's Land earth'.*

During the first few years of the European presence, encounters had been sometimes friendly, sometimes hostile, and mostly just mystifying on both sides. Then, as white settlements became established, relationships followed divergent patterns in different areas. Immigrants to the north-western coastal and island parts were mainly solitary male sealers, at least until the Van Diemen's Land Company arrived, and there was a lot of sexual contact between them and the indigenous women. In the central districts, where Jorgenson was now working, the situation was different. Personal contacts were rarer: the settlers

---

* Standard interpretations of Tasmanian Aboriginal history have recently undergone upheaval following a dramatic revisionist attack by Keith Windschuttle questioning both the interpretations and much of the data relied upon by more established historians. Counter-attacks and defences have since been mounted, but at the time of writing it is not clear how things will look when the dust has fully settled. Boyce's remark is aimed at Windschuttle, but it could apply to anyone who attempts a too-tidy explanation of the subject.

often lived with their own families, and had no need for companion-ship. Some trading and gift-giving took place, but on the whole meet-ings were non-existent or downright unfriendly. The settlers and their hired stockmen probably took pot shots at Aboriginal passers-by to keep them at bay, and if they killed any they were unlikely to report the matter to the authorities. In turn, the local people occasionally filched items from remote huts; they developed a particular liking for blankets (desirable in the freezing Tasmanian winter), tea, sugar and flour, as well as miscellaneous knick-knacks. Jorgenson once found a stash of loot including sheep shears, bottles, mirrors, a teapot and a pair of trousers.

But at first there was no systematic plan of plunder or mob violence on the Aboriginal side. Things were not completely tranquil, but the settlers found their own situation quite liveable. Some prided them-selves on having achieved a friendly understanding with the indige-nous population; others simply did not trouble their minds about them much. In the mid-1820s, however, the situation changed.

The first signs came in 1824, with several seemingly random attacks on settlers and their servants; two houses were set on fire. Each year after that there were more arson attacks, more assaults and more robberies, many committed by Aboriginal groups of a hundred or more. These were not done purely for gain: the purpose was un-mistakably to inflict damage for its own sake. Livestock were killed, women and children in farmhouses were attacked while the men were out in the fields, and the men themselves were often stalked and speared while at their work. In 1828, the year Jorgenson joined the police force, there were seventy-eight assaults on individuals, and around seventy attacks on huts and dwellings. Clearly, the members of the two central tribes – known to the Europeans as the Big River and Oyster Bay people – had decided to change tactics and to launch what looked very much like a guerrilla war against their invaders.

This shift may have been a response to a rise in the numbers of settlers' farms and fences in the Midlands, which surged in the early 1820s. Most farmers did not bother with fences, but enough were prob-ably built to interfere with seasonal kangaroo hunts. There was also direct competition for kangaroo: the whites had always shot a lot of game.* But it cannot have been a simple matter of hunger and desperation, as is sometimes suggested, for when the Tasmanians killed sheep and cattle they rarely ate them. Nor would this explain the arson and random assaults. The same objection applies to another theory: that the two tribes were led (by a disaffected Aboriginal mainlander from Sydney and two detribalized Tasmanians) into an orgy of bushranger-style crime for gain. Others have proposed a very different explanation: that it was an act of deliberate resistance designed to repel the settlers. But the evidence for this more glamorous interpretation is also shaky. Even at the time, there was considerable speculation about the causes, but no one was in sufficient communication with the tribes to ask them.

Whatever the reasons, the attacks shocked the settlers out of their complacency. Working in the Field Police, Jorgenson witnessed the effects at first hand, and his employer Thomas Anstey, who doubled as coroner, often had to perform autopsies on the victims. This gave them both a close, horrifying view of what was going on in the remotest areas. Jorgenson had been predisposed to feel sympathetic towards the Tasmanians, having liked their architecture and craftsmanship so much in the north-west, but his experiences now made him less tolerant. He particularly deplored the fact that their assaults seemed so arbitrary, showing no more mercy to those who treated them considerately than to those who abused them. One acquaintance of his, who had always made a point of being friendly and generous, had been killed in 1826 simply because they had been frustrated in their attempts to attack a neighbour; Jorgenson found this impossible to comprehend (although, of course, the unrecorded attacks by whites may be presumed to have been equally indiscriminate). Anstey's report certainly made this man's death sound like one inflicted in a frenzy of hatred: he had spear wounds in his thigh, torso, cheek and right eye, craters in his skull, missing teeth, and wounds all over his arms where he had been trying to protect his head.

* It has been argued that the already declining Aboriginal numbers would have offset any decline in kangaroo, but it is noteworthy that when Jorgenson wrote about Aboriginal languages, his translated examples included the following: 'When I returned to my country I went hunting but did not kill one head of game. The white men make their dogs wander, and kill all the game, and they only want the skins.'

The anger motivating assaults was often made explicit. During an attack on the family of a Patrick Gough in October 1828, the mother pleaded for the lives of her three young daughters to be spared: one of the attackers replied in English, 'No you white bitch we'll kill you all.' They beat her and two of the girls over the head with waddies – short sticks used as clubs. The mother, one four-year-old daughter, and a female neighbour all died of their injuries. Survivors of other assaults also heard remarks like, 'Go away you white buggers – what business have you here?' In a case reported by Jorgenson, a man speared a stock-keeper and then demanded his weapon back from his victim's body, saying 'Give me that Spear you white ———: you die.'

Spears and waddies were the weapons of choice. The Tasmanians did steal guns and ammunition from huts, but rarely used them except for hunting birds. This is not surprising: the muskets of the time were notoriously unreliable, and took a long time to reload as a ball had to be inserted into the barrel afresh for each shot, as if loading a minia-ture cannon.* But they could cause devastating damage in a direct hit, and the Tasmanians certainly feared firearms – this being one probable reason why they attacked women or unarmed convict servants more often than free male settlers, unless they could ambush the latter unseen and make a quick getaway.

This they could often do, however, for ambush and invisibility were skills they excelled in. Besides lying in wait for unprotected individ-uals, they would often watch a house for days before attacking it. Any house occupied by armed men would be left alone, but if the men went away a mob might descend within hours. The whites were profoundly unnerved: their attackers seemed to emerge from nowhere and dissolve after they had finished, melting away like dreams. Even in full view, they could be elusive. One settler was in the very act of levelling his gun at a man who, he said, 'disappeared as if by magic and I could see no more of him'. Another time, a party of Field Police chased a woman and a boy down to a creek: seeing the pair fall down

---

* This is one of the arguments advanced against the assumption that large-scale massacres were conducted by small groups of whites, for it would have been technically impossible using such weapons. On the other hand, there is evidence that other kinds of weapons were sometimes used and that muskets could be loaded with shot or multiple smaller balls instead.

behind a pile of logs surrounded by bare land, they thought they had them trapped. Yet when they reached the logs they found no one there.

The settlers no longer felt so at home in this deceptively English-looking rural landscape. Jorgenson described the sense of fear everywhere: 'the fields are deserted, the harvest delayed; no person venturing to leave a stock hut for fear of having it burned to the ground, stacks of corn destroyed by fire, and the mother turning round looking about her with conscious paleness, on observing her infant child a few yards from her, or crawling towards the scrubby hill.' Some settlers were defiant, and barricaded themselves in for a battle: one shored up his hut with logs around the walls and put an Icelandic-style covering of turf on the roof, so it could not be set alight. But many decided to abandon their farms and preserve their own lives, at least until the problem somehow resolved itself. By the end of the 1820s, the hills were full of eerie, deserted buildings. On a journey to the west, Jorgenson found a flock of sheep without a shepherd or any sign of human life near them; later his party heard barking and looked up to see several dogs on a hill in the distance, chasing a bullock. They tried to catch up with the dogs, but lost them. The next hut they saw was abandoned; it contained 'two old Beds, two Iron pots, a frying pan, and a table', but no provisions or blankets. Jorgenson suspected that the original residents had not fled, but had been taken out and killed in the bush somewhere.

Many colonists deplored the Aboriginal actions: newspaper articles spoke of 'savagery', 'cunning, treachery and cowardice', 'ingratitude', and 'a wanton and savage spirit'. But other writers were impressed by their talents and strategy. The *Hobart Town Courier* pointed out that these gave the lie to anyone who thought them an inferior race, and especially those phrenological faddists who believed Aboriginal people lacked the 'intellectual bumps' for sophisticated life. Others openly recognized that the problem was the fault of the Europeans themselves, going all the way back to the early violence at Risdon Cove in 1804. The Aboriginal response was what should have been expected all along: they were merely defending their natural rights, as any self-respecting people must.

This attitude was more common among the urban, administrative population in Hobart and Launceston than it was in the rural areas, where people were in immediate danger and had no time for soul-searching. Jorgenson himself, working on the front line, poked fun at the comfortable folk of Hobart who were so quick to condemn the early settlers – though in fact he too believed that everything was traceable to the events in Risdon, and had argued ever since his arrival in Tasmania that the indigenous people deserved better treatment than they received. He was certain that many had been brutally murdered, for the coarser class of rural whites still went around boasting of such killings. In any case it seemed 'scarcely possible not to suppose that the black natives must have had some cause for pursuing the whites with such unrelenting perseverance'.

Among those who were sure that the colonists were originally to blame was Lieutenant-Governor Arthur himself, and he was at first reluctant to meet Aboriginal violence with yet more white violence in return. He wrote: 'I cannot divest myself of the consideration that all aggression originated with the white inhabitants, and that therefore much ought to be endured in return before the blacks are treated as an open and accredited enemy by the government.'

On the other hand, it was becoming increasingly apparent that the administration must address the problem: it could not ignore the chaotic unravelling of colonial intentions that was going on in the remote areas. The settlers were clamouring for action, and they were a powerful lobby. Besides, many of the victims were unarmed convicts; the government felt it had a particular duty to protect them, for they had not chosen to be in Tasmania and had been sentenced only to punitive labour, not violent death.

There was another reason to act, too. If nothing decisive were done, white vigilantes were likely to plunge the Midlands into a vengeful blood-bath from which none would suffer more than the Aboriginal people themselves. As Jorgenson had written to Arthur in January 1828 (before he started working for the Field Police), failure to intervene must be considered the worst sin of all. 'Should nothing be done to improve the condition of the aborigines, we shall see a race of beings removed from the face of the earth, a race whom God has planted in this particular spot.' He even noted, wisely, that direct killings were not the only danger: demoralization and decline in territory were just as destructive. Unless the government took control of the situation, the white population would spread like a mould over the island, hunting grounds would shrink even further, and in the end nothing would be left but barren rocks and wastes, where the Aboriginal people would die in despair.

What must then be the feelings of our descendants, when reflecting that they could not hold their possessions but for the fatal policy which had delivered over to extermination a people who were guilty of no other crime than accidentally coming into contact with strangers from a far country, and who by no title of law nor justice could exercise the right of despoiling them of their national inheritance. Heaven avert so foul a stain on the British character!

In the same letter, he argued that questions of original cause and culpability were now less pressing than the need to deal with the immediate problem at hand. 'Who were the original aggressors; – to whom most blame is attached, cannot now become a subject of enquiry: it would be useless to enter upon a topic of that nature; and should we ever do so, I doubt whether after all the truth could be fairly elicited. We must take things as they stand.' Jorgenson's letter was splendidly eloquent (it may have helped him get the Oatlands job) but, as with his letters to Banks about Iceland in 1808, he was orating to the converted. Arthur himself wrote a fortnight later that it was 'in vain to trace the cause of the evil which exists; my duty is plainly to remove its effects'. This was hard to argue with, but it was much less clear what could or should be done.

One solution that might suggest itself to a twentieth- or twenty-first-century mind, but never to a nineteenth-century one, was to acknowledge the evils of colonial invasion and withdraw from the island altogether. This was unimaginable – indeed, most would have considered it actually unethical. It would have been an abdication of the colonist's various responsibilities: to bring the Tasmanians into the Christian fold, to share with them the technological and educational benefits of British civilization and, by hard work, to educe the maximum agricultural and economic potential of the island itself. The

Tasmanians were, as Jorgenson put it, a people 'whom it is our duty, if possible, to enlighten and protect'. To back away because of a few practical difficulties would be a cowardly betrayal. It could never have resulted from self-doubting, anti-imperialist reflections; the only thing that could cause it would be attacks on a scale too devastating to be dealt with. And the intermittent Aboriginal assaults fell well short of this.

In his letter to Arthur, Jorgenson had proposed a rather absurd early solution of his own, and although it represents Jorgenson at his most fantastic, it also functions as an emblem of the Christian Evangelical world-view then dominant among the governing classes. His idea was that one could not wait in Hobart for the indigenous people to convert to the European way: human nature did not work like that. They thought they were better off as they were, and indeed they might be right, but for one thing: they were missing out on the spiritual dimension of life. This was why 'the philanthropist would wish to see the black population of this country enter into our views, and arrive at that state of perfection which eventually brings the character of man in harmony with the character of God'. It remained only to convince the Aboriginal people of this, and the best way to do it was by example.

Colonists should therefore go into the wilderness themselves, not as scruffy settlers (and certainly not as all-too-human hypocrites like the Tahitian missionaries) but as heroic exemplars. Huts should be set up in key spots, and each one occupied by six whites of elevated character and fine appearance, led by 'a man of singular humanity and penetration, and guided by those nobler considerations which are not common to ordinary minds'. The six must radiate peaceful benevolence; even their garments must be different from other people's, 'to excite veneration'. Once there they need do little, for their main function would be to live graciously and be observed. They would be a little zoo exhibit, not of animals but of angels. Intrigued, the Aboriginal tribes would eventually come and seek peace voluntarily, though the angels should keep muskets concealed about their person in case things went wrong.

N.J.B. Plomley, editor of Jorgenson's book on the Aboriginal Tasmanians, once speculated that Jorgenson could take a more rational and tolerant approach than most because he was a Dane, 'and therefore

not endowed with an ingrained emotionalism and belief in the right-
ness of everything British'. Yet in fact almost everything Jorgenson
said on the matter reflected the assumptions of the British Evangelical
establishment, never more so than with his conversion scheme.
Evangelicals (of whom Arthur was one) were freedom-lovers and
believers in equality: they had, after all, been the force behind the
abolition of slavery. But they had no doubts at all about the superiority of their own philanthropic, freedom-loving, egalitarian Christian
culture. To reap the benefits of it, the world's peoples needed to convert
to Christianity, to learn the value of property (if they did not already
know it),* and to aspire to the approved moral ideals. Many did. But
if a population showed little or no interest in the things held up for
their admiration, it turned out that there was no Plan B. This was the
problem facing well-meaning policy-makers in Tasmania. Jorgenson's
scheme was an unwitting *reductio ad absurdum* of the kind of thinking
that could never work there. But what else could be done?

Between the unacceptable extremes of abandonment and massacre,
the few intermediate options were regarded with varying degrees of
distaste. A few coldly contemplated the idea of turning a blind eye
while maverick settlers and their men fired at will until the Tasmanians
were all dead, or driven into remote bush areas. Most considered this
repugnant, however. Where mentioned, it was usually cited as the
nightmare scenario, the consequence of doing nothing.

A more widely approved strategy was to impose a government ban
on hostile tribes entering settled areas at all, and to cut off all contact
between them and the colonists until they could be 'civilized'. But

* British ideas of property and land ownership were hard for Aboriginal people to
appreciate at the best of times, but there was one particularly alien concept governing
nineteenth-century British attitudes to Australian territory, that of *terra nullius*, or 'land
of no one'. This asserted that a people who merely occupied the land without using it
(which meant farming, not hunting and gathering) could have no property claim over
it. In agricultural work, a worker mixed his labour with the land; as his labour was his
property he thus acquired proprietorial rights over the land too. Indigenous Australians
could have claimed this right, had they used the land in this way – but of course they
did not, whereas the colonists, as descendants of Central Asian farmers, had no difficulty
fulfilling their own requirement. Agriculture came naturally to them, and they thought
it only natural that it should be the foundation of land rights.

there was no hope of communicating this ban to the tribes, let alone negotiating any agreement. The main problem was not language, but the more fundamental one of access: the settlers now rarely saw Aboriginal people in the central districts at all except when an attack was in progress, and then they dared not approach them except with a raised gun, at the sight of which the group would flee.

In any case, why should the tribes agree to such a compromise? Everything they saw in the rural areas suggested that they were winning. Settlers and their families were fleeing, the sheep were disappearing, the fields were emptying. The few remaining whites seemed incapable of tracking or pursuing anyone effectively, and when they tried they always gave away their location in the clumsiest of ways. As Jorgenson noted, the Aboriginal people had no reason to doubt that they were the superior forces in the art of war.

The only possibility, therefore, was to impose the ban by sheer unannounced force. Some means had to be found of fencing the tribes out, or of cornering them and then sending them to a reservation well away from the settlers, perhaps in a remote section of Tasmania itself or on an island in Bass Strait. It would not be Jorgenson's white angels who would live in a zoo, but the indigenous people, who would be fed and protected but also restrained. Few denied that this would be yet another affront to their rights, but it seemed the best of a bad range of options. Arthur was far from happy about it, and also recognized that it would be difficult to achieve. 'I confess I feel the subject exceedingly perplexing.' But something of the sort must be tried, he concluded. '[I]t is but justice to make the attempt.'

So, in April 1828 – just before Jorgenson joined the Field Police – Arthur issued his first proclamation on the subject, officially ordering Aboriginal people out of the settled areas and announcing the creation of a line of military posts to enforce the exclusion. Army and police officers at these posts could use violence to ensure that the ban was respected, but only within strict restrictions. Aboriginal people could not be interfered with outside the designated area, and even the two hostile tribes must be allowed to follow their annual migrations to the coast for shellfish, one of which was due soon. In the last few clauses, Arthur seemed to forget that they could not be communicated with, for he declared that their leaders should be issued with special passports during the migrations and that they should complain to the authorities if any rules were infringed. If it were that simple to establish mutual understanding, laws such as this one might not have been needed at all.

For a brief moment, however, it seemed to be working. The country became noticeably more peaceful in the few months following the proclamation. Arthur himself suspected that this was merely because of the shellfish season, and he was right. In the spring of 1828, when the tribes returned to the central district, an even more violent wave of attacks burst upon the remaining settlers. The war was on again. The two tribes were clearly signalling 'their intention to destroy, without distinction of sex or age, all the white inhabitants who should fall within their power'. The police and military detachments seemed to have no deterrent effect at all. They were not numerous, and the soldiers' uniforms made them stick out like red berries in the bush: the attackers simply kept away from them and carried on in nearby areas as usual. Arthur therefore decided to take the next fateful step. On 1 November 1828, he introduced martial law.

Until now, Aboriginal Tasmanians had technically been British subjects whose violence breached criminal law, and who were liable for trial if captured. In practice, individuals were rarely identified, and when they were the trials were visibly absurd, since the defendants had no understanding of the court process. This was no impediment in law, however, and four hangings of Aboriginal individuals did take place in 1825 and 1826.* But many colonists were aware that this did not go to the heart of the problem.

There had already been discussion about the legal aspects of the situation, which were well summarized in a letter written later, in

* Reportedly, when the chaplain urged one of them to pray during his last moments, the man said he was 'too b[loody] scared to pray', and added: 'Hanging's no good for black fellows – white fellow he used to it.' The law was supposed to apply equally to whites and blacks, but there were no hangings of whites in Tasmania for killing Aboriginal victims, and just one execution has been traced in New South Wales, in 1820. Trials of whites did occasionally take place, but usually ended in acquittal or in relatively mild penalties. Meanwhile, the inability of Aboriginal defendants to understand the trial process could inspire strange perversions of legal principles: during one New South Wales trial it was suggested that, since trial by a jury consisting at least in part of Aboriginal peers was not possible, 'the retributive laws of nature and of Moses' should prevail instead.

1831, by a 'J.E.' (undoubtedly J.E. Calder) to the *Launceston Advertiser*. He asked:

> Are these unhappy creatures the *subjects* of our king, in a state of rebellion? or are they an injured people, whom we have invaded and with whom we are at war? Are they within the reach of our laws; or are they to be judged by the laws of nations? Are they to be viewed in the light of murderers, or as prisoners of war? Have they been guilty of any crime under the laws of nations which is punishable by death, or have they only been carrying on war *in their way*? Are they British subjects at all, or a foreign enemy who has never yet been subdued, and which resists our usurped authority and dominion?

His own conclusion was that the second alternative of each pair was true. 'We are at war with them: they look upon us as enemies – as invaders – as their oppressors and persecutors – they resist our invasion. They have never been subdued, therefore are they not rebellious subjects, but an injured nation . . . What we call their crimes is what in a white man we should call patriotism.'

Paradoxically, Arthur's declaration of martial law reflected this sympathetic line of thought: it implicitly recognized members of the hostile tribes as military opponents rather than mere criminals. But it also reflected sheer desperation, and it was a drastic step, one that could only be approved in time of extreme national emergency. For, in practical terms, it meant that anyone who now killed an Aboriginal person (within certain restrictions) was immune from even theoretical prosecution for murder. This changed the situation considerably.*

In a letter justifying his action to the Colonial Office in London, Arthur expressed the hope that this admittedly 'strong measure' would put a stop to the 'lawless warfare which has been lately carrying on

---

* Martial law did not technically strip Aboriginal Tasmanians of citizenship, nor did it declare them members of an enemy nation. It applied to them the same rules that could be applied in Britain in cases of riot or attempted revolutionary uprising – that is, they remained subjects but could be treated *as if* they were a military enemy. In normal conditions one could kill Britons during a civil disturbance only if specifically sanctioned to do so by a magistrate: martial law acted in effect as a universal magistrate's sanction.

between the Natives and the settlers and stockmen', and so minimize bloodshed on both sides. Its purpose was the typically Arthurian one of preventing greater suffering in the long term by means of a precise injection of fear and mayhem in the short term. 'Terror may have the effect which no proffered measures of conciliation have been capable of inducing,' he wrote; if it did, lives would be saved.

The restrictions on its application were stringent: he listed them in the proclamation, and explained them further in an emphatic letter sent to all district magistrates on the same day. Martial law would apply only within the central, settled districts, and only to the two hostile tribes: others must not be touched. Arms should never be used if other options were available, and non-violent approaches must always be tried first. Women and children should not be attacked. Nothing must be left to 'undirected convicts, or other unauthorized persons'. Weekly reports must be sent to the Colonial Secretary, and everything should still be done to seek terms of peace. All involved must understand that the law had been introduced 'by no means whatever with the view of seeking the destruction of the Aborigines': the motive was quite the opposite, and the actions of all police and magistrates must reflect that.

But there *was* a bottom line and, like Icelanders seeing nothing in Jorgenson's proclamations but the cancellation of their debts, people naturally tended to seize on that one factor to the exclusion of all else. Martial law, in essence, was a licence to kill.

As before, the Aboriginal people knew nothing about the new situation, and the only way of communicating it was to impose it. To supplement the parties of soldiers already in the field, a new type of police 'roving party' was inaugurated under the overall command of Thomas Anstey in Oatlands. The roving parties' job was to patrol the settled districts in teams and to track down members of the hostile tribes. They could shoot to kill, within the restrictions, but they were not expected to act as assassination squads: capture was the aim.

Nine roving parties were created altogether, each containing six men, mostly convicts who volunteered in exchange for promised tickets of leave. Each party had a leader, and three overall supervisors were appointed to co-ordinate three parties each. Two of these were eminent free colonists: Gilbert Robertson, the Chief Constable of the Richmond district (the man who had caught William Sheldon), and John Batman, a settler originally from New South Wales who was later to become famous as a founder of Melbourne. Both men were experienced bushmen; both also happened to be rather bumptious characters.

The other triad of parties was entrusted to Jorgenson, still only a ticket-of-leave man, but singled out by Anstey for his skills and leadership ability. As the person with the best knowledge of the western districts, he was assigned this direction as his special responsibility – though the western wilderness itself was outside the martial law limits. In practice, he also often went east, whenever he heard rumours of an Aboriginal presence in that area.

The work was exhausting: only the irresistible promise of a ticket of leave could have induced most of the other employees to take part. The parties were expected to cover large tracts of territory, carrying many days' or weeks' worth of food on their backs. Horses were not supplied, though they would have been useful in this relatively open landscape. Treks were often done overnight, to avoid the heat and to stay out of sight – a tactic particularly favoured by the early-rising Jorgenson. (There could be 'no necessity for taking them out of a settlement at that time of night', grumbled his men sometimes, as they were dragged from their blankets at two-thirty in the morning and pushed out on the path by moonlight.) After one 'extraordinary and rapid' overnight trek, his men threw themselves on the ground without troubling to make camp, and fell into such a deep sleep that it was only when they woke up hours later that they realized they were drenched to the skin. It had been pouring with rain, and they had not felt it.

But Jorgenson himself was the toughest of all, and he inspired his teams by example. He never lagged behind, although he was now nearly fifty and the other men were mostly 'young and robust'. As he proudly stated, he never failed to take the lead 'in ascending and descending mountains – in crossing rapid rivers heavily laden with provisions – forcing our way through almost impenetrable scrubs and deep gullies'.

The work was dangerous as well as laborious. Apart from the prospect of doing battle with Aboriginal opponents, there was constant risk of accident and injury in the hills, or of getting lost. Jorgenson himself became separated from his party once, and wandered lost for days: he nearly died. He had no food. The mist and lashing rain made it hard to get his bearings, and the scrubland was almost as formidable as the Walls of Jerusalem. He somehow staggered on, even when assailed by hallucinations: someone addressed him in a loud voice, and he had visions of a farmhouse with a man and woman standing in front of it. The vapour from the rain seemed to turn into a kind of sea-mist, with the waving tree-tops resembling small islands; he lost all sense of where he was. He was on the point of complete collapse when he happened across an occupied hut and was saved.

Jorgenson often praised his men in his reports, and willingly put them forward for tickets of leave when they did well. Anstey sometimes had to quash these recommendations in order not to lose all the staff too quickly. Jorgenson also filled his letters with complaints and suggestions on administrative matters: he drew attention to poorly fitting boots, which made it painful to walk, and 'wretched' knapsacks, so small that they had to be overstuffed and made an awkward lump on the walker's back. Worse, some parties were better equipped than others, which caused resentment. Some of these problems were solved, but Jorgenson continued to feel that operations were not as well supported as they might have been.

Over the next year or two, he and his parties repeatedly covered the western agricultural districts and the nearby forests and tiers. Occasionally he ventured outside the area covered by martial law, for what he called reconnaissance purposes, but he never saw Aboriginal people there.* He sometimes took all three parties with him, or arranged for them to rendezvous at a certain point; more often, two parties would be sent in different directions under trusted sub-leaders

* Jorgenson was well aware of the geographical restriction: when one of his deputy leaders, Richard Tyrrell, went AWOL in 1830 and was suspected of pursuing Aboriginal people outside the correct area, both Jorgenson and Anstey were worried, and Jorgenson wrote, 'He has not been heard of for thirty-eight days. Much do I fear that these men have proceeded to attack some of the peaceable tribes either on the Western Sea coast, or without the limits where martial law is not in force.' Anstey noted that Tyrrell and his men would be gaoled and subjected to an inquiry as soon as they were found. Tyrrell had left the controlled area, but apparently he had not attempted to kill anyone there; Jorgenson suspected it was to allow a man in his party to visit a friend nearby.

while he took charge of the third himself.

Jorgenson's reports usually indicate that he understood the limitations of what he was expected to do, namely 'to place the native tribes in a situation that they may be captured without the parties in pursuit being compelled to shed more human blood than should be necessary to bring them to a sense of justice and moderation'. But his language sometimes became careless or ambiguous enough to attract censure from Anstey, and this makes his reports an important source for anyone trying to divine the true nature of the 'Black War', as these operations became known.

In one report, Jorgenson referred to the hostile tribes' being 'captured, or otherwise disposed of'. In another, forwarding an account by one of his deputy leaders, he remarked: 'You will see by Tyrrell's report that he at length fell in with the natives, shot one, killed a number of dogs etc. There can be no doubt had his party been stronger, <u>he might have done more good</u>.' The underlining was either Jorgenson's or Anstey's; Anstey wrote in the margin here, 'Did he do any?' And when Jorgenson went on '<u>I feel more and more convinced that some effectual good would be done were the parties quickly filled up</u>', Anstey added in disgust: 'Not if they were to commit such acts as this.' Jorgenson may have meant 'with more men he could have captured a large number instead of shooting at a few', not 'with more men he could have shot more', but Anstey apparently did not think so. A few weeks later, Jorgenson blithely spoke of 'capturing and destroying' Aboriginal people, and he once castigated a settler for failing to fire on a large crowd when he had the chance, although the man could not have captured any of them unhurt without back-up. All he could have achieved was to kill one or two, which Jorgenson seemed to think he should have done.

Yet Jorgenson still firmly believed that the work of the roving parties was ultimately for the indigenous people's benefit: expulsion from the settled areas would 'constitute the greatest act of humanity toward the Aboriginal tribes'. And, whatever he and his parties may have considered themselves entitled to do in theory, it made little practical difference; the embarrassing truth was that, in all their months of purposeful roving, they hardly saw any Aboriginal people. Even those historians who are most inclined to estimate high numbers of Aboriginal casualties do not state that the roving parties killed more than a handful between them. The person shot by Tyrrell's group was the only casualty noted among any of Jorgenson's parties.

The only Aboriginal people definitely recorded as shot dead by other roving parties were two murdered with particular brutality in September 1829 by Jorgenson's fellow supervisor John Batman – though a remark by Arthur that Batman had 'much slaughter to account for' does suggest that there might have been more. (To be fair, at other times Arthur spoke of highly of him, and noted his general belief in the use of kindness rather than severity.) On this occasion his party tracked down a large camp and charged it, guns blazing; most people escaped into the bush, but a woman and a toddler were captured. The next day two men were found nearby, incapacited by wounds received during the attack. Batman tried to take all four captives back to base, but the two men could not walk, so he executed them. That this was not approved behaviour is clear from the fact that, in a formal interview two weeks later, Batman changed his story, and claimed that one had died of his injuries while the other had to be shot in self-defence after attacking a member of the party. The first version was obviously the true one. All in all, it seems likely that the death toll at the hands of official roving parties was low – but that this had more to do with lack of opportunity than with a sensitive reading of Arthur's instructions.

The journals of all the party leaders make it clear that sightings were rare, and actual combat even rarer. One of Jorgenson's journals, of a tour in deep-frozen winter conditions, records their trying every trick they could think of to take Aboriginal camps unawares – avoiding the usual paths, staying up all night keeping watch – but all they ever saw were empty huts. The settlers' houses were mostly abandoned too; the few remaining residents invariably told horror stories of recent violent encounters. Wherever Jorgenson went, it seemed that an Aboriginal mob had just left; of a later trip, he wrote: 'We every moment fell in with their fires yet warm . . . we saw Kangaroo speared which had been left hanging on the trees'. In one place, they arrived in time to find a man who had been speared in the lungs just an hour previously.

Jorgenson himself tackled the question of the roving parties' failure in clear-eyed detail, and presented Anstey with a list of likely causes, still often cited in histories of the conflict. The first five were:

1. Want of a plan of combined operations.
2. A total absence of discipline.
3. Inveterate laziness which induces the parties to proceed over the best ground they can find from one place to another, and the natives thus knowing their customary tracks can easily avoid them.
4. That the men forming the parties have been promised indulgences at the expiration of a certain time, without the additional condition that none would be granted unless the natives were fallen in with, captured, or otherwise disposed of.
5. The imposition and deceit practised by prisoner leaders, wishing to stand well, and be called good fellows, by their fellow prisoners, and thus indulge the parties in idleness, and stifle all complaints.

After these came two particularly interesting reasons. One was the possibility that the Aboriginal guides they were using – taken from among the few captives, or from the tribes near Hobart, or even from New South Wales – were deliberately misleading their parties. Jorgenson advanced this 'with great caution', but John Burnett at the Colonial Secretary's Office in Hobart added in the margin: 'I think it extremely probable.' The final reason was '[t]he imposition practised to screen idleness, to hold out that the Aborigines are men of superior cunning, and amazingly swift runners'.

It was shrewd of Jorgenson to realize that the myth that their opponents were virtually superhuman could act as a kind of excuse. Yet Aboriginal bush skills were real, and Jorgenson suffered the same problem himself: no matter how hard he tried to do his job (and his journals suggest that he tried very hard indeed), the Aboriginal Tasmanians slipped into the landscape as if they had never existed. It was as if they only manifested themselves to do damage, and then became mere figments again. Looked at from the other side, of course, they were simply making their way around the bush in a normal human way, while the whites were crashing around like giant Tasmanian devils.

They stank like Tasmanian devils, too, smoking their pipes wherever they went and thus broadcasting their location for miles. It was Jorgenson who first pointed this out to his bosses, having been alerted to it by one of his Aboriginal trackers – indicating that their advice was not completely useless after all.

All the roving parties used Aboriginal guides, and Jorgenson was right that some deceived them deliberately. One man bearing the common appellation 'Black Jack' admitted to him that he had misled an earlier party to get revenge because they beat him. Jorgenson was sure his own well-treated trackers were more faithful, however, particularly the one he trusted most, a boy of about sixteen whom the men called 'Mungo', although the boy himself preferred the more common Jack. (He objected to 'Mungo' after meeting a man with a pet monkey in the town of Bothwell, and coming to the conclusion that he had been named after the creature.)

Mungo/Jack was from the Ben Lomond tribe, who were not involved in the conflict, but he had become hungry for revenge against one of the two hostile tribes, the Big River people, because they had killed members of his family. He proved a source of all kinds of interesting information, though he did not seem entirely to trust the roving parties and never actually led them to the tribes they were looking for. He would show them where a mob had recently been roasting kangaroo, or where they had assembled for a meeting: he pointed out the prints of women's and children's feet, and a thicket from which new spears had been cut. He also helped the party to find water and food in places where the whites would never have thought of looking for it: Jorgenson marvelled at his skills.

Indeed, Jorgenson had even higher hopes, thinking that Mungo/Jack might one day make a good peace negotiator. Arthur had always emphasized the desirability of finding a mediator: it did not matter from which race he came, so long as he was trusted by the colonists and could persuade the hostile tribes into some sort of treaty. Jorgenson enthusiastically set about Mungo/Jack's education with this in mind: he taught him the English alphabet and made sure that no one in his parties used indecent language in his hearing, so he would not be corrupted. 'I hope by the End of nine months, he may be sufficiently taught to become an able interpreter and negociator,' he wrote confidently. But he knew there were problems, the main one being that Mungo/Jack hated the Big River tribe so much that it was hard to imagine his ever sitting down to negotiate with them. He was also more distrustful of the whites than Jorgenson realized. One day he was told to accompany a party of men he did not know: frightened, he refused, and was thrown into a gaol cell overnight as punishment. This so horrified him that he ran away the minute he was freed, and never came back. It seemed that Jorgenson had allowed his fondness for the lad to blind him to the obvious, for Mungo/Jack did later confess (truthfully or not, we shall never know) to leading the parties astray.

When at last the sought-after 'conciliator' and negotiator was found, it would be a white man, George Augustus Robinson. Mungo/Jack eventually died with many others in Robinson's ill-managed sequel to the conflict; he became not the chief negotiator of the conciliation plan, as Jorgenson had hoped, but one of its victims.

Some of Jorgenson's schemes were less ambitious, and more practical. For example, he proposed that instead of trying to hide by not lighting fires at night, the parties should light lots of fires wherever they went, 'to baffle and confound the calculations of the Natives, and make them believe that they are nearly surrounded and hotly pursued'. Anstey was often impressed by Jorgenson's suggestions, and passed several of them on to higher authorities. He also appreciated Jorgenson's reports and reprimanded the other supervisors for not doing so well with theirs. Jorgenson proudly wrote: 'With reference to this race of people the Colonial Archives contain no less than eleven large Octavos. – Volume no. 1 – is upwards of one thousand pages, more than five hundred written by me, in the shape of reports to the local government – and so on in other volumes.' This is a slight exaggeration, but not much. Jorgenson believed in rigorous accountability, always potentially something of a nuisance to the occupants of superior posts, though Anstey never seemed to mind. (He confined himself to occasionally advising his own superiors to skip parts.) Jorgenson even apologized to Anstey for his verbosity, and once remarked that a report was less 'simple' than he wished because he had not had time to revise it in a second draft.

It was a job well suited to all Jorgenson's talents, but he soon started to feel the strain, and even to feel his age. He did not enjoy the work as much as he should: the inefficiency of his colleagues troubled him (especially that of Gilbert Robertson, with whom he fell out), and he took his own setbacks very much to heart. In July 1829 he wrote to Anstey: 'The extreme anxiety I have laboured under for some time past, the almost total absence of rest and sleep, I fear have in no shape been beneficial to my health, though I hope, a constitution natural[ly] strong may not be subdued altogether by any thing but actual sickness.' He could not help approaching the job 'with all the zeal and enthusiasm which my character is capable of' – which was a great deal – and he weighed in his mind 'by day and night' how best to achieve the roving parties' aims. 'I know the tribes are to be captured, and the war ought to be terminated this very Summer, but ignorance, sloth, imposition, and want of energy and vigorous discipline on our part have been the best friends of the natives.'

He kept going, however, and it was almost another year before he gave vent to his weariness again, in March 1830. This time he asked Anstey to relieve him of his duties. He was hoping to get his conditional pardon soon (he did, a few months later), and wanted to be free to find something more congenial. Again, in May, he wrote to Anstey:

I beg to state to you that although it may not be visible to others, my constitution is breaking down fast, I feel it every hour with sensible symptoms of decay naturally incident to an advance[d] age of life. I have now stood four winters campaigns in this country, and am certain one more would feel too much for me. In stormy weather, in wet, and in cold, I have exerted myself.

He asked Anstey to intercede for him with Arthur, 'that I may be permitted to retire from all connexion with the Police into some more peaceful and quiet mode of life than the one I am at present engaged in. – I am heartily sick of it.' Anstey did forward this request, and added his own note saying that Jorgenson was highly capable and by his diligence had created enemies 'who would readily go all lengths to ruin him'. On the other hand: 'It must at the same time be admitted that Jorgenson's greatest enemy is himself.' He hoped Arthur would provide 'some employment suitable to his talents, and in which he might render himself useful to the Colony'.

But this quiet, civilized job did not yet materialize. Jorgenson's conditional pardon came through in early June, albeit with conditions ordered personally by Arthur forbidding him ever to return to Britain.*
Otherwise a free man, he wrote to Anstey asking permission to leave his job, and his resignation was accepted.

Jorgenson's life away from the police service did not last long, however, for a plan was in preparation and his services would soon be commandeered again. Arthur knew the roving parties were not working. He was pondering a new approach, one for which he would need all the personnel at his disposal.

---

* Arthur was generally reluctant to allow 'educated convicts' to leave, as he preferred to keep them working towards the island's future. But it is possible that Jorgenson was still considered a potential revolutionary, too dangerous for Britain – the home government being jumpy about such matters at the time. Jorgenson did not mind the restriction much, and told Anstey: 'I would not chuse to return to the troubles of the old world.' He also later told his brother that he never wanted to see Britain again: 'it was the bane of my hopes and the grave of my happiness.'

12

A precarious existence

The world's first *levée en masse* had been ordered in revolutionary France, in August 1793. At the height of its own Terror, and under attack from enemies on all sides, the French leaders had decreed a total public mobilization. Civilians as well as military men were supposed to come forward for the defence of the republic: all material resources were re-directed into the task. Women and children had to contribute whatever work they could, and even elderly men were to 'have themselves carried to public places, there to stir up the courage of the warriors' in this emergency. Thirty-seven years later, Lieutenant-Governor Arthur decided to launch a similar *levée en masse* in the very different battlefield of Tasmania, to defend the colony against its internal threat. The great mobilization was referred to by the French term at the time, but it has since become known as the 'Black Line'.

The idea of a mass deployment may have been borrowed, but even France had never attempted anything quite like what Arthur had in mind. He did not merely want a crowd of volunteers to swell the ranks of ordinary police and militia. He wanted to assemble all the men he could and string them out in a human cordon all the way across the settled zone: a cordon that would sweep southwards like a giant broom, harrying all members of the two hostile Aboriginal tribes ahead of it. Eventually it would sweep them across a narrow bottleneck into the Tasman Peninsula, in the island's south-east, where they would be trapped in a small space. There the broom would metamorphose into a fishing net: they would be scooped up and eventually transferred to a well-appointed, government-approved fish-tank somewhere, probably on an island in Bass Strait.

The policy was designed in August 1830; by the first week of October the Line was ready to start. It took a tremendous effort of organization: over two thousand men participated in the Line itself, around three-quarters of them civilians, and they all had to be properly deployed and supplied. The army and the Field Police took part in full force; many free volunteers joined in, and all the island's ticket-of-leave men had to report for duty unless they could find someone to take their place. Others on the island were made to contribute their efforts: inmates of the women's prison in Hobart were set to work making hundreds of pairs of thick trousers, while other convict workshops made boots and knapsacks. Staff were employed to distribute food, clothing and weapons. Around a thousand muskets and thirty thousand rounds of cartridges were issued, plus three hundred pairs of handcuffs. Further depots were set up along the Line's path and stocked with more supplies. It was immensely expensive: the Line cost the government thousands of pounds in equipment and pay.

Having been the nucleus of the roving parties' operations, Oatlands was the natural choice as the administrative centre, and through September the small town blazed with activity. Men arrived from all over the island. Jorgenson was at the centre of it all, and described the atmosphere: 'an ardour and spirit manifest themselves to a high degree amongst all classes in the District. – Arms are coming in, offers made of Carts free of expence to the Government to convey provisions, Volunteer parties of free men offering their Services – Assigned Servants eager to enter the List – the Ticket of Leave men determined to distinguish themselves – and every other ready assistance.'

Jorgenson did not hesitate to put himself forward both for administrative work and for leadership in the field. The opportunity actually came as a relief to him; without regular employment he had been becoming restless, and impoverished. He wrote to Anstey offering to meet men as they arrived in Oatlands and to pick out more experienced individuals 'with a quick eye', assigning each to the place where he would be of most use. He would supply everyone and sort out financial accounts, then conduct the parties to their appointed spot on the Line. When all was prepared, he would join in himself as a party leader. Anstey accepted the plan willingly.

By 7 October, the Line stretched across 190 kilometres of the northern settled district, its separate parties arranged like beads on a string. As soon as everyone was in position and all was ready, it began to move – slowly and awkwardly, like the behemoth it was. Each group was instructed to stay within hailing distance of its neighbours, and to make sure that it moved at an even rate and in the right direction, so that gaps did not develop. This required astonishing organization: it was like moving troops around a complex European battlefield, but on much more uneven territory and with poor visibility. It was indeed, as the contemporary writer Henry Melville remarked, 'a great war in miniature'.

Like a Napoleonic battle, it was also a noisy business. The old roving parties had been told to act stealthily, laying ambushes and following tracks, but this was different. The Line men were supposed to crash through the bush as loudly as they could, for the main aim at this stage was not to take captives but to create such an intimidating front line that everyone fled before it. The easiest way to keep in touch with neighbouring parties' positions was for all personnel to shout, whistle, fire muskets and blow bugles, and this they did with abandon. They also wrought havoc on the landscape, again with deliberate intent. A traveller the following year described in his diary the scenes of chaos where the Line had passed by: 'The ground was torn up by the trafficking of carts, horses, bullocks &c in conveying supplies. Shoes of a light description, worn out, were strewn about. It had all the appearance of a great assemblage of persons having met, and vast destruction was effected among the trees of the forest' – their bark having been stripped and their branches cut for fires.

The problem was that the spirit of chaos extended beyond the noise-making, and the Line almost immediately started disintegrating into a confused rabble. Some sections went faster than others; they often had to stop for the others to catch up, and inevitably gaps and weak points developed. It was rumoured that, when the scrub seemed too impenetrable, some parties gave up and walked in single file along established footpaths.

None of Jorgenson's parties would have got away with this. He was horrified by the prevailing disorder, describing how his part of the Line had become scattered in all directions by an officer's confused order and how, after regrouping, they kept meeting groups of lost men from other parties – first a gaggle of six, then another three, then three more. When night fell, Jorgenson heard gunshots and noises in the bush; he went alone to investigate, and found several huts filled with even more odds and ends of soldiers, all out of position.

Yet somehow, despite the disarray, the Line managed to keep going at a roughly even pace and in roughly the right direction. By early November, the men found themselves converging on the narrow isthmus leading to the Forester Peninsula, which in turn led to the Tasman Peninsula. The Line was less than fifty kilometres wide by this time, stretching from coast to coast, and the parties were bunched together. There seemed little possibility of anyone slipping through the gaps now. The Aboriginal tribes were somewhere ahead, getting closer and closer to the peninsula where they would be trapped. Indeed, a large camp was soon seen: a party rushed it and shot two people, bringing the total of recorded Aboriginal deaths during the Line operation to three. Two more were captured, an old man and a teenaged boy. The rest escaped, but clearly they would still be trapped in the bush ahead, so it did not matter too much. More reinforcements arrived, and a detachment of four hundred men was sent to comb the scrub in front of the Line, to see how many they could capture before the isthmus was reached.

This team stormed through the bush, cutting a broad path so that no one could hide or flee unseen. The isthmus was watched at one end; the Line remained solid at the other. Hundreds of fugitives were expected. But after several days of futile searching, it was concluded that the number of people captured by the Black Line was not going to exceed the unexpectedly low figure of two – these being the man and the boy already taken. The rest had melted unseen through the gaps along the way, including even the dozens who had run off from the camp just days before, when the Line was at its densest.

This outcome was seized by Arthur's enemies on the island with delight as evidence of total, risible, expensive failure. Not only had he used a sledgehammer to crack a nut: he had even missed the nut.

At a meeting near the end of that year, where a vote of thanks to Arthur was proposed, one speaker said that a man 'might go to the top of Mount Wellington, with a harpoon in his hand to kill a whale, and his exertions in so attempting such an absurdity might be tremendous' – but that was no reason to thank him for it.

Jorgenson too was sometimes harsh about the Line débâcle. He wrote to the Colonial Secretary's Office blaming it on 'lukewarmness, sleepishness, and want of zeal and activity' among those involved. The obstacles now being put forward as excuses were well known in advance, he said, and could have been prepared for. 'I suppose in descanting on those subjects I shall raise enemies, but this cannot be helped, I have seen no hearty co-operation, and I do not for my part ascribe the causes of failure more to the obstacles of nature than I do to a want of vigilance, to slugginess, and total inattention.'

The Line was not an obvious success, and its brutal-sounding nature – all rigid lines and armed, booted men – has led to its going down in history, wrongly, as an orgy of murder, complete with corpse-strewn landscapes and Aboriginal parents killing their babies lest they cry and give their position away. There is no evidence of bodies being found in the bush, however; nor is there reason to think that many more were shot than appear in the records – since by this stage, and with plenty of witnesses, there would have been little reason to conceal it. It was no massacre. On the other hand, what was largely true of the roving parties is even more likely to be true here: the low death toll was the result of incapacity, not deliberate restraint. The parties crashing through the bush were armed and inexperienced; there was a sense of all-out war by this stage. Had more Aboriginal people had been seen, more would undoubtedly have been killed.

The Black Line did not achieve precisely what it set out to do, but in a strange way it turned out to be effective. The sheer scale and noise of it seemed to have an impact on the Tasmanians, and its devastation of the landscape gave them a shocking insight into what they were up against – not isolated stock-keepers and incompetent police after all, but an apocalyptic monster that barged through the island and left it looking like the aftermath of the greatest flood ever seen. They did not know that the Line had been cripplingly expensive, or that it could not easily be repeated. Things became much quieter afterwards, as if the two hostile tribes were thoroughly chastened and subdued.

There was another factor, however. Over the last few years, including the two years of the 'Black War', the Aboriginal population had been so reduced that there simply were not many left. The mobs that had once terrorized settlers no longer existed in full force. Their depletion must have resulted at least in part from colonists' violence, though much of it was probably committed by isolated vigilantes holed up in their farms rather than by the hapless official parties. No one suspected that it had happened until, during the early 1830s, the remaining population was gradually persuaded to come forward and surrender. Even counting all the members of the western tribes, who had mostly stayed out of the conflict, they numbered only a few hundred.

The character behind this final act in the drama was George Augustus Robinson, the 'Conciliator', who was to become an almost legendary figure in Tasmania. From early 1830 to 1834, he travelled around the island accompanied by small parties of Aboriginal companions, at first drawn from communities near Hobart, later from other surrendering tribes. These people helped him to track down the Aboriginal groups scattered over the island, and to establish contact with them. It worked so well that, a year after the Black Line, everyone in the two hostile tribes had given themselves up, and others surrendered in small hesitant clusters over the next year or two, until they had all been removed from Tasmania and shipped off to Flinders Island in Bass Strait – into the state of exile that Arthur had been planning for years.

The fact that the indigenous people turned themselves over to Robinson so readily has been attributed mainly to his personal persuasiveness and to his use of Aboriginal intermediaries. But it is unlikely that his efforts would have worked so well without the shock inflicted by the Black Line. He had been at work for many months before the Line began, yet it was only after it that he started getting results. Indeed, he was not above openly threatening the Line's return, if he encountered reluctance: he knew that this would be effective. Jorgenson was an admirer, but he too pointed out that Robinson could not have 'allured the Blacks to follow him' had the Line not demonstrated the colonists' brute strength.

Robinson was a peculiar character, not entirely unlike Jorgenson. He too was a fantasist and poseur, who loved to think of himself as a great defender of human rights, like Jorgenson in Iceland. His supporters spoke of him in hushed tones as 'no ordinary man', a sort of Moses leading the Aboriginal people out of the wilderness to safety. In truth he was more of a Pied Piper, and he was leading them not into the promised land but into a forlorn and hopeless state of exile. Robinson pitied the Tasmanians, but he was also excessively interested in the money to be earned from turning them over – he collected a bounty for every captive, even for members of his own travelling party, whom he turned in when he had finished with them. In the most respectful, sympathetic and warm-hearted way, he was selling the Aboriginal people to their enemies for personal profit.

As with so much in the story of the Tasmanian war, the Flinders Island camp was a deadly institution run with the best intentions. By the time the Aboriginal exiles arrived there, their numbers were so low and they were in such poor psychological and physical health that it is hard to imagine what arrangement could still have saved them, but certainly the one at Flinders Island was not it. Removed from their homeland and accommodated like prisoners of war, they pined and sickened. Two hundred or so were sent to the island, over the years, but by 1847 over 130 of these had died. Most deaths were from respiratory diseases – cold, influenza, pneumonia, tuberculosis – which may already have claimed innumerable lives on mainland Tasmania as well.

Robinson was officially the supervisor on Flinders Island, and thus responsible for conditions. In fact he left its management to commandants who had little understanding of how to rescue the almost irredeemable situation. They concentrated on education and on schemes of moral improvement: there was much emphasis on religion, and on teaching concepts of money and trade. Makeshift markets were set up once a week, where the Aboriginal people were encouraged to sell things – shell necklaces, feathers, and spears – and to buy fishing-lines, shirts, clay pipes, sugar plums and cricket bats. They were encouraged to wear British clothing, and introduced to the joys of British food and sport. At a celebration day to welcome Robinson to the island in October 1835, they feasted on mutton, rice, and plum pudding, played a cricket match after dinner, and watched a firework display in the evening. This was what the philanthropists had always wanted – but they had never intended it to be like this. It was a sham, a theatrical dream acted by people who were already ghosts. They still kept getting ill, and their numbers kept declining; no new generation was born. Meanwhile most Tasmanian colonists, feeling safe again, went back to their farms. They got on with building the new Tasmania, while the Aboriginal people continued to die.

The Flinders Island establishment endured for over a decade. In 1847 it was abandoned at last, and the few survivors were returned to their home island, but they were not saved. The last fully Aboriginal individual to die was long thought to have been a woman named Truganini or Trugernanna, in 1876. In fact, a few other women outlived her by several years, not in Tasmania but on Kangaroo Island off South Australia, where they had gone with white sealers: the last of these died in 1888. There remained only people of mixed race, who survived both in Tasmania itself and on the Bass Strait islands and became the foundation of what is now generally recognized as the modern Aboriginal community in Tasmania – a community which has had to be reborn out of a memory.

There is no consensus on how many deaths were involved in this seventy-year decline, since the starting population is not known. And there is no agreement on how much of the fall from this initial figure to the paltry few hundred shipped to Flinders Island is attributable to direct killings. Adding up the killings recorded in the documentary evidence produces the very low figure of around 120, which is actually lower than the number of whites (187) recorded as being killed by Aboriginal attackers. The difference, of course, is that the second figure is likely to be fairly accurate, while the first certainly cannot be. The alternative hypotheses put forward – European diseases, disruption in sexual and reproductive relations, or general cultural decline and maladaptation to the changed environment – remain too speculative to be real solutions to the mystery: they merely deepen and extend it.

Returning to Jorgenson's formulation of the problem, we are left with a vague but powerful conviction that countless atrocities must have occurred during the first three decades of white occupation, without (insofar as we try to be scrupulous) being able to state this as fact. The more minutely the evidence is examined – and it is now being examined more carefully than ever before, to salutary effect – the more profound the sense of perplexity. One can do little more in the end than stand in silent, respectful contemplation before Tasmania's empty tomb: before the unknown.

The Black Line had been a respite for Jorgenson. After resigning from the roving parties, he had lost the sense of urgency and responsibility that had suited him so well, and had gone haywire for a while – beginning with an arrest for drunkenness while celebrating the news of his conditional pardon. 'The fact is,' he wrote of his disoriented response, 'a man who has long been deprived of his liberty, may be compared to one who has been long bed-ridden, and when allowed to walk does not at once feel his legs under him.' This was true enough: Jorgenson got completely legless, and was fined five shillings for it. He also wrote: 'Take the chain off the dog, he commits various pranks, and his ferocity leaves him.' But the wildness did not leave Jorgenson, except during his interlude in the Line.

He had even been given an opportunity to become a farmer, for his pardon had been followed by a government grant of a hundred acres (forty hectares) of land near Oatlands, with the promise of another hundred if he used it well. But he had no money to invest in sheep, nor any idea how to manage them, or how to exploit the land for any other purpose. The grant lay fallow until eventually it was re-sold to Anstey. Jorgenson was one of life's hunter-gatherers: the instincts of the agriculturalist seemed as alien to him as they were to the Aboriginal people.

He did settle down in one way, though it was hardly the best route to a restful life: he married Norah, on 25 January 1831, in St Matthew's Church in New Norfolk – a town chosen because no one knew them there, for they still feared their old enemies. Officially required (as Jorgenson's employer) to give Arthur his opinion on the marriage, Anstey had written:

I have often told Jorgenson that his ruin is inevitable if he marries this woman. His infatuated attachment to her has now existed a long time, and as it cannot be subverted by reason or reflection, I most respectfully beg leave to solicit His Excellency's permission for the man and woman to be married. Norah Corbett did most undoubtedly render very great service to the Police, some time since, in breaking up several Gangs of desperate villains. I know nothing to the woman's prejudice, save that of being much addicted to liquor, and of her propensity to beat and scratch Jorgenson when she is intoxicated.

The most dangerous aspect of Norah's behaviour for Jorgenson, apart from the risk of cuts and bruises, was that her alcoholism helped to drag him back into the heavy-drinking habits that had almost ruined him in London – though he managed never to go back to gambling. He and Norah were often seen staggering in the streets of Hobart and the various Midlands towns where they lived over the next few years, she often laying into him verbally or physically. Jorgenson himself was no lamb – there had been the violent Waterloo Tavern incident in 1829 – but her attacks on him seemed more frequent and more frenzied; she was half his age and twice as ferocious. It has been said, rather unreliably, that the favourite Saturday night entertainment wherever they lived was to watch her chasing him down the road after the pub closed, armed with a rolling-pin or broom-handle.

But, as Anstey recognized, Jorgenson was in love, and there was no reasoning with him. Norah was charismatic when at her best, and Jorgenson felt protective towards her. He also considered himself responsible for her persecution by fellow convicts, which had much to do with her loss of mental equilibrium. For Jorgenson, infatuation and guilt made a powerful combination.

As a married man, Jorgenson felt a heightened sense of financial duty – but neither of them found it easy to make money. Norah earned a little by taking in laundry; Jorgenson resumed writing for the newspapers, though this paid only a pittance. The literary project that most fired his enthusiasm was more long-term: a book about the Aboriginal Tasmanians and the recent conflict. He wanted to be the Black War's first historian. Indeed, he did produce one of the earliest studies of the subject, but his work took him many years, and was never properly completed. It did not see full publication until 1991, after sitting unidentified for 150 years in another man's archives.*

In this work, Jorgenson approved the government's reasons for its operations, but also spoke warmly of the Aboriginal people and showed intense interest in their disappearing way of life. He made a particular study of the various languages of the island, using data earlier collected by himself and others, probably mainly from Mungo/Jack and other guides. His linguistic work, which proved of considerable value since so few other people had attempted it, was published separately just after his death in the *Tasmanian Journal of Natural Science.*[†]

Jorgenson worked from stacks of papers and notebooks, asking the Colonial Secretary's Office for copies of his own reports and filling his room with a 'mass of journals'. He did not get everything he wanted: he was still asking for materials nine years later, in 1840. By then he had been tinkering with the manuscript for too long: perhaps the true reason for its non-publication was that, like the painter in Balzac's 'The Unknown Masterpiece', he could not call it finished until it had developed into a hopelessly overworked (if fascinating) mess. If so, this was a sign of a change in his character: he liked to revise his work, but his final versions were usually produced fluently and at speed. The fact that many of the manuscript pages are 'badly waterstained,

---

* It was discovered by N.J.B. Plomley in the papers of a schoolmaster named Thomas Henry Braim, to whom Jorgenson had apparently lent or sold much of his material for use in Braim's own book about Australia. Jorgenson mentioned the arrangement in a letter to Hooker, adding: 'It would hardly be fair to Mr Braim to let it be generally made known that I have contributed so largely to his book.' Plomley recognized Jorgenson's handwriting, and edited the manuscript for publication as *Jorgen Jorgenson and the Aborigines of Van Diemen's Land.*

† Another researcher who compiled an early vocabulary, Joseph Milligan, described some of the formidable difficulties involved, apart from the lack of easy contact with most Aboriginal groups. The languages seemed simple, for there was no fixed word order, no mood, no tense, and no number. But this was the very thing that made them difficult to study, for all these things were conveyed by tone or gesture. The words themselves were highly mutable, taking affixes whose precise meanings often defeated outsiders: '*la, lah, le, leh, leah, na, ne, nah, ba, be, beah, bo, ma, me, meah, pa, poo, ra, re, ta, te, ak, ek, ik*'. Words could be pronounced differently at different times, even by the same person, and their use could be discontinued by taboo. If a person died whose name meant, say, 'kangaroo' or 'thunder', that word had to be abandoned and a new one adopted in its place.

usually by what appears to have been a wet circular object' (as their editor N.J.B. Plomley put it) may have had something to do with the problem.

He had more success with another book called *Observations on the Funded System*, which came out in instalments in Henry Melville's *Colonial Times* and was re-issued separately in late 1831. Jorgenson claimed to have made about a hundred guineas from it: it was something of a bestseller, mainly because Tasmanian readers were pleasantly surprised, on picking up a book about a subject that seemed to have little to do with them (Britain's National Debt), to discover much enjoyable gossip of strictly local interest, as well as some rousing blasts on a new, anti-imperialist trumpet.

Among other subjects, the book did touch fleetingly on the National Debt. Britain had borrowed heavily from banks and private individuals to finance the wars with France, and was now having difficulty keeping up interest payments; many people felt that future generations had been mortgaged to fund the exigencies of the present. Jorgenson was among them, but he also adopted a distinctively colonial viewpoint. He argued that the home country was now trying to solve its problem by exploiting and impoverishing its colonies. In particular, Britain's debt had led it to deprive Tasmania of £30,000 originally promised for road- and bridge-building and other needs, not least the cost of the Aboriginal conflict. Yet they still expected the colonists to send taxes home: the injustice was apparent.

He was radical as well as eloquent. Not since Icelandic days had he written such rousing political material as this:

England having burdened its children with an intolerable load, is now laying about to the right and the left, ransacking the whole world for that which is unworthy of her acceptance, to patch up for a little while that system which will soon be exploded, catching like the drowning man at the feeble straw for salvation.

Or even this:

[T]he great mass of the human race has been considered as being born for no other end than administering and pampering to the arrogant pretensions, luxury, vice, and debauchery of a very limited number, who, to the eternal degradation of man's character, assume titles and lordly honors and names, which alone ought to be bestowed on the Holiest Holy.

Anyone in the administration who believed rumours that Jorgenson was a dangerous revolutionary would not have been reassured by such passages. In his most extreme moments, he seemed to be inciting the poor to rise up against the rich, or the marginal against the central. In truth, his political position was as equivocal as ever: he mixed firebrand radicalism with underlying conservatism. But there was a new element here. He seems to have acquired a new sense of himself as a Tasmanian, and as a spokesman for the distant, disregarded southern colonies against the careless arrogance of London. He was among the first in Tasmania to voice sentiments of local pride and resentment.

But, of course, this is still Jorgenson, and so the rebellious energy of the *Observations* is lost in a herd of hobby-horses. The book touches on hypocrisy in the Church, abuse of the law, mismanagement of the press, and much else besides, including the evils of the Malthusian theory of population. This he deplored because it encouraged contraception and tried to stop the poor procreating so the rich could keep the good things to themselves. That could not be just: 'If eternal happiness is the true end of creation, the more that are the partakers of the feast, the better.'

One assumes from this that, although he and Norah never had children, it was not because of deliberate prevention, at least not on Jorgenson's part. Perhaps it was something to do with his health, or Norah's. She had had a child before leaving Ireland,* but by now her general state was much more disordered and toxic. In 1832, she was arrested twice, once for an assault on two people and once for theft. While she was awaiting trial for the second offence, Jorgenson wrote seeking Arthur's help: she had displayed 'such a visible derangement of intellect' recently that he actually hoped she would be confined for a few months, preferably not in an ordinary prison but 'in a hospital

---

* This was a daughter, born when Norah was only seventeen or so. The child was left in Ireland and brought up under the name of Mary Macdonald by another family. Jorgenson tried to trace her with Arthur's assistance in 1834, but apparently without success.

or elsewhere, to cool the fermentation of her blood'. Instead, Norah was acquitted on a technicality, and remained in Jorgenson's care.

Her violence and dipsomania were apparently evolving into something worse. In mid-July Jorgenson wrote again to Arthur, saying that her 'mental delusions' were more serious than ever, and that she had tried to commit suicide by swallowing a piece of poisonous copper sulphate or 'Blue Stone'. 'This is the fourth desperate attempt she has made on her own life, and each one nearly successful. She is certainly not fit to be at large.' He hoped that Arthur would, in his goodness, help her by placing her in secure custody. 'I do not write under the influence of passion, she is not innately depraved, and I have been taught to forgive seven times seventy.'

This time Arthur did order her imprisonment, albeit in a place hardly likely to improve her sanity: the Factory, Hobart's dreaded women's prison, where conditions were bestial and inmates ran amok. She was released by the end of the month. Almost immediately afterwards Jorgenson himself was arrested for assault, not on her, but on a constable who had called to investigate neighbours' reports of a commotion at their lodgings. The constable found Jorgenson sitting half-naked and distraught outside his house; his boots and breeches were burning in the fireplace, where he had apparently thrown them. It emerged that he had come home, drunk, to find Norah with another man, a local butcher. *The Tasmanian* newspaper ran a gleeful report headed 'Liberty of the Subject, and a Man's House his Castle', which annoyed Jorgenson even more when he read it, especially because it made fun of his accent.

Defending himself, he tried to prove that the constable had barged into his house by force, that he had not been drunk but merely angry, and that in any case he had a right to set fire to his own breeches; but no one bought the story. During the trial, Norah became hysterical, shouting 'Jergo – Jergo', with what the newspaper described as a 'faint and discordant scream'. She was removed from court and taken downstairs for air – though Jorgenson later said that she had not been led down, but thrown down brutally. When she returned, having recovered her self-possession, she had two butchers with her. The one presumed to be her lover paid Jorgenson's bail.

Over the next few years there were several financial ups and downs.

An *up* was when he got a job working as a overseer on a farm, Norah also being employed to work in the dairy. A *down* was when he lost the job within a month, because he knew nothing about farm life. ('It is true that I had never paid the slightest attention to farming or gardening, so I did not know a turnip top from a potato top.') Next he was imprisoned in Hobart for debt for several weeks in November 1832, but things looked up again when he received a letter from his family telling him he was due property from his mother's estate.* This money took a long time to arrive, however, and when it did come he wasted it all immediately. He learned that (as he was no longer considered a traitor) he was due some prize money from the *Admiral Juul* – but this never materialized at all.

Meanwhile, he continued writing for the *Hobart Town Chronicle* and for Andrew Bent's *Colonist* newspaper. Looking back later, he claimed that he had 'exercised great influence over the colonial press' during these years. This was an exaggeration, but he was a well-known figure among the island's vibrant journalistic community. It was later said that he managed for some years to support 'a precarious existence by his pen'.

So precarious was the existence that he soon had to look for a proper job. He wrote to Arthur in mid-1833, hinting that he would like to be appointed to a post in a new settlement he had heard was being founded.

I am now advancing in years, though my activity remains unabated, still I cannot help looking towards the future with some degree of uneasiness and anxiety. I have another person depending on me for support. – Whatever attempts I have latterly made to place myself above want they have failed. The Press might have opened to me a field for competence, but in these matters it is hard to be over-ruled and subject to unjust dictation.

He would consider anything, he said: 'Either as taking charge of a

* She had died in 1828, which he would not have known until receiving this letter, so it was not entirely good news. On the other hand, it enabled him to re-establish contact with the rest of his family – especially with his most loyal brother, Fritz – after many years of silence.

Store – superintending men sent to public works – managing a Government farm – further exploring a new country, or collecting such cattle as may be claimed by the Government.' He was aware that his wife might be regarded as a problem; but she had improved recently: 'for months past a happy reformation has been effected, which I shall be able to prove to Your Excellency's satisfaction by the attestations of high respectable gentlemen and magistrates, and some of those had formerly expressed an opinion that reformation was hopeless.' He congratulated himself on having achieved this through his own patience and perseverence. This was speaking too soon: on 3 June and again on 19 June 1833 she was arrested for drunkenness.

Arthur did not find him a job as a storekeeper or cattle-collector. But, perhaps recalling an earlier letter in which Jorgenson had hinted that he was ready to 'engage in any special Service' that might be required, he did apparently help to procure him a much more suitable post. The official appointment was as Division Constable in the small town of Ross, not far from his old territory at Oatlands. In reality, he was being employed once again to act as a spy.

13

Jorgenson the Australian

When Jorgenson and Norah moved to Ross in July 1833, there was no stone bridge over its river; there was only a half-collapsed log construction. Work had begun on a new bridge in 1828, on Arthur's orders. Teams of convicts worked for five years under a succession of supervisors; stone was continually dug from nearby quarries and conveyed to Ross by labour crews. Yet by 1833 there was no sign of any bridge, nor of most of the stone. It became a local joke: 'Our bridge will bridge nothing but a gap in conversation.' Meanwhile, new stone buildings were going up on private land all over the Ross area. It was obvious that the convicts, supervisors and many local settlers were all in on a giant scam: even local magistrates and government officials were suspected of involvement, since any attempt to bring corruption charges was invariably thrown out of court.

Arthur had been alerted to the problem, and he chose Jorgenson to sniff out the true explanation – Jorgenson being 'peculiarly quali-fied' for such work by his experience of espionage and detection both in Europe and in Tasmania, as Arthur noted. It was a chance to prove himself again.

Renting a simple hut for himself and Norah on a nearby estate, Jorgenson got to work in Ross with a messianic spirit. But he had an impossible job, for everyone in town knew why he was there, and there began what the Ross Bridge's historian has called 'a grand conspiracy of innocence'. All illicit work paused while Jorgenson snooped about, diligently inspecting the bridge, the quarry, the workers' quarters, and the settlers' new homes. An explanation was provided for everything: when he asked about two extra brick kilns found operating, the convicts said it was their spare-time occupation to bake bricks. Whenever he averted his gaze, the abuses continued as before.

At the end of September, the rented hut was sold and Jorgenson and Norah were made homeless. Finding nowhere else affordable on Jorgenson's low salary,* they moved into a derelict pub called the Man o' Ross Inn on the other side of the river, across the wreck of the old bridge. This was not thought proper: his employers felt that Jorgenson was setting himself beyond the pale. Indeed, with Norah and Jorgenson in residence the Man o' Ross became infamous. Once, the couple were caught boozing with a woman Jorgenson was supposed to have arrested. Another time, he had to call on a friend called Dodd to protect him from Norah's violence; unable to cope alone, Dodd eventually ran to the police station for help. The constable on duty left two prisoners unattended to deal with the emergency, and the prisoners escaped. The whole disaster was firmly blamed on Jorgenson.

His worst misjudgement came when he developed a grudge against a local publican named John Headlam, whom he suspected (probably rightly) of being involved in criminal activities. Headlam kept visitors at bay with ferocious guard dogs, and Jorgenson became so frustrated that he and four armed constables broke into the inn one night and shot two of the dogs. Headlam heard the gunfire and shouted out of his bedroom window; according to him, a man carrying a sword – obviously Jorgenson – called up haughtily that 'it was the King's orders'. Jorgenson denied this and claimed that he had acted legally in destroying two dangerous dogs which were preventing him from conducting investigations. The local magistrates reprimanded Jorgenson, and Arthur himself recorded his displeasure.

The matter might have ended there, but more episodes of drunken disorderliness at the Man o' Ross ensued, and in November Jorgenson was ordered to resign. He did so, though his letter of resignation struck

---

* Like all police officers, he was expected to supplement it with fines and rewards – but he was not catching anybody.

a far from penitent note: he alleged that the whole problem had its origins in the town conspiracy, and that things had only gone well as long as everyone thought he was blind. Now that he was starting to uncover secrets (which, he hinted, implicated the local magistrates who were now treating him so severely) a system of 'annoyance' had broken out to discredit him. He threatened that it would all come to light one day, though he would bide his time for now.

Jorgenson was becoming a conspiracy theorist, but, as is always a possibility with paranoiacs, he may have been partially right. There is no doubt that abuses were still going on in Ross, involving some of the most established settlers. After he was sent away, the corruption continued undisturbed for another year or two. The big change, when it came, was initiated not by government-appointed functionaries but by two of the convicts sent to work there: Daniel Herbert and James Colbeck, the creators of the artwork on the bridge. They were sent to join the gang as punishment for a drunken spree; instead of going along with the prevailing practices, they seemed to become inspired by a vision. Their enthusiasm (particularly Herbert's) infected everyone else, and the bridge was finished promptly in 1836. It emerged as a creative masterpiece, complete with the twin royal portraits of King Jorgen and Queen Norah. Two convict mischief-makers succeeded where, alas, Jorgenson's policemanly righteousness had failed. But he had his reward, too, being preserved in the ridiculous but not unkind stone portrait: a sign that he was already remembered in Ross as pure myth.

Jorgenson and Norah drifted from town to town for a while; Norah was arrested several times for drunkenness and violence. She even lost her ticket of leave, but amazingly went on to receive a full pardon in September 1836. Jorgenson received his a year before her, in August 1835.

He continued to write, penning newspaper articles as well as letters and petitions for anyone who would pay him. He sold little packets of eloquence, epistle by epistle, writing at length on any subject his clients chose. Most of these letters were addressed to Matthew Forster, the Chief Police Magistrate, and over the next few years Forster became thoroughly tired of seeing the familiar handwriting. He rarely replied, but he did develop a certain exasperated fondness for Jorgenson.

In late 1834, Jorgenson published a pamphlet called *An Address to* the *Free Colonists of Van Diemen's Land, on Trial by Jury, and our other Constitutional Rights*, under the pseudonym 'Publicola'.* The specific topic was jury trial, which was not usually granted in Tasmania, even though in Britain – as in Iceland – it was considered the essence of democratic freedom. Many in Tasmania wished for reform (though they did not immediately get it).† 'Publicola' went even further, and urged a radical extension of Tasmanian civil rights in general. Recent meetings on the jury issue had not gone far enough: 'an opportunity was lost of more fully declaring the whole of our undoubted rights as free subjects'. All British colonies must, in time, follow America in confronting the issue of self-determination. If democratic representation were not granted, a violent revolution might one day be expected, and it would be justified, too. London should take warning: 'with respect to the Colonies, the British Government has not derived wisdom from experience, continuing in the same impudent, headstrong, and obnoxious policy, which has always marked its proceedings towards British Settlements, in various parts of the globe.' Jorgenson was becoming quite the colonial freedom fighter.

Such arguments had little effect on Arthur, and in Britain too the government continued to think of Tasmania as a sort of remotely moored, tree-covered prison hulk, rather than as a young, second England. The recent Aboriginal conflict hardly helped to raise the island's status in their eyes. But, exasperated by the indifference of London, the settlers were developing a new image of themselves. Even freed convicts like Jorgenson, now settled there for life, were acquiring considerable self-respect.

The years 1834 and 1835 brought Jorgenson good tidings; he heard

---

* Jorgenson himself later claimed it as his own, and internal textual evidence bears out the idea. The preliminary advertisements, published in the *Colonist*, state that the writer is 'no native of any British dominion'. The text itself includes an otherwise inexplicable historical disquisition on Scandinavia, with special reference to Denmark – and, at the end of this section, the author remarks in classic Jorgenson style that he has been writing from memory. The only aspect that does not fit is a spirited attack on Arthur, but this was the one period when Jorgenson seems to have doubted the Lieutenant-Governor's wisdom.

† Limited reforms did take place in 1834, allowing for small four-man juries in civil cases only, but full jury trial was only achieved under the next Lieutenant-Governor, in 1837.

from Denmark, was granted his full pardon, and got a job briefly working for the famous 'Conciliator', George Augustus Robinson. His task was to travel around the island extracting the rewards promised in the heat of the moment by grateful settlers. He continued working on his Black War book, and published the first instalment of his *Shred of Autobiography* in his old friend Ross's *Almanack*, finding plenty of appreciative readers. This work continued to attract more interest than any other, though it is flawed, and not just by factual errors. He wrote elsewhere that his intention was to undertake a 'stern survey' of his life and character: to draw a map of the interior topography of his head to set alongside the external one which he was still hoping the Phrenological Society of Edinburgh wanted to cast. He intended to describe all his 'propensities, inclinations, vices, properties of the mind, and virtues (if any)', and to provide a self-portrait of unrivalled honesty. But the *Shred of Autobiography* did not turn out like this; his soul-map took him little further than the confession of puzzlement he had already made to Hooker a few years earlier: 'Even in my most solitary hours and in the midst of deepest meditation, I cannot understand myself.'

Unknown to Jorgenson, far away in Scotland, Hooker actually got hold of a copy of his old friend's autobiography, sent to him by a Tasmanian correspondent. Hooker was no longer a bright-eyed young naturalist: he was the perfect nineteenth-century patriarch and an extremely eminent botanist. Like most scientific men of the era, he wrote regularly to professional and amateur colleagues all over the world, who sent him dried plants and anything else they thought might be of interest. He must already have asked R.W. Lawrence, one of his Tasmanian friends, about Jorgenson, for in 1832 Lawrence replied correcting his misconception that Jorgenson was a government surveyor: in fact, Jorgenson was not much of anything at the moment. In December 1833 Hooker mentioned Jorgenson again to another correspondent, Ronald Campbell Gunn, and offered to send Gunn his own *Journal of a Tour in Iceland*, with its account of this 'extraordinary man':

> By accident I was thrown much with him during a rather adventurous voyage I made when quite a young naturalist to Iceland . . . I stood him friend as long as I could; but he proved too bad

for me . . . That man's life would form a perfect Romance if written with the strictest attention to truth . . . I should like to hear how he is conducting himself, from you or your Brother. His talents are of the <u>highest order</u>: but for his character, moral & religious, it was always of the lowest order.

Gunn's brother told Jorgenson that Hooker had been asking after him; by coincidence, Jorgenson had just ended many years' silence by posting Hooker a long letter. Hearing from family in Denmark had melted his resolution to break off communication with those he loved in Europe, he said, and a new river of emotion was opened up: 'I remembered you my Hooker – and I burst into a flood of tears. I was then determined to write, and if possible to hear from you – and once more to see your hand-writing, ere the grave closes upon me for ever.'

When Gunn sent Hooker the *Almanack*, he warned that Jorgenson's standing was 'very low' on the island. 'He married a woman here of abandoned character and very drunken habits, – I do not know how he earns a subsistence just now, but I believe he is not devoting his talents to any profitable or industrious pursuit.' Writing again six months later, Gunn added that Jorgenson seemed shabbily dressed and miserable: 'he is evidently a clever man, but has turned his talents to a wrong account'. These descriptions may have scared Hooker off, for he left Jorgenson's letter unanswered. He never again wrote directly to him, though he continued to make discreet enquiries. Jorgenson wrote several more times, and at least he knew from Gunn that Hooker took some interest in his fate.

The year 1835 brought more stories of drunkenness: he became a familiar shambling figure on the streets of Hobart. As 'His Icelandic Majesty', however, he was also developing into a legend in his own lifetime, especially once his autobiography had come out. 'Everyone knows me in this island,' he boasted to Hooker, and it was true.

Somehow Jorgenson and Norah were still together, despite his occasional attempts to get her removed from his care, and his own frequent incapacity. But she provided little satisfactory companionship. He was still lonely, and knew it was his own fault that things had ended this way. Describing the Tasmanian landscape to Hooker, he wrote:

But here again, when I rested under the Honey Suckle, the Waddle tree, or other elegant shrubbery, my mind became insensibly affected, both melancholy and despondent, I wanted one like you to communicate my feelings to, for those about me took no delight in the beauties of nature ... my broken heart wandered back to former associations and past days. I felt an intolerable vacancy within, for such a friend I might forever have preserved in you, but I have lost you with many others.

And to his brother Fritz, in September 1835, he confessed: 'I am here solitary, and far distant from the scenes of my youth . . . I feel the deepest sorrow, the bitterest grief.' He knew that he had been a source of pain to his family. They had lived 'in continued apprehension and terror' on his account; that was why he had decided not to bother them further. He felt differently now, though he found that he could not bear to write to them about personal matters in Danish, and had to use English. As he put it to Hooker: 'the fragments of my poor heart are widely scattered over the surface of the globe'.

It was Fritz who had told Jorgenson that their father lived to be sixty-five, rather than the dreaded sixty-three, thus liberating him from his obsession. He was now fifty-five himself; the feared age had been creeping closer. Yet he still felt astonishingly fit. Toughened by his years at sea, his vigorous constitution somehow weathered the ocean of alcohol as well. He told Fritz happily that he enjoyed 'uncommonly good health, I feel little difference now and when I was thirty-years of age. Constant exercise, and [being] exposed to the free air in a salubrious climate, have preserved my constitution greatly unimpaired.' It seemed as if, despite his tribulations, he could go on for ever.

Jorgenson had threatened that his Ross reports would come back to haunt his enemies, and the prophecy turned out to be true. During 1835, his need for money was so great that he sold a stack of them to a litigious settler named William Bryan, who had undertaken a legal campaign against Arthur's administration in the attempt to clear his own name of corruption charges. Taking his case all the way to London, Bryan backed it up using Jorgenson's documents. These did not accuse

Arthur directly, but they did convey a damaging picture of a colony in which corruption was rife, and this hardly made Arthur look good. Jorgenson seems never to have intended to use this material against Arthur, merely against the Ross officials and he may have been unaware of Bryan's purposes. He found himself caught up in something he surely would not have wanted: a small but effective plot to bring down the Lieutenant-Governor he respected so much.

Arthur defended himself, dismissing Jorgenson's reports as nonsense and Bryan's motives as suspicious. The Colonial Office did not find Arthur culpable, but the affair did remind them that, in any case, he had been in Van Diemen's Land long enough – twelve years. It seemed time for a change, so they recalled him in 1836, later sending him to a similar post in Canada. Jorgenson was sad to see him go. He continued to write warm letters even after Arthur had left the colony, and he also sang his praises publicly in Tasmania, addressing a meeting of colonists in November 1836 in support of a motion of thanks to Arthur's government. He spoke as an official representative of that hitherto neglected but increasingly important third category of Tasmanian residents, after settlers and prisoners: liberated convicts. It was a role he also assumed in his *Shred of Autobiography*, writing in 1837, 'I have purposely given the progress of a convict; I have done so with the utmost sincerity of heart.'

Jorgenson missed Arthur, but he was by no means disappointed to see the next Lieutenant-Governor arrive, for it turned out to be another man he idolized: Sir John Franklin, a veteran of voyages of exploration in both Australia and the Arctic. He had even met him once before, briefly, during the Flinders expedition. Now he started a one-sided correspondence with Franklin just as he had with Arthur, and proudly presented him with a copy of his inflammatory *Observations on the Funded System*. Franklin did not seem to mind, though he paid Jorgenson little attention.

In early 1835, from the addresses on his letters, Jorgenson was staying at or near an inn called the Labour in Vain, an apt enough name. By April 1836, he was in prison for debt, while Norah broke her leg and was kept in hospital for a while. This was expensive, so Jorgenson asked to have her transferred to the Factory, where she would at least be fed and housed. Hobart was suffering a particularly bad autumn, and the winter became the coldest in the history of the colony: it was no time to be destitute, drunk and broken-legged on the streets. The request was granted. Meanwhile, Jorgenson put his time in prison to constructive use, writing notes for Forster on prison conditions. He was eventually released, after being officially declared bankrupt.

He received another letter from his brother, containing the sad news that Fritz himself was ill and that his wife had incurable breast cancer. Many of those Jorgenson loved in Denmark were dead: both parents, his impeccable elder brother Urban and four of Urban's children; now it seemed Fritz and his wife would soon follow. Fritz wrote (in a translation by Jorgenson): 'While I write this tears stream from my eyes, when I think how happily we could have lived together in our latter days.' He also added something Jorgenson recognized as 'a gentle and brotherly hint': 'Sense and talents God has given us all, but alas! we have not exercised them with that knowledge we might have done.'

Jorgenson himself was now showing signs of wear and tear, and in June 1839 wrote to Forster: 'I have not been able to stir out for many days, I met with a terrible crash on Thursday evening last, when it was dark, wet and slippery – in one of the holes which are very deep, and not filled up in Williamson street. I am shook all to pieces – extremely weak, and shall not be well for sometime to come.' But he worked on: in March 1840 he was engaged in 'a mass of writing', and said that he hoped soon to 'have sufficient leisure and quiet to finish some productions which I have long since commenced'. He continued to take an interest in prison conditions, and also in the pros and cons of convict constables, writing a series of letters on the subject to the *Colonial Times*. This was mainly inspired not by his having been a convict constable himself, but by his having recently been arrested by one during a drunken scene with Norah. Naturally he took a more critical attitude than he had done a few years previously.

He was still struggling to cope with his wife's difficulties, which were again worsening. During 1840, he came to the conclusion that she was in a hopeless condition, and in March asked a magistrate to 'put her for about six weeks where she can get rid of her extremely drunken habits'. The magistrate apparently thought Jorgenson was trying to evade his marital responsibilities, and did not oblige. Some weeks later Jorgenson wrote to Forster: 'Norah is irrecoverably lost –

totally insensible to proper habits and decorum. She is past redemption, she is continually dragging me downhill, and her associates are of the most disreputable character.' He announced that he had left her, but he did not actually go, or if he did he soon returned. In May she fell downstairs and again broke a bone, this time in her arm.*

Norah was in a serious decline, and a couple of months later, on 17 July 1840, she died. The cause is recorded in the death register as 'Visitation of God', which sounds dramatic but was merely the standard form used when no precise diagnosis was available. Some form of alcohol-related illness was presumably the underlying cause. She was buried in Hobart's Catholic cemetery: a young woman of thirty-five.

Her tumultuous marriage with Jorgenson had lasted for nearly ten years. It had never exactly settled down into an understanding – he was trying to get rid of her to the end – but it had become a routine of sorts, and there was a certain companionship as they slid downhill together. Now Norah was gone: according to Jorgenson's own estimation, his own decline should have levelled out. Instead, it continued at the same rate. Her loss was not such a liberation after all. Now he was solitary and diminished: smaller than his own legend, which was rapidly overtaking him.

He did have one glorious moment in 1840. On 29 April, a public meeting of colonists took place in Hobart to protest against the abolition of the assignment system, a change which had been decreed from London. Instead of convicts being sent to work for individual settlers, as before, there would be a new centralized approach, with all work being done on vast government projects and and all convicts housed in large prison buildings. This ignored the economic interests of the colonists, who relied on convict servants and stock-keepers to run their businesses. They were outraged by the way it had been imposed from the other side of the world, without discussion or appeal, by people who knew nothing of Tasmanian conditions.

The meeting was well attended: the boxes, pit and stage were all crowded, as if for a popular benefit concert. Speakers included impor-

* One has to wonder if violence from Jorgenson was involved here, but it is just as likely to be a drunken tumble. Both had become very accident-prone by this time.

tant landowners, a barrister speaking for the professional classes, a clergyman speaking for the Church, and the merchant who had lived longest in the colony – Anthony Fenn Kemp – representing the commercial sector. Then, at the very end, there rose one unscheduled extra speaker: Jorgen Jorgenson, addressing the assembly in his new role as spokesman for the ex-convict population.

According to the *True Colonist*'s report, he asked the assembly: 'Will you permit me to speak a few words?' Several voices said, 'Yes; hear him, certainly; every man has a right to be heard.' And so he began, reading from an extremely dignified text:

I thank you; and as I am, from being a foreigner, unable to express myself readily and correctly in English, I hope you will allow me to read from this paper the few observations which I crave to offer on the very important matters now under your consideration. The present is a subject which deeply interests every class and every individual member of the community – both rich and poor, free and bond. And although it would be out of the question, to permit any one of the latter class to take a part in your deliberations, yet I trust, that you will not only consider it pardonable, but really desirable and advantageous to the ends you have in view, that some one of my class should come forward to express his opinions on a subject in which all are alike interested, and, in which all are so unanimous.

He then dealt in turn with each of the arguments advanced by the government, none of which satisfactorily addressed the problem of lost labour. One could not change such arrangements overnight: 'The system took its origin in the necessities of the earlier days of the two penal colonies; it is so interwoven with their existence, that it cannot be interrupted without causing a violent shock, the effects of which will not be fully perceived until much mischief is done – mischief not foreseen by those who are advocates for a change.'

It was plain, he said, that things had not been thought through by the supposed experts in prison discipline and colonial politics, sitting in their offices in London. 'Without a perfect knowledge of the tempers of prisoners – without a skill in human nature – without experience

... they have presumed to form hasty conclusions from very imperfect materials.' It was symptomatic of more fundamental misunderstandings: he cited 'the barefaced calumnies heaped on our colonial society, charging the Colonists of all classes with utter depravity, and general demoralization'. If that was what they thought, he said, they should look into any church on the island to see how full the congregations were, and how decent was their dress and deportment: 'Van Diemen's Land will in these respects yield to no other country under the British Crown.'

Those at home might speechify, 'and misrepresent facts of which they are ignorant, and slander a whole community, equal at least, if not greatly superior, to that to which their cruel misrepresentations are addressed', but the truth would prevail. As far as he was concerned, Hobart could hold its head high against any town of the world.

Jorgenson's views accorded with those of the assembly in general, and there is no reason to doubt that he was applauded by his audience. When the meeting drew to a close, its resolutions were voted on and carried unanimously. The colonists' objection to the new system was registered with Franklin; but the matter had been decided, and there could be no appeal. It would be a long time before expressions of Antipodean irritation such as this produced any real effects, or generated any kind of independence movement. Canada was slightly ahead in this respect, for a major rebellion there in 1837 had forced Britain to make compromises.

Just as in Iceland in 1809, self-government was not yet a viable concept and, once again, Jorgenson was ahead of his time. In his final public appearance, he stood up not only as an unashamed representative of the newly defined community of free ex-convicts, but as an advocate of colonial self-determination – and a proud Australian.

14

We, Jorgen Jorgenson

Jorgenson's memories of his oldest and still best beloved friend were revived one more time in August 1840, when he met Hooker's son, the naturalist Joseph Dalton Hooker, a man destined to become even more famous than his father. Like William Jackson Hooker before him, he was on his youthful apprenticeship tour. Instead of Iceland, he was travelling to a frozen region even further from home: Antarctica. He sailed with the expedition led by James Clark Ross, on the *Erebus* and *Terror* – the same ships in which the island's present Lieutenant-Governor Sir John Franklin was to go missing eight years later while searching for the Northwest Passage. Franklin was enthusiastic about the Ross expedition, which called at Hobart for several months on its way south; he was also keen to meet Joseph Hooker, for he too knew his father well. Jorgenson was even more eager, and sought the young man out several times.

But Joseph was a different kind of person from his father. He was rather aloof and cool, with none of William's easy charm; in Hobart he avoided society as much as he could and spent his time botanizing in the surrounding bush. The colony appeared contemptible to him: people here tried to imitate English culture, he observed languidly, but local literature was 'at a low ebb', and 'except a few English families, there are none who take the better periodicals, or would comprehend them if they did. There are lots of splendid Pianos and Harps, and few who can use them.'

It is not surprising, therefore, that Joseph greeted the shambling, weepingly sentimental Jorgen Jorgenson with distaste. He wrote later that Jorgenson appeared 'in a half tipsy state and in rags, and begged for half a crown'; and to his father he remarked, 'Jorgen Jorgensen had nearly slipped my mind. I have seen him once or twice, but he is quite incorrigible; his drunken wife has died and left a more drunken widower; he was always in that state when I saw him, and used to cry about you.' Jorgenson asked him if he had a spare copy of the *Journal of a Tour in Iceland*, as he had lost his – but the naturalist Ronald Campbell Gunn warned Joseph that he had lent Jorgenson his own copy just a few months earlier (the one sent by Hooker, presumably), and had not yet had it returned.

Even fifty years later, Joseph Hooker was irritated by the mention of Jorgenson's name. A Mrs Lyell wrote asking him about the famous 'Uncrowned King', as she had just read a book about him, presumably J.F. Hogan's *Convict king*. He replied with a dismissive mish-mash of wrong information. She wrote asking for more, and this time he replied crossly: 'You say he does not seem to be anything worse than a gambler – but did you read my letter? My father had scores of letters from him *from the condemned cell in Newgate*, and I found him a *convict* in Tasmania. I have often heard my father tell the tale of his iniquities. He was the most plausible rascal he ever knew, and narrowly escaped the gallows.' If anything, this probably increased Mrs Lyell's enthusiasm for the subject, but she gave up asking Hooker.

The Ross expedition left for Antarctica towards the end of the year, as the summer season came on. It was successful, penetrating as close to the southern magnetic pole as was possible by sea and claiming several new areas with British flags. In April 1841, the two ships again called at Hobart. But by this time, Jorgen Jorgenson was dead. After living for years in fear of the Grand Climacteric, he had not made it that far. He died on 20 January 1841, a few months short of his sixty-first birthday.

Some weeks earlier, on 4 December 1840, Jorgenson had written his final letter to William Jackson Hooker: a letter that would not arrive until after his death. His writing was as lucid and legible as ever. He actually seemed to be feeling better, and he described Joseph's visit and laid out his own plans for the future with optimism. Despite his ungenerous reception, he had been overjoyed to meet Hooker's son, especially as the young man looked just like his father. It threw Jorgenson's mind back to their adventures on the other side of the world all those years ago, adventures which played in his memory still – 'although at this time of life the images which lurk round my mind partake of the character of a dream'.

'My history since my arrival here has been (as in all other instances of my life) one of strange fortunes and great activity', he wrote, truly enough. 'I am now advanced to that time of life, next March 29th Sixty one years, that I cannot much longer expect to linger in this world.' He wanted to gather together his publications to leave a 'memorial' of himself; not having them all to hand, he asked Hooker to trace the missing ones, including the Danish book about the Pacific, the English book about the Copenhagen expedition, and various manuscripts and newspaper articles. He seemed to be trying to compile a sort of auto-bibliography, to leave his mark on the world in words. But his chaotic habits throughout life made this almost impossible.

It is sometimes said that Jorgenson died in a ditch, an idea derived from one of Joseph Hooker's throwaway remarks. He may have collapsed in one, but if so he was scooped up and taken to Hobart's Colonial Hospital, around the corner from his lodgings. It was there that he died. The cause of death was given as an inflammation of the lungs, possibly pneumonia. As with Norah's final illness, it was probably the result of alcoholic debilitation.

The Governor himself noted the death in a letter to the elder Hooker: 'Jorgen Jorgenson died in the hospital after a short illness. – He had been long breaking – Dr [J.D.] Hooker saw him and perhaps had from him a request for a little money as I occasionally had on the score of being an old ship mate.'

Several of the island's newspapers printed a fine obituary. It read:

It becomes our duty to record the death of one of the most extraordinary men of his time . . . His political career is so well known that any detail of it would be superfluous – suffice it to say that Mr Jorgenson has figured in every sphere of life, from the Supreme Governor of Iceland, down to a bush constable in Van Diemen's Land. Few men had a stronger mind, and the works he has left behind him, on a variety of subjects, are the best proofs of his talent. Among these perhaps the most conspicuous is 'the Religion of Christ, the Religion of Nature,' published in England about 18 or 20 years ago. He was also the author of several other pamphlets, on the corn laws, currency, and various political subjects, and a contributor to almost every journal in the colony. Although a Dane by birth he wrote and spoke the English language with propriety and force, and was also master of the Latin, French, and German languages, and deeply read in the authors of each. Of late years he has been considerably reduced, and supported a precarious existence by his pen, and the occasional remittances of his friends in Denmark. It is our province merely to record his death – to portray his character would be impossible. That was in truth like his life, a mingled yarn of good and evil; but he is gone, and let his faults be buried with him. He died in the Colonial Hospital on Tuesday last, at the advanced age of 72 years [*sic*], and there are many in this colony and elsewhere who will lament the death of 'Jorgen Jorgenson'.

Jorgenson and Norah left no children. There was also no will, and Jorgenson died a pauper. But acquaintances may have helped with funeral expenses, for he received a proper burial alongside Norah on 31 January 1841 in the Catholic cemetery, although he had never been a Catholic himself. The cemetery fell into decay during the later nineteenth century, and a college was built over the site in 1911, obliterating almost all trace of the graves. There is just one reminder of the past: the workers came across a number of bones during construction, and laid them aside to be cremated. The ashes of these bones are kept in a small memorial box near the entrance to the college; and they may well include some grey ghosts of the bodies of Jorgenson and Norah.

Jorgenson's biographer J.F. Hogan noted in 1891 that his career formed 'one of the most striking confirmations of the trite saying that truth is stranger than fiction. The most daring and unconventional of novelists would never dream of crowding into the life of a hero of the circulating libraries such a rapid succession of extraordinary adventures.'

Alan Villiers in *Vanished Fleets* agreed that if Jorgenson had been a fictional character in a book, that book would never have been published. 'It would have been thought to strain probability to breaking point.' In fact, some have tried to re-create him in fiction, and these often bizarre attempts form perhaps the most fitting memorial to this mutable man, who was himself such a fabulist of his own life.

He was resurrected first in an early Tasmanian novel by William Moore Ferrar, called *The Maxwells of Bremgarten*, in which he appears as a tracker of bushrangers in the north-west: his life is related in a version avowedly lifted from the *Shred of Autobiography*. This in turn inspired the novelist Marcus Clarke, who in 1870 retold the *Shred of Autobiography* again in a non-fiction article in the *Australasian* newspaper, and then recycled aspects of it for his famous novel *His Natural Life*. His newspaper piece ended: 'All the raven-haired, hot-headed, supple-wristed soldiers of fortune that ever diced, drank, duelled, kissed and escaladed their way through three volumes octavo never had such an experience!'

In a 1922 novel by Roy Bridges, *The Cards of Fortune*, Jorgenson is reborn as a sinister but capable bushman with glittering blue eyes and a sardonic smile, who leads a party in pursuit of a bushranger's gang through the Tasmanian wilderness – which is all rank vegetation and rotting ferns, filled with 'festoons of bloated fungus' and miasmic exhalations. As a 'fat black snake' slithers out from under a decaying log, the novel's heroine asks, 'Are you sure of your ground, Jorgenson?' He replies: 'I am quite confident. You needn't be afraid', and explains that his own fate rests on the success of the trip, for his pardon application is soon to be considered, and he longs to be freed. 'I, Jorgen Jorgenson, in Van Diemen's Land, like Napoleon at St Helena!'

Another novel of the 1920s, Vernon Williams's *The Straitsman*, also features Jorgenson as a bush trekker, but this time there is nothing of the marshland creature about him. His bearing is bold and commanding, and his chin is firm; 'his head was peculiarly large, with brown cheeks laced with furrows, a sharp, hawk-like nose, and large blue eyes lit with a cunning gleam.' The narrator's father hails him with the unlikely words, 'Hey there, Cap'n Jorgenson, this here island's not another pesky Iceland. 'Tain't Arctic here, but something a darned sight hotter.' Jorgenson greets him affectionately and delivers a brief run-down of his life story, interspersed with sailor's cries of 'now, my hearties' and 'shiver my timbers!' He finishes almost wonderingly, 'Ay, God bless me, once I was King of Iceland.'

Even in non-fictional accounts, the urge to dramatize is irresistible. Rhys Davies's 1940 quasi-biography *Sea Urchin* unashamedly took leave of reality; Frank Clune and P.R. Stephensen's *The Viking of Van Diemen's Land* of 1954 used fictional devices to ornament their more traditional research. A splendidly peculiar children's book was issued by the Tasmanian Education Department in 1970: *Jorgen Jorgenson: a Convict King*. It begins with Jorgenson sitting down to write his autobiography; we then see him as a boy, leaving Denmark and travelling to Australia on the *Lady Nelson* ('How he loved that little ship!'), killing the first whale in the Derwent River ('There she blows!'), and returning to a hero's welcome in Copenhagen. But then: 'The King of Denmark decided to join Napoleon, the Emperor of France, and make war against England.' In Iceland, Jorgenson heroically arrests the Danish Governor: an illustration shows him standing open-armed while the happy Icelanders gaze up at him. He is captured and sent to Britain, then freed, and sent to the Continent as a spy. 'He would be well paid for his work. What good luck!' It could almost have been written by Jorgenson himself, and in a sense it was, since, like so many re-tellings, it is based uncritically on his *Shred of Autobiography*.

Eventually the story follows him out to Tasmania, and touches on the Aboriginal conflict. Once again, we see him writing at the table – but then 'a sudden noise made him drop his pen. Into the room came his wife Norah.' On this page there appears a glorious Ladybird-style illustration of the dishevelled Norah clinging to the door-frame for support and clutching a bottle. Even Jorgenson's fairy-tale imagination could never have predicted that his life would receive quite this kind of treatment.

The same flashback structure (from writing desk to real-world adventures and back again) was used by the writer Craig Cormick for his 1998 story 'The last history of Jorgen Jorgensen', which portrays Jorgenson fabricating his memoirs and then destroying them with the intention of starting again: 'This time the truth'. Another recent fictional appearance, taking the fabulation theme even further, has been in Richard Flanagan's 2001 novel *Gould's Book of Fish*. Here, in keeping with the novel's deliberately fantastical nature, Jorgenson is more transformed than ever. He is relocated to the prison colony of Sarah Island, where he never set foot, and given the job of clerk and archivist, recording the prison's activities in a flowery hand unlike his real one. His life is rearranged with garbled dates and details, and his physical appearance is reversed: he is given an elongated, angular physique and a sallow complexion. Later he metamorphoses into an evil demiurge whose falsified ledgers magically create an alternative universe while he hovers in his prison library making baleful pronouncements: "'Doomed'", continued he, savouring the word, "to suffer torment for all eternity." Jorgenson would perhaps have enjoyed the joke.

A noticeable feature of most fictional accounts, like most non-fictional ones, is that they concentrate either on the swashbuckling side of his nature or on the sleazy side – whose existence cannot be denied. But he is no more defined by either of these extremes than he is by the more subtle elements of his makeup: his literary ambition and energy, his intelligence and prodigious memory, his physical endurance, his uninhibited warmth towards friends, his romantic sense of the sublime, or his tendency to sabotage his own chances just when everything was going smoothly.

Frank Clune and P.R. Stephensen started a different trend by interpreting his life mainly in terms of his literary efforts rather than real-world adventures. They were also keen to find a 'philosophical meaning' of sorts in his life, an attempt which is rather becalmed by Jorgenson's own opaque, almost surreally deadpan brand of philosophy – as when he writes that 'every tub should stand upon its own bottom, and every herring hang by its own tail', or (of death) that 'when a cannon-ball takes a man's head off, which he does not expect, there is an end of him'. And of human liberty, in the final sentence of his manuscript on the Aboriginal Tasmanians:

I would not give myself the slightest concern or trouble about it; reflecting on the shortness of human life, instability of fortune and the uncertainty of all transitory enjoyments, I would rather rush on in as quiet a manner as possible.

But the idea that literary endeavour, rather than a piratical spirit of adventure, is the key to his life is persuasive. He applied himself to his writerly apprenticeship with dedicated patience and effort, especially in Britain after the Iceland adventure, and he never rested for more than a day or two in prison without producing some fluent disquisition on Afghanistan or religion or smuggling or Danish history. His writings, despite their digressions, are invariably full of entertaining detail. Jorgenson's greatest desire, never fully realized, was to be taken seriously as a man of letters, as his last request to Hooker suggests.

Clune and Stephensen concluded: 'He was a man of action who was also a man of thought. This is the chief fascination in the study of his life. He was not one personality, but two.' In fact he was a double man through and through, divided between wisdom and folly, between conservatism and rebellion, between the roles of liberator and colonist, between countries, between languages and between impulses. As he himself realized, he was also divided between brilliance and madness. Jorgenson was actually more than two people in one: he was many, and he spoke more truly than he realized when he began his Icelandic proclamations: 'We, Jorgen Jorgenson'.

In many ways he was a literary Romantic of the type described in *Doubles*, Karl Miller's study of the era's cloven minds. All the torments endured by such a man are generated by his fissile nature: he 'is not of common clay. His nerves are peculiarly susceptible. He is highly-strung. He is suspended between heaven and earth, torn between the two as he is between reason and imagination. He has his ups and downs, is neither here nor there . . . He is a specialist in contrasts and cross-purposes, and in misfortune.' He is all over the place, like a knot of ropes.

Yet Jorgenson himself invariably ended any bout of self-examination by asserting that, in spite of everything, 'even with a hundred nooses around my neck, I still have a good heart, and have done many good deeds'. He was not wrong in this, and it seems only right to remember Jorgen Jorgenson as a unified man after all: a man with 'a good and feeling heart'.

Acknowledgements

Foremost among those I would like to thank are Anna Agnarsdóttir and Dan Sprod, who were both extraordinarily generous with their time and expertise. I am also grateful to Jette Nielsen for her fantastically patient and helpful work on translations from the Danish, and to my mother Jane Bakewell for bibliographical research.

Special thanks are due to Lesley Albertson, J.M. Bruce, Stephanie Burbury, Jørn Dyrholm, Alan Magnusson, Kim Peart, Axel Pedersen, Chandak Sengoopta, Sigurður Hjartarson, Hanne Tylén, and to Inga Lara Baldvinsdóttir of the National Museum of Iceland; also to Steffen Heiberg and Irene Falnov of the Frederiksborg Museum, Mette Bruun Beyer of the Københavns Bymuseum, Lucy Waitt of the National Maritime Museum, Roxanne Peters of the Victoria & Albert Museum, Kathy Wilkinson of the Council for World Mission, and Jora Johannsdóttir of Iceland's RUV television archives. As always, the staff in all the libraries and archives I've used have been most helpful, and I am particularly grateful to Michele Losse of the Library and Archive of the Royal Botanic Gardens (Kew), Judith Magee of the Natural History Museum's Botany Library, Lesley Price of the University of London's SOAS Library, Palle Ringsted and Bodil Østergaard-Andersen of Det Kongelige Bibliotek, Henrik Stissing Jensen of Rigsarkivet, Marian Minson of the Alexander Turnbull Library, Fiona Macfarlane and Robyn Eastley of the Archives Office of Tasmania, Carmel McInerny of the National Library of Australia, Warwick Hirst of the Mitchell Library (SLNSW), Tony Marshall and all the Heritage Collections librarians of the State Library of Tasmania, Gail Davis of the State Records of New South Wales, and Jill Rosenshield of the University of Wisconsin-Madison's Memorial Library.

Finally, thanks to my zestful agent Zoë Waldie, to Alison Samuel and to my terrific editor Jenny Uglow at Chatto & Windus, to Ray Bakewell for the close reading and to Rowan Taylor for the dashes. Above all, to Simonetta Ficai-Veltroni, for the whole *ambaradan*.

Notes

Abbreviations:

(a) Archives and libraries

AOT	Archives Office of Tasmania (Hobart)
BL	British Library (London)
BLARS	Bedfordshire and Luton Archives and Records Service (Bedford)
BNA	British National Archives (London)
KB	Det Kongelige Bibliotek (Copenhagen)
ML	Mitchell Library, State Library of New South Wales (Sydney)
NHM	Botany Library, Natural History Museum (London)
RA	Rigsarkivet (Copenhagen)
RBG	Library and Archive of the Royal Botanic Gardens, Kew (London)
ThÍ	Thjóðskjalasafn Íslands (Reyjkavík)

(b) Jorgenson's works

AFC by	*An Address to the Free Colonists of Van Diemen's Land, on Trial by Jury* . . .
ATW	*The Adventures of Thomas Walter*
CE	*The Copenhagen Expedition* . . .
HA1	*Historical Account of a Revolution on the Island of Iceland* . . . [Version 1]
HA2	*Historical Account of a Revolution on the Island of Iceland* . . . [Version 2]
HVDLC	*History of the . . . Van Diemen's Land Company*
NHMC	'A narrative of the habits, manners, and customs of the Aborigines of Van Diemen's Land', N.J.B. Plomley's edition
OFS	*Observations on the Funded System* . . .
OPT	*Observations on Pacific Trade* . . . (English translation of *Efterretning* . . .)
RC	*The Religion of Christ is the Religion of Nature*
RJJ	'Report of Mr Jorgen Jorgenson . . .' in Van Diemen's Land Company: *Report made to the third Yearly General Meeting* . . .
SA	*Shred of Autobiography*, J. Dally's edition
SC	*State of Christianity in the Island of Otaheite* . . .
TFG	*Travels through France and Germany* . . .

Full publication details of other references can be found in the bibliography.

A note on the name

vii   Jorgenson's affidavit: 12 Sept. 1834, enclosed with Arthur to Lefevre, 17 Sept. 1834, BNA CO 280/49, ff. 156r–v.

Jorgen Jorgenson on a bridge

3   Norah on the bridge: Greener and Laird pp. 167, 125.

4   Damper an excellent thing: SA p. 56.

4   Description of Jorgenson from his entry in Tasmanian convict register: AOT CON 31/23.

4   Tasmanian commemoration: *The Advocate* (Burnie), 12 May 2001, p. 30; *The Mercury*, 6 Nov. 1968, p. 32; *The Mercury Westerner*, 22 May 1986, p. 30(B); *The Mercury*, 1 Feb. 1988, p. 8 (letter from F. Bradshaw).

5   Crown Prince Frédérik's wedding speech (14 May 2004): *Sunday Mail (Australia)*, 16 May 2004.

5   Literary comparisons: Phelps (1817) p. 60; Haygarth, N., *A view to cradle* (Canberra: the author, 1998), p. 14; L. Huxley in Hooker, J.D., v. 2, p. 483; Oehlenschlæger v. 1, p. 53; http://www.adventourers.com; *The Mercury*, 28 Aug. 2003, p. 22; Ibsen p. 8.

6   'Rudderless barque' etc.: Hogan pp. 37–9.

6   'What a list!' Villiers p. 99.

Chapter 1: A Danish boy

7   Birth: church register of St Nikolaj, Landsarkivet for Sjælland. Jorgenson celebrated his birthday on 29 March and gave that as his date of birth in official documents throughout his life: see his affidavit of 12 Sept. 1834, BNA CO 280/49, ff. 156r–v; JJ to Anna Jørgensen, 22 March 1825, RA Samlingspakke no. 2679; JJ to Hooker, 4 Dec. 1840, RBG DC v. 76, no. 47; Sprod pp. 1, 632.

7   Roaring: ATW p. 23, where he writes as 'Thomas Walter', in a work mixing fantasy with genuine autobiography.

7   Father and house: JJ to Hooker, 22 July 1820, BL Ms. Eg. 2070; Fritz Jürgensen to JJ, as translated and quoted by the latter in JJ to Forster, 31 March 1840, AOT CSO 19/2 pp. 195–8; Sprod pp. 4, 634. Jorgenson's father's clocks can be seen at Frederiksborgmuseet in Hillerød, Denmark, and in the Fitzwilliam Museum in Cambridge.

8   Father, mother and wet-nurse: ATW pp. 21–5.

8–9   Siblings: JJ to Fritz Jürgensen, 11 Sept. 1835, KB NBD IX 8, Haandskrift Afd. 163; JJ affidavit of 12 Sept. 1834, BNA CO 280/49, ff. 156r–v; church register of St Nikolaj, Landsarkivet for Sjælland. On Fritz the younger: Nygaard pp. 741–9; Bjerring; *Dansk biografisk leksikon* v. 7, pp. 504–6; Axel West Pedersen, personal communication.

9   Strength and charisma: ATW pp. 24–5; Fritz Jürgensen to JJ, as translated by the latter and enclosed with a plea for pardon on 14 May 1829,

AOT CSO 1/426.

9   First school and truancy: ATW pp. 25–6.

10   Efterslægtens Skole: ATW pp. 28–39, 49–50, 53; Oehlenschlæger v. 1, pp. 55–6; SA p. 9.

10   Oehlenschlæger's anecdotes: Oehlenschlæger v. 1, pp. 55–6. Fruit-seller anecdote: ATW pp. 54–6. For Fritz's cartoons: Nygaard pp. 743, 749.

11–12   Songstress: JJ to Fritz Jürgensen, 11 Sept. 1835, KB NBD IX 8, Haandskrift Afd. 163.

12   Expulsion: ATW pp. 76–7.

12   Practical jokes and depression: ATW p. 94.

12   Fire: SA pp. 9–10. The following year, after Jorgenson left, there was an even more terrible fire which destroyed nearly a thousand buildings in the city, including the church where he had been christened.

12–13   Countryside, revolution, uncle and England: ATW pp. 92, 121–4, 136–40, 146, 149, 155–9.

14   Seafarers and the ship dream: ATW p. 93; SA p. 10; see also JJ to Fritz Jürgensen, 11 Sept. 1835, KB NBD IX 8, Haandskrift Afd. 163.

14   Conrad: Conrad pp. 49, 5 (*A personal record*).

15   'From my earliest youth . . .': JJ to Hooker, 17 Dec. 1810, BL Ms. Eg. 2070.

15   Father, the *Jane*, and farewell: ATW, pp. 164, 172–3; Sprod p. 6.

15–16   Crossing to England: *Letters from Albion* v. 1, pp. 26, 39; Geijer p. 76.

16   'I served my time out . . .' and 'I perfected myself . . .' ATW p. 174; SA p. 10.

16–17   First glimpse and second home: JJ to Macleay/Hooker, 24 Nov. 1809, BL Ms. Eg. 2070. 'A great many books': SA p. 10.

17   London: Simond v. 1, p. 25; *Letters from Albion* v. 1, pp. 60, 66, 43, 86, 97; Sydney Smith: Pearson, Hesketh, *The Smith of Smiths* (London: Hamish Hamilton, 1934) pp. 85–6.

18   'A second father': JJ to Castlereagh, 31 May 1820, BNA FO 22/86 f. 151v.

Chapter 2: Dreams fulfilled

19   Britain's confidence: Martin Lynn, 'British policy, trade, and informal empire in the mid-nineteenth century', in Porter and Low p. 102.

19–20   Ralegh on trade: see Padfield (1999) p. 2.

20   Press-ganging and journey to Cape: ATW pp. 174–83.

20   Life at sea: Lloyd pp. 214–5; Porter, David: *Journal of a cruise made to the Pacific Ocean . . .* 2nd edn (New York: Wiley & Halsted, 1822) v. 1, pp. 2–3. Psychological problems: Lamb pp. 118–127.

21–22   Piracy: ATW pp. 185–6, 190; OPT p. 26; Richards pp. 108 ff.

22   Quicksilver mines: SA p. 22. Thomas Walter's bawdy story: ATW pp. 190–244.

22 The *Lady Nelson/Harbinger* conundrum: SA p. 11; *Lady Nelson* pay list in King Papers, ML A1976 v. 1, pp. 28–9; Grant p. 53; BNA ADM 103/61 (entry 846); AOT CON 31/23; Richards pp. 107–13; Sprod pp. 15–21.

23 *Lady Nelson* trips: Grant pp. 87, 123 ff., 149 ff.; Lee (1915) pp. 33–67.

23–4 Sealing: Lee (1915) pp. 103, 117–20; Grant p. 123; OPT pp. 21, 23–4; Dunbabin pp. 13–14, 22. Sealers and Aboriginal women: Ryan, L., p. 3; NHMC pp. 126–7.

24–5 *Lady Nelson* encounter: Lee (1915) pp. 137–40, and pp. 110–11 for a similar, earlier incident.

25 Flinders and the *Lady Nelson*'s keels: Lee (1915) pp. 3, 176, Grant pp. v–xxvi; Sprod p. 27; Flinders v. 2, pp. 9, 18.

26 Taking the ground: Conrad p. 191 (*The Mirror of the Sea*), Lee (1915) pp. 186–7, Flinders v. 2, p. 64.

26 Mangrove and coral: Flinders v. 2, pp. 20, 26–9, 88; Lee (1915) p. 195.

27 Broken anchor and separation from *Investigator*: Lee (1915) pp. 197, 200; Flinders v. 2, pp. 90–1, 96.

27 Reshuffling and Jorgenson's promotions: Lee (1915) pp. 200–1, 215; Flinders v. 2, p. 98; Sprod p. 31.

27 Journey to Sydney: Lee (1915) pp. 205–6; SA p. 12.

27–8 Journey to Risdon: Nicholson p. 11; Sprod p. 36. On reasons for expanding the Sydney colony: *Historical Records of Australia* Series I, v. 4, p. 249, cited in Sprod p. 33.

28 Naming of landmarks: Mortyn, p. 7; Dunbabin p. 7.

28 Second journey to Risdon: Lee (1915) pp. 221–5, 229; *Australian Dictionary of Biography* v. 1, pp. 236–40 (entry for Collins) and pp. 136–7 (entry for Bowen); Humphrey pp. 94–6; Robson (1983) p. 41. On the Tamar detour: Lee (1915) p. 228; Humphrey p. 83; Sprod p. 38.

29 Sullivan's Cove and Mount Wellington: SA p. 13; *Hobart Town Gazette*, 6 May 1826 (stating that Jorgenson climbed it with Humphrey – but this is not mentioned in Humphrey's journal); Hügel pp. 112–14.

29 Sermon: Knopwood p. 45 (26 Feb. 1804).

29–30 Risdon shootings: Reynolds pp. 76–7; Windschuttle p. 16–26; Tardif, 'Risdon Cove', in Manne pp. 218–24; SA p. 65.

30 Departure, other trips, and *Lady Nelson*'s subsequent career: Lee (1915) pp. 230–2; Sprod p. 41.

30–31 Tasmanian whaling and sealing: SA p. 14 ('oleaginous remains'); Villiers p. 114; Collins to King, 28 Sept. 1805, quoted Dunbabin p. 25; Pink and Ebdon p. 10.

31 Journey on *Contest*: OPT p. 32 (note by Richards); Richards pp. 53–4; *Sydney Gazette*, 10 Feb., 11 Feb. 1805; Sprod pp. 42–3; SA p. 14.

31   *Alexander*: SA pp. 13–14; Richards pp. 62–4; *Sydney Gazette*, 16
            Dec. 1804, 6 Jan. 1805; Cumpston, J.S., *Shipping Arrivals and
            Departures: Sydney 1788–1825* (Canberra: Roebuck Press, 1964)
            p. 51.

32   The *Contest/Alexander* conundrum: Knopwood pp. 57 ff.; Rhodes's
            Alexander accounts, ML A1442, pp. 1–5; Richards pp. 57, 64;
            Nicholson pp. 12 ff.; Sprod pp. 45–6.

33   Delays: OPT p. 17; Melville, H., *Typee*, Everyman edn (London: J.M.
            Dent, 1993) pp. 23–4.

33   Smuggling: Richards p. 65.

33   Maori passengers: Richards pp. 75–7; see also Richards pp. 103, 80,
            citing a letter from Jorgenson to the *Courier*, 15 Oct. 1817.

33   Tahiti: SA p. 14; Davies, J., pp. 71, 79–80; Villiers pp. 101–2. The
            missionaries' journals also record that one of the two ships that called
            on them during this period was blown off-course by contrary winds:
            School of Oriental and African Studies, University of London, CWM
            South Seas Journals, Box 2, no. 26, p. 1 (Journal 29 July 1805–8 March
            1806).

34   Maniacal missionary: this was William Waters. See Davies, J., pp. 26–7,
            74. Davies, points out however, that Waters had already shown signs
            of mental instability on the voyage out.

34   Jorgenson's impressions: SC pp. 15–18.

34   Difficulty in keeping to the right path: Introduction by C.W. Newbury
            to Davies, J., pp. xl–xli n.; letter from John Eyre, 1806, copy in School
            of Oriental and African Studies, University of London, CWM South
            Seas Journals, Box 2, no. 26, p. 3.

34–5   Jefferson: SC pp. 21*–3* (numbering sequence is repeated); School
            of Oriental and African Studies, University of London, CWM South
            Seas Journals, Box 2, no. 26, pp. 4–5; Davies, J., pp. 76, 80–1, 104.

35   'Serious and long faces': SC p. 25.

36   War and Pomare II: SC, pp. 26*–7* (numbering sequence is repeated);
            see also Ramsden p. 43. Banks's description from 'Some observations on
            a Bill for admitting the produce of New South Wales to entry at the
            Customs-house of the United Kingdom, 7 July 1806', cited McNab,
            Robert (ed.), *Historical records of New Zealand* (Wellington: J. Mackay,
            1908–14) v. 1, p. 278.

37   'The *ignorance, bigotry* . . .': SC p. 12.

37   Noble savages and Evangelical movement: SC pp. 29–30, 93; Salmond,
            Anne, *The Trial of the Cannibal Dog* (London: Allen Lane, 2003)
            p. 109; Gascoigne pp. 148 ff., 155, 164.

38   Albion's Aborigines: Gascoigne p. 151.

38   Tahitian passengers: Davies, J., pp. 100, 109; SA p. 15.

38   Missionaries and tattoos: Davies, J., p. 81; Darwin, Charles (ed. Richard

Darwin Keynes), *Charles Darwin's* Beagle *diary* (Cambridge: Cambridge University Press, 1988) p. 366. Jorgenson's entries in convict registers mention no tattoos under 'distinguishing marks'.

38–9   Return: log-book of the *Thames*, 25 Dec. 1805, cited Richards p. 66 (beef stew); convoy: SA p. 15; ATW p. 247; Sprod p. 51; Hill p. 61.

39   The lost journal: ATW pp. 301–4; HA1 ff. 99r–101r.

Chapter 3: English Jorgenson

40   Rhodes: Richards p. 67; SA p. 38.

41–1   Tahitians: ATW pp. 257–61.

41   London: Geijer pp. 90, 82 (forest and smog); Simond v. 1, p. 38 (soot); *Letters from Albion* v. 1, pp. 78–80 (shops); Rush, Richard, *A Residence at the Court of London* [abridged edn], (London: Century, 1987) p. 28 (traffic).

42   Banks and the Tahitians: ATW p. 253; SA p. 15.

43   Denmark: ATW p. 277; JJ to Fritz Jürgensen, 11 Sept. 1835, KB NBD IX 8, Haandskrift Afd. 163. Lionized and courted: ATW pp. 305–6, 301.

44   *Efterretning*: OPT pp. 14, 25.

45   Loss of journal: HA1 ff. 99r–101r; ATW pp. 301–4. On the later fate of the journal: ATW pp. 301–4; JJ to Anna Jørgensen, 6 May 1823, RA Samlingspakke no. 2679.

45   'I had during my servitudes . . .': HA1 ff. 97v–98r.

46   Napoleonic fascination: H.C. Andersen, *The Fairy Tale of My Life*, cited in Wullschlager, J., *Hans Christian Andersen* (London: Allen Lane, 2000) p. 22; Kierkegaard pp. 53–60, 71; Geyl, Pieter (tr. O. Renier), *Napoleon: For and Against* (Harmondsworth: Penguin, 1976) p. 31; *Narrative of the Expedition to the Baltic* (BL copy, with annotations) p. 211. Both British writers were soldiers, stationed there during the British occupation.

47   Jorgenson and Napoleon: CE pp. 55–8; HA1 ff. 155r–v.

47–9   Anglophilia and arguments: ATW pp. 279–300. 'English Jørgensen' is a translation from ATW's pseudonymous equivalent, 'Capricornian Walter'.

49   Continental Anglophilia: Constant pp. 45, 53; Buruma, pp. 24, 48–50. Jorgenson the Burkean: ATW pp. 297–8.

49–51   Background to Copenhagen 1807: Ryan, A.N. (1953) pp. 37–55; Muir pp. 23–4; Ruppenthal pp. 7–23.

51   Arrival of ships: CE p. 3; Crookes pp. 5–6.

51–2   'Wooden clog army': CE pp. 7–8. On clogs: Macdonald p. 26.

52   Fire: Browne p. 56; *Narrative of the Expedition to the Baltic* p. 143.

52–3   First attack: Sommer p. 31; *An Authentic Account of the Siege of Copenhagen* p. 24; *Narrative of the Expedition to the Baltic* p. 143.

53 Congreve rockets: Winter, Frank H., *The First Golden Age of Rocketry: Congreve and Hale Rockets of the Nineteenth Century* (Washington, DC: Smithsonian Institution Press, 1990); Ford p. 237.

54–5 Second and third attacks: *Narrative of the Expedition to the Baltic* pp. 147 ff.; Crookes p. 19; Grahame pp. 4–9; Browne p. 56; Sommer pp. 32–3; *An Authentic Account of the Siege of Copenhagen* pp. 25–7.

55 Casualties and damage: Gates p. 82; Holland p. 204 n. (note by Andrew Wawn); *An Authentic Account of the Siege of Copenhagen* pp. 27; CE pp. 16–17.

55–6 Aftermath: CE p. 18; Lauring p. 196; *Narrative of the Expedition to the Baltic* pp. 194, 208.

56 The loot: Lauring pp. 196, 198; Muir p. 25; *An Authentic Account of the Siege of Copenhagen* pp. 79–81; *Narrative of the Expedition to the Baltic*, map and p. 173.

56–7 Responses in Britain: Longford p. 135; Ryan, A.N. (1953), p. 37; *The real state of the case* pp. 2–13.

57–9 Jorgenson's reactions: JJ to Fritz Jürgensen, 11 Sept. 1835, KB NBD IX 8, Haandskrift Afd. 163; ATW pp. 314–15, 320–2; HVDLC p. 8; CE pp. 2–5, 30 ('politically just' and 'masterstroke'), 31 ('It is but a poor excuse . . .'), 39–40.

59 Trine's farm: JJ to Fritz Jürgensen, 11 Sept. 1835, KB NBD IX 8, Haandskrift Afd. 163. Wellesley: HA1 ff. 101v–102r; see also ATW pp. 319–20.

60 British fellow-feeling: *The Life and Opinions of Gen. Sir Charles Napier* (1857), cited in Longford p. 135; JJ's manuscript on Spain and Portugal (1812), BLARS Whitbread papers W4848, f. 34v; Mahan, A.T., *The Life of Nelson* (1899), cited in Padfield (2003) p. 182.

60 Wellesley and Popham: CE pp. 18–20.

61 Danish declaration: Gans and Yedida ff. 2–3.

61 Jorgenson's predictions and later response: ATW p. 324; CE p. 26.

62 Danish attitudes to British and French: Macdonald pp. 24, 33, 42.

62 Rebuilt fleet, and the *Admiral Juul*: Anderson p. 320 ff.; Ruppenthal pp. 19–20; Sprod p. 57. Portrait: Halldór J. Jónsson pp. 45–49; personal communication with Steffen Heiberg of Frederiksborgmuseet and Inga Lara Baldvinsdóttir of the National Museum of Iceland.

63–4 Battle with *Sappho*: HA1 f. 104v; HMS *Sappho* log (16 Feb. 1807 to 23 April 1808), BNA ADM 51/1726, nos. 4–5; *London Gazette*, 1–5 March 1808, Sprod pp. 59–61; James p. 307; JJ to Fritz Jürgensen, 11 Sept. 1835, KB NBD IX 8, Haandskrift Afd. 163; SA pp. 15–16.

64–5 Jorgenson's remarks: HA1 ff. 137r–139r; ATW pp. 331–3. Accusations of treachery, and Jorgenson's anger: HA1 ff. 108r–v; see also Trampe to Jones, 20 Aug. 1809, BNA ADM 1/1995.

65 London and Spread Eagle: Sprod pp. 61, 86; TFG p. 133; Groom,

Arthur, *Old London Coaching Inns and their Successors* (Euston Station: London Midland and Scottish Railway Company, [1928]) p. 25; *Letters from Albion* v. 1, p. 71.

66   Lottery: HA1 ff. 111v–112r, 6r; ATW pp. 336, 349.

66–7   Icelandic plans: HA1 ff. 4v–5v; Phelps (1817) p. 51 ff.; JJ to Banks, 27 May 1808, in Gans and Yedida, ff. 72–74.

68   Cargo and departure: Phelps (1817) p. 52; HA1 f. 7r; ATW p. 349; *Colonial Advocate*, 1 June 1828, p. 193.

Chapter 4: Uprising in Reykjavík

69   Icelandic weather: W. Morris, *Icelandic Journals*, cited in Wawn (2000) p. 254; Strabo (tr. H.L. Jones), *Geography*, Loeb edn (London: W. Heinemann, 1917–23), p. 399 (2.4.1).

70   Trading monopolies and debts: Gunnar Karlsson (2000) pp. 139–41, 182; ATW p. 413–14.

70–71   Poverty, food and housing: Banks to Castlereagh, 24 Feb. 1808, NHM Banks correspondence v. 17, f. 132; Olafsen and Povelsen p. 15; Holland p. 225; Holinshed cited in E. Seaton, *Literary Relations of England and Scandinavia in the Seventeenth Century* (1935) and thence in Wawn (2000) p. 14; Auden, W.H., and MacNeice, Louis, *Letters from Iceland* (London: Faber & Faber, 1937) pp. 42, 44; Hooker, W.J., v. 1, pp. 21, 26, xxxi; Nicol p. 200.

71   Temperament: Dillon v. 1, pp. 295, 133, 106; Hooker, W.J., v. 1, pp. lxxxix–xc; see also Henderson v. 1, p. xxxiv.

72   Skaftá and population fluctuations: Nicol pp. 38–41; Gunnar Karlsson (2000) pp. 178–81.

72   Imports and trade: Jorgenson claimed that the *Justitia* had no useful imports in its cargo, but this is doubtful: HA1 ff. 12v–13r; Anna Agnarsdóttir (2000) p. 104; Hooker, W.J., v. 2, p. 13; RC (annotated copy), ML C672; HA1 ff. 7v–8r; Banks to Bjarni Sívertsen, 3 March 1808, NHM Banks correspondence v. 17, ff. 138–9 (discussing the question of whether ships can make the journey in winter).

72–3   Arrival of *Clarence* and negotiations with Ísleifur: HA1 ff. 7r–8r; Savignac to Phelps, 19 March 1809, in Great Britain: Historical Manuscripts Commission: *Report on the Manuscripts of Earl Bathurst*, pp. 84–6; Helgi P. Briem (1943) p. 123; Sprod pp. 89–92, translating letters from Savignac to Ísleifur Einarsson and from JJ to same, both 14 Jan. 1809, both in ThÍ (Stiftamtmanns-Innkomin Bref no. 266 and Jörundarskjöl XLV, folder 11); Helgi P. Briem (1936) p. 101; HA1 ff. 8v–9r.

74   Reasons for lack of customers: HA1 ff. 10r–v, 12r; Phelps (1817) pp. 52–3; Gunnar Karlsson (1995) pp. 36–7. On Trampe's reasons: Trampe's submission to Bathurst, BL Ms. Eg. 2067, ff. 194v–196r; Phelps

(1817) p. 52. On the reluctant Icelander (Markús Magnússen of Garðar): JJ to Banks, undated (1809), NHM Banks correspondence v. 1, ff. 40–1. On Gilpin: Anna Agnarsdóttir (1989) p. 71.

74–5   Failure, ballast and Savignac's behaviour: HA1 ff. 11r, 12v; Sprod p. 93.

75   Reaction of Phelps: HA1 f. 13v.

76–6   Discussions with Banks: JJ to Banks, 14 April 1809, and Banks to Wellesley Pole (i.e. Bathurst), 16 April 1809, both NHM Banks correspondence v. 1 ff. 38–9, ff. 42–3; Anna Agnarsdóttir (1989) pp. 84, 96 n. ; Phelps (1817), p. 75.

76   Annexation: Anna Agnarsdóttir (1989) pp. 13 ff., 98–9; Hawkesbury to Banks, 29 Nov. 1807, and Banks to Hawkesbury, 30 Dec. 1807, both NHM Banks correspondence v. 17, ff. 72, 78–9; Gunnar Karlsson (1995) pp. 43–5; Banks: 'A brief recital . . .', State Library of South Australia: York Gate Library, M/F Reel 1 (174), pp. 41–2 ('ancient Hereditary Dominion'); Banks: 'Remarks concerning Iceland', 30 Jan. 1801, BL Add. Ms. 38356, ff. 39–48 ('much inclined to become dependent'); Banks: 'A project for the conduct of S.J.B. in respect to Iceland', in Gans and Yedida f. 70 (cod plan); HA2 f. 117v; Anna Agnarsdóttir (1989) p. 29.

77   Proverb: MacKenzie p. 271; Phelps (1817) p. 21.

77   Banks's letter: Banks to 'Mr Stephensen of Reikiavick', NHM Banks correspondence v. 12, undated (1808?); Halldór Hermannsson pp. 30–2; Anna Agnarsdóttir (1989) Appendix and p. 44 n.; Anna Agnarsdóttir (1994) p. 42.

77   '500 men with a very few Guns . . .': Banks: 'A brief recital . . .', State Library of South Australia: York Gate Library, M/F Reel 1 (174) pp. 41–2.

77   Opinion of Phelps: Phelps (1817) p. 6; JJ to Banks, 27 May 1808, in Gans and Yedida, f. 75; HA1 ff. 39v–40r.

78   Conspiracy theory: Helgi P. Briem (1943) pp. 124–7; see Anna Agnarsdóttir (1989) pp. 97–9.

78   Despatch of *Rover*: Phelps to Banks, 21 April 1809 and 22 April 1809, both NHM Banks correspondence v. 1, ff. 44, 45; Sprod p. 99; Anna Agnarsdóttir (1989) p. 101; Phelps (1817) p. 54; Helgi P. Briem (1943) p. 125.

78–9   Trampe's return, and his interests: Trampe's submission to Bathurst, BL Ms. Eg. 2067 ff. 196v–197r; Ordinances of 24 Dec. 1807 and 30 Oct. 1807, nos. 1951–2 respectively, *Stiftamtsjournal* I (1803–9), cited Helgi P. Briem (1943) pp. 113–14 and Anna Agnarsdóttir (1989) p. 103; HA1 ff. 18v–19r; Phelps (1817) p. 54; Anna Agnarsdóttir (1989) pp. 103, 106; *Dansk biografisk leksikon* v. 14, pp. 666–7 (entry for Trampe); for Magnús's proposals of May 1808, see Anna Agnarsdóttir (2000) pp. 104–5.

79–80   Negotiations and the Nott Convention: Trampe to Nott, 12 June 1809, and Savignac to Nott, 13 June 1809, both BNA ADM 1/692; Stiftamtsplakat, 13 June 1809, RA Rtk. 373.133; Anna Agnarsdóttir (1989) pp. 105–6; Convention signed by Nott and Trampe, 16 June 1809: English manuscript copy in BNA ADM 1/1995, Danish printed copies there and in ThÍ Jörundarskjöl XLV, folder 8; Sprod p. 124.

80   Trampe's failure to enforce the convention: Phelps (1817) p. 56; Hooker, W.J., v. 2, p. 23; Holland p. 256 (introduction by A. Wawn); Trampe's submission to Bathurst, BL Ms. Eg. 2067 f. 198v; Trampe to Jones, 21 Aug. 1809, BNA ADM 1/1995; Hooker, W.J., v. 2, pp. 18–20; Sprod p. 123.

80–1   *Margaret & Anne*'s cargo: M.C. Fell: 'Invoice of sundry goods shipped [by] Capt. Liston for Iceland by and on account of Messrs Phelps and comp. in London', ThÍ Jörundarskjöl XLV, folder 13; see also HA1 f. 14v.

81   The Vancouvers: HA1 ff. 15r–v; ATW pp. 361–2; *Dictionary of National Biography* v. 20, pp. 96–7 (entries for Charles and George Vancouver).

81   Hooker: Hooker, J.D., v. 1, p. 21; *Dictionary of National Biography* v. 9, pp. 1190–2 (entry for W.J. Hooker); Allan p. 44; Banks to Olafur Stephensen, 28 May 1809, RA RTK 373.133.

82   Arrival of *Margaret & Anne*: Hooker, W.J., v. 1, pp. 8–17, v. 2, p. 22; Phelps (1817) p. 56. On Holland's impressions of Reykjavík: Holland pp. 314, 139.

82–3   Hooker's stroll: Hooker, W.J., v. 1, pp. 17–29, v. 2, p. 23; JJ to Hooker, 29 March 1811, BL Ms. Eg. 2070; Holland p. 93; JJ to Hooker, 23 Nov. 1810, BL Ms. Eg. 2070.

84–7   The revolution: Hooker, W.J., v. 2, p. 25; Trampe's submission to Bathurst, BL Ms. Eg. 2067 ff. 200r–201r, 224r–v; Phelps (1817) pp. 57–8; Hooker, W.J., v. 1, pp. 53, 56; HA1 f. 32v; SA pp. 16–17. In his autobiography Jorgenson takes credit for leading the operation, but other accounts agree that the actual uprising was led by Liston.

86–7   Icelanders' non-resistance: RC (annotated copy), ML C672; SA p. 17; Gunnar Karlsson (2000) p. 196; Trampe's submission to Bathurst, BL Ms. Eg. 2067 ff. 202r–v; Jörginsáttur Gísla Konráðssonar, Landsbókasafn Lbs. 4186 4to; Jón Espólín v. 12, pp. 27–30; last two both cited in Anna Agnarsdóttir (1989) pp. 128–9; Phelps (1817) p. 58.

87–8   Phelps's deliberations, and appointment of Jorgenson: Phelps (1817) pp. 59–60; HA1 ff. 34r–v; ATW pp. 393–5; Hooker, W.J., v. 1, p. 26.

88   Napoleon comparison: Phelps (1817) pp. 59–60; HA1 f. 52r; ATW p. 416.

Chapter 5: Jorgenson the Protector

89   Trading fair: Phelps (1817) p. 60; Holland pp. 224–5.

89–90   Proclamation no. 1: Jorgenson's own English version in HA2 ff.

28r–29v; originals in Danish in BNA ADM 1/1995 (2 copies) and RA RTK 373.133; Icelandic in Jón Thorkelsson p. 151; HA2 ff. 51r–v.

90 Proclamation no. 2: Jorgenson's own English version in HA2 ff. 29v–32r; Danish and Icelandic versions in BNA ADM 1/1995, ThÍ Jörundarskjöl XLV, folder 7 and RA RTK 373.133; Icelandic in Jón Thorkelsson p. 152; HA1, f. 40v.

91 Collecting of weapons: Hooker, W.J., v. 2, p. 35, v. 1, pp. 56–7.

92–3 Lunch with Olafur: Hooker, W.J., v. 1, pp. 57–78; on a similar visit, see Holland p. 90.

93–4 Rumours of bloodshed, and Jorgenson's response: HA1 ff. 52r–v, 84v–85r, 136v–137r; Trampe's submission to Bathurst, BL Ms. Eg. 2067 f. 210r; ATW p. 455.

94 Proclamation no. 3: Jorgenson's English version in HA2 ff. 32r–v; Icelandic version in Jón Thorkelsson p. 163. His treatment of the 'sneaking fellow': HA2 ff. 52r–v.

94 Proclamation no. 4: Jorgenson's English version in HA2 ff. 32v–33r; Icelandic version in RA RTK 373.133 and Jón Thorkelsson pp. 163–4.

95 Petition: 'A petition from Biarne Thorlevsen', Jorgenson's own translation in HA2 ff. 62v–63v, also in Hooker, W.J., v. 2, pp. 29–30; Icelandic original in BNA FO 95/648.

95–6 Magnús Stephensen: Hooker to Banks, 27 July 1810, NHM Banks correspondence v. 18, ff. 50–2; HA1 ff. 74r–v. On Magnús's 1807 approach to Banks: Magnús Stephensen to Banks, 17 Oct. 1807, NHM Banks correspondence v. 17, ff. 69–63; see Anna Agnarsdóttir (2000) pp. 105–6; Holland p. 99.

96–7 Ísleifur Einarsson: HA2 ff. 45r–48v, 53v–54r; Hooker, W.J., v. 1, pp. 87–9; Trampe's Enclosures S–T, Landsbókasafn Lbs 168 fol., Sprod pp. 355–60.

97 Officials' responses: BNA ADM 1/1995; English translations by Jorgenson in HA2, ff. 37r–51r, including (ff. 49r–50r) the one cited here: S. Snorrasen to JJ, 15 July 1809; Hooker, W.J., v. 2, p. 33. See Holland p. 26 (discussion by A. Wawn).

97 Magnús's request: HA2 ff. 36r, 43v–44r; HA1 f. 74v.

98 Jón Guðmundsson: Jón Guðmundsson, Sysselmand of Vesturskafta-fellssysla, to JJ, 10 Aug. 1809, copies in Landsbókasafn ÍB 382 and RA RTK 373.133, Sprod p. 134.

98 Finnur Magnússon's poem: this translation from MacKenzie pp. 454–5; Icelandic and Latin in Hooker, W.J., v. 2, pp. 295–308. On its recitation the following year: Holland p. 147. Even MacKenzie (p. 453) remarks that the language 'certainly assumes some license in the poetic embellishment of facts'.

99 Political framework: Ibsen p. 136; see Gunnar Karlsson (1995) p. 35. Karlsson also quotes a description of a nineteenth-century

widow by the Icelandic poet Guðmundur Friðjónsson: 'She did not love her country, only her plot and shack, / A few yards of the stream, and the lava, rough and black' (p. 36). On Icelandic perspectives, see Holland p. 26 (discussion by A. Wawn); Gunnar Karlsson (2000) p. 199; Gunnar Karlsson (1995) p. 33; Anna Agnarsdóttir (1989), p. 129.

100   Jorgenson's militia: Helgi P. Briem (1936) pp. 202–3; list of prisoners in RA RTK 373.133 and Sprod pp. 346–7; Hooker, W.J,. v. 2, p. 35; ATW p. 412; HA1 f. 49r. See Trampe's submission to Bathurst, BL Ms. Eg. 2067 ff. 211r–v; M. and S. Stephensen, 'Being a Remonstrance . . .', 22 Aug 1809, copies in BNA ADM 1/1995 and RA RTK. 373.133.

100   Delusions of grandeur: Trampe's submission to Bathurst, BL Ms. Eg. 2067 f. 205r.

100   Guðrún Einarsdóttir Johnsen: Holland p. 104 (note by A. Wawn); Wawn (1985) pp. 97–133; Anna Agnarsdóttir (2001), pp. 123–39; Memorial Library, University of Wisconsin-Madison: Ms. 3 (Banks correspondence): JJ to Banks, 24 Aug.–6 Oct. 1813.

101–2   Proclamation no. 5: on revolutionary spirit: Anna Agnarsdóttir (1989) p. 125; on the 'we': HA2 ff. 33v, 57r; HA1 ff. 47r–48r; ATW p. 433. The proclamation: Jorgenson's English translation in HA2 ff. 33v–36v; Danish and Icelandic versions in BNA ADM 1/1995, ThÍ Jörundarskjöl XLV, folder 7, and RA RTK 373.133; Jón Thorkelsson pp. 169–71.

102–3   The flag: Banks: 'A brief recital . . .', State Library of South Australia: York Gate Library, M/F Reel 1 (174), and NHM Banks correspondence v. 18, ff. 20–7; Hooker, W.J., v. 2, p. 39; M. and S. Stephensen, 'Being a Remonstrance . . .', 22 Aug. 1809, BNA ADM 1/1995 and RA RTK 373.133.

103   Clerical salaries: SA p. 17.

103   Instincts: SA p. 17; RC (annotated copy), ML C672; Villiers p. 105.

103–4   Abolition of passes: M. and S. Stephensen, 'Being a Remonstrance . . .', 22 Aug. 1809, BNA ADM 1/1995 and RA RTK 373.133; HA1 f. 42v; Hooker, W.J., v. 2, p. 39.

104   Tour to the north: Sprod pp. 138–41, 650 (n. 31); SA pp. 17–18; HA1 f. 51v. On the horses: Henderson v. 1, pp. 23–5.

105   Quarrels: SA p. 18; Banks: 'A brief recital . . .', State Library of South Australia: York Gate Library, M/F Reel 1 (174), and NHM Banks correspondence v. 18, ff. 20–7; HA2 f. 55r; Sprod pp. 139–41; ATW pp. 413–14; HA1 ff. 50r–v.

105–6   Phelps's activities and the question of profits: HA1 ff. 52v–53r; Trampe's submission to Bathurst, BL Ms. Eg. 2067 ff. 209v, 201v; see letter from C.C. Strube, included as Enclosure M in Trampe's submission, Landsbókasafn Lbs 168 fol., cited in Sprod p. 351; Hooker, W.J.,

v. 2, p. 48 n.; HA2 ff. 73–109; Sprod pp. 133–4. The receipts do slightly outweigh the expenses, showing a total 'profit' of 103 *riksdaler*, 3 marks and 10 shillings – about seven pounds sterling – which, as Jorgenson remarks, hardly amounts to a large-scale plunder.

106   Latin School: Hooker, W.J., v. 1, pp. 352–4; HA2 ff. 113r–v; Holland pp. 118–19; Henderson pp. 371–2.

107   Arrival of Jones: Sprod p. 283; Jones to Nagle, 23 Aug. and 4 Sept. 1809, both BNA ADM 1/1995; HA1 ff. 58v–59r.

107   Trampe's complaints: Trampe's submission to Bathurst, BL Ms. Eg. 2067 f. 224v–225r; Trampe to Jones, 20 Aug. 1809, Jones to Nagle, 23 Aug. 1809, both BNA ADM 1/1995. On Jorgenson's response: JJ to Hooker, 29 Nov. 1810, BL Ms. Eg. 2070. Hooker's opinion: Hooker to Banks, 20 June 1810, RBG Banks letters v. 2, no. 334 and NHM Banks correspondence v. 18, f. 43.

107–8   Jones's investigations: Jones to Nagle, 23 Aug. 1809, Phelps to Jones, 16 Aug. 1809, Jones to Phelps, 19 August 1809 and Phelps to Jones, 23 Aug 1809, all BNA ADM 1/1995; ATW p. 450.

108   The Stephensens' document: M. and S. Stephensen, 'Being a Remonstrance . . .', 22 Aug. 1809, BNA ADM 1/1995 and RA RTK. 373.133.

108–9   Deliberations and judgement: Hooker, W.J., v. 1, p. 325; ATW pp. 452–3, f. 234r (facing p. 453); Jones to Phelps, 19 Aug. 1809, Jones to Phelps, Liston and JJ, 20 Aug 1809, and Phelps to Jones, 23 Aug 1809, all BNA ADM 1/1995. Jorgenson on the flag issue: HA1 f. 76r. The agreement: Samnignur/Agreement, 22 Aug. 1809, copies in BNA ADM 1/1995, RA RTK 373.133, Landsbókasafn JS 111 fol. and ThÍ XLV Jörundarskjöl, folder 8; English and Danish text also in Helgi P. Briem (1936) pp. 455–9.

110   Jorgenson's response: JJ to Hooker, 3 Oct. 1809, BL Ms. Eg. 2070; JJ to Whitbread, 14 Nov. 1811, BLARS Whitbread papers W 4832; HA1 f. 69v.

110   Jones's sympathy and the Savignac issue: Jones to Hooker, 1 Sept. 1810, RBG DC v. 1, no. 183; Hooker to Banks, 27 July 1810, NHM Banks correspondence v. 18, ff. 50–2; McKay p. 89; Halldór Hermannsson p. 69. On Savignac's later life in Iceland, and the reported later conspiracy with Magnús: Magnús Stephensen to Banks, 8 Aug. 1812, BL Ms. Add. 8100, f. 142v; Holland pp. 226, 101–2; Hooker to Banks, 22 July 1810, NHM Banks correspondence v. 18, ff. 48–9.

111   *Margaret & Anne* passengers and cargo: Hooker, W.J., v. 1, p. 358. On the dresses, see also JJ to Franklin, 26 Oct. 1839, RBG Misc. correspondence (in which Jorgenson claims that he bought them himself, though an added pencil note by Hooker's son contradicts this). On Phelps's cargo: Jorgenson estimated it as £35,000: RC (annotated

copy), ML C672. Phelps later put in an insurance claim for £40,000: Phelps (1817) p. 66; Anna Agnarsdóttir (1989) p. 159.

111–113 Fire: Hooker, W.J., v. 1, pp. ii, 359–60, 363; RC (annotated copy), ML C672; HA1 f. 89r; Jones to Nagle, 23 Aug 1809, BNA ADM 1/1995; Phelps (1817) p. 66; Anna Agnarsdóttir (1989) p. 159; SA p. 18. On the idea that Danish prisoners started the fire: Hooker, W.J., v. 1, p. 364.

113–4 Changes while in Reykjavík: Trampe to Jones, 31 Aug. 1809, BNA ADM 1/1995; Magnús Stephensen to Jones, 29 Aug. 1809, RA RTK 373.133; Sprod pp. 318–19.

114 Return to Britain: JJ to Hooker, 13 Dec. 1810, BL Ms. Eg. 2070; Jones to Nagle, 23 Aug., 4 Sept., and [20 Sept.], all BNA ADM 1/1995; Anna Agnarsdóttir (1989) p. 159; Sprod p. 313.

115 Press reports and survival of story: *Dagen*, 15 Sept. and 18 Sept. 1809; Anna Agnarsdóttir (1989) p. 130; JJ to Hooker, 7 Dec. 1810, BL Ms. Eg. 2070; *Household Words*, v. 14 (20 Dec. 1856) p. 352; Dillon v. 1, pp. 69–70; Gunnar Karlsson (2000) p. 195; Jónas Árnason; *The Mercury* 15 Aug. 1987, p. 65. Heroic version: JJ to Fritz Jürgensen, 11 Sept. 1835, KB NBD IX 8, Haandskrift Afd. 163. *Síðasti Víkingurinn*: Inði Einarsson; Holland p. 26 (A. Wawn's introduction).

115 Jorgenson's motives: HA1 ff. 126v–127r; RC (annotated copy), ML C672; JJ to Hooker, 10 Nov. 1810, BL Ms. Eg. 2070; HA1, f. 177v, ff. 167v–168r; JJ to Anna Jørgensen, 24 Dec. 1822, RA Samlingspakke no. 2679; JJ to Fritz Jürgensen, 11 Sept. 1835, KB NBD IX 8, Haandskrift Afd. 163.

117–18 Speculation: *Memoir on the causes* . . . pp. 32–3. On this work's authorship, see Anna Agnarsdóttir (1989) p. 221 ff. On Icelanders' response: Gunnar Karlsson (1995) p. 39.

118 Admiralty judgement on Jorgenson and Phelps: Anna Agnarsdóttir (1989) pp. 160–1, 201.

118 Changes in Icelandic affairs: BNA FO 40/1 ff. 21–2; Anna Agnarsdóttir (1989) pp. 158, 154; Helgi P. Briem (1943) p. 131; Hooker, W.J., v. 2, p. 62. On consequences of the Order in Council for annexation plans, see Anna Agnarsdóttir (1989) pp. 155, 221, 279–80.

119 Subsequent governors, and later life of Trampe: Anna Agnarsdóttir (1989) pp. 161–3, 181–4; Trampe to Magnús Stephensen, 29 March 1810, RA RTK 373.133; Sprod p. 396; *Dansk biografisk leksikon* v. 14, pp. 666–7. On Magnús's response to his dismissal: Magnús Stephensen to Mackenzie, 8 June 1810, RA RTK 373.133. On Trampe's later life: Sprod pp. 377–8. On British control: Anna Agnarsdóttir (2000) p. 111.

119–120 Iceland's later history: Gunnar Karlsson (2000) p. 314; United Nations: *Human development report 2003* (New York: Oxford University Press USA, 2003).

Chapter 6: Prisoner

121   Jorgenson in London: JJ to Hooker, 3 Oct. 1809, 24 Nov. 1809, both BL Ms. Eg. 2070.

121–2   Banks: JJ to Hooker, 3 Oct. 1809, BL Ms. Eg. 2070; Banks, 'A brief recital . . .', State Library of South Australia: York Gate Library, M/F Reel 1 (174) pp. 45–50; Banks to Lord Liverpool, 11 Dec. 1809, BNA FO 40/1 ff. 5–7; Banks to Hooker, 15 June [1813], RBG DC v. 1, no. 38. Jorgenson's response: HA1 ff. 132r–v; ATW p. 470; JJ to Hooker, 22 Dec. 1809, BL Ms. Eg. 2070. Hooker's mediation: Hooker to Banks, 27 July 1810, NHM Banks correspondence v. 18, f. 52.

122–3   Arrest and imprisonment: ATW p. 493; BNA FO 40/1 ff. 29–30; Trampe's submission to Bathurst, BL Ms. Eg. 2067 ff. 193–229; HA1 f. 114r; JJ to Hooker, 23 Oct. 1809 and 24 Nov. 1809, both BL Ms. Eg. 2070; Macdonald pp. 36–7; Partridge pp. 205–8; Jorgenson's illustration of the *Bahama* in ATW f. 266v (facing p. 496); JJ to Hooker, 24 Nov. 1809 and 7 Dec 1810, both BL Ms. Eg. 2070; HA1 f. 139r.

123–4   On his writings: ATW p. 491, f. 4r; JJ to Hooker, 18 May 1810, BL Ms. Eg. 2070. On ships made from animal bones: Sotheby's, London: *The marine sale*, 18 June 2003; *The Guardian*, 14 June 2003, p. 7.

124   Jorgenson's command of English: JJ to Fritz Jürgensen, 11 Sept. 1835, KB NBD IX 8, Haandskrift Afd. 163; RC (annotated copy), ML C672; *The Tasmanian*, 3 Aug. 1832, cited in Dally (1993) pp. 9–11, 14.

124   Banks's response: Banks to Hooker, 16 June 1810, 15 June [1813], 2 Sept. 1813, all RBG DC v. 1, nos. 31, 38, 40.

124–5   Plays and other projects: JJ's *Robertus Montanus* and *The duke d'Angiens*, both BL Ms. Eg. 2069; JJ to Hooker, 28 June 1810, BL Ms. Eg. 2070; Buruma p. 78 (Napoleon and Ossian); Jermyn to JJ, 4 Sept. 1810, BNA FO 95/648. On the Scandinavian craze, see Wawn (2000).

125–7   Jorgenson's illness: Jones to Hooker, 1 Sept. 1810, RBG DC v. 1, no. 183; JJ to Jermyn, 16 Jan. 1816, JJ to Hooker, 7 Oct. 1810, JJ to Macleay, 24 Nov. 1809, and JJ to Hooker, 22 Dec. 1809, all BL Ms. Eg. 2070; JJ to Castlereagh, 31 May 1820, BNA FO 22/86 ff. 151–2. On porphyria: I. MacAlpine and R. Hunter, *George III and the Mad-Business* (London: Pimlico, 1991), pp. 172–5; www.porphyriafoundation.com. I am also indebted to Chandak Sengoopta, though he is not responsible for my rash speculation.

127   Release: JJ to Hooker, via Macleay, 13 Sept. 1810, BL Ms. Eg. 2070; Hooker to Banks, 27 July 1810, NHM Banks correspondence v. 18 ff. 50–2. On Hooker's efforts and Macleay's involvement, see also Hooker to Brown, Oct. 1810, BL Ms. Add. 32439, f. 337v; Hooker to Gunn, 30 Dec. 1833, National Library of Australia Ms. 5831.

127–8   Job-hunting: JJ to Hooker, 11 Sept., 27 Sept., 1 Oct. ('My dear friend . . .'), 3 Oct., 4 Oct., 7 Oct. 1810, all BL Ms. Eg. 2070.

128   Reading: JJ to Hooker, 3 Oct and 7 Oct. 1810, both BL Ms. Eg. 2070.

129–130   *Historical Account* and Hooker's *Tour*: JJ to Hooker, 2 [i.e. 12?] Oct. 1810, BL Ms. Eg. 2070. Epistolary debate derived from JJ to Hooker, [12] Oct., 10 Nov., 20 Nov., 22 Nov., 23 Nov., 29 Nov., 7 Dec., 13 Dec. and 17 Dec. 1810, all BL Ms. Eg. 2070.

130   Jorgenson's appreciation of Hooker's *Tour*: JJ to Hooker, 10 Nov. 1810 and 12 Feb. 1811, both BL Ms. Eg. 2070; Hooker, J.D., v. 1 p. 108.

130   Graphomania: JJ to Hooker, 31 Oct., 11 Nov., 29 Nov. and 17 Dec. 1810, all BL Ms. Eg. 2070.

131   Shandaria: JJ: *Description of the Kingdom of Shandaria*, BL Ms. Eg. 2069 pp. 193–4, 204–5, 321, 358.

132   Feelings about Britain: JJ to Hooker, 17 Dec. 1810, BL Ms. Eg. 2070.

132–3   Feelings about Hooker: JJ to Hooker, 17 Dec. 1810 ('one friend'), 3 Nov. 1809 ('peculiar pleasure' and 'something else'), 28 Oct. 1810 ('I see good nature'), 10 Nov. 1810 ('which proceeds'), 17 Aug 1817 ('a strong and lasting interest' etc.), 17 Dec. 1810 ('And do not dear friend wonder'), all BL Ms. Eg. 2070.

133   Hooker's activities: Allan pp. 56–7; JJ to Hooker, 28 Oct. and 31 Oct. 1810, both BL Ms. Eg. 2070. On Jorgenson's response to Hooker's business career: JJ to Hooker, 3 Nov. 1809, 24 Nov 1809, 28 June 1810, all BL Ms. Eg. 2070; ATW pp. 291–2.

133–4   *The State of Christianity*: JJ to Hooker, 10 Nov., 7 Dec., 26 Dec. 1810, 3 Feb., 12 Feb. 1811, all BL Ms. Eg. 2070; SC p. 74.

134–5   Theological doubts: RC pp. 6–9; SC p. 90.

135   Reaction: JJ to Hooker, 24 March and 18 April 1811, both BL Ms. Eg. 2070.

135   Reading: JJ to Hooker, 3 Feb., 26 March 1811, 7 Oct 1810, all BL Ms. Eg. 2070.

136   More writing: JJ to Hooker, 24 March and 26 March 1811, both BL Ms. Eg. 2070.

Chapter 7: Spy

137   Sponging-house and falling out with Hooker: JJ to Hooker, 13 Sept., 3 Oct. 1811, 10 Jan. 1813, all BL Ms. Eg. 2070.

137   Whitbread: JJ to Whitbread, 14 Nov. 1811, BLARS Whitbread papers W4832 (and see also JJ to Whitbread, 21 Nov., 25 Nov., 30 Nov., 2 Dec. 1811, 31 May 1813, all BLARS Whitbread papers W4833–5, W4838, W4844); JJ to Hooker, 6 April 1812, BL Ms. Eg. 2070.

138   Gambling: JJ to Hooker, 14 Aug. 1820, BL Ms. Eg. 2070; *Colonial Advocate*, 1 June 1828, pp. 192–3; SA p. 19; TFG pp. 93–6.

138   King's Bench: BNA PRIS 4/25, f. 58v; JJ to Whitbread, 22 Dec. 1811, BLARS Whitbread papers W4949.

139   Father's death: SA p. 47; *Brewer's Dictionary of Phrase and Fable*, 15th edn (rev. A. Room) (London: Cassell, 1996) p. 226.

139   Release and Bloomsbury: BNA PRIS 4/25 f. 58v; JJ to Hooker, 6 April 1812, BL Ms. Eg. 2070.

139–40   Spain and Portugal: SA p. 19; JJ to Whitbread, [4?] March 1813, W. Hamilton to JJ, 15 June and 22 June 1812, all BLARS Whitbread papers W 4841, W4838–9. On the British: JJ to Whitbread. 10 Jan. 1813, and JJ, [Report from Lisbon], 5 Nov. 1812, both BLARS Whitbread papers W5518, W4848 (ff. 34r–36r); JJ, [Fragment on Portugal], BNA FO 95/648.

141   Gibraltar and illness: SA p. 20; JJ to Hooker, 10 Jan. 1813, BL Ms. Eg. 2070; JJ: petition, 29 Aug. 1834, BNA CO 286/49; *Colonial Advocate*, 1 June 1828, p. 193; JJ to Hooker, undated [1813?], BL Ms. Eg. 2070.

141–2   Portsmouth and tour of friends: JJ to Whitbread, 25 Feb. and 2 March 1813, BLARS Whitbread papers W5718 and W4842; Hooker to JJ, 28 March 1813, BNA FO 95/648; see also JJ to Hooker, 11 March and 25 March 1813, both BL Ms. Eg. 2070; SA p. 20 ('King of Iceland').

142–3   French plot: JJ to Whitbread, 8 June 1813, BLARS Whitbread papers W 4846; *Historical Records of Australia* Series I, v. 8, pp. 72 ff., 241, 653–6, reprinting JJ's 'Information respecting a plan for attacking the colony', Bathurst to Macquarie 19 Aug. 1813 and Macquarie's reply, 30 April 1814, and H. Stuart of the Colonial Secretary's Office to the Admiralty, June 1813; Scott (1910) p. 21, 122 ff.; Scott (1917); Inglis p. 251; James p. 146; SA pp. 21, 24.

143–4   Fleet: he was released on 22 Nov. 1813 and re-imprisoned on 21 Jan. 1814 after a two-month break. BNA PRIS 1/27 p. 313; PRIS 1/28 p. 110; SA p. 24; JJ to Dawson Turner, [13] Aug. 1813, and JJ to Hooker, 4 Sept. 1813, both BL Ms. Eg. 2070; JJ to W. Hamilton, 18 May 1814, BNA FO 22/69 ff. 84r–85r. On his writings: SA pp. 19, 24; Banks to Hooker, 2 Sept. 1813, RBG DC v. 1, no. 40; JJ to Whitbread, 5 Sept. 1813, BLARS Whitbread papers W4847.

145   Foreign Office and release from Fleet: JJ to W. Hamilton, 21 March and 18 May 1814, JJ to C. Dundas, 18 May 1813 and Dundas to Hamilton, 19 May 1814, all BNA FO 22/69; Sprod p. 493. For the 1820 letters: Birnie to Hamilton, 20 Jan. 1820, Hamilton to Birnie, 20 Jan. 1820 and Hamilton to JJ, 8 Feb. 1820, all BNA FO 22/86; see Sprod p. 504. Jorgenson was released on 27 May 1815, having been in (apart from a two-month break) since 18 Aug. 1813: BNA PRIS 1/27, PRIS 1/28, PRIS 3/14. On the nature of his employment: *Colonial Advocate*, 1 June 1828, p. 193; SA pp. 25, 39; JJ to Hooker, 17 Aug. 1817, BL Ms. Eg. 2070. Channel crossing: SA p. 25.

146   Waterloo and Low Countries: SA pp. 25–6; TFG pp. 1–3, 13; Dallas
     p. 397; Allan p. 66; *Edinburgh Review* v. 28 (March–Aug. 1817)
     pp. 371–90.

146–7   Paris: TFG pp. 140, 209 (coat); Calder (1878) 29 July (coat); TFG
     pp. 123–4 (snuffbox), 69–87, 126, 143–6, 149–50; Mme de Staël, *De*
     l'Allemagne (Paris: 1968), cited Dallas p. 130. Gambling houses: TFG
     pp. 89–97; SA p. 26.

147–8   Journey to south and illness: JJ to Jermyn, 16 Jan. 1816, BL Ms. Eg.
     2070.

148–9   Northern France: SA p. 26; TFG pp. vi, 174–5, 179–81 (Irish pilgrim),
     173, 208–9 (soldiers and wagoners). Jorgenson's knowledge of French
     is mentioned in his obituary, *Hobart Town Advertiser*, 22 Jan. 1841.

149–51   Frankfurt: TFG pp. 218–19, 224, 237; SA p. 27; JJ to Hooker, 14 Aug.
     1820, BL Ms. Eg. 2070 (on Maria); TFG pp. 236–7 (dance); JJ to
     Jermyn, 16 Jan. 1816, BL Ms. Eg. 2070 (museum).

151   Weimar, Leipzig and Berlin: TFG pp. 258–64, 270–1, 286–7, 292–8;
     SA pp. 28–9; Editor's introduction to Pückler-Muskau, Hermann (tr.
     S. Austin, ed. E.M. Butler), *A Regency Visitor* (London: Collins, 1957)
     p. 9; Buruma p. 88.

152   Hamburg: SA p. 30; TFG pp. 386–9.

152   On Germany: *Edinburgh Review*, v. 28 (Aug. 1817) p. 382; TFG
     pp. 414–16.

152   *Travels in France and Germany*: *Edinburgh Review*, v. 28 (Aug. 1817)
     pp. 371–90; JJ to Jermyn, 25 July 1817, BL Ms. Eg. 2070.

153   Government reports, gambling and journalism: JJ to Jermyn, 25 July
     1817, and JJ to Hooker, 17 Aug. 1817, both BL Ms. Eg. 2070; J.J. to
     Sidmouth, 9 March 1820 BNA HO 44/1 f. 41; SA p. 31.

153–4   Letter to Hooker: JJ to Hooker, 17 Aug. 1817, BL Ms. Eg. 2070.

Chapter 8: In a dreadful scrape

156   Old Bailey trial: *The Whole Proceedings* . . . (1820) pp. 422–3 (no.
     701), Jorgan [sic] Jorgenson, 25 May 1820.

157   Request to transport himself: JJ to Castlereagh, 31 May 1820, BNA
     FO 22/86, ff. 151–2; JJ to Hooker, 22 July 1820, BL Ms. Eg. 2070.

157–8   Newgate: JJ to Hooker, 22 July, 14 Aug., 25 Aug. and 18 Sept. 1820,
     all BL Ms. Eg. 2070.

158   Hospital job: JJ to Hooker, 26 Sept., 30 Sept., 11 Oct. and 23 Oct.
     1820, all BL Ms. Eg. 2070.

159–   Writings: JJ to Hooker, 6 Oct., 20 Oct. 1820, 11 Oct, 31 Oct. 1821,
     all BL Ms. Eg. 2070; printed prospectus for RC, dated 18 July 1825,
     bound in BL Ms. Eg. 2070; SA p. 32.

159   Release, freedom and re-arrest: BNA HO 13/37 (entry 391); see Noble
     to Dundas, [18 Nov. 1825], ML A2209; AOT CON 31/23 (entry 299),

identifying this release as a 'transportation'. JJ to Sidmouth, 24 Nov. 1821, BNA HO 17/53/1 Ih07; SA p. 39; Sprod pp. 527–8; JJ to Hooker, 4 Jan 1823, BL Ms. Eg. 2070. On Davis's harassment: Fritz Jürgensen to JJ, translated by latter and enclosed in JJ to Arthur, 14 May 1829, AOT CSO 1/426; JJ to Anna Jørgensen, 6 May 1823, RA Samlingspakke no. 2679. Second trial: JJ to Hooker, 4 Jan. 1823, BL Ms. Eg. 2070; *The Whole Proceedings* . . . (1822) p. 3 (no. 2): Jorgan [sic] Jorgenson, 4 Dec. 1822.

160–61   Letters from Newgate: JJ to Anna Jørgensen, 24 Dec. 1822, RA Samlingspakke no. 2679; JJ to Hooker, 4 Jan. 1823, BL Ms. Eg. 2070.

161   Sentence commuted: Hooker to R. Gunn, 30 Dec. 1833, National Library of Australia Ms. 5831. Box's assistance: *Morning Chronicle*, 27 July 1825 (letter to editor from John Clarke); JJ to Anna Jørgensen, 24 June 1823, 6 May 1823, both RA Samlingspakke no. 2679.

161–2   Life in Newgate: *Morning Chronicle*, 30 July 1825 (letter to editor from JJ); JJ to Anna Jørgensen, 6 May, 24 June 1823, both RA Samlingspakke no. 2679; JJ to Hooker, 22 July 1820, BL Ms. Eg. 2070.

162–3   Religion: RC pp. 10–11; SA p. 47; Partridge p. 188 (on laziness of chaplain); JJ to Arthur, 3 June 1826, ML A2209 Arthur papers v. 49; RC (annotated copy), ML C672; see JJ to Hooker, 12 Sept. 1834 and 15 Oct. 1834, both RBG DC v. 72, nos. 140–1; prospectus for RC, 18 July 1825, BL Ms. Eg. 2070.

163–4   *Religion of Christ*: RC pp. xv, 312–13; Bede (tr. L. Sherley-Price, rev. R.E. Latham), *A History of the English Church and People*, II:13 (Harmondsworth: Penguin, 1968), p. 127. On the twins and phrenology: RC pp. 55–7. On the Golden Rule: RC pp. 291–4. Reviews: *Gentleman's Magazine* v. 97 (2) (1827) pp. 518–20; *Sydney Gazette*, 7 May 1828.

165   Jorgenson and the Deists/Carlilites: JJ's sermon on the text 'Be ye always ready; for in such an hour as ye think not the final summons cometh', BL Ms. Eg. 2070; Wiener pp. 88–9; *Dictionary of National Biography* v. 3, pp. 1009–12 (entry for Carlile); *Morning Chronicle*, 27 July and 30 July 1825 (letter to editor from John Clarke and Jorgenson's reply); *The Republican*, v. 12 (14), 7 Oct. 1825, pp. 446–7; JJ to Arthur, 3 June 1826, ML A2209 Arthur papers v. 49; JJ petition to Arthur, 4 May 1829, ML Aj 19/2.

165–6   Removal to *Justitia*: JJ to Hooker, 26 Oct. 1825, written on copy of printed prospectus for RC, 18 July 1825, BL Ms. Eg. 2070; SA pp. 43–4; Noble to Dundas, [18 Nov. 1825], ML A2209 Arthur papers v. 49.

167–9   *Woodman*: SA pp. 48, 36, 40, 46. Experiences in ship's hospital: Sprod p. 539; Noble to Dundas, [18 Nov. 1825], ML A2209 Arthur papers

v. 49; SA pp. 46–9; Arthur to Hay, 1 June 1826, in *Historical Records of Australia* Series III, v. 5, pp. 276–7; see also JJ to Arthur, 3 June 1826, ML A2209 Arthur papers v. 49.

Chapter 9: A species of gloomy delight

169   Arrival in Hobart: Arthur to Hay, 1 June 1826, in *Historical Records of Australia* Series III, v. 5, pp. 276–7; *Hobart Town Gazette*, 6 May 1826, also repeated in *Sydney Gazette*, 24 May 1826. *Lady Nelson* convict theory: Richards, pp. 115–16. Jorgenson's entry in convict register: AOT CON 31/23 (entry 299).

169–70   Transformation of Hobart: SA pp. 13, 51, 50. Clark p. 408; on convict numbers, put at 6,762 in 1826), *Colonial Times*, 6 July 1827; Goodrick p. 70; *Hobart Town Gazette*, 6 May 1826.

171   Convict assignment and discipline: Melville (1835) pp. 235–6; Gascoigne p. 135; Robson (1965) pp. 101, 105.

171–2   Arthur and his system: *Australian Dictionary of Biography* v. 1, p. 37 (entry for Arthur); *Colonial Times*, 11 May 1827; Robson (1983) p. 147; Jackman p. 50; Gascoigne pp. 135, 131. On espionage in Hobart, see *Colonial Times*, 10 Aug. 1831. Gascoigne notes that Arthur knew Bentham's work; Bentham had also tried (without success) to interest Tasmania's earlier Governor David Collins in using an actual panopticon. 'They looked at me . . .': evidence given by Edward White to an 1830 Committee for the Affairs of the Aborigines, cited Windschuttle p. 19.

173   Jorgenson in Customs House: SA p. 52; *Colonial Times*, 12 Jan. and 19 Jan 1827; *Hobart Town Gazette*, 23 June, 30 June and 7 July 1827; 'Memorial in behalf of Jorgen Jorgenson', to Arthur, 15 Jan. 1827, in *Historical Records of Australia*, Resumed Series III, v. 7, p. 475. On his salary: Sprod p. 543. On Childs's execution: *Hobart Town Gazette*, 7 July 1827.

174   Van Diemen's Land Company: Sprod p. 555; Pink and Ebdon pp. 32–3.

175   Jorgenson's exploring party: Curr to Inglis, 25 Aug. 1826, AOT VDL 5/1; Meston pp. 108 ff., reproducing Scott's map in part facing p. 110 (original in AOT); Curr to JJ, 2 Sept. 1826, AOT MM 71/5 20/255; Binks pp. 47–8; JJ's journal, ML C125, 22 Sept. 1826; Curr to Inglis, 5 Oct. 1826, AOT VDL 5/1; HVDLC p. 31. On Colbert: AOT CON 31/6; AOT CON 23/1. On Robinson's racial background: C. Pybus, 'Robinson and Robertson', in Manne (pp. 258–76) p. 274.

176–7   Setting out: JJ's journal, ML C125, 3 Sept., 4 Sept., 5 Sept. 1826; HVDLC pp. 18–20. Equipment: HVDLC pp. 19, 22; JJ's journal, ML C125, 5 Sept., 9 Sept. (and following undated pages), 18 Sept. 1826. In the journal he says that they were carrying about 50 lb (almost 23 kilos), excluding weapons, but his HVDLC estimate of 70 lb each (almost 32 kilos) matches the journal's itemized list more closely. On the journal and its rescue: JJ's journal, ML C125, introductory notes in unknown hand; RJJ pp. 63–81; HVDLC p. 30; Bruce (1995) p. 8.

177   The sword: SA p. 53, p. 60.

177–180 The journey: crossing the Shannon: RJJ pp. 64–5; JJ's journal, ML C125, 14–21 Sept. 1826; HVDLC p. 20. Great Lake: JJ's journal, ML C125, 21–2 Sept. 1826; RJJ pp. 69–70, Binks p. 49. Ouse: JJ's journal, ML C125, 22–3 Sept. 1826; RJJ p. 66; Meston reproduces the skyline Jorgenson would have seen from his ridge, facing p. 114; Binks pp. 52–3, p. 72. Jorgenson's contemplations: SA p. 56; JJ to Hooker, 12 Sept. 1834, RBG DC v. 72, no. 140. Pragmatic version for Curr: JJ's journal, ML C125, 24 Sept. 1826. Continued attempts to cross: JJ's journal, ML C125, 25–6 Sept. 1826. Return: JJ's journal, ML C125, 27 Sept. 1826; HVDLC pp. 26–7; Binks p. 53; RJJ p. 72; SA p. 55.

180   Curr's report: Curr's despatch of 5 Oct. 1826, AOT VDL 5/1; Curr to JJ, 2 Oct. 1826, AOT VDL 23, cited in Bruce (1995) pp. 125–8.

180–82   Second journey: RJJ pp. 73–4; Meston pp. 108, 118. Walls of Jerusalem: HVDLC pp. 28–9; RJJ pp. 75–7; Meston pp. 107, 120; Binks, p. 8. Barren country: RJJ pp. 77–8. Return: RJJ pp. 78–80; Meston p. 121; HVDLC pp. 31–2. Curr's report: Curr's despatch of 13 Nov. 1826, AOT VDL 5/1.

183   Meston's and Binks's conclusions: Meston pp. 107, 122; Binks pp. 77, 50, 55–6.

Chapter 10: A rogue in grain

184–8   Third attempt: Curr's despatch of 13 Nov. 1826, AOT VDL 5/1; Binks pp. 69–71; Plomley (1991) p. 8; HVDLC p. 33. On Lorymer: Bruce (1993) pp. 12–16. First stages of journey: Binks pp. 69–70, with map; HVDLC p. 33; JJ's journal, ML C125, 27 March 1827 (on Lorymer's method of pacing); 3, 4, 9, 10 March 1827 (on Aboriginal encounter); HVDLC pp. 36–7 (encounter, and second disagreement with Lorymer). Heading inland: HVDLC pp. 37–42; Binks pp. 74–5; JJ's journal, ML C125, 19 March 1827. Attempt abandoned: HVDLC pp. 42–4; JJ's journal, ML C125, 21 March 1827. Dogs: JJ's journal, ML C125, 23, 27, 31 March 1827; HVDLC p. 45; Curr's despatch of 17 April 1827, AOT VDL 5/1.

189–91   Return along coast: HVDLC pp. 46–50; JJ's journal, ML C125, 31 March–3 April, 18 March 1827 ('The natives seem . . .'); Binks p. 77; Ian McFarlane, 'Cape Grim', in Manne (pp. 277–98) pp. 291–4. Lack of rope: JJ's journal, ML C125, 7 April 1827. Dogs: HVDLC pp. 49–50; JJ's journal, ML C125, 5, 8 April 1827.

190   Short cut through mudflats: HVDLC p. 50; JJ to Hooker, 12 Sept. 1834, RBG DC v. 72, no. 140.

190–1   Duck River: JJ's journal, ML C125, 7–8 April 1827; HVDLC pp. 50–1.
191–2   Curr's report: Curr to Ingle, 17 April 1827, AOT VDL 5/1. Jorgenson's
         disagreement with Curr: JJ to Hooker, 12 Sept. 1834, RBG DC v. 72,
         no. 140; HVDLC pp. 52, 14, 12 (on Curr's book); Curr, despatch of
         5 Jan. 1829, AOT VDL 5/1 (accusations of 'fabrication').
193   Ticket of leave: Hobart Town Gazette, 9 June 1827; AOT POL 452/1
         (entry 299); AOT CON 31/23 (entry 299); SA p. 59.
194   Writing: HVLDC p. 18. On Arthur's repression of Bent: Miller, pp.
         81–3; Australian Dictionary of Biography v. 1, pp. 86–7 (entry for
         Bent). Phrenology: Colonial Advocate, 1 May 1828; R.W. Lawrence
         to W.J. Hooker, 29 June 1832, in Burns and Skemp p. 20; Sprod
         p. 679 (n. 35); RC p. 56; JJ to Hooker, 12 Sept. 1835, RBG DC
         v. 72, no. 140. Jorgenson's later work for Bent: SA p. 60; Colonial
         Times, 20 Nov. 1832; Tasmanian, 5 April 1833; Austral-Asiatic Review,
         16 April 1833; Miller p. 40. Jorgenson on James Ross: JJ to Hooker,
         12 Sept. 1834 and 4 Dec. 1840, both RBG DC, v. 72, no. 140 and
         v. 76, no. 47.
195   Jorgenson on Arthur: JJ to T. Anstey, 27 July 1828, ML Aj 19/5; SA
         pp. 87–8; JJ to Hooker, 28 Oct. 1836, RBG DC v. 73, no. 204; JJ to
         Forster, 17 May 1837, cited in Levy p. 355.
195–7   Field Police: SA pp. 87–8; Hobart Town Gazette, 24 May 1828; Hobart
         Town Courier, 24 May 1828; JJ to Anstey, 27 July 1828, ML Aj 19/5.
         For early starts: JJ's Report, 4 June 1829, Allport Library (State
         Library of Tasmania), p. 3. On the Midlands: SA pp. 63–4; Mortyn
         p. 12. Enjoyment of his service, sly grog-shops and reverse morality:
         all SA p. 61.
197   Anstey: SA pp. 60–1; Australian Dictionary of Biography, v. 1, pp. 19–21
         (entry for Anstey). On his estate: Stieglitz (1960) p. 48; Weeding
         (1994) pp. 7–9.
198   Sheldon gang: JJ's petition to Arthur, undated (30 April or 1 May
         1829), AOT CSO 1/426/9583 p. 99 (on exerting himself 'in a manner
         never before done'); AOT CON 23/3, CON 31/38 and CON 31/1
         (entries for Sheldon and Axford); Hobart Town Courier, 6 Dec. 1828;
         Tasmanian, 12 Dec. 1828.
198   Norah Corbett: AOT CON 40/1 (entry 97); Tardif, pp. 1060 ff.; Hobart
         Town Gazette, 12 July 1828, containing advertisement that she is
         missing, repeated in subsequent weeks; Sprod pp. 560–1.
199   Capture of Sheldon, and fears for safety: Hobart Town Courier, 4 April,
         14 March 1829. Rumours about Norah: Hobart Town Courier, 4 April
         1829. There were a few William Elliotts among the convicts on the
         island at this time, but Axford seems more likely to be meant. Petition
         for marriage (and also Norah's application for permission to marry
         Houskie, 18 Jan. 1830): AOT CSO 1/378/8600.

199–201 Trials in Hobart: AOT CON 31/38 (entry 315, for Sheldon); JJ's petition to Arthur, undated (30 April or 1 May 1829), AOT CSO 1/426/9583 p. 99, with Anstey's note dated 4 May 1829. Jorgenson and Norah in Hobart: AOT CON 31/23 (entry 299, for Jorgenson); JJ to A. Stephen, 10 May 1829, ML Aj 19/3 ('I do know . . .', 'actually came out in the street', 'In the man who is giving himself up . . .', 'by the manner of throwing out my arms . . .'); JJ to Arthur, 12 May 1829, AOT CSO 1/426/9593, pp. 102–5 ('certain very unmannerly', 'handy-work', 'Here is this busy fellow . . .')

201–2 Outcome of trials, and assignment of Norah: Sprod pp. 562–3; AOT CON 31/38 (entry 315, for Sheldon); Petition for marriage: CSO 1/378/8600, p. 137; Tardif p. 1061 ff.

Chapter 11: The unknown

203–4 Aboriginal Tasmanians: Ryan, L., pp. 9–12, 14; Pardoe pp. 1 (land bridge), 11 (population); Reynolds pp. 4, 52; Windschuttle pp. 364–71; T. Murray and C. Williamson, 'Archaeology and history', in Manne (pp. 311–33) p. 314; Jones p. 321; Plomley (1992) pp. 10–11, 25 (table 1), 29 (graph 1); NHMC pp. 123–4; J. Boyce, 'Fantasy island', in Manne (pp. 17–78) p. 69.

204–5 Relations with settlers: JJ's 'Report of the proceedings . . .', 12 Jan. 1830, AOT CSO 1/320/7578, 7D (pp. 351–5) p. 353; Plomley (1992) pp. 17–20, 26–7; for a more detailed breakdown of the tribes on the island, and the bands within them, see Ryan, L., pp. 15–16.

204 Suggested causes of change: Morgan pp. 13, 22, 57–8; Plomley (1992) p. 6; J. Boyce, 'Fantasy island', in Manne (pp. 17–78) pp. 47–57, 61; Windschuttle pp. 65–114, 129–30, 399; Reynolds pp. 30–2, 66; Connor pp. x, 20–1.

205 Attacks: SA pp. 67, 53; *Hobart Town Gazette*, 11 Nov. and 18 Nov. 1826; Bruce (1995) pp. 207–9; documents on Gough inquest, 11 Oct. 1828, AOT CSO 1/316/ 7578, pp. 166–8, 759; Reynolds p. 31 and Connor p. 85, both citing testimony of John Sherwin, 23 Feb. 1830; JJ to Anstey, 25 Jan. 1830, AOT CSO 1/320/7578 7D, p. 338 (i.e. 358) – Jorgenson writes 'your' for the first 'you'; here corrected for clarity. On the kangaroo question: Windschuttle p. 89; NHMC p. 63; Plomley (1992) p. 18.

207 Weapons: Reynolds pp. 41–3, 72; Connor pp. 18–19, 89. On the musket question: Windschuttle pp. 260–1; Ian McFarlane, 'Cape Grim', in Manne (pp. 277–98) pp. 285–7; JJ to Anstey, 28 July 1829, AOT CSO 1/320/7578 7D, p. 309.

207 Ambush and invisibility: JJ to Anstey, Report for Dec. 1830 to March 1831, AOT CSO 1/320/7578 7D, p. 403; Reynolds p. 35.

208 Settlers' fear: JJ to Anstey, 18 Feb. 1830, AOT CSO 1/320/7578 7D,

p. 364; Robinson p. 508; JJ's 'Report of the proceedings . . .' AOT CSO 1/320/7578 7D, p. 342.

208 Colonists' reactions: Reynolds pp. 67, 70, citing *Hobart Town Courier*, 11 Sept. 1830; Arthur to Goderich, 10 Jan. 1828, in Great Britain: Parliament . . .: *Van Diemen's Land*, pp. 3–4.

209 Jorgenson's views: NHMC p. 118; JJ's report of 18 Feb. 1830, AOT CSO 1/320/7578 7D, pp. 364–5; SA p. 65; JJ's journal, ML C125, 18 March 1827.

209 Government's problem: Arthur to Goderich, 10 Jan. and 17 April 1828, in Great Britain: Parliament . . .: *Van Diemen's Land* pp. 3–7; NHMC pp. 50–1 (duty to convicts).

210 Jorgenson's letter: JJ to Arthur, 5 Jan. 1828, ML A2209 Arthur papers v. 49.

211 Jorgenson's solution: JJ to Arthur, 5 Jan. 1828, ML A2209 Arthur papers v. 49; Plomley (1991) pp. 43–4.

212 Evangelical Christianity: James p. 137; Gascoigne pp. 148 ff. On *Terra nullius*: Locke, John (ed. J.W. Gough), *The second treatise of civil government* (Oxford: Basil Blackwell, 1946), sections 27, 32 and 34, pp. 15–8; Gascoigne p. 8; Frost pp. 513–23.

213 Signs of Aboriginal victory: JJ to Anstey, 18 Feb. 1830 and JJ's report of 25 March 1830, both AOT CSO 1/320/7578 7D, pp. 360, 374.

213–14 Exclusion plans, and Arthur's proclamation: Arthur to Goderich, 10 Jan. and 17 April 1828, in Great Britain: Parliament . . .:*Van Diemen's Land* pp. 3–7.

214 Peaceful interlude, and return of violence: Reynolds p. 104; Windschuttle p. 150; Arthur to Huskisson, 5 July 1828, and Arthur to Murray, 4 Nov. 1828, both in Great Britain: Parliament . . .: *Van Diemen's Land* pp. 8–9.

214 Legal situation before martial law: Connor p. 58; Windschuttle pp. 36, 104. On hangings: Calder (1875) pp. 46–7; Weeding (1994) pp. 26–7; NHMC p. 75; Connor pp. 58, 67; Windschuttle pp. 189–91. On the law of Moses: *Hobart Town Gazette*, 16 June 1827.

215 J.E.'s questions in *Launceston Advertiser*, 26 Sept. 1831, cited in Reynolds pp. 83–4.

215–16 Martial law: Connor p. 58; Reynolds pp. 110–12; Arthur to Murray, 4 Nov. 1828, and Minutes of Executive Council 30–31 Oct. 1828, both in Great Britain: Parliament . . .: *Van Diemen's Land* pp. 9–11; J. Boyce, 'Fantasy island', in Manne (pp. 17–78) p. 28. Restrictions: Proclamation, 1 Nov. 1828, and Arthur's letter to magistrates, 1 Nov. 1828, both in Great Britain: Parliament . . .: *Van Diemen's Land* pp. 12–13.

216–17 Roving parties: *Hobart Town Courier*, 13 July 1829; T. Anstey, 'General orders', 27 June 1829, AOT CSO 1/320/7578 7D, p. 295. On Batman:

Australian Dictionary of Biography v. 1, pp. 67–70; Serle v. 1, pp. 23–5; Bonwick (1867 and 1883). On Robertson: C. Pybus, 'Robinson and Robertson', in Manne, pp. 258–76; *Australian Dictionary of Biography* v. 2 pp. 384–7; Serle v. 2, pp. 283–4. Duties of roving parties: Reynolds p. 71; Connor pp. 100–1; JJ to Anstey, 28 July 1829 and report of 18 Feb. 1830, both AOT CSO 1/320/7578 7D, pp. 303 (early start), 360 (sleeping in rain); JJ memorial to Glenelg via Arthur, 5 Dec 1836, ML A2209 Arthur papers, v. 49.

218   Jorgenson lost: 'Jorgenson's account . . .', [March 1829], AOT CSO 1/320/7578 7D, pp. 271–2; SA p. 63.

218   Jorgenson's praise and complaints: JJ, 'Extract of Journal . . .', 14 July 1829, AOT CSO 1/320/7578 7D, pp. 292–3. Ticket of leave recommendations: e.g. JJ's Report, 4 June 1829, Allport Library (State Library of Tasmania) p. 38, with Anstey's note dated 6 June.

218–20   Jorgenson's understanding of restrictions. Geographical limits: JJ to Anstey, undated (early 1830), AOT CSO 1/320/7578 7D, pp. 352–3. Tyrrell incident: AOT CSO 1/320/7578 7D, pp. 362–3, 377–80. Restrictions on violence: JJ to Anstey, 18 June 1829 ('to place the native tribes . . .'), 29 July 1829 ('captured, or otherwise disposed of'), 18 Jan. 1830 ('You will see by Tyrrell's report . . .'), Feb. 1830 ('capturing and destroying'), 28 July 1829 (castigating the settler who failed to shoot), and his Report of 25 March 1830 ('constitute the greatest act of humanity'), all AOT CSO 1/320/7578 7D, pp. 275, 321–2, 335 (i.e. 355), 368–9, 309, 374. On estimates of casualties: L. Ryan, 'Who is the fabricator?', in Manne (pp. 230–57) p. 251; Windschuttle pp. 152–3; Connor p. 93.

220   Batman's killings: Windschuttle pp. 156–7; Reynolds p. 81; NHMC p. 119; Campbell p. 32; Billot, C.P., *The Story of John Batman and the Founding of Melbourne* (Melbourne, Hyland House, 1979) p. 48; J. Boyce, 'Fantasy island', in Manne (pp. 17–78) pp. 31–2; *Australian Dictionary of Biography* v. 1, p. 68; Bonwick (1867) p. 2.

220   On rarity of sightings: see Gilbert Robertson's diaries, AOT CSO 1/332/7578, pp. 114–55; Windschuttle pp. 154–5; Batman's diaries in Bonwick (1883) pp. 151ff; JJ's 'Extract of Journal . . .', 14 July 1829, JJ to Anstey, 18 Feb. 1830, and JJ to Anstey, 28 July 1829, all in AOT CSO 1/320/7578 7D, pp. 279–82, 363, 297–316.

220–22   Jorgenson's assessment of reasons for failure: JJ to Anstey, 29 July 1829 and (for pipe-smoking) 18 Feb. 1830, both in AOT CSO 1/320/7578 7D, pp. 321–2, 360.

222–3   Mungo/Jack: JJ to Anstey, 18 Feb. 1830, 25 Jan. 1830, and his Report for Dec. 1830 to March 1831, all in AOT CSO 1/320/7578 7D, pp. 344–5, 358–64, 341, 405–6; NHMC p. 83.

223   Jorgenson's proposals and reports: JJ to Anstey, 18 June 1829, AOT

CSO 1/320/7578 7D, pp. 275–8. For Anstey's use of them, see e.g. his General Orders, 27 June 1829, based on JJ to Anstey, 18 June 1829; Plomley (1991) pp. 27–9. 'With reference to this race . . .': JJ to Hooker, 4 Dec. 1840, RBG DC v. 76, no. 47. Jorgenson's signed reports are in AOT CSO 1/320/ 7578, no. 7: Reports and Journals of Roving Parties. Section D: 'Jorgen Jorgenson's Reports'. Apologies for length: JJ, 'Extract of Journal . . .', 14 July 1829, and JJ to Anstey, 28 July 1829, both AOT CSO 1/320/7578 7D, pp. 295, 297; JJ's Report, 4 June 1829, Allport Library (State Library of Tasmania), pp. 8–10, with Anstey's note of 6 June advising his superiors to skip parts.

223– Jorgenson's dissatisfaction and requests to leave: JJ to Anstey, 31 July 1829, in ML A2209 Arthur papers v. 49; Windschuttle p. 155 (on JJ and Robertson); JJ, Report, 25 March 1830, AOT CSO 1/320/7578 7D, p. 376; JJ to Anstey, 22 May 1830, AOT CSO 1/426, pp. 121–3 with Anstey's added note.

224–5 Conditional pardon: AOT CON 31/23 (entry 299 for Jorgenson) (Conditional Pardon no. 161, 3 June 1830); Arthur's Minute no. 59 and draft version of pardon, both 3 June 1830, both AOT CSO 1/426/9583 pp. 124–5, 133–4. Jorgenson's reaction to ban on returning to Britain: JJ to Anstey, 28 June 1830, AOT CSO 1/320/7578 7D, pp. 383–4; JJ to Fritz Jürgensen, 11 Sept. 1835, KB NBD IX 8, Haandskrift Afd. 163.

Chapter 12: A precarious existence

226–8 Black Line: Ford p. 127; Connor pp. 93–8, with map p. 96; memo by Arthur, 20 Nov. 1830, cited Windschuttle p. 153. Jorgenson's account of the Line: NHMC pp. 99–109. Preparations: Connor pp. 94–5, 98; West v. 2, p. 295; Windschuttle p. 178 n.; Reynolds pp. 117–18; JJ to Arthur, 20 Sept. 1830, ML A2209 Arthur papers v. 49; JJ to Anstey, 16 Sept. 1830, with Anstey's added note dated 17 Sept., AOT CSO 1/320/7578 7D, p. 385–90.

228–9 Movement of the Line: Connor pp. 95, 98; Melville (1959) pt 2, pp. 30, 38 n.; Windschuttle p. 174; Robinson p. 315; JJ's Report, Nov. 1830, AOT CSO 1/320/7578 7D, pp. 396–8. End of the Line: Connor p. 97; Windschuttle pp. 174–5.

229–31 Assessments of the Line: Melville (1959) pt 2, p. 40, with editor's note identifying the speaker at the meeting as T.G. Gregson; JJ to Charles Arthur, 30 Nov. 1830, AOT CSO 1/320/7578 7D, pp. 394–5. On misconceptions: Windschuttle, pp. 168, 175–6; see e.g. Davies, D.M. p. 126 for crying babies. Impact of Line: NHMC pp. 99, 109; Reynolds p. 51; Ryan, L., p. 112; Windschuttle pp. 179–81; JJ's Report for Dec. 1830 to March 1831, AOT CSO 1/320/7578 7D, pp. 399–406; SA p. 80.

Notes to pages 231 to 236

231 Remaining Aboriginal population: no exact figures are known, but Plomley (1992) says 350 (p. 10) and Ryan, L., says 300 (p. 183), while Windschuttle criticizes these figures and says 200 (pp. 224–6), citing the Flinders Island commandant's return of 1836 in V. Rae-Ellis, *Black Robinson* (Melbourne: Melbourne University Press, 1988). Jorgenson himself put it at around 200: SA, p. 81.

231–2 Robinson: Robinson p. 428 (n. 44), cited Windschuttle p. 179; NHMC p. 99; SA p. 80; Reynolds p. 51, p. 135; Connor p. 100; *Australian Dictionary of Biography* v. 2, pp. 385–7 (entry for Robinson); Reynolds p. 135; Hughes, R., *The Fatal Shore* (London: Harvill Collins, 1987), p. 423; Windschuttle, pp. 207–14; C. Pybus, 'Robinson and Robertson', in Manne (pp. 258–276).

232 Flinders Island: Windschuttle pp. 226, 247. On disease: Windschuttle pp. 372–6; J. Boyce, 'Fantasy island', in Manne (pp. 17–78) pp. 42–4; *Australian Dictionary of Biography* v. 2, pp. 385–7 (entry on Robinson); Ryan, L., p. 183. On Flinders Island, see Plomley (1987).

233 Kangaroo Island: Ryan, L., p. 220; Windschuttle p. 13 (n. 8); Tindale, N., 'Tasmanian Aborigines on Kangaroo Island', *Records of the South Australian Museum*, v. 6, no. 1 (1937), pp. 29–37. On modern Aboriginal community: Ryan, L., pp. 222–61 and particularly pp. xxiv–xxv, describing the processes of cultural reconstruction.

233–4 Speculation as to death toll and causes: Reynolds pp. 75–6, 81–2; Ryan, L., pp. 122, 174; Windschuttle pp. 358–64, 372–86, 387–97 (table 10), with revisions to latter on www.sydneyline.com; Ryan, L., 'Who is the fabricator?', in Manne (pp. 230–57) pp. 252–3; S. Breen, 'Re-inventing social evolution', in Manne (pp. 139–59) pp. 142–5; T. Murray and C. Williamson, 'Archaeology and history', in Manne (pp. 311–33) pp. 315–29. On perplexity: NHMC p. 124; J. Boyce, 'Fantasy island', in Manne (pp. 17–78) p. 69.

234 Jorgenson's arrest and land grant: SA p. 73; AOT CON 31/23 (entry 299 for Jorgenson); JJ to Arthur, 12 July 1830, ML A2209 Arthur papers v. 49; order dated 25 Aug. 1830, cited in Hawkings p. 194; *Hobart Town Gazette*, 25 Dec. 1835; *Hobart Town Courier*, 1 Jan. 1836.

234–5 Marriage: JJ and Norah Corbett, Petition for marriage, with Anstey's notes: AOT CSO 1/378/8600, p. 137; St Matthew's Church register, AOT NS 489/1, p. 17 (entry 65); SA pp. 40–1; Villiers p. 109. Jorgenson's protectiveness and sense of responsibility are expressed in the marriage petition.

235–6 Jorgenson's Black War book: JJ to Arthur, 24 May 1831, ML A2209 Arthur papers v. 49; JJ to Hooker, 12 Sept. 1834, RBG DC v. 72, no. 140; JJ to Anstey, 28 June 1830, AOT CSO 1/320/7578 7D, pp. 383–4; JJ to Arthur, 12 July 1830, ML A2209 Arthur papers v. 49. On the discovery of the Braim manuscript: Plomley (1991) pp. 3, 39–42; JJ to Hooker, 4 Dec. 1840, RBG DC v. 76, no. 47. On Aboriginal languages: 'Aboriginal languages of Tasmania', in *Tasmanian Journal of Natural Science* v. 1, no. 4 (1842), pp. 308–18; NHMC pp. 58–65; Milligan, J., *Vocabulary of the Dialects of some of the Aboriginal tribes* ([Hobart]: James Barnard, 1866) pp. 33–5. Jorgenson's work and papers: JJ to C. Arthur, 30 Nov. 1830, AOT CSO 1/320/7578 7D, pp. 392–3; JJ to Hooker, 4 Dec. 1840, RBG DC v. 76, no. 47; Plomley (1991) pp. 41–2, 142 (n. 76).

237–8   *Observations on the funded system: Colonial Times*, 15, 22, 29 June, 28 Sept. 1831; SA p. 84; review in *The Independent* (Launceston), 22 Oct. 1831; OFS pp. 47–8 (on debt and withdrawal of Tasmanian funds), 75–6 ('England having burdened its children . . .'), iv ('the great mass . . .'), viii–ix (on Malthus).

238–9   Norah: JJ to Colonial Secretary, 24 Oct. 1834, AOT CSO 1/763/16363, pp. 8–10 (enquiring about her daughter). Her present difficulties: JJ to Hooker, undated (1813?), BL Ms. Eg. 2070; Tardif p. 1061; JJ to Arthur, 9 June and 11 July 1832, both in ML A2209 Arthur papers v. 49; AOT LC 219/1 (entry no. 96); AOT CON 31/23 (entry 299).

239   Jorgenson's arrest: *The Tasmanian*, 3 Aug. 1832, with Jorgenson's unpublished response, both cited in Dally (1993) pp. 9–11, 23, with note on p. 35 n. identifying the butcher as probably W.J.T. Clarke.

239–40   Jorgenson's ups and downs, and his writing: SA pp. 84–5; JJ to Arthur, 6 Nov. 1832, ML A2209 Arthur papers v. 49; JJ to Robinson, 1 Dec. 1832, ML A7056 Robinson papers, v. 35; JJ to Hooker, 4 Dec. 1840, RBG DC v. 76, no. 47; Jorgenson's obituary in *Hobart Town Advertiser*, 22 Jan. 1841.

240–41   Job-hunting: JJ's petition to Arthur, undated (May 1833?) and JJ to Arthur 12 July 1830, both ML A2209 Arthur papers v. 49; Tardif p. 1062 (Norah's arrests).

Chapter 13: Jorgenson the Australian
242–3   Ross: Greener pp. 97–9, 104–7; Arthur to Glenelg, 24 Dec. 1835, BNA CO 280/76, f. 75r. Jorgenson's appointment announced in *Hobart Town Gazette*, 19 July 1833. Greener and Laird p. 10. Man o'Ross Inn and drunken scenes: JJ to Burnett 1 Oct. 1833, Horne to Forster 28 Oct. 1833, and Leake to Forster, 4 Nov. 1833, all in BNA CO 280/76 and ML A1214; Greener p. 108; AOT CON 31/23 (entry 299 for Jorgenson). Headlam affair: Headlam, undated letter (1833), and JJ's Report, 11 Sept. [1833], both in BNA CO 280/76 and ML A1214; Greener p. 107.

243–4   Resignation: Arthur to Glenelg, 24 Dec. 1835 and JJ to Leake, 20 Nov. 1833, both in BNA CO 280/76 and ML A1214; Sprod p. 590; Greener pp. 100–1, 109–13; Greener and Laird pp. 14–16.

244   Drifting and writing: Tardif pp. 1061–2; AOT CON 31/23 (entry 299 for Jorgenson); Forster to Colonial Secretary, 24 Dec. 1835, BNA CO 280/76 and ML A1214; Hooker, J.D., v. 1, p. 108; Sprod p. 596.

244–5   *An Address to the Free Colonists*: Gascoigne pp. 52–3; AFC pp. 4, 9, 12, 14. On Jorgenson's authorship: JJ to Hooker, 4 Dec. 1840, RBG Directors' Correspondence v. 76, no. 47; *The Colonist*, 22 July 1834; AFC pp. 22–4, with notes concerning authorship in State Library of Tasmania's copy.

246   Work for Robinson: JJ to Robinson, correspondence from 24 Sept. 1834 to 20 Aug. 1835, with various undated letters, ML Robinson papers vols 35, 37 and 39, ML A7056, A7058, A7060; Robinson, pp. 927, 912 (n.13); Plomley (1991) p. 33.

246   Autobiography: JJ to Hooker, 12 Sept. 1834, RBG DC v. 72, no. 140 ('stern survey'); JJ to Hooker, 17 Aug. 1817, BL Ms. Eg. 2070 ('Even in my most solitary hours . . .').

246–7   Hooker: Hooker to Gunn, 30 Dec. 1833, National Library of Australia Ms. 5831; R.W. Lawrence to W.J. Hooker, 29 June 1832, in Burns and Skemp p. 20; JJ to Hooker, 12 Sept. and 15 Oct. 1834, both RBG DC v. 72, nos. 140–1; Gunn to Hooker, 30 March and 26 Sept. 1835, both in Burns and Skemp pp. 41–2, 50.

247–8   Jorgenson's life in 1834/5: AOT LC 83/1 (drunkenness); JJ to Hooker, 12 Sept. 1834, RBG DC v. 72, no. 140; JJ to Fritz Jürgensen, 11 Sept. 1835, KB NBD IX 8, Haandskrift Afd. 163.

248–9   Bryan affair and departure of Arthur: file of documents at BNA CO 280/76; Sprod pp. 587–9; *Australian Dictionary of Biography* v. 1, pp. 172–3 (entry on Bryan). Jorgenson's letters to Arthur: JJ to Arthur 8 Aug. 1835, 26 Oct. 1836, JJ to Glenelg with covering letter to Arthur, 5 Dec. 1836, JJ to Arthur, 24 June 1837, all ML A2209 Arthur papers v. 49; JJ, 'To his Majesty's Executive Government of VDL', 5 Nov. 1836, AOT CSO 1/889/18867, in Dally (1977) pp. 245–6; SA p. 92.

249   Franklin: OFS (presentation copy in ML, C813); Franklin to W.J. Hooker, 6 Aug. 1841, Burns and Skemp p. 90.

249   Jorgenson in prison and Norah in hospital: JJ to Robinson from the Labour in Vain, undated (but probably Sat. 23 April 1836, a subsequent letter of the same day being dated 'Saturday evening') and 29 April 1836, ML Robinson papers vol 42, ML A7063; JJ to Forster, 3 May 1836, ML A2209 Arthur papers v. 49; Goodrick pp. 182–3 (weather); *Hobart Town Courier*, 13 May 1836; JJ to Forth, 17 Oct. 1837, ML Aj 19/4; JJ to C. Swanston, 12 Oct. 1838, State Library of Tasmania: Crowther Pamphlet Q.CRO.PQ 920.JOR.

250   Letter from Fritz, as translated by Jorgenson and included in JJ to Forster, 31 March 1840, AOT CSO 19/2, pp. 195–8.

250   Jorgenson's accident and his writing: JJ to Forster, 12 June 1839, 31 March 1840 and 9 Nov. 1840, all AOT CSO 19/2 pp. 320–2, 195–8, 222–3; *Colonial Times*, 17 March, 21 April, 12 May 1840; *Hobart Town Courier*, 28 Feb. 1840.

250–51   Norah's decline and death: JJ to J. Price, 15 March 1840, National Library of Australia Ms. 5831; JJ to Forster, 31 March 1840, AOT CSO 19/2 pp. 195–8; JJ to Swanston, 22 May 1840, State Library of Tasmania: Crowther Pamphlet Q.CRO.PQ 920.JOR; AOT RGD 35/1 (entry 512: Norah's death); AOT NS 1052/53, p. 10 (Norah's burial); Sprod p. 608.

251–3   Public meeting on assignment system: Wiedenhofer pp. 13–15; Robson (1965) p. 92; Woodward pp. 365–81; *True Colonist*, 15 May 1840.

Chapter 14: We, Jorgen Jorgenson

254–5   Joseph Dalton Hooker: Hooker, J.D., v. 1, pp. 107–8, v. 2, pp. 346–8, citing a letter to his father (1841) and two to Mrs Lyell (nee Katharine Horner), 11 April and 16 April 1892.

255–6   Jorgenson's final letter: JJ to Hooker, 4 Dec. 1840, RBG DC v. 76, no. 47.

256–7   Jorgenson's death and burial: AOT RGD 35/1 (entry 578: JJ's death); AOT NS 1052/53, p. 12 (his burial); J.D. Hooker to Mrs Lyell, 11 April 1892, in Hooker, J.D., v. 2, p. 347; Sprod pp. 609–10; Franklin to W.J. Hooker, 6 Aug. 1841, in Burns and Skemp p. 90; obituary in *Hobart Town Advertiser*, 22 Jan. 1841, *Hobart Town Courier*, 26 Jan. 1841, and *Cornwall Chronicle*, 30 Jan. 1841. With thanks to Dan Sprod for showing me the burial site.

257–8   Truth stranger than fiction: Hogan p. 4; Villiers p. 99.

258–60   Novels: Ferrar; Clarke (1870 etc.); Clarke (1874); Bridges pp. 120–30; Williams pp. 28–47; Davies, R.; Clune and Stephensen; *Jorgen Jorgenson: a Convict King*; Cormick p. 38; Flanagan pp. 146, 253, 292.

260–61   Literature and philosophy: Clune and Stephensen p. 470; SA pp. 41, 15–16; NHMC p. 131.

261   Double man: Clune and Stephensen p. 470; JJ to Hooker, 17 Aug. 1817, BL Ms. Eg. 2070; Miller, Karl, *Doubles: Studies in Literary History* (Oxford: Oxford University Press, 1985) p. 40.

Bibliography

Jorgenson's Main Works

'Aboriginal Languages in Tasmania', in *Tasmanian Journal of Natural Science*, v. 1, no. 4, 1842, pp. 308–18. (Jorgenson is credited as the main source in the opening words of the text.)

An Address to the Free Colonists of Van Diemen's Land, on trial by jury, and our other constitutional rights. By Publicola. ([Hobart]: Andrew Bent for the author, 1834)

The Adventures of Thomas Walter. Manuscript: British Library Ms. Eg. 2066

The Copenhagen Expedition traced to other causes than the Treaty of Tilsit; with observations on the history and present state of Denmark. By a Dane. (London: T. Harper, jun., and sold by W.H. Wyatt, 1811)

Description of the Kingdom of Shandaria and Adventures of King Detrimedes. Manuscript: British Library Ms. Eg. 2069

The Duke d'Angiens. Manuscript: British Library Ms. Eg. 2069

Efterretning om Engelændernes og Nordamerikanernes fart og handel paa Sydhavet. (Kiobenhavn: A. Seidelin, 1807)

— English translation: *Observations on Pacific Trade and Sealing and Whaling in Australian and New Zealand Waters before 1805.* (Tr. Lena Knight, ed. Rhys Richards) (Wellington, NZ: Paremata Press, 1996)

Historical Account of a Revolution on the Island of Iceland in the Year 1809

— [Version 1] Manuscript: British Library Ms. Eg. 2067

— [Version 2] Manuscript: British Library Ms. Eg. 2068

— A composite edition of the two versions is published in Sprod, Dan, *The Usurper* (Hobart: Blubber Head Press, 2001), pp. 146–282.

History of the Origin, Rise, and Progress of the Van Diemen's Land Company (London: Robson, Blades, 1829). Originally published serially in fuller form in *Colonial Advocate, and Tasmanian Monthly Review and Register*, from May to Oct. 1828. Also reprinted in facsimile with added folded map of north-western Tasmania. (Hobart: Melanie Publications, 1979)

'A Narrative of the Habits, Manners, and Customs of the Aborigines of Van Diemen's Land.' Manuscript in Braim papers at State Library of New South Wales's Mitchell Library: A614. Edited version later published in Plomley, N.J.B., *Jorgen Jorgenson and the Aborigines of Van Diemen's Land*. (Hobart: Blubber Head Press, 1991)

Observations on the Funded System: a summary view of the present political state of Great Britain and the relative situation in which the colony of Van Diemen's Land stands towards the mother country (Hobart Town: H. Melville, 1831). Originally published serially in the *Colonial Times*, 15–29 June 1831

The Religion of Christ is the Religion of Nature (London: Joseph Capes, 1827). With biographical preface by H.D.M.

— Printed prospectus for above 'In the press and will be immediately published, a work entitled The religion of Christ is the religion of Nature, by Jorgen Jorgenson, a prisoner in Newgate' (18 July 1825)

'Report of Mr Jorgen Jorgenson of a journey undertaken for discovery of a practicable route from Hobart Town to Circular Head, dated 8th November, 1826', in Van Diemen's Land Company: *Report made to the third Yearly General Meeting . . .* (London: Robson, Blades, 1828), pp. 63–81

Robertus Montanus, or The Oxford Scholar. Manuscript: British Library Ms. Eg. 2069

'A Shred of Autobiography', in *Ross's Hobart Town Almanack, and Van Diemen's Land Annual for 1835* [pt 1] and *The Hobart Town Almanack, and Van Diemen's Land Annual for 1838* [pt 2]. Later published as *A shred of autobiography* ([ed. James Dally]) ([Adelaide]: Sullivan's Cove, 1981).

State of Christianity in the Island of Otaheite, and a defence of the pure precepts of the Gospel, against modern Antichrists, with reasons for the ill success which attends Christian missionaries in their attempts to convert the heathens. By a foreign traveller. (London: J. Richardson, 1811)

Travels through France and Germany in the Years 1815, 1816 and 1817, comprising a view of the moral, political, and social state of those countries. Interspersed with numerous historical and political anecdotes, derived from authentic sources. (London: T. Cadell and W. Davies, 1817)

Bibliography

Manuscript and Archival Sources

British Library

Ms. Add. 8100, ff. 141–4: Magnús Stephensen to Banks, 8 Aug. 1812

Ms. Add. 32439, v. 1, ff. 311–2, ff. 336–9: Hooker to R. Brown (3 letters), 1810

Ms. Add. 38356, ff. 39–48, Banks, 'Remarks concerning Iceland', 30 Jan. 1801

Ms. Eg. 2067, ff. 193–229: Count Frédérik Trampe's submission to Lord Bathurst, bound with Jorgenson's *Historical account of a revolution* [Version 1]

Ms. Eg. 2070: Letters from Jorgenson, mainly to W.J. Hooker, 3 Oct. 1809 to 26 Oct. 1825, with two sermons and the printed prospectus for *The religion of Christ*

British National Archives

ADM 1/692: Savignac to Nott, 13 June 1809

ADM 1/1995 (Cap.J.7): collection relating to Iceland revolution, 1809

ADM 1/3899: documents on Iceland after the revolution

ADM 2/893: Admiralty correspondence relating to Iceland

ADM 51/1726 (*Sappho*), ADM 51/1940 and ADM 52/4630 (*Talbot*), ADM 51/1954/3 (*Rover*), ADM 51/4019 and 52/4170/3 (*Lady Nelson*): ships' logs

ADM 99/204: Transport Board register noting Jorgenson petition, 16 Aug. 1810

ADM 103/01: Chatham Entry Books

CO 286/49: Jorgenson petition and affidavit, 29 Aug. 1834 and 12 Sept. 1834

CO 280/76: documents on Ross and Bryan affairs, 1833–5. (See also Mitchell Library and Archives Office of Tasmania.)

FO 22/69: Foreign Office correspondence regarding Jorgenson, 1814

FO 22/86: Foreign Office correspondence regarding Jorgenson, 1820

FO 40/1: Banks and Foreign Office correspondence regarding Iceland revolution, 1809–10

FO 83/2293: Foreign Office documents on Iceland, 1810

FO 95/648: miscellaneous Jorgenson material, 1810–13, including fragment of his Report to the Foreign Office on Portugal and Spain, 1813

HO 13/37 (entry 391): pardon on condition of self-transportation, 21 Oct. 1821

HO 17/53/1 Ih07: Jorgenson petition to Lord Sidmouth with covering letter from Sheriff Garratt, 24 Nov. 1821

PRIS 1/27, PRIS 1/28, PRIS 3/14 (Fleet Prison commitment and discharge books)

PRIS 4/25 (King's Bench discharge books)

Library and Archive of the Royal Botanic Gardens, Kew
Directors' correspondence (DC): vols 1, 49, 72, 73, 76
Miscellaneous correspondence: Jorgenson to Sir John Franklin, 26 Oct. 1839
Banks letters, v. 2, no. 334: W.J. Hooker to Banks, 20 June [1810]

Botany Library, Natural History Museum, London
Banks correspondence, Dawson Turner transcriptions: vols 1, 12, 17, 18

School of Oriental and African Studies (University of London)
CWM South Seas Journals, Box 2, no. 26

Bedfordshire and Luton Archives and Records Service, Bedford
Whitbread papers, nos. W4831–4848, 4949–50, 5518, 5718

Det Kongelige Bibliotek (Royal Library), Copenhagen
NBD IX 8, Haandskrift Afd. 163: Jorgenson to Fritz Jürgensen, 11 Sept. 1835

Rigsarkivet (National Archives), Copenhagen
RTK 373.133: 'Akter til Jörgen Jörgensenske Usurpations Historie 1809–10'
Samlingspakke no. 2679: Privatarkiv, Anna Jørgensen, f. Leth Bruun. Letters from Jorgenson to his mother, 1822–5. (Copies of originals in Odense Regional Archives)

Landsarkivet for Sjælland (Zealand Regional Archives)
Church register of St Nikolai, Copenhagen

Thjóðskjalasafn Íslands (National Archives of Iceland)
Jörundarskjöl XLV
Stiftamtmanns-Innkomin Bref, no. 266, 267, 268, Ar. 1808–9

Landsbókasafn (National Library of Iceland)
ÍB 382
JS 111 fol. (miscellaneous, including copy of Trampe's submission to Lord Bathurst, with attachments)
Lbs 168 fol. (ditto)
Lbs 197 fol.
Lbs 4186 4to: Jörginsáttur Gísla Konráðssonar

National Library of Australia
Ms. 5831: Hooker to R. Gunn, 30 Dec. 1833, and Jorgenson to John Price, 15 March 1840, both bound with Gunn's copy of Hooker's *Journal of a Tour in Iceland*, v. 1
Ms. 4213: Nan Kivell Collection: Jorgenson to Anstey, 23 June 1829, with Anstey's note and Jorgenson's reply to the note

Mitchell Library, State Library of New South Wales
A605: Calder papers, pp. 513, 555, 795–80: J.E. Calder's notes on Jorgenson for his *Tribune* article, 1878
A614: Braim papers: includes the manuscript 'Narrative of the habits, manners, and customs of the Aborigines of Van Diemen's Land', later attributed to Jorgenson
A1059/2, p. 188: indent of *Woodman*, 29 April 1826
A1214: documents on Ross affair, 1833–4. (See also British National Archives and Archives Office of Tasmania.)
A1442: *Alexander* accounts, 1801–6
A1976: King papers, v. 1, pp. 28–9: *Lady Nelson* pay list for 1 July to 31 Dec. 1801
A2015: King letter books, ff. 306, 394, 482–4: letters from King to Foveaux, 11 Sept. 1803, 31 May 1804, 1 May 1805
A2209: Sir George Arthur papers, v. 49: Letters from Jorgenson to Arthur, Anstey and others, 1826–37; also Noble to Dundas, 18 Nov. [1825?]
A7056, A7058, A7060, A7063: G.A. Robinson papers, vols 35, 37, 39, 42: letters from Jorgenson to Robinson, 1832–6

Aj 19/2: Petition from Jorgenson to Arthur, 4 May 1829

Aj 19/3: Jorgenson to A. Stephen, 10 May 1829

Aj 19/4: Jorgenson to Forth, 17 Oct. 1837

Aj 19/5: Jorgenson to T. Anstey, 27 July 1828

C125: Jorgenson's journals of his explorations for the Van Diemen's Land Company, 1826–7

C672: Jorgenson's presentation copy to T. Anstey of his *The Religion of Christ . . .* with inscription and extensive Ms. notes

C813: Jorgenson's presentation copy to Sir John Franklin of his *Observations on the funded system,* with letter to Franklin's secretary A. Maconochie, 27 Aug. 1837

ML Doc 60: Jorgenson to Anstey, 23 June 1829 (copy of original in NLA: Nan Kivell Collection), with typescript notes by Phyllis Mander Jones, 7 Sept. 1962

State Records of New South Wales

Accession A4110, Jorgenson to A. Macleay, 27 Jan. 1827 (formerly in Mitchell Library as Aj 19/1)

State Library of Tasmania

Crowther Pamphlet Q.CRO.PQ 920.JOR: three letters from Jorgenson to Charles Swanston and one to F. Roper, 1838–40

Allport Library and Museum of Fine Arts: Jorgenson: 'Report to Thomas Anstey, of an expedition from Oatlands to Waterloo Point . . . 24 May–3 June 1829', 4 June 1829

Archives Office of Tasmania

CON 23/1, CON 23/3, CON 31/1, CON 31/6, CON 31/23, CON 31/38, CON 40/1: convict registers and records

CSO 1/316/7578

CSO 1/320/7578: reports of roving parties. Vol. 7, Section D for Jorgenson's reports

CSO 1/332/7578

CSO 1/378/8600: Jorgenson and Norah's petition to marry, 7 Sept. 1830

CSO 1/426/9583: Jorgenson petition to Arthur [30 April or 1 May 1829]

CSO 1/763/16363: Jorgenson to Colonial Secretary, 24 Oct. 1834

CSO 19/2: letters from Jorgenson to Forster, 1839–40

GO 1/18, GO 1/19: documents re. Ross and Bryan affairs, 1833–5 (See also British National Archives and Mitchell Library.)

GO 2/9/29: Lefevre to Arthur, 25 Jan. 1834, enquiring about Jorgenson

LC 83/1, LC 219/1: arrests of Jorgenson and Norah

LSD 1/6/ 239: Jorgenson to George Frankland, 26 April 1837

MM 71/5 20/255: Edward Curr's instructions to Jorgenson, 2 Sept. 1826 (copies of originals in Dixson Library, State Library of New South Wales)

NS 23: Van Diemen's Land Company archives

NS 489/1: marriage register (entry 65: Jorgenson and Norah's wedding)

NS 690/26: W.H. Hudspeth file on Jorgenson

NS 1052/53

POL 452/1

RGD 35/1

VDL 5/1

State Library of Victoria

Australian Manuscripts Collection: Calder papers, p. 211: Jorgenson to J. Spode, 9 Dec. 1828

Ms. 8222, Marcus Clarke papers. Box 455/10(a): clippings. Undated clipping from the *Herald*, signed T.F.M., responding to Clarke's article on Jorgenson

State Library of South Australia

York Gate Library, Royal Geographical Society of Australasia, South Australia Branch: M/F Reel 1 (174). Banks, Sir Joseph: 'Notes on Iceland 1807–1809', including 'A brief recital of some of the enormities lately committed in Iceland . . .' (ff. 40–50)

Memorial Library, University of Wisconsin-Madison

Ms. 3: correspondence of Sir Joseph Banks

Periodicals

British:
Edinburgh Review, v. 28 (Aug. 1817), pp. 371–90
Gentleman's Magazine, v. 97 (2) (1827), pp. 518–20
Household Words, v. 14 (20 Dec. 1856), pp. 529–32
London Gazette, 1–5 March 1808
The Morning Chronicle, 27 July, 30 July 1825
The Republican, v. 12 (14) (7 Oct. 1825), pp. 446–7

Danish:
Dagen, 4 July, 15 Sept., 18 Sept., 7 Oct., 11 Dec., 18 Dec., 19 Dec., 29 Dec. 1809
Kjøbenhavns-posten, 18 Oct., 25 Oct., 27 Oct., 30 Oct., 24 Nov. 1832

Australian:
The Advocate (Burnie), 16 Aug., 23 Aug. 1975; 8 Aug. 1981; 12 May 2001
Austral-Asiatic Review, 16 April 1833; 1 Dec. 1840
Bent's News, 14 April 1838
Colonial Advocate, and Tasmanian Monthly Review and Register, 1 May–1 Oct. 1828
Colonial Times, 12 Jan., 19 Jan., 11 May, 6 July 1827; 15, 22, 29 June, 20 July, 10 Aug., 28 Sept. 1831; 20 Nov. 1832; 17 March, 21 April, 12 May 1840
The Colonist, 22 July 1834
Cornwall Chronicle, 30 Jan. 1841
The Examiner (Launceston), 6 April 1867–17 Oct. 1868
Hobart Town Advertiser, 22 Jan. 1841
The Hobart Town Almanack, and Van Diemen's Land Annual for 1838
Hobart Town Courier, 24 May, 6 Dec. 1828, 14 March, 4 April, 23 May, 13 July, 5 Sept. 1829; 16 Nov. 1832; 7 June 1833; 1 Jan., 13 May 1836; 28 Feb., 1 May, 27 Nov. 1840; 26 Jan. 1841
Hobart Town Gazette, 6 May, 11 Nov., 18 Nov. 1826; 9 June, 16 June, 23 June, 30 June, 7 July 1827; 24 May, 12 July, 11 Dec. 1828; 19 July 1833; 25 Dec. 1835; 16 Sept. 1836
The Independent (Launceston), 22 Oct. 1831

Bibliography

The Mercury, 6 Nov. 1968; 22 April, 4 May 1976; 15 Aug. 1987; 1 Feb. 1988; 28 Aug. 2003

The Mercury Westerner, 24 April, 22 May 1986

Ross's Hobart Town Almanack, and Van Diemen's Land Annual for 1835

Sunday Mail (Australia), 16 May 2004

The Sunday Tasmanian, 3 June, 10 June, 17 June 2001

Sydney Gazette, 16 Dec. 1804; 6 Jan., 10 Feb., 11 Feb. 1805; 24 May 1826; 7 May 1828

The Tasmanian, 12 Dec. 1828; 5 April 1833

The Tasmanian Mail, 16 Sept. 1980

The Tribune (Hobart), 24, 26, 27, 29 July 1878

True Colonist, 15 May 1840

The Weekender, 18 April 1987

Other Printed Sources

Agnar Thórðarson, *Hundadagakóngurinn: leikrití thremur tháttum* (Reykjavík: Helgafell, 1969)

Allan, Mea, *The Hookers of Kew, 1785–1911* (London: Michael Joseph, 1967)

Anderson, R.C., *Naval Wars in the Baltic 1522–1850* (London: Francis Edwards, 1969)

Anna Agnarsdóttir, *Great Britain and Iceland, 1800–1820* (PhD thesis, London School of Economics) (London: 1989)

— 'Sir Joseph Banks and the exploration of Iceland', in Banks, R.E.R., et al. (eds), *Sir Joseph Banks: A Global Perspective* (Kew: Royal Botanic Gardens, 1994)

— 'Centre and periphery in wartime: Iceland and Denmark during the Napoleonic wars', in Ingi Sigurðsson and Jón Skaptason (eds), *Aspects of Arctic and Sub-Arctic History: Proceedings of the International Congress on the history of the Arctic and Sub-Arctic Region, Reyjkavík, 18–21 June 1998* (Reykjavík: University of Iceland Press, 2000), pp. 101–112

— 'Hundadagadrottningin heldur út í heim, 1812–1814', in *Kvennaslóðir: rit til heiðurs Sigríði Th. Erlendsdóttir sagnfræðingi.* (Reykjavík: Kvennasögusafn Íslands, 2001), pp. 123–39

Australian Dictionary of Biography (ed. D. Pike) (Melbourne: Melbourne University Press, 1966–2002)

An Authentic Account of the Siege of Copenhagen, by the British, in the Year 1807 . . . (London: W. Faden, 1807)

Binks, C.J., *Explorers of Western Tasmania* (Launceston, Mary Fisher Bookshop, 1980, reprinted Devonport: Taswegia, 1989)

Bjerring, Claus, *Fritz Jürgensen* (København: C. Ejler, 1999)

Bonwick, James, *John Batman, the Founder of Victoria* (Melbourne: S. Mullen, 1867)

— *Last of the Tasmanians.* (London: Sampson Low, 1870)

— *Port Phillip Settlement* (London: Sampson Low, 1883)

Braim, T.H., *A History of New South Wales, from its Settlement to the Close of the Year 1844* (London: R. Bentley, 1846)

Bridges, Roy, *The Cards of Fortune* (Sydney: NSW Bookstall Co., 1922)

Browne, Thomas Henry (ed. R.N. Buckley), *The Napoleonic War Journal of Captain Thomas Henry Browne, 1807–16.* (London: The Bodley Head for the Army Records Society, 1987)

Bruce, J.M. (ed.), *Journal of Henry Hellyer 1826, together with two dispatches by Edward Curr . . . Stephen Adey's Account of his Expedition to Circular Head, and Clement Lorymer's Journal* ([Burnie, Tas.]: J.M. Bruce, 1993)

— *Loitering in a Tent: Jorgen Jorgenson in the High Country* ([Burnie, Tas.]: J.M. Bruce, 1995)

Burns, T.E., and Skemp, J.R., *Van Diemen's Land Correspondents: Letters from R.C. Gunn, R.W. Lawrence, Jorgen Jorgenson, Sir John Franklin and others to Sir William J. Hooker, 1827–1849* ([Launceston]: Queen Victoria Museum, 1961)

Buruma, Ian, *Voltaire's Coconuts* (London: Weidenfeld & Nicolson, 1998)

Calder, James Erskine, *Some Account of the Wars, Extirpation, Habits, &c. of the Native Tribes of Tasmania* ([Hobart], Tasmania: Henn & Co., 1875)

— 'J. Jorgenson. A biographical sketch', in *The Tribune* (24, 26, 27, 29 July 1878)

Campbell, A.H., *John Batman and the Aborigines* (Melbourne: Kibble Books, [1987])

Carter, Harold B., *Sir Joseph Banks, 1743–1820* (London: British Museum (Natural History), 1988)

Bibliography

Clark, Charles Manning Hope (ed.) (with L.J. Pryor), *Select Documents in Australian History 1788–1850* (Sydney: Angus & Robertson, 1950)

Clarke, Marcus, 'Old stories retold: the adventures of Captain Jorgensen', published serially in the *Australasian*, 4 June, 18 June, 25 June 1870, and then issued as 'Adventures of Captain Jorgenson' in his *Old Tales of a Young Country* (Melbourne: Mason, Firth & M'Cutcheon, 1871), pp. 66–105, and 'Jorgen: king of adventurers', in his *The Austral Edition of the Selected Works* (Melbourne: Fergusson & Mitchell, 1890), pp. 71–101

— *His Natural Life* (Melbourne: G. Robertson, 1874)

Clune, F., and Stephensen, P.R., *The Viking of Van Diemen's Land: The Stormy Life of Jorgen Jorgenson* (Sydney: Angus & Robertson, 1954)

Connor, John, *The Australian Frontier Wars 1788–1838* (Sydney: UNSW Press, 2002)

Conrad, Joseph (ed. M. Kalnins), *A Personal Record and The Mirror of the Sea* (London: Penguin, 1998)

Constant, Benjamin (tr. and ed. B. Fontana), 'The spirit of conquest and usurpation', in *Political Writings* (Cambridge: Cambridge University Press, 1988), pp. 44–167. Translation of *De l'esprit de conquête et de l'usurpation*, 4th edn (Paris: 1814)

Cormick, Craig, 'The last history of Jorgen Jorgensen', in *Unwritten Histories* (Canberra: Aboriginal Studies Press, 1998), pp. 31–8

Craig, Clifford, *Notes on Tasmaniana* (Launceston: Foot & Playsted, 1986)

Crookes, Septimus, *Particulars of the Expedition to Copenhagen . . .* (Sheffield: the author, 1808)

Curr, Edward, *An Account of the Colony of Van Diemen's Land* (London: G. Cowie, 1824)

Dallas, Gregor, *1815: The Road to Waterloo* (London: R. Cohen, 1996)

Dally, James, 'Jorgen Jorgenson's last voyage to Van Diemen's Land', *Tasmanian Historical Research Association Papers and Proceedings*, v. 2 (1952), pp. 55–9

— (ed.), *Mortmain: a collection of choice petitions, memorials and letters of protest and request from the convict colony of VDL . . . collected and transcribed from the originals by Eustace FitzSymonds* [i.e. James Dally] (Hobart: Sullivan's Cove, 1977)

— (ed.), *Jorgen Jorgenson's Fiery Breeches displayed in Hobart Town by*

Mr Henry Melville, M.DCCC.XXXII (Adelaide: Sullivan's Cove, 1993)

Dansk Biografisk Leksikon 3rd edn (ed. Sv. Cedergreen Bech) (København: Gyldendal, 1979–84)

Davies, David Michael, *The Last of the Tasmanians* (London: Muller, 1973)

Davies, John (ed. C.W. Newbury), *The History of the Tahitian Mission 1799–1830* (Cambridge: Hakluyt Society, 1961)

Davies, Rhys, *Sea Urchin: Adventures of Jorgen Jorgenson* (London: Duckworth, 1940)

Dich, Preben, *Hundedagekongen: beretningen on Jørgen Jürgensen* (Skive: C. Erichsen, 1985)

Dictionary of National Biography (ed. Sir Leslie Stephen and Sir Sidney Lee) (Oxford: Oxford University Press, 1917)

Dillon, Arthur, *A Winter in Iceland and Lapland* (London: Henry Colbourn, 1840)

Dunbabin, Thomas, 'Whalers, sealers and buccaneers', in *Proceedings of the Royal Australian Historical Society*, v. 11, no. 1 (1925), pp. 1–32

Elliott, Brian, 'The Viking of Van Diemen's Land and Marcus Clarke', *Biblionews*, v. 8, no. 2 (1955), pp. 4–6.

Feldborg, A.A. ('J.A. Andersen'), *A Dane's Excursions in Britain* (London: Mathews & Leigh, 1809)

Fenton, James, *A History of Tasmania* (Hobart: Walch, 1884)

Ferrar, William Moore, *The Maxwells of Bremgarten*, published serially and anonymously in the *Examiner* (Launceston), 6 April 1867 to 17 Oct. 1868

Fitzpatrick, Kathleen, *Sir John Franklin in Tasmania, 1837–1843* (Melbourne: Melbourne University Press, 1949)

Flanagan, Richard, *Gould's Book of Fish: a Novel in Twelve Fish* (London: Atlantic Books, 2002) (Originally published Sydney: Picador, 2001)

Flinders, Matthew, *A Voyage to Terra Australis* (London: G. and W. Nicol, 1814)

Ford, Franklin L., *Europe 1780–1830*, 2nd edn (London: Longman, 1989)

Forsyth, W.D., *Governor Arthur's Convict System: Van Diemen's Land 1824–36: a Study in Colonization* (London: Longmans, Green for the Royal Empire Society, 1935)

Franks, Shirley M., *Land Exploration in Tasmania 1824–42, with special reference to the Van Diemen's Land Company* (University of Tasmania MA thesis) (Hobart, 1958)

Frost, Alan, 'New South Wales as *terra nullius*: the British denial of Aboriginal land rights', in *Historical Studies*, 19 (1981), pp. 513–23

Fulford, R.T.B., *Samuel Whitbread 1764–1815: a Study in Opposition* (London: Macmillan 1967)

Gans, A.I., and Yedida, A. (eds.), *New Source Material on Sir Joseph Banks and Iceland from the Original Manuscripts in the Sutro Branch California State Library* (San Francisco: California State Library, 1941)

Gascoigne, John (with Patricia Curthoys), *The Enlightenment and the Origins of European Australia* (Cambridge: Cambridge University Press, 2002)

Gates, David, *The Napoleonic Wars 1803–1815* (London: Arnold, 1997)

Geijer, Erik Gustaf (tr. E. Sprigge and C. Napier), *Impressions of England 1809–10* (London: J. Cape, 1932)

Gjerset, Knut, *History of Iceland* (London: Allen & Unwin, 1924)

Goodrick, Joan, *Life in old Van Diemen's Land* (Adelaide: Rigby, 1977)

Grahame, James, *The Siege of Copenhagen, a Poem* (London: Longman, Hurst, Rees, & Orme, 1808)

Grant, James, *The Narrative of a Voyage of Discovery, performed in His Majesty's Vessel the 'Lady Nelson' . . . in the Years 1800, 1801, and 1802, to New South Wales* (London: T. Egerton, 1803)

Great Britain: Historical Manuscripts Commission, *Report on the manuscripts of Earl Bathurst, preserved at Cirencester Park* (London: HMSO, 1923)

Great Britain: Parliament: House of Commons paper no. 259, of 1831: *Van Diemen's Land: Copies of all correspondence between Lt.-Gov. Arthur and His Majesty's Secretary of State for the Colonies, on the subject of the military operations lately carried on against the aboriginal inhabitants of VDL. Reprinted with historical introduction by A.G.L. Shaw.* (Hobart: Tasmanian Historical Research Association, 1971)

Greener, Leslie, 'The Bridge at Ross', *Tasmanian Historical Research Association Papers and Proceedings*, v. 14, no. 3 (1967), pp. 97–115

Greener, Leslie, and Laird, Norman, *Ross Bridge and the Sculpture of Daniel Herbert* (Hobart: Fullers Bookshop, 1971)

THE ENGLISH DANE

Grotius, Hugo (tr. R. Van Deman Magoffin, ed. J. Brown Scott), *The Freedom of the Seas or the Right which belongs to the Dutch to take part in the East Indian trade* (New York: Oxford University Press, 1916). Translation of *Mare liberum* (Leyden: 1633, originally published 1608)

Gunnar Karlsson, 'Icelandic nationalism and the inspiration of history', in R. Mitchison (ed.), *Roots of Nationalism: Studies in Northern Europe* (Edinburgh: Donald, 1980), pp. 77–89

— 'The emergence of nationalism in Iceland', in Tägil, S. (ed.), *Ethnicity and Nation-building in the Nordic World* (London: Hurst, 1995), pp. 33–62

— *The History of Iceland* (Minneapolis: University of Minnesota Press, 2000) (First published London: C. Hurst, 2000)

Halldór Hermannsson, 'Sir Joseph Banks and Iceland', *Islandica*, v. 18 (1928), pp. 1–99

Halldór J. Jónsson, 'Myndir af Jörundi hundadagakóngi', *Árbók hins Íslenzka fornleifafélags, 1967* (Reykjavík: Ísafoldarprentsmiðja, 1968), pp. 45–9

Hawkings, D.T., *Bound for Australia* (Chichester: Phillimore, 1987)

Heckscher, Eli F., *The Continental System: an Economic Interpretation* (Oxford: Clarendon Press, 1922)

Helgi P. Briem, *Byltingin, 1809* (PhD thesis) (Reykjavík, 1936)

— *Sjálfstæði Íslands 1809* (Reykjavík: E.P. Briem, 1936)

— '"King" Jörgen Jörgensen: an episode in Iceland's history', *American-Scandinavian Review*, v. 31 (1943), pp. 120–31

Henderson, Ebenezer, *Iceland, or the Journal of a Residence in that Island, during the Years 1814 and 1815* (Edinburgh: Oliphant, Waugh & Innes, 1818)

Hill, Richard, *The Prizes of War: the Naval Prize System in the Napoleonic Wars, 1793–1815* (Stroud, Glos.: Sutton Publishing and Royal Naval Museum, 1998)

Historical Records of Australia (Canberra: 1914–97) Series I: v. 3, 4, 5, 8. Series III: v. 5, 6. Resumed series III: v. 7

Hobsbawm, Eric, *The Age of Revolution: Europe 1789–1848* (London: Weidenfeld & Nicolson, 1975)

Hogan, J.F., *The Convict King, being the Life and Adventures of Jorgen Jorgenson* (London: Ward & Downey, 1891)

Holland, Henry (ed. A. Wawn), *The Iceland Journal of Henry Holland, 1810* (London: Hakluyt Society, 1987)

Hooker, Joseph Dalton (ed. L. Huxley), *Life and Letters of Sir Joseph Dalton Hooker* (London: John Murray, 1918)

Hooker, William Jackson, *Journal of a Tour in Iceland, in the Summer of 1809*, 2nd edn (London: Longman, Hurst, Rees, Orme, and Brown & Murray, 1813)

Hovde, J., *The Scandinavian Countries, 1720–1865* (Boston: Chapman & Grimes, 1943)

Hügel, Carl, Freiherr von (tr. and ed. D. Clark), *New Holland Journal, November 1833–October 1834* (Melbourne: Melbourne University Press, 1994)

Hull, H.M., *Statistical Summary of Tasmania, from the Year 1816 to 1865 inclusive* (Hobart: Government Printer, 1866)

Humphrey, A.W.H. (ed. J. Currey), *Narrative of a Voyage to Port Phillip and Van Diemen's Land with Lieut.-Governor Collins 1803–1804* (Melbourne: the Colony Press, 1984)

Ibsen, Henrik (tr. C. Fry and J. Fillinger), *Peer Gynt* (Oxford: Oxford University Press, 1989)

Indriði Einarsson, *Síðasti víkingurinn, eða, Jörgen Jörgensen* (Reykjavík: Guðm. Gamalíelssonar, 1936)

Inglis, K.S., *The Australian Colonists: an Exploration of Social History 1788–1870* (Carlton, Vic.: Melbourne University Press, 1974)

Íslenzkar Æviskrár (ed. Páll Eggert Ólasson) (Reykjavík: Íslenzka Bókmenntafélag, 1948–52)

Jackman, S.W., *Tasmania* (Melbourne: Wren, 1974)

James, William, *The Naval History of Great Britain, during the French Revolutionary and Napoleonic Wars*, vol. 4: 1805–1807 (London: Conway Maritime, 2002)

Johansen, J.C., *Kapitan Kong Jørgen Jørgensen* (København: Særtryk af Museum, 1892)

Jón Espólín, *Íslands árbækur í söguformi* (Kaupmannahöf: Íslendska Bókmenntafélag, 1821–55): pt 12 (1855)

Jón Thorkelsson: *Saga Jörundar Hundadagakóngs* (Kaupmannahöfn: Gyldendal, 1892)

Jónas Árnason, *Thiðmunið hann Jörund* (Reykjavík: Leikfélag Reykjavíkur, 1970)

— (Danish translation): *I husker vel Jørgen? kongen af Island* (Graasten: Drama, 1984)

Jones, Rhys, 'Tasmanian tribes', Appendix to N.B. Tindale, *Aboriginal Tribes of Australia* (Canberra: Australian National University Press, 1974), pp. 317–54

Jorgen Jorgenson: a Convict King (Hobart: Department of Education, 1970)

Kierkegaard, Søren (tr. A. Hannay), *A Literary Review* (London: Penguin, 2001)

Knopwood, Robert (ed. Mary Nicholls), *The Diary of the Reverend Robert Knopwood 1803–1838* (Hobart: Tasmanian Historical Research Association, 1977)

Lamb, J., *Preserving the Self in the South Seas 1680–1840* (Chicago and London: University of Chicago Press, 2001)

Lauring, Palle (tr. D. Hohnen), *A History of the Kingdom of Denmark* (Copenhagen: Høst & Søn, 1960)

Lee, Ida (ed.), *The Logbooks of the Lady Nelson with the Journal of her first commander Lieutenant James Grant* (London: R.N. Grafton, 1915)

— 'Jorgensen's journeys', in her edition of R. Hare, *Voyage of the Caroline from England to Van Diemen's Land* (London: Longmans, Green, 1927), pp. 116–59

Letters from Albion to a Friend on the Continent, Written in the Years 1810, 1811, 1812 and 1813 (London: Gale, Curtis, & Fenner, 1814)

Levy, M.C.I., *Governor George Arthur* (Melbourne: Georgian House, 1953)

Lewis, Michael, *A Social History of the Navy, 1793–1815* (London: Allen & Unwin, 1960)

Lloyd, C. *The British Seaman 1200–1860: a Social Survey* (London: Paladin, 1970) (Originally published London: Collins, 1968)

Longford, Elizabeth, *Wellington: the Years of the Sword*. (London: Weidenfeld & Nicolson, 1969)

Macdonald, James, *Travels through Denmark, and part of Sweden, during the Winter and Spring of 1809* (London: R. Phillips, 1810)

McKay, Derek, 'Great Britain and Iceland in 1809', in *Mariner's Mirror*, v. 59 (Feb. 1973), pp. 85–95.

MacKenzie, Sir George Steuart, *Travels in the Island of Iceland, during the Summer of the Year* MDCCCX, 2nd edn (Edinburgh: A. Constable, 1812)

Manne, Robert (ed.), *Whitewash: on Keith Windschuttle's Fabrication of Aboriginal history* (Melbourne: Black Inc. Agenda, 2003)

Melville, Henry, *The History of the Island of Van Diemen's Land, from the Year 1824 to 1835 inclusive. To which is added, A few words on prison discipline* (London: Smith & Elder, 1835)

— (the same, ed. and annotated by George Mackaness) (Sydney: D.S. Ford, 1959)

Memoir on the Causes of the Present Distressed State of the Icelanders, and the easy and certain means of permanently bettering their condition, by an Icelander (London: J.J. Stockdale, 1813)

Meston, A.L. (ed. W. Meston and R.A.V. McCulloch), 'Jorgenson's journey across the Central Plateau – September–October 1826', *Papers and Proceedings of the Royal Society of Tasmania*, v. 89 (1955), pp. 107–23.

Miller, E. Morris, *Pressmen and Governors: Australian Editors and Writers in early Tasmania* (Sydney: Angus & Robertson, 1952)

Morgan, Sharon, *Land Settlement in Early Tasmania* (Cambridge: Cambridge University Press, 1992)

Mortyn, S.M., 'The nomenclature of the Oatlands district', *Tasmanian Historical Research Association: Papers and Proceedings*, v. 15, no. 1, 1967, pp. 4–17

Muir, Rory, *Britain and the Defeat of Napoleon 1807–1815* (New Haven, CT: Yale University Press, 1996)

Narrative of the Expedition to the Baltic: with an account of the siege and capitulation of Copenhagen . . . by an officer employed in the expedition (London: W. Lindsell, 1808)

Nicholson, Ian Hawkins, *Shipping Arrivals and Departures: Tasmania*, vol. 1: 1803–1833 (Canberra: Roebuck, 1983)

Nicol, J., *An Historical and Descriptive Account of Iceland, Greenland, and the Faroe Islands* (Edinburgh: Oliver & Boyd, 1840)

Nygaard, Georg, 'Between the ramparts', *The American-Scandinavian Review*, v. 17, no. 12 (1929), pp. 741–9

O'Brian, Patrick, *Joseph Banks: a Life* (London: Harvill, 1997) (Originally published London: Collins Harvill, 1987)

Oehlenschlæger, Adam, *Erindringer* (Kiøbenhavn: A.F. Høst, 1850)

Olafsen, E., and Povelsen, B., *Travels in Iceland: performed by order of His Danish Majesty. Translated from the Danish* (London: Richard Phillips, 1805). In Blagdon, F.W. (ed.), *A Collection of Modern and Contemporary Voyages and Travels . . .* (London: R. Phillips, 1805–10), v. 2.

Padfield, Peter, *Maritime Supremacy and the Opening of the Western Mind* (London: John Murray, 1999)

— *Maritime Power and the Struggle for Freedom* (London: John Murray, 2003)

Pardoe, Colin, 'Isolation and evolution in Tasmania', *Current Anthropology*, v. 32, pt 1 (Feb. 1991), pp. 1–21

Partridge, S.G., *Prisoner's Progress* (London: Hutchinson, [1935])

Pétur Sigurðsson, 'Tvær greinar um byltingu Jörgensens árið 1809', *Saga: Tímarit Sögufélags*, v. 2, no. 2 (1955), pp. 161–81

Phelps, Samuel, *Observations on the Importance of Extending the British Fisheries, and of Forming an Iceland Fishing Society . . . Also, an account of the first introduction of British trade with Iceland, &c.* (London: W. Bulmer, 1817)

— *The Analysis of Human Nature, or an investigation of the means to improve the condition of the poor, and to promote the happiness of mankind in general* (London: W. Simpkin & R. Marshall, 1818)

Pink, Kerry, and Ebdon, Annette, *Beyond the Ramparts: a Bicentennial History of Circular Head* (Hobart: Mercury-Walch, 1988; reprinted with corrections, 1992)

Plomley, N.J.B., *Weep in Silence: a History of the Flinders Island Aboriginal Settlement* (Hobart: Blubber Head Press, 1987)

— *Jorgen Jorgenson and the Aborigines of Van Diemen's Land* (Hobart: Blubber Head Press, 1991)

— *The Aboriginal/Settler Clash in VDL 1803–1831* ([Launceston]: Queen Victoria Museum & Art Gallery, in association with the Centre for Tasmanian Historical Studies, University of Tasmania, 1992)

Porter, Andrew, and Low, Alaine (eds), *Oxford History of the British Empire*, vol. 3: *The Nineteenth Century* (Oxford: Oxford University Press, 1999)

Pretyman, E.R., 'The Lady Nelson and how she came to sail in Australian waters', *Tasmanian Historical Research Association Papers and Proceedings*, v. 2 (1952), pp. 70–1

Ramsden, Eric, '"King" Jorgen Jorgensen: when Iceland's future king visited Tahiti', *Pacific Islands Monthly* (Dec. 1940), pp. 42–3

The Real State of the Case respecting the Late Expedition (London, J. Ridgway, 1808)

Reynolds, Henry, *Fate of a Free People* (Ringwood, Vic. and Harmondsworth: Penguin, 1995)

Richards, Rhys, 'Jorgen Jorgenson in New Zealand in 1804 and 1805', in his edition of Jorgenson's *Observations on Pacific Trade and Sealing and Whaling in Australian and New Zealand Waters before 1805* (Wellington, NZ: Paremata Press, 1996)

Robinson, George Augustus (ed. N.J.B. Plomley), *Friendly Mission: the Tasmanian Journals and Papers of George Augustus Robinson, 1829–1834* (Hobart: Tasmanian Historical Research Association, 1966)

Robson, L.L., *The Convict Settlers of Australia: an Enquiry into the Origin and Character of the Convicts transported to New South Wales and Van Diemen's Land 1787–1852* (Carlton, Vic.: Melbourne University Press; London and New York: Cambridge University Press, 1965)

— *A History of Tasmania*, vol. 1: *Van Diemen's Land from the earliest times to 1855* (Melbourne and Oxford: Oxford University Press, 1983)

Royle, Edward, *Revolutionary Britannia? Reflections on the Threat of Revolution in Britain 1789–1848* (Manchester and New York: Manchester University Press, 2000)

Ruppenthal, R., 'Denmark and the Continental system', *Journal of Modern History*, v. 15, no. 1 (1943), pp. 7–23

Ryan, A.N., 'The causes of the British attack on Copenhagen in 1807', *English Historical Review*, v. 68 (1953), pp. 37–55

— 'The defence of British trade with the Baltic, 1808–1813', *English Historical Review*, v. 74 (1959), pp. 443–66

— 'Documents relating to the Copenhagen operation, 1807', in N.A.M. Rodger (ed.), *The Naval Miscellany*, v. 5 (London: Allen & Unwin for the Naval Records Society, 1984), pp. 297–324

Ryan, Lyndall, *The Aboriginal Tasmanians*, 2nd edn (Sydney: Allen & Unwin, 1996)

Schulesen, Sigfus, *Jörgen Jörgensens Usurpation i Island i aaret 1809* (Copenhagen: Jacobsen, 1832)

Scott, Ernest, *Terre Napoléon: a History of French Explorations and Projects in Australia* (London: Methuen, 1910)

— 'An Australian spy', *Argus* (Melbourne), 24 Feb. 1917

Selden, John (tr. Nedham, Marchamont), *Of the Dominion, or, Ownership of the Sea.* (London: William Du-Gard, 1652) Translation of *Mare clausum* (Leyden: 1636)

Serle, Percival, *Dictionary of Australian Biography* (Sydney: Angus & Robertson, 1949)

Shaw, A.G.L., *Convicts and the Colonies: a Study of Penal Transportation* (London: Faber, 1971)

— *Sir George Arthur* (Melbourne: Melbourne University Press, 1980)

Simond, L., *Journal of a Tour and Residence in Great Britain, during the Years 1810 and 1811* (Edinburgh: A. Constable, 1815)

Sommer, F.L., *A Description of Denmark; and a Narrative of the Siege, Bombardment, and Capture of Copenhagen* . . . 2nd edn (Colchester: I. Marsden, [1808?])

Sprod, Dan, *The Usurper: Jorgen Jorgenson and his Turbulent Life in Iceland and Van Diemen's Land 1780–1841* (Hobart: Blubber Head Press, 2001)

Stephenson, P.R., 'An author replies to a critic', *Biblionews*, v. 8, no. 4 (1955), pp. 11–13

Stieglitz, K.R. von, *A Short History of Ross* (Evandale, Tas.: K.R. von Stieglitz, 1949)

— *A History of Oatlands and Jericho* (Evandale, Tas.: K.R. von Stieglitz, 1960)

Tardif, Phillip, *Notorious Strumpets and Dangerous Girls: Convict Women in Van Diemen's Land 1803–1829* (Sydney: Angus & Robertson, 1990)

Turnbull, Clive, *Black War* (Melbourne and London: Cheshire, 1948)

Villiers, Alan, *Vanished Fleets* (London: Geoffrey Bles, 1931)

Wawn, Andrew, 'Hundadagadrottningin. Bréf frá Íslandi: Guðrún Johnsen og Stanleyfjölskyldan frá Cheshire, 1814–16', *Saga: Tímarit Sögufélags*, v. 32 (1985), pp. 97–133

— *The Vikings and the Victorians* (Cambridge: Brewer, 2000)

Weeding, J.S., *A History of Oatlands* (New Norfolk: Derwent Printery, 1988)

— *A History of the Lower Midlands*, 4th edn (Launceston: Regal Publications, 1994) (Originally published 1975)

West, John (ed. A.G.L. Shaw), *The History of Tasmania* (Sydney: Angus & Robertson for the Royal Australian Historical Society, 1971) (Originally published Launceston: 1852)

The Whole Proceedings on the King's Commission of the Peace Oyer and Terminer, and Gaol Delivery for the City of London, and also the Gaol Delivery for the County of Middlesex, held at Justice Hall, in the Old Bailey; on Wednesday, 17th of May, 1820, and following days . . . (London: H. Buckler, 1820)

The Whole Proceedings on the King's Commission of the Peace, Oyer and Terminer, and Gaol Delivery for the City of London, and also the Gaol Delivery for the County of Middlesex, held at Justice Hall, in the Old Bailey; on Wednesday, 4th of December, 1822, and following days . . . (London: H. Buckler, 1822)

Wiedenhofer, Margaret, *The Convict Years: Transportation and the Penal System 1788–1868* (Melbourne: Lansdowne Press, 1973)

Wiener, Joel H., *Radicalism and Freethought in Nineteenth-century Britain: the Life of Richard Carlile* (Westport, CT: Greenwood Press, 1983)

Williams, Vernon, *The Straitsman* (London: Cassell, 1929)

Windschuttle, Keith, *The Fabrication of Aboriginal History*, vol. 1: *Van Diemen's Land 1803–1847* (Sydney: Macleay Press, 2002)

Woodward, Llewellyn, *The Age of Reform: England 1815–1870*, 2nd edn (Oxford: Oxford University Press, 1962)

Index

Aboriginal Australians/Tasmanians 203–4; architecture 188–9; kangaroo hunts 28, 29–30, 205–6; land ownership 212n; languages 236 *and* n; and property 25n; early relations with Europeans 24–5, 29–30, 172, 185–6, 196, 197, 204–9, 221, 233–4; and 'roving parties' 216–23; and 'Black Line' (1830) 226–31, 234; at Flinders Island camp 231, 232–3; Jorgenson's views on 206, 209–12, 219, 220–1, 235–6

Admiral Juul (ship) 62–4, 88, 123, 240

Alexander (ship) 31–3, 35, 36, 38–9

Alexander I, of Russia 50

Althing 90, 97, 101, 106, 119

Ambrister, Robert 153

Angoulême, Duchesse de 148

Anstey, Thomas 4, 195, 206, 216, 218n; relationship with Jorgenson 197, 200, 217, 224, 225, 227, 228; opinion of Jorgenson's marriage 234–5; Jorgenson's reports to 218, 219, 221, 223

Arbuthnot, Alexander 153

Arthur, Sir George 2; treatment of convicts 171–2, 225n, 245; ignores Jorgenson's petition for pardon 173–4; supported by Jorgenson 194–5; and creation of Field Police 195, 197; further petitions from Jorgenson 199–200, 201; attitude towards Aboriginal Tasmanians 209, 210, 212, 213–14, 215–16, 220, 222; gives Jorgenson conditional pardon 224–5; launches 'Black Line' 226, 229–30; imprisons Jorgenson's wife 238, 239; employs Jorgenson as spy 240–1, 242, 243; leaves Tasmania 248–9

Auden, W.H.: *Letters from Iceland* 70

Australasian, The (newspaper) 258

Axford, William 198, 199, 201–2

Bahama (prisonship) 122–3, 126, 127, 129

Banks, Sir Joseph 14, 42; and the 'noble savage' 37; sadness at Tahiti's fate 36–7; takes Tahitians off Jorgenson's hands 42; agrees to read Jorgenson's journal 45; supports Jorgenson's plans 66, 67–8, 75; attitude to Iceland 70, 75–8, 120; pays Hooker's passage to Iceland 81; recommends Phelps 81n; and Olafur and Magnús Stephensen 81, 91, 95, 96; attitude to Jorgenson on his return to England 114, 118, 121–2, 127; hates Jorgenson's *Historical account* 124, 144

Bass Strait 22n, 23, 27, 30, 31, 231, 233

Bathurst, Earl of 142, 143

Batman, John 217, 220

Bede, Venerable 164

Bent, Andrew 194, 195, 240

Bentham, Jeremy 172

Berlin (1816) 151, 152

Bessastaðir: Latin School 106

Binks, C.J. 183

Bjarni Sívertsen 66

Index

Index

Vancouver, Charles 81, 88, 107, 109, 111, 124

Vancouver, Mrs Charles 81, 88, 108–9, 111, 124

Vancouver, George 81n

Viðey island (Iceland) 92–3

Villiers, Alan: *Vanished Fleets* 258

Walls of Jerusalem (Tasmania) 179, 180–1, 183 *and* n

Waterloo, battle of (1815) 146, 147, 152

Weimar (1816) 151

Wellington, Arthur Wellesley, Duke of 59, 60

whaling/whale-ships 30–3, 38–9

Whitbread, Samuel 56, 137, 138, 140, 141, 142, 144–5

Williams, Vernon: *The Straitsman* 258–9

Windschuttle, Keith: *The Fabrication of Aboriginal History* 204n

Woodman (convict transport) 166–8, 169, 170